Ferguson

CRIMINAL EVIDENCE FOR POLICE

SECOND EDITION

Paul B. Weston

Professor,
Department of Criminal Justice,
California State University—Sacramento

Kenneth M. Wells

Public Defender
Sacramento County, California;
Adjunct Professor of Law,
McGeorge School of Law,
University of the Pacific, Stockton, California

Prentice-Hall, Inc., Englewood Cliffs, New Jersey

Library of Congress Cataloging in Publication Data

WESTON, PAUL B.
 Criminal evidence for police.

 (Prentice-Hall series in criminal justice)
 Bibliography: p.
 Includes indexes.
 1. Evidence, Criminal—United States. I. Wells,
Kenneth M., joint author. II. Title.
KF9660.W38 1975   345'.73'06   75-5736
ISBN 0-13-193391-4

Printed in the United States of America

10 9 8 7 6 5 4

Prentice-Hall of Australia, Pty. Ltd., Sydney
Prentice-Hall International, Inc., London
Prentice-Hall of Canada, Ltd., Toronto
Prentice-Hall of India Private Limited, New Delhi
Prentice-Hall of Japan, Inc., Tokyo
Prentice-Hall of Southeast Asia, (Pte.) Ltd., Singapore

Contents

Chapter Three

Police Responsibility for Evidence: Standards   39

Chapter Four

Witnesses and Testimonial Proof   53

Chapter Five

Hearsay Evidence   69

Chapter Six

Chapter Seven

Chapter Eight

Chapter Nine

Chapter Ten

Chapter Eleven

Chapter Twelve

Chapter Thirteen

Chapter Fourteen

Discovery and Disclosure   313

Chapter Fifteen

Evidence of Electronic Surveillances   333

Chapter Sixteen

The Defense Case   359

Preface

The first edition's theme of criminal evidence for police has been retained, and the book's primary objective is unchanged: to present as simply as possible those areas of evidence important to police officers, the investigation of crimes, and the prosecution of persons accused of crime.

The text of the first edition has been updated and expanded. New federal rules of evidence have been integrated with the basic text, and corrections made for emerging or changing case law.

A feature of the second edition is emphasis on evidence in action: application of procedural rules to varying factual situations. Eight cases have been added to the case studies of the first edition for this purpose. Four of these cases relate to non-testimonial evidence, two of them to testimony, and one each to electronic surveillance and pre-trial discovery. All are decisions post-dating the first edition.

Two new chapters have been added. They are now Chapters 2 and 3. Chapter 2 details the roles of prosecutor and defense counsel in the trial of persons accused of crime, citing various responsibilities to their clients as well as the ethical dimensions of the role of advocate. Another new case study concludes this chapter. It reveals the quality of legal representation that is the right of all defendants. Chapter 3 presents authoritative standards for police in collecting, preserving, and presenting evidence within the framework of the police responsibility for on-the-scene investigations and the enlargement of the basic role of police to serve the defense as well as the prosecutor (police reports are generally available to defense through pretrial discovery).

Together with Chapter 1, From Evidence to Proof, these new chapters offer an introductory segment to the core area of this text: the rules of evidence and their exclusions and exceptions, the procedural regulations for the introduction of evidence and the examination of witnesses; and doctrine on offers of proof and motions to suppress or strike out inadmissible evidence.

Many innovative teaching aids are used in this edition. Key words throughout the text are printed in boldface type to focus reader attention and serve as a ready reference in review reading. Each chapter begins with a list of *chapter objectives* to foreshadow the chapter content. Each chapter ends with a *summary* and a *glossary*. One offers a synopsis of chapter content; the other provides definitions of words in the chapter likely to be unfamiliar to many readers. Discussion Questions in the first edition have been retained and additional questions developed to cover new and updated material.

The authors believe their text-and-cases chapter development is a logical treatment of criminal evidence, and a style that encourages scholarly inquiry and promotes reader understanding of the rules of evidence and their rationales.

Paul B. Weston

Kenneth M. Wells

1 From Evidence To Proof

CHAPTER OBJECTIVES

1. In discussing the refinement of evidence for use in criminal proceedings, this chapter will show the importance of admissibility of evidence; also,

2. Proof will be shown to be of legal significance in its impact upon the triers of fact (judge or jury) and

3. The doctrine of presumed innocence and the requirement of proof beyond a reasonable doubt will be described in their relationship to

4. The operation of the two-party adversary system, which distinguishes the American legal system.

In a criminal case the truth of the accusation against a defendant must be proved beyond all reasonable doubt. The doctrines of presumed innocence and reasonable doubt protect persons accused of crime from injustice. The role of evidence in the trial of criminal cases is to prove guilt or indicate innocence.

Evidence is defined as any matter of fact, the effect, tendency, or design of which is to produce in the mind a persuasion, affirmative or disaffirmative, of the existence of some other matter of fact. To sum up: evidence means testimony, writings, material objects, or other things presented to the senses that are offered to prove the existence or non-existence of a fact.[1]

Court procedures limit the exhibits and testimony that may be given in evidence. If there were no rules for the admissibility of evidence, and if any exhibit or testimony with the slightest bearing on the issue before the court could be presented in evidence, it would be impossible to conduct criminal trials within a reasonable span of time. The rules of evidence are designed to enable courts to reach the truth and, in criminal cases, to secure a fair trial for persons accused of crime.[2]

Guilt vs. Innocence.   In a criminal trial the community—"the people"—is represented by a prosecutor and the defendant is represented by a private attorney or a public defender. At trial, exhibits and testimony admitted as evidence are examined from opposite directions to establish the **innocence or guilt** of the defendant. Evidence is presented in such a manner and of such character that a decision can be made about the defendant's guilt or innocence.

In the apparatus of criminal justice the process of discovering truth and making decisions is entrusted to a judge or jury. A person accused of crime may waive trial by jury and accept the trial judge as a decision-maker, but juries usually function as the "triers of fact" in criminal cases. Most major felony cases in the United States in which defendants claim to be innocent are tried before a jury. The jurors review all the evidence—exhibits and testimony—admitted during the criminal trial in order to make their decision as to guilt or innocence. The trial judge instructs jurors to avoid any passion, bias, prejudice, or sympathy toward either the victim or the defendant in arriving at their verdict, and he excludes evidence offered exclusively to play on their passions or prejudices. The jurors decide all questions of fact and, under the control of the trial judge, determine the effect and value of the evidence presented to them, including the credibility of witnesses.[3]

It is sometimes difficult to distinguish between evidence and proof. **Proof** is the effect or result of evidence. Evidence is the medium of proof. More accurately, evidence is the means by which the facts are established, and proof is the effect or the conclusions drawn from such evidence.

---

[1]California Evidence Code, Section 140.
[2]Rule 102, Proposed Rules of Evidence for United States Courts and Magistrates, promulgated by the U.S. Supreme Court in 1973, and hereinafter termed **Federal Rules of Evidence.**
[3]California Evidence Code, Section 312.

Evidence may be either direct or circumstantial. Direct evidence means evidence which in itself, if true, conclusively establishes a fact in issue. Circumstantial evidence goes to prove a fact or series of facts which, if proved, may tend by logical inference to establish a fact in issue.

The weight of the evidence indicating guilt or innocence depends on the impact of the evidence on the trier of fact. Therefore it is important that evidence be considered in relation to (1) its admissibility, and (2) its value as proof of a significant point or element of the prosecution or the defense case. The value of any exhibit or testimony as evidence is based on its nature and on its being recalled and understood by the triers of fact.

THE ADVERSARY SYSTEM

Rational judgments depend on relevant, factual information being brought to the attention of the triers of fact for full assessment. The system of criminal justice in the United States is known as the adversary system and it is based on **fight theory**—each party fights to discover and disclose evidence favorable to his side. This system of opposing interest lets us hope to discover facts that will prove or disprove the accusation against the defendant. If there were not two sides, each presenting exhibits and testimony in evidence, there would be no trial. The accusation alone would prove the case against the accused.

Under this system of adversary proceedings, lawyers are necessary for both parties. The assistance of counsel for defendants in criminal prosecutions is a right provided under the Sixth Amendment to the Constitution. In fact, counsel is necessary because of the complexity of modern court procedures. The belief that the presiding judge can see that procedures are fair during a criminal trial without defense counsel has been rejected. As early as 1938, the U.S. Supreme Court commented on the necessity of legal counsel for both sides in a criminal prosecution, saying, "The Sixth Amendment stands as a constant admonition that if the constitutional safeguards it provides be lost, justice will not 'still be done.' It embodies a realistic recognition of the obvious truth that the average defendant does not have the professional legal skill to protect himself when brought before a tribunal with power to take his life or liberty, wherein the prosecution is presented by experienced and learned counsel."[4]

The concept that a person accused of crime cannot be assured a fair trial without legal counsel has become so strong that recent de-

---

[4] Johnson v. Zerbst, 304 U.S. 458 (1938).

cisions of the U.S. Supreme Court* require that legal counsel be assigned when accused persons are too poor to hire an attorney, and extend this right to legal representation to juveniles. In *Gideon v. Wainwright*[5] the court noted that great emphasis had always been placed on procedural and substantive safeguards designed to assure fair trials before impartial tribunals in which every defendant stands equal before the law. "This noble ideal," the majority opinion states, "cannot be realized if the poor man charged with crime has to face his accusers without a lawyer to assist him." In *Gault v. Arizona*[6] a juvenile claimed his basic rights were denied in a juvenile court hearing. In reversing the lower court, the U.S. Supreme Court rejected the parent and probation officer as adequate resources to protect the juvenile's interests, saying, "The child requires the guiding hand of counsel at every step in the proceedings against him."

The prosecutor represents the "people" in criminal cases. Defendants who have the necessary funds are represented by legal counsel of their choice, while indigent defendants are assigned counsel by the court. The office of public defender has been playing a role in the administration of justice similar to that of the prosecutor, but serving as defense counsel. The public defender offers indigent defendants a formal organization for defense against accusations of crime or juvenile delinquency.

The concept of a fair trial in an adversary system also requires that the entire criminal proceeding be conducted by an unbiased judge. Kinship, personal bias, or conflict of interest can disqualify a judge. A direct, personal, substantial pecuniary interest in ruling against a defendant certainly disqualifies. Any circumstance that would offer a possible temptation to the average judge to forget the burden of proof required to convict the defendant, or that might lead him not to hold the balance clearly and truly between the state and the accused person denies the defendant due process of law.[7]

Trial procedure is keyed to the fight theory. Each side, in turn, is given an opportunity to overcome its adversary. Because the people are making the accusation, the prosecutor opens a criminal trial with his side of the case. His goal is to prove the **"corpus delicti"** of the crime and the "identity" of the criminal agent. "Corpus delicti" is commonly termed the "body of the crime" or "the essential elements of the crime." The essential elements of most criminal cases include the prohibited *act* and the necessary criminal *intent*. After proving these elements, the prosecutor tries to show that the defendant is the person guilty of

*See Case List for guide to case references.
[5]372 U.S. 335 (1963).
[6]387 U.S. 1 (1967).
[7]Tumey v. Ohio, 273 U.S. 510 (1927).

the crime charged. When the prosecution's case has been completed, the defense has its opportunity. In the closing stages of trial both sides are allowed time to repair their cases and answer the opposition's evidence.

Orderly trial procedure consists of presenting evidence in the following order:

1. The people's main case is presented. This is evidence "in chief."
2. The defense presents its evidence and answers the people's "case in chief."
3. "Rebuttal" by the prosecutor in answer to the defense case, which closes the people's case.
4. "Rejoinder" by defense to the evidence presented in the prosecutor's rebuttal.

No party to a criminal action is allowed a piecemeal presentation of evidence. The judge is expected to make sure that a party introduces all the evidence he will rely on when he first presents his case. During the rebuttal and surrebuttal or rejoinder the parties are allowed to amend the evidence structure of their case if they have been surprised by their adversary's evidence.

The proffering of exhibits and witnesses, and specific questions and lines of questioning are also keyed to the adversary system. Proffered evidence and questions may be objected to by opposing counsel. The trial judge examines the substance, purpose, and relevance of the proffered evidence or the evidence sought by questioning, and the form of questions, and scans the grounds of an objection, or a motion to exclude or strike evidence.

The prosecution's advantage in being first to present evidence can be negated by defense counsel through effective cross-examination. Capable defense attorneys often seize this opportunity to begin the defense case during the presentation of evidence in chief. Of course, the prosecutor has a similar opportunity to destroy witnesses presented by the defense, but this never seems quite as effective because the people must develop convincing evidence of guilt, and the defense need only produce a reasonable doubt of guilt.

THE BURDEN OF PROOF

Most criminal trials in the United States result from the police apprehension process. An incident is reported to the police or discovered by them. They respond and investigate the incident. If it constitutes a crime, the search for the criminal is begun. Police continue the investigation until it is closed by arrest, or by administrative action when no arrest is possible. When the police investigator reports to the prosecutor that a crime under investigation has been solved, and forwards the investigation report and the collected evidence to the prosecutor, the investigating officer has assumed the burden of proving the accused person guilty.

The prosecutor, after a review of the police case and a pretrial investigation, makes a formal accusation against the individual identified by police as the guilty person. By preparing the accusatory pleading against the defendant, and preparing for the trial, it is the **prosecutor's burden of proof** to show that the defendant is guilty. This burden of proof remains on the prosecution throughout the case. "The party claiming that a person is guilty of crime or wrongdoing has the burden of proof on that issue."[8]

Accused persons do not have the burden of proof, but rather the burden of overcoming the case made against them by the prosecution. Although the defendant only has to create a reasonable doubt of his guilt, defense counsel attempts the strongest defense and tries to create the highest degree of reasonable doubt so that the defendant will be acquitted.

When the defendant introduces evidence that he was not present when the alleged offense was committed, the burden of proof is not shifted; it remains with the prosecution. The same rule applies when the defendant offers evidence of self-defense or of any of the other common defenses.

At the end of a trial, the presiding judge explains the presumption of innocence and the definition of reasonable doubt to the jury. He does this to orient the members of the jury to the method of weighing the evidence presented by the prosecution to prove the guilt of the defendant, as well as the evidence produced by the defendant to create a **reasonable doubt** of his guilt. Usually this instruction is worded to highlight the presumption that a defendant in a criminal action is presumed innocent until the contrary is proved and to emphasize that in case of a reasonable doubt, the defendant is entitled to acquittal. This presumption places the burden of proving the defendant guilty beyond a reasonable doubt upon the state—that is, the prosecution. Reasonable doubt is defined as "not a mere possible doubt; because everything relating to human affairs, and depending on moral evidence, is open to some possible imaginary doubt. It is that state of the case, which after the entire comparison and consideration of all the evidence, leaves the minds of the jurors in that condition that they cannot say they feel an abiding conviction, to a moral certainty, of the truth of the charges."[9]

[8]California Evidence Code, Section 520.
[9]California Penal Code, Section 1096.

BURDEN OF PRODUCING EVIDENCE

A party has the burden of producing evidence about a particular fact if a finding against him on that fact would be required in the absence of further evidence. The prosecutor is the first party to produce evidence. If he develops a *prima facie case* and the defendant does nothing to answer, the defendant fails. The burden of producing evidence is a rule for deciding who must continue presenting evidence.

Even when a negative allegation is made, the party asserting it has the burden of producing evidence despite the inconvenience of proving a negative, but in such instances less evidence will usually shift the burden of producing evidence to the other party. Any evidence that shows the existence of the negative should shift this burden.

During a criminal trial the burden of producing evidence shifts from one side to the other. When a fact is peculiarly within the knowledge of one of the parties, only slight evidence from the other side is enough to satisfy the initial burden. In determining the amount of evidence necessary to shift this burden, the presiding judge considers the opportunities for either the prosecution or defense to secure exhibits or testimony about the fact to be proved.

If the defendant enters a plea of "Not guilty by reason of insanity" the burden of proving insanity is on the defendant. The legal presumption that the defendant is sane must be overcome by evidence which proves the defendant is insane. When the defendant presents evidence of insanity the burden of producing evidence to the contrary shifts to the prosecution. This is one of the general types of defense called an **affirmative defense,** one in which the defendant has the burden of proof.

Another affirmative defense is the proof of defendant's age when it is a possible defense to the crime. The burden will be on the defendant to prove by a preponderance of the evidence he is a certain age, or under a certain age. If, on the other hand, the victim's age is an essential element of the crime, the prosecution has the burden of proof beyond a reasonable doubt.

A derivative pretrial issue illustrating this shifting burden of proof occurs when a criminal trial is pending. The defendant may apply for a change of venue on the ground that a fair and impartial trial is impossible in the county in which the case has been developed and brought to trial. The burden of producing evidence on this issue is on the defendant. The defense makes the application for removal in open court and in writing. At the hearing, the prosecutor has an opportunity to rebut the claim. If the court is satisfied that the defendant's application is true, the action is transferred to the proper court of a convenient county free from a similar objection.

PRELIMINARY DETERMINATIONS ON ADMISSIBILITY

Evidence to which timely objection has been made often requires proof of the existence or nonexistence of a **preliminary fact**.[10] Usually, the party proffering the evidence has the burden of producing evidence about the preliminary fact. Sometimes, however, the judge decides which party has the burden of producing evidence on the disputed issue. The courtroom procedure varies with the evidence and its nature. The trial judge may invite opposing counsel to approach the bench or he may grant a short recess to permit discussion in his chamber. The jury may be directed to leave the room while evidence about a preliminary fact is produced. It is viable legal strategy for either counsel to request this. The preliminary fact is determined by the judge based upon the relevancy of the proffered evidence and the sufficiency of the preliminary fact. A preliminary fact may be the determination of a privilige, the qualifications of a witness to testify, the existence of unlawful police action, authenticity of documents, or other preliminary fact determining relevance of the proffered evidence.

Problems arise when:

1. The relevance of the proffered evidence is questioned.
2. An objection has been made that the expected testimony is not based on the witness' personal knowledge.
3. The authenticity of a writing is questioned.
4. The proffered evidence concerns a statement or other conduct of a particular person and there is reason to doubt that the person made the statement or so conducted himself.
5. The admissibility of a defendant's confession or admission is questioned.
6. Tangible evidence is claimed to have been seized illegally.
7. Proffered evidence is claimed to be incriminatory.

When these problems arise, the following are the standards for admission:

When the problem involves:	*Enough evidence must be introduced to:*
Relevancy	warrant a finding of the preliminary fact.

[10]California Evidence Code, Sections 310, 400 **et seq.**; Rule 104, Federal Rules of Evidence.

Personal knowledge	sustain a finding of the witness' personal knowledge.
Authentication of writings	sustain a finding by the court of the authenticity of the writing.
Hearsay declarations	justify a finding that the hearsay declarant made the statement or acted as specified, and that the circumstances of the statement or act satisfy the minimum standards of trustworthiness required by the applicable exception to the hearsay rule.
Admission of a party	justify a finding that the party made the statement.
Admissions—authorized or adoptive	justify a finding that the admission was made by an authorized agent of the party, or by the party's adoptive conduct.
Admissions—co-conspirator	justify finding that there was a conspiracy.
Admissions and confessions — voluntariness	justify finding that the admission or confession was voluntary.

JUDICIAL NOTICE

Judicial notice is a shortcut used by judges to do away with the necessity for evidence when the proposed testimony concerns a matter of **common knowledge.** The three requirements for this judicial shortcut are that matter be: common and general knowledge, well-established and authoritatively settled, and practically indisputable in the jurisdiction where the case is being tried. It should be noted that what may be common knowledge in one jurisdiction may not be, or is unlikely to be, common knowledge in another.[11]

Courts may often take judicial notice in the following general areas:

1. *Laws:* Including federal and state constitutions and statutes; treaties with foreign countries; municipal charters and ordinances; executive orders and proclamations of the president of the United States and the governor of the state; and certain administrative and departmental regulations.

2. *Geographical and Historical Facts:* Such as the name, size, and statistical data regarding states, counties, and cities, or foreign countries, boundaries, and their historical origin; distances computed from a map.

3. *Judicial Proceedings:* The existence, organization, and operation of

[11]Rule 201 **et seq.**, Federal Rules of Evidence.

courts will be judicially noticed. Notice may be taken of well-known conditions such as the fact that the descriptions of witnesses may vary. Memory is not infallible. Jurors are generally without knowledge in the law. The court will also notice its own records of a case.

4. *Public Officials and Records:* Judicial notice includes the identity of holders of state and county offices and of local offices within the court's own county, and of the content of journals and records of the state legislature.

5. *Scientific Principles and Procedures:* The commonly known laws of nature such as the quality of matter, that fruit rots, eggs develop noxious odors, glass cuts, and gasoline burns; the nature of certain diseases; various facts regarding narcotics; the alcoholic content of whisky, gin, wine, beer; and the operation, use, and effect of weapons and poison when commonly known.

6. *Other Matters Subject to Judicial Notice:* Certain characteristics or behavior of humans such as the general period of gestation, knowledge that a person with good character is less likely to commit a crime than someone with bad character, that persons write their names differently at different times and places, that it is difficult to see dark objects at night; the nature of some games such as baseball; modus operandi or patterns of some crimes; the validity of fingerprints; the significance of blood tests; and the habits and instincts of some animals.

RULES OF EVIDENCE

The rules for presenting evidence are designed to help the court and jury establish truth and administer justice. There is no question that evidence should be previewed in some manner before a jury is allowed to speculate on it.

The rules prescribe the manner of presenting evidence; the qualifications and privileges of witnesses, and the manner of examining them; and which things are logically, by nature, evidential. The rules of evidence appear to be highlighted by negativism. They often exclude exhibits and testimony offered in evidence.

Generally, no evidence is admissible unless it is relevant, and except as provided by state laws, all **relevant evidence** is admissible. Relevance is the connection between a fact offered in evidence and the issue to be proved. Briefly, "relevant" implies a traceable and significant connection.

The admissibility of evidence and its relevance are not synonymous. An item of evidence may be relevant but not admissible. However, to be admissible, the evidence must be relevant.

To be admitted, **evidence must also be material.** An item of evidence is material if it is important or substantial, capable of properly influencing the outcome of the trial. Evidence is considered immaterial when it is so unimportant compared to other easily available evidence that the court should not waste its time admitting it.

Another major test of evidence is the **competence of the witness** in general, or in relation to specific testimonial areas. With certain statutory exceptions, anyone who can perceive and communicate his perceptions can be a witness.

Evidence collected by means that violate the constitution may be excluded on the grounds that its admission would violate the doctrine of due process or the right to a fair trial.

Police investigators should know which evidence is likely to be inadmissible. They must also know about hearsay and opinion evidence which may be barred if defense counsel objects. Police investigators are not expected to know the legal interrelationships necessary for the conduct of a trial, but they are expected to know the general ground rules for admitting various forms of evidence.

Investigators who have learned the rules of evidence can carry this procedure one step further and preview evidence likely to be offered by the defense to which the prosecutor might object. By doing this, he can use the rules for excluding evidence to support the state's case and its burden of proof.

After thoroughly investigating a case, the investigator should know the facts disclosed and the facts likely to be disputed at trial. Then, in analyzing the evidence collected the police investigator can project the evidence's admissibility. Like the prosecutor, the investigator should determine disputed facts and answer the following questions:

1. What relevant and material evidence is there about each disputed fact?*

2. Is the witness to any of the disputed facts mentally competent to testify? Is his testimony the result of his own perception or the perception of someone else?

3. What witnesses and testimony may be barred by rules excluding privileged communications, hearsay, or opinion evidence? Can defense objections be overcome?

4. What physical evidence is involved, and is there a sufficient foundation for admitting it? Who can testify to its connection to the crime, its

---

*Every essential element of the crime charged is a disputed fact. In the crime of robbery the following are always matters of dispute: the taking and carrying away of personal property of another, whether the taking was from the person or immediate presence of the victim (possession), the means used for the taking was force or fear, and the identity of the robber.

discovery, and that it has been safely kept between discovery and trial?
5. Is the admissibility of any evidence jeopardized by lawless searches
and seizures, coerced confessions, or some other violation of the Constitution?

Jurors must make impartial findings based on evidence presented
to them during a criminal trial. However, the rules of evidence are
designed to keep evidence that would be speculative or confusing from
the jury. Therefore, evidence must be fit to pass the tests of admissibility
so that it can reach and convince the triers of fact.

SUMMARY

This introductory chapter provides a framework for the remaining chapters of this text. It is an exposition of the screening process by which
raw evidence is refined under judicial supervision to its end product:
proof.

The role of evidence in criminal proceedings is to prove guilt or
innocence. Proof is the effect or result of evidence. The adversary system is based on a two-party criminal process in which each "side" has
the assistance of legal counsel, and trial procedure insures an orderly,
sequential array of evidence. The prosecution has the burden of proof
in criminal cases; either party may have the burden of producing evidence; and the party proffering the evidence usually has the burden of
showing its admissibility when the opposing party objects to its presentation. Certain facts need not be proved by in-court presentation; judicial notice obviates the need to prove matters of common knowledge.
Rules of evidence are guidelines which aid the functioning of the adversary system by restrictions that tend to keep speculative or confusing evidence from being presented to the triers of fact (jury). Relevance
and materiality of proffered evidence and the competency of witnesses
are the common tests of the admissibility of evidence.

DISCUSSION QUESTIONS

1. Is the adversary system the best means for discovering truth in jury
   trials?
2. What is the legal significance of evidence?
3. What advantages does the prosecution have in being first to present evidence in a criminal trial?
4. Why are all witnesses exposed to cross-examination?
5. How does studying the rules of evidence help a police officer prepare a
   better case for the prosecutor?

6. Why should jurors be kept ignorant of many items of evidence known to both attorneys and the trial judge?
7. Discuss the difference between judicial determination of preliminary facts and judicial notice.
8. What are the major objectives of the rules of evidence? How are the rules designed to achieve these objectives?

GLOSSARY*

ACQUITTAL. Court or jury certification of the innocence of a defendant during or after trial.

ADMISSIBILITY. Determination of whether evidence, exhibits, or testimony will be allowed in trial; inadmissible evidence cannot be allowed and is therefore not presented in court and is not heard or examined by the triers of fact.

ADMISSION. A statement inconsistent with innocence of a crime; defendant admits a damaging fact.

BENCH. The presiding judge (and his position at the front of the courtroom).

CASE IN CHIEF. The main case of the prosecution or defense; their original array of evidence.

CRIMINAL ACT. Act or omission prohibited by law.

CRIMINAL INTENT. A determination of the mind; an intelligent purpose to do an act prohibited as criminal by law: *mens rea*.

CONFESSION. A statement acknowledging guilt; defendant's statement that he committed the crime charged.

CROSS-EXAMINATION. Questioning of witness by counsel for opposing party; follows the *direct examination* of a witness by the party calling the witness to court.

HEARSAY. Second-hand evidence; testimony of evidence not based on the personal knowledge of a witness, but information someone else has seen or heard and related to a testifying witness.

IDENTITY. Proof of a person's identity as being the individual alleged in the accusatory pleading.

JUVENILES. Persons under a specified age (usually eighteen) who may be processed in a special juvenile court on the issues of neglect and delinquency.

OBJECTION. Opposition to the introduction of certain evidence or questions during a criminal proceeding, or to judicial rulings. Linked with a "request to strike," to remove from the record any portion of the opposed evidence or question already before the triers of fact. The objection is granted when the presiding judge *sustains* it; it is *overruled* when denied.

PRESUMPTION. The inference of one fact from the existence of a related fact.

PRIMA FACIE. On the face of; at first view; uncontradicted.

REBUTTAL. The answer of the prosecutor to the defense case in chief; an opportunity for the prosecution to repair portions of the prosecution's case damaged by defense evidence.

*Terms not defined in the chapter text.

REJOINDER (SURREBUTTAL).   The answer of the defense to the prosecutor's rebuttal; an opportunity for the defense to repair portions of the defense
   case damaged by prosecution evidence during the rebuttal stage of a
   trial.

VENUE.   Place or area in which a crime was committed; *situs delicti*. Change
   of venue is to transfer a pending trial to another county or district.

The Roles of
Prosecutor
and
Defense Counsel

CHAPTER OBJECTIVES

1. In this chapter, the duties and responsibilities of the prosecutor in preparing accusatory pleadings and in prosecuting persons accused of crime will be explained, as will

2. The circumstances under which prosecutors can decline to prosecute, divert selected defendants from the criminal justice system, or engage in plea negotiations for a reduced charge or sentence in return for a guilty plea.

3. The client-attorney relationship between defendant and defense counsel will be examined, as well as the right of defendants to effective representation by their legal counsel, including complete loyalty and service in good faith to the best of counsel's ability.

4. In addition, the chapter will show the inability of an attorney to equitably defend his client when he is convinced of his client's guilt to the extent that he cannot or will not give his undivided

allegiance and conscientious services. Defense counsel's obligation to disprove charges against an apparently guilty defendant will also be outlined, as well as the

5. Development of the idea of the adversary system as a structure for the use of evidence to prove guilt or to demonstrate innocence.

Too often the basis for misunderstanding and hostility between the police and defense counsel and, at times, even the prosecuting attorney is a lack of knowledge of the role of defense counsel and prosecutor and an inadequate perception of how both are necessary for the proper administration of justice. Police frequently believe that the prosecutor is either protecting the criminal or is incompetent because he fails to prosecute or dismisses a pending case. The prosecutor has a dual role; as well as being an **advocate for the people,** he is also responsible for **administration and promotion of justice** for the accused under our laws and accusatory system. It is not uncommon for police to believe defense counsel morally, if not legally dishonest because he zealously defends a "guilty" client. Again, an understanding of his professional and ethical position within the justice system can help dispel such beliefs.[1]

The role of all attorneys in criminal cases is to see that justice is accomplished according to law and within the procedural processes of the adversary system; the adversary system depends for its vitality upon vigorous and proper challenges to assertions of governmental authority and accusations of crime, and upon the advocacy of conscientious prosecutor and defense counsel participating in a judicial search for truth.

The fundamental freedoms of individuals are always threatened by the power of government. Even in the so-called free world the relationship of the state to individual freedom can only be balanced by a government operating under reasonable laws and, in the case of persons accused of crime and threatened with a possible loss of freedom, an adversary system in which each participant is represented by legal counsel.

The prosecutor represents the people of the jurisdiction in which the trial is held, and defense counsel represents the defendant(s). In acting out these roles, both attorneys serve as advocates for their clients; the prosecutor presents the cause of the state, and the defense counsel presents the defendant's position by witnesses and argument.

Standards relating to the prosecution and the defense in criminal proceedings are fundamental dimensions of conduct acceptable in the role of advocate. Standards developed by the American Bar Association, state bar associations, and legislative enactment are more than ethical

---

[1] Johns v. Smyth, 176 F. Supp. 949 (1959).

guidelines and rules of decorum or propriety—they represent collected data as to the past conduct of the best prosecutors and defense counsel.[2] Although the roles of prosecution and defense counsel differ, each of these advocates are bound in the interests of justice to adhere to accepted standards of conduct throughout a criminal proceeding. Their activities range from duties to their clients to the advoidance of unprofessional conduct.[3]

The institution of advocacy and the adversary system seek justice by the production of evidence under fixed rules of procedure whenever there is a confrontation between the community (the people) and an individual accused of crime.

THE PROSECUTOR

The prosecutor ensures that the laws of his state or government are faithfully executed and enforced. He is an administrator of justice and an advocate; and in each capacity he must exercise a sound discretion.

The public prosecutor should be an attorney who is subject to the legal and ethical standards of his profession, and he should avoid any real or apparent conflict of interest with respect to his official duties. He should maintain the reality and appearance of the independence and integrity of his office.

A prosecutor's contact with the courts must be professionally correct. He must not engage in unauthorized ex parte* discussions with or submission of material to a judge relating to a particular case without affording the defense attorney the opportunity to be present, unless an in camera** inspection of evidence is authorized by law.

DECISION TO CHARGE

The prosecutor is the legal adviser to the grand jury and may explain the law and express his opinion on the legal significance of the evidence. He should not attempt to influence grand jury action in any manner that would be impermissible at trial before a petit jury.

However, because a grand jury is a body of citizens selected from the community without regard to any legal education, for a grand jury indictment the prosecutor must present sufficient available evidence to

---

[2]American Bar Association, **Standards Relating to the Prosecution Function and the Defense Function** (New York: American Bar Association, 1971), pp. 1–15.
[3]Raymond L. Wise, **Legal Ethics**, 2nd ed. (New York: Matthew Bender, 1970), p. 303 **et seq.**
*Outside the presence of the opposing party.
**Evidence viewed only by the court.

allow the members of the grand jury to decide whether or not the evidence warrants prosecution. Grand juries require a quorum of their membership to be present and a vote of twelve of those jurors is necessary to return an indictment.

A prosecutor should present to the grand jury only evidence which he believes would be admissible at trial. However, in appropriate cases he may present witnesses to summarize that evidence. He should disclose to the grand jury any evidence which he knows will tend to negate guilt, and he should recommend that the grand jury not indict the accused if he believes the evidence presented does not warrant an indictment under governing law.

If the prosecutor believes that a witness is a potential defendant he should not seek his testimony before the grand jury without informing him that he may be charged and that he should seek independent legal advice concerning his rights, and he should not compel the appearance of a witness whose activities are the subject of the inquiry if the witness states in advance that if called he will exercise his constitutional privilege not to testify.

Preliminary Hearing: Information.   In many jurisdictions, prosecutors are given the authority to route a case through court instead of the grand jury and the indictment process. The first step is the **preliminary hearing,** where the prosecutor assumes an adversary role presenting evidence before the presiding judge in an effort to secure a judicial ruling that there is sufficient evidence to warrant further prosecution. If the decision favors the prosecutor, he then files an **information** (accusatory pleading) in the trial court. In grand jury sessions the prosecutor is not confronted by opposing counsel; at a preliminary hearing the defendant and his legal counsel have an opportunity to be heard in response to the accusation.

Diversion from Criminal Justice.   The decision to institute criminal proceedings is initially and primarily the responsibility of the prosecutor. He should establish standards and procedures for evaluating complaints to determine whether or not criminal proceedings should be instituted.

Where the law permits a citizen to complain directly to a judicial officer or the grand jury, the citizen complainant should be required to present his complaint for prior approval to the prosecutor.

The prosecutor should explore the availability of a noncriminal disposition, including programs of rehabilitation, formal or informal, in deciding whether to press criminal charges. He should be familiar with the resources of social agencies that can assist in the evaluation of cases for **diversion from the criminal process.**

The prosecutor should first determine whether there is evidence

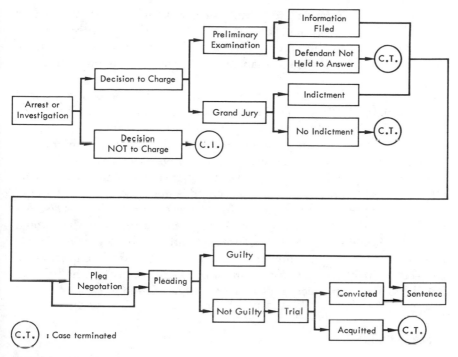

FIGURE 1.   Route of the accusatory pleading in felony prosecutions.

that would support a conviction. However, he is not obliged to present all charges which the evidence might support. He may, in some circumstances and for good cause consistent with the public interest, decline to prosecute. Some factors used in exercising his discretion to charge are:

1.   His reasonable doubt that the accused is in fact guilty
2.   The extent of the harm caused by the offense
3.   The disproportion of the authorized punishment in relation to the particular offense or the offender
4.   Possible improper motives of a complainant
5.   Prolonged nonenforcement of a statute, with community acquiescence
6.   Reluctance of the victim to testify
7.   Cooperation of the accused in the apprehension or conviction of others
8.   Availability and likelihood of prosecution by another jurisdiction

In making the decision to prosecute, the prosecutor should give no weight to the personal or political advantages or disadvantages that might be involved or to a desire to enhance his record of convictions. He should not be deterred from prosecution by the fact that in his jurisdiction juries have tended to acquit persons accused of the particular kind of criminal act in question, particularly when the offense involves a serious threat to the community, and he should not bring charges greater in number or degree than he can reasonably support with evidence at trial.

If the prosecutor is present at the first appearance of the accused before a judicial officer, he should cooperate in obtaining counsel for the accused. He should cooperate in good faith in arrangements for release under the prevailing system for pretrial release. He should not encourage an uncounseled accused person to waive preliminary hearing by securing an indictment, or seek delay in the preliminary hearing after an arrest has been made if the accused is in custody.

It is unprofessional conduct for a prosecutor to fail to disclose to the defense at the earliest feasible opportunity evidence that would tend to negate the guilt of the accused or mitigate the degree of the offense or reduce the punishment, and it is unprofessional conduct for a prosecutor intentionally to avoid pursuit of evidence because he believes it will damage the prosecution's case or aid the accused.[4]

DEFENSE COUNSEL

Counsel for the accused is an essential component of the administration of criminal justice. A **court** properly constituted to hear a criminal case must be viewed as a tripartite entity consisting of the judge (and jury, where appropriate), counsel for the prosecution, and counsel for the accused.

The basic duty of the defense attorney is to serve as the accused's counselor and advocate with courage, devotion, and to the utmost of his learning and ability, and according to law. He has no duty to execute any directive of the accused which does not comport with the law; and it is unprofessional conduct for an attorney intentionally to misrepresent matters of fact or law to the court.[5]

Defense counsel must disclose to his client any matter that might involve a conflict of interest or the defendant's choice of attorney.

Except for preliminary matters such as initial hearings or applications for bail, lawyers who are associated in practice should not undertake to defend more than one defendant in the same criminal case if the duty to one of the defendants may conflict with the duty to another.

In accepting payment of fees by one person for the defense of another, a lawyer should be careful to determine that he will not be con-

[4]Canon 7, Disciplinary Rule 7-103, Code of Professional Responsibility, American Bar Association.
[5]Canon 7, Disciplinary Rules 7-101, 7-102, Code of Professional Responsibility, American Bar Association.

fronted with a conflict of loyalty because his entire loyalty is due the accused. There must be an explicit understanding that the lawyer's entire loyalty is to the accused who is his client and that the person who pays his fee has no control of the case.

Whether privately engaged, judicially appointed, or serving as part of a legal aid or public defender system, the duties of a lawyer to his client are to represent his legitimate interests, and considerations of personal and professional advantage should not influence his advice or performance.

Defense counsel should seek to establish a relationship of trust and confidence with the accused. The lawyer should explain the necessity of full disclosure of all facts known to the client for an effective defense, and he should explain the obligation of confidentiality which makes privileged the accused's disclosures relating to the case.

As soon as practicable, defense counsel should seek to determine all relevant facts known to the accused. He should probe for all legally relevant information without seeking to influence the direction of the client's responses.

The lawyer may not instruct the client or intimate to him in any way that he should not be candid in revealing facts so as to afford the lawyer free rein to take action which would be precluded by the lawyer's knowing of such facts.

The decisions which are to be made by the accused after full consultation with counsel are: what plea to enter, whether to waive jury trial, and whether to testify in his own behalf. The decisions on what witnesses to call, whether and how to conduct cross-examination, what jurors to accept or reject, what trial motions should be made, and all other strategic and tactical decisions are the exclusive province of the lawyer after consultation with his client.

If a disagreement on significant matters of tactics or strategy arises between the lawyer and his client, the lawyer should make a record of the circumstances, his advice and reasons, and the conclusion reached. The record should be made in a manner that protects the confidentiality of the lawyer-client relation.

If the defendant has admitted to his lawyer facts which establish guilt and the lawyer's independent investigation establishes that the admissions are true, but the defendant insists on his right to trial, a lawyer must advise his client against taking the witness stand to testify falsely.

If, before trial, the defendant insists that he will take the stand to testify falsely, the lawyer must withdraw from the case, if possible. If withdrawal from the case is not possible, or if the situation arises during the trial and the defendant insists upon testifying falsely in his own behalf, the lawyer may not assist the perjury. Before the defendant takes the stand in these circumstances, the lawyer should make a record of the fact that the defendant is taking the stand against the advice of counsel in some appropriate manner without revealing the confidential communication to the court. The lawyer must confine his examination to identifying the witness as the defendant and permitting him to make his statement to the trier or triers of the facts; the lawyer may not engage in direct examination of the defendant as a witness in the conventional manner and may not later argue the defendant's known false version of facts to the jury as worthy of belief and he may not recite or rely upon the false testimony in his closing argument.

It is a lawyer's duty to advise his client to comply with the law, but he may advise concerning the meaning, scope, and validity of a law. However, it is unprofessional conduct for a lawyer to agree in advance of the commission of a crime that he will serve as counsel for the defendant (except as part of a bona fide effort to determine the validity, scope, meaning, or application of the law, or where the defense is incident to a general retainer for legal services to a person or enterprise engaged in legitimate activity). The attorney may not counsel his client or assist his client to engage in conduct which the lawyer believes to be illegal.[6]

Many important rights of the accused can be protected and preserved only by prompt legal action. Defense counsel should immediately inform the accused of his rights and take all necessary action to exercise such rights. He should consider all procedural steps which in good faith may be taken, including, for example, motions seeking pretrial release of the accused, obtaining psychiatric examination of the accused when a need appears, moving for a change of venue or continuance, moving to suppress illegally obtained evidence, moving for severance from jointly charged defendants, or seeking dismissal of the charges.

The duties of defense counsel are the same whether he is privately retained, appointed by the court, or serving in a legal aid or public defender system. He has the continuing duty to keep his client informed of developments in the case and the progress of preparing the defense.

After informing himself fully on the facts and the law, defense counsel should advise his client with complete candor concerning all aspects of the case, including his estimate of the probable outcome. It is unprofessional conduct to intentionally understate or overstate the risks, hazards, or prospects of the case in order to influence the accused's decision as to his plea.

The defense counsel should caution his client to avoid communication about the case with witnesses, except with his approval, to avoid any contact with jurors or prospective jurors, and to avoid either the reality or the appearance of any other improper activity.[7]

[6]*In re* **De Pamphilis**, 30 N.J. 470 (1959).
[7]*In re* **Robinson**, 136 N.Y.S. 548 (1912).

PUBLIC STATEMENTS

Neither the prosecutor nor the defense attorney should exploit the case for his own personal advantage. Neither attorney should utilize the news media for the purpose of influencing public opinion generally, or prospective or serving jurors individually. The attorneys in a case should obey the orders of the court regarding publicity and when they are of a different opinion than the court order they should seek a legal remedy rather than unilateral disobedience of the court order. There should be no public statements made which could interfere with the defendant's, and the people's, right to a fair trial.[8]

PLEA NEGOTIATIONS

The Guilty Plea. The process of plea negotiations has also been termed **plea bargaining.** This is consultation between prosecutor and defense counsel for the purpose of entering into an agreement advantageous to the defendant (a reduction in the charges, or a less severe sentence) in return for a **plea of guilty.** Prosecutors enter these agreements because justice is served by the guilty plea, statistically a conviction is noted in the case, and the local justice system avoids the expenses of a trial. It is a prosecutor's technique to avoid crowding the local courts and at the same time close out cases with convictions.

The prosecutor should be willing to consult with defense counsel concerning disposition of charges by plea. It is unprofessional conduct for a prosecutor to engage in plea discussions directly with an accused who is represented by counsel, except with counsel's approval. If the accused refuses to be represented by counsel, the prosecutor may properly discuss disposition of the charges directly with the accused. It is unprofessional conduct for a prosecutor knowingly to make false statements or representations in the course of plea discussions with defense counsel or the accused.

Defense counsel, whenever the nature and circumstances of the case permits, should explore the possibility of an early diversion of the case from the criminal process through the use of other community agencies. When a full investigation and study disclose that under controlling law and the evidence a conviction is probable, he should so

[8]American Bar Association Project on Standards for Criminal Justice, **Standards Relating to Fair Trial and Free Press** (New York: American Bar Association, (1968). See also Sheppard v. Maxwell, 384 U.S. 333 (1966); Estes v. Texas, 381 U.S. 532 (1965).

advise the accused and seek his consent to engage in plea discussions with the prosecutor, if such appears desirable. In these discussions it is unprofessional conduct for counsel knowingly to make false statements concerning the evidence in the course of plea discussions with the prosecutor, or to seek or accept concessions favorable to one client by any agreement that is detrimental to the legitimate interests of any other client.

A prosecutor may not properly participate in a disposition by plea of guilty if he is aware that the accused persists in denying guilt or the factual basis for the plea, without disclosure to the court; and if the accused discloses to his lawyer facts that negate guilt and the lawyer's investigation does not reveal a conflict with the facts disclosed but the accused persists in entering a plea of guilty, counsel may not properly participate in presenting a guilty plea, without disclosure to the court.

A prosecutor may properly advise the defense what position he, as prosecutor, will take concerning disposition, but he should avoid implying a greater power to influence the disposition of a case than he possesses.

If the prosecutor finds he is unable to fulfill an understanding previously agreed upon in plea discussions, he should give notice to the defendant and cooperate in persuading the court to allow the defendant to withdraw the plea and to restore the defendant to the position he was in before the understanding was reached or the plea made.

THE INVESTIGATION

The Prosecutor

A prosecutor is the **chief law enforcement official** of his jurisdiction, and ordinarily relies on police and other investigative agencies for the investigation of alleged criminal acts. He also has an affirmative responsibility to investigate suspected illegal activity when this is not adequately done by other agencies.

A prosecutor may not use illegal means to obtain evidence, and he should not obstruct communication between prospective witnesses and defense counsel, or advise any person to decline to give information to the defense.

The prosecutor may not promise a witness immunity from prosecution for some prospective criminal activity, except where such activity is part of an officially supervised investigative and enforcement program.

It is the duty of the defendant's attorney to conduct a prompt investigation of the circumstances of the case and explore all avenues leading to facts relevant to guilt and degree of guilt, or penalty. The investigation should always include efforts to secure information in the possession of the prosecution and law enforcement authorities. The duty to investigate exists regardless of the accused's admissions or statements to his attorney of facts constituting guilt or his stated desire to plead guilty. The defense attorney must not use illegal means to obtain evidence or information or to employ, instruct, or encourage others to do so; or to advise a person (other than a client) to refuse to give information to the prosecutor or counsel for co-defendants.

The defense attorney or prosecutor should interview prospective witnesses in the presence of a third person unless they are prepared to forego the impeachment of that witness by their own testimony as to what the witness stated in the interview, or to withdraw from the case in order to present his impeaching testimony.

Both the prosecutor and defense counsel should utilize available **discovery** procedures to supplement their investigation. An investigation by defense counsel is not completed until he has secured the data in the hands of the prosecutor as to the evidence against his client.

RELATIONS WITH EXPERT WITNESSES

A defense counsel or prosecutor who engages an expert for an opinion should respect the independence of the expert and should not seek to dictate the formation of the expert's opinion on the subject. To the extent necessary, the expert should be advised of his role in the trial as an impartial expert called to aid the fact-finders and the manner in which the examination of witnesses is conducted.

Neither the defense counsel nor the prosecutor may pay an excessive fee for the purpose of influencing the expert's, or other witness', testimony. Neither attorney may fix the amount of the fee contingent upon the testimony the expert or other witness will give or the verdict in the case.[9]

COURTROOM DECORUM

As officers of the court the prosecutor and the defense counsel should support the authority of the court and the dignity of the trial courtroom by strict adherence to the rules of decorum and by manifesting an attitude of professional respect toward the judge, opposing counsel, witnesses, and jurors.

Each attorney should comply promptly with all orders and directives of the court, but each has a duty to make **objections** to have the

[9]**In re Schapiro**, 128 N.Y.S. 852 (1911).

record reflect adverse rulings or judicial conduct which he considers prejudicial to his client's legitimate interests. Both attorneys have a right to make respectful requests for reconsideration of adverse rulings.

SELECTION OF JURORS

The prosecutor and defense attorney should be prepared, prior to trial, to function effectively in the selection of the jury and in the exercise of jury challenges.

Each attorney should be prepared to raise any appropriate issues concerning jury panel selection.

Where it appears necessary to conduct a pretrial investigation of the background of jurors, both the prosecutor and defense counsel should restrict inquiries to investigatory methods which will not harass or unnecessarily embarrass potential jurors or invade their privacy and, whenever possible, should restrict this investigation to records and sources of information already in existence.

In jurisdictions where both advocates are permitted personally to question jurors on **voir dire,*** this opportunity should be used solely to obtain information for the intelligent exercise of challenges. *Voir dire* should not be used by either the prosecutor or defense counsel to present factual matter which is not likely to be admissible at trial or to argue a case to the jury. Jurors should be treated with deference and respect. Neither attorney may communicate privately with persons summoned for jury duty or impaneled as jurors concerning the case prior to or during the trial.

The attorneys for the people or defendant should not make comments to or ask questions of a juror for the purpose of harassing or embarrassing the juror in any way that will tend to influence judgment in future jury service.

If the lawyer has reasonable ground to believe that the verdict may be subject to legal challenge, he may properly, if no statute or rule prohibits such course, communicate with jurors for that limited purpose, upon notice to opposing counsel and the court.

OPENING STATEMENTS

In their opening statements the prosecutor and defense counsel should confine their remarks to evidence each advocate intends to offer, and which they believe in good faith will be available and admissible.

A prosecutor or defense counsel may not offer false evidence,

---

*Examination under oath as to qualifications.

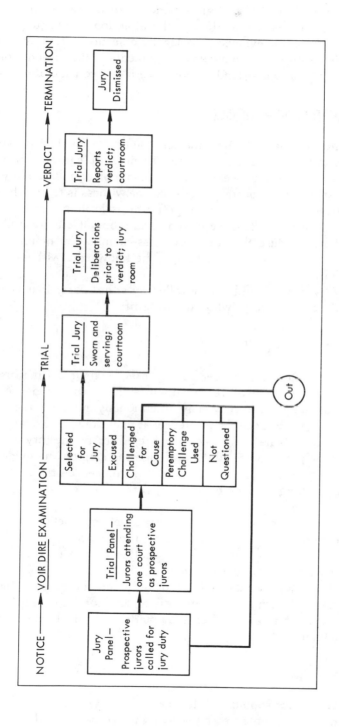

FIGURE 2. The jury process in criminal prosecution.

27

whether by documents, tangible evidence, or the testimony of witnesses; or bring inadmissible matters to the attention of the judge or jury, or offer inadmissible evidence, ask legally objectionable questions, or make other impermissible comments or arguments in the presence of the judge or jury which would tend to prejudice a fair consideration of the case.

EXAMINATION OF WITNESSES

The interrogation of all witnesses should be conducted fairly, objectively, and with due regard for the dignity and legitimate privacy of the witness, and without seeking to intimidate or humiliate the witness unnecessarily. An advocate's belief that the witness is telling the truth does not necessarily preclude appropriate cross-examination in all circumstances, but may affect the method and scope of cross-examination. No one should misuse the power of cross-examination or impeachment to discredit or undermine a witness if he knows the witness is testifying truthfully.

A witness should not be called by either party if it is known that he will claim a valid privilege not to testify.

ARGUMENT TO THE JURY

The prosecutor and the defense counsel, in their closing arguments to the jury, may argue all reasonable inferences from evidence in the record, but neither attorney may intentionally misstate the evidence or mislead the jury as to the inferences it may draw, or use arguments calculated to inflame the passions or prejudices of the jury or that would divert the jury from its duty to decide the case on the evidence, by injecting issues broader than the guilt or innocence of the accused under the controlling law, or by making predictions of the consequences of the jury's verdict.

An attorney should not express a personal belief or opinion as to the truth or falsity of any testimony or evidence or the guilt of the defendant, or attribute the crime to another person unless such an inference is warranted by the evidence.

The attorney may refer to or argue on the basis of facts, outside the record, if such facts are matters of common public knowledge based on ordinary human experience or matters of which the court can take judicial notice.

SENTENCING

The prosecutor should seek to assure that a fair and informed judgment is made on the sentence and to avoid unfair sentence disparities. Where sentence is fixed by the judge without jury participation, the prosecutor ordinarily should not make any specific recommendation as to the appropriate sentence unless his recommendation is requested by the court or he has agreed to make a recommendation as the result of plea discussions. Where sentence is fixed by the jury, the prosecutor should present evidence on the issue within the limits permitted in the jurisdiction, but he should avoid introducing evidence bearing on sentence which will prejudice the jury's determination of the issue of guilt.

The prosecutor should disclose to the defense and to the court at or prior to the sentencing proceeding all information in his files which is relevant to the sentencing issue.

In the interests of **post-conviction justice,** defense counsel should be familiar with the sentencing alternatives available to the court and should endeavor to learn its practices in exercising sentencing discretion. The consequences of the various dispositions available should be explained fully by the lawyer to his client. He should present to the court any ground that will assist in reaching a proper disposition favorable to the accused.

The prosecutor should assist the court and the probation agency in securing complete and accurate information for use in the **pre-sentence report.** He should disclose to the court any information in his files relevant to the sentence. If incompleteness or inaccurateness in the pre-sentence report comes to his attention, he should take steps to present the complete and correct information to the court and to defense counsel.

If a pre-sentence report or summary is made available to the defense lawyer, he should seek to verify the information contained in it and should be prepared to supplement or challenge it if necessary. If there is no pre-sentence report, or if it is not disclosed, he should submit to the court and the prosecutor all favorable information relevant to sentencing, and in an appropriate case be prepared to suggest a program of rehabilitation based on his exploration of employment, educational, and other opportunities for his client made available by community services.

Counsel should alert the accused to his right of addressing the court, and also to the possible dangers of making a judicial confession which might tend to prejudice his appeal.

The trial lawyer's responsibility includes presenting appropriate motions, after verdict and before sentence, to protect the defendant's rights.

After conviction, counsel should explain to the defendant the meaning and consequences of the court's judgment and his right of appeal. The lawyer should give the defendant his professional judgment as to whether or not there are meritorious grounds for appeal and as to the probable results of an appeal. He should also explain to the defendant the advantages and disadvantages of an appeal. The decision whether or not to appeal must be the defendant's own choice, but the lawyer should take whatever steps are necessary to protect the defendant's rights of appeal.

If counsel for a convicted defendant, after investigation, is satisfied that another lawyer who served in an earlier phase of the case did not provide effective assistance, he should not hesitate to seek relief for the defendant on that ground. However, if he is satisfied after investigation that another lawyer who served in an earlier phase of the case provided effective assistance, he should so advise his client and he may decline to proceed further.

Illustrative of the demands of trial practice in criminal actions, and the concern of attorneys as to their duty to clients, is that the zealously guarded confidentiality of lawyer and client can be breached by an attorney accused by the client of ineffective advocacy. A lawyer whose conduct of a criminal case is drawn into question by his former client is entitled to testify concerning the matters charged and is not precluded from disclosing the truth concerning the accusation, even though this involves revealing matters that were given in confidence.

DEFENSE COUNSEL FOR INDIGENT DEFENDANTS

Beginning with *Gideon v. Wainwright*,[10] the U.S. Supreme Court has made it clear that states have an obligation to ensure that defendants in criminal cases are provided with defense counsel, regardless of their economic means. A basic question since the *Gideon* mandate is whether the state should leave it up to local communities to provide defense counsel, or whether it should provide the service directly.

The U.S. Advisory Commission on Intergovernmental Relations suggests standards:

> **Recommendation 31, State Responsibility for Providing Defense Counsel for the Indigent:** The Commission recommends that each state establish and finance a statewide system for defense of the indigent, making either a public defender or coordinated assigned counsel service readily available to every area of the state.[11]

Every community should be served by the defense counsel system best suited to its needs—either a full-time public defender office or a coordinated assigned counsel system—provided that minimum standards

---

[10]372 U.S. 335 (1963).
[11]*State-Local Relations in the Criminal Justice System* (Washington, D.C.: U.S. Government Printing Office, 1971), p. 52.

of performance are observed. Minimum standards include such requirements as the following:

> Legal representation for every person who is without financial means to secure competent counsel when charged with a felony, misdemeanor or other charge where there is a possibility of a jail sentence.
>
> Standards of eligibility that effectively screen out those with sufficient funds to procure competent private counsel, but, at the same time, not so stringent as to create a class of unrepresented accused.
>
> Representation available immediately after a person has been taken into custody or arrested, at the first and every subsequent court appearance, and at every stage in the proceeding.[12]

TO REMEDY ERROR OR INJUSTICE

Representation should be available to persons convicted of crime at appeal or other post-conviction proceedings to remedy error or injustice, including parole and probation-violation proceedings, extradition proceedings, and proceedings involving possible detention or commitment of minors or alleged mentally ill persons. Probation and parole revocation hearings may involve both disputed issues of fact and difficult questions of judicial or administrative judgment. These hearings lack some of the evidentiary and other technical complexities of trials, but where the facts are disputed, the same process of investigating, marshaling, and exhibiting facts is often demanded as at trial. A lawyer for the defense is needed in these proceedings because of the range of facts which will support revocation, the breadth of discretion in the court or agency to refuse revocation even though a violation of the conditions of release is found, and the absence of other procedural safeguards which surround the trial of guilt.

CASE STUDY

Raleigh Johns v. W. Frank Smyth, 176 F. Supp. 949 (1959).*

Petitioner is a state prisoner serving a life sentence for the murder of one Melvin Childress in accordance with a final judgment of the Circuit Court of the City of Richmond, Virginia, entered on December 17, 1942. Petitioner and Childress were inmates at the State Penitentiary when the killing took place on October 7, 1942. While there is no tran-

---

[12]Ibid., pp. 52–53.
*Headings added by authors for reader's convenience.

script of the evidence available from the state court, as no court reporter was present, the petitioner's signed statement given on the day following the crime is to the effect that he killed Childress with a knife in the cell of the latter, when Childress took hold of the petitioner and suggested an unnatural sexual act. An investigation by prison authorities points to other motives for the killing but, for the purpose of this proceeding by way of habeas corpus, we are not particularly concerned with the details of the crime.

On some date following the return of an indictment on October 14, 1942, the state court assigned counsel to represent petitioner. The record reveals that the court-appointed attorney had been practicing for a period of approximately fifteen years at the time of petitioner's trial. There is nothing in this proceeding which would reflect that the trial judge or prosecutor were negligent in the performance of their duties with respect to the appointment of court-assigned counsel and the ensuing trial.

While the Attorney General now states that petitioner has not exhausted his state court remedies before turning to the federal court, this is apparently in conflict with a prior concession stated in the brief that such remedies had been exhausted. The record discloses that petitioner has, on two prior occasions, instituted habeas corpus proceedings in the state court. The first case alleged the incompetency of assigned counsel and was dismissed without a plenary hearing. A petition for a writ of error to the Supreme Court of Appeals in Virginia was filed too late, but the latter court nevertheless treated the request as an original petition and denied same. Apparently certiorari was not requested in the United States Supreme Court. On April 19, 1955, petitioner made application to the Hustings Court of the City of Richmond, Part II, which court declined to consider the question of incompetency of counsel because of the prior adjudication of this point, but granted a plenary hearing on an entirely different issue. On June 30, 1955, the state court denied the petition. Subsequent appeals to the Supreme Court of Appeals of Virginia and the United States Supreme Court were to no avail; a petition for a writ of certiorari having been denied on February 25, 1957. The present proceeding was instituted in this court on May 29, 1957, but has been delayed due to petitioner's alleged inability to secure what he considered to be pertinent evidence.

At no time during the state court proceedings did petitioner waive his right to allege the incompetency of his court-appointed counsel. True, he did not appeal the initial adverse ruling on habeas corpus to the United States Supreme Court, but he properly excepted to the action of the state court in declining to consider this point in his later petition which thereafter followed the course of exhaustion of state remedies. Indeed, the Assistant Attorney General candidly stated that if the matter reverted to further proceedings in the state court, the Attorney General would take the position that the point had been previously adjudicated. Under such circumstances petitioner has exhausted his state court remedies and has not been accorded a plenary hearing on the sole question before this court.

While the petition alleges several points for consideration, it is only necessary to determine whether petitioner had a fair trial by reason of the actions of court-appointed counsel. All too often the incompetency of counsel is assigned in vague allegations which are invariably without merit. It is on the basis of the testimony now given by court-assigned counsel that this court has arrived at the conclusion that petitioner's constitutional rights have been invaded.

Client-Attorney Relationship: Fair Trial. One of the cardinal principles confronting every attorney in the representation of a client is the requirement of complete loyalty and service in good faith to the best of his ability. In a criminal case the client is entitled to a fair trial, but not a perfect one. These are fundamental requirements of due process under the Fourteenth Amendment. United States ex rel. *Weber v. Ragen,* 7 Cir., 176 F.2d 579, 586. The same principles are applicable in Sixth Amendment cases (not pertinent herein) and suggest that an attorney should have no conflict of interest and that he must devote his full and faithful efforts toward the defense of his client. *Glasser v. United States,* 315 U.S. 60, 62 S.Ct. 457, 86 L.Ed. 680; *Von Moltke v. Gillis,* 332 U.S. 708, 725, 726, 68 S.Ct. 316, 92 L.Ed. 309.

With this in mind, let us examine the facts to determine (1) whether the representation afforded petitioner at his murder trial was so totally lacking that it cannot be said that he had a fair trial in the usual sense of the word, and (2) whether the court-appointed attorney was so prejudiced and convinced of his client's guilt of *first degree murder* that he was unable to, and did not, give his client the "undivided allegiance and faithful, devoted service" which the Supreme Court has held to be the right of the accused under the Constitution, and (3) whether the attorney's interest in his client was so diverted by his personal beliefs that there existed a conflict in interest between his duty to his client and his conscience.

The importance of the attorney's undivided allegiance and faithful service to one accused of crime, irrespective of the attorney's personal opinion as to the guilt of his client, lies in Canon 5 of the American Bar Association Canon of Ethics, in effect during 1942, where it is said:

> It is the right of the lawyer to undertake the defense of a person accused of crime, regardless of his personal opinion as to the guilt of the accused; other-

wise innocent persons, victims only of suspicious circumstances, might be denied proper defense. Having undertaken such defense, the lawyer is bound, by all fair and honorable means, to present every defense that the law of the land permits, to the end that no person may be deprived of life or liberty, but by due process of law.

The difficulty lies, of course, in ascertaining whether the attorney has been guilty of an error of judgment, such as an election with respect to trial tactics, or has otherwise been actuated by his conscience or belief that his client should be convicted in any event. All too frequently courts are called upon to review actions of defense counsel which are, at the most, errors of judgment, not properly reviewable on habeas corpus unless the trial is a farce and a mockery of justice which requires the court to intervene. *Diggs v. Welch*, 80 U.S.App.D.C. 5, 148 F.2d 667. But when defense counsel, in a truly adverse proceeding, admits that his conscience would not permit him to adopt certain customary trial procedures, this extends beyond the realm of judgment and strongly suggests an invasion of constitutional rights.

Little need be said of the trial. The accused did not testify. No proposed instructions were submitted to the trial judge in behalf of the defendant, although under the law of Virginia it was possible for the defendant to have been convicted of involuntary manslaughter and received a sentence of only five years. The defense attorney agreed with the prosecutor that the case would be submitted to the jury without argument of counsel. The instructions given by the court were generally acceptable in covering the categories of first and second degree murder, but failed to mention the possibility of a manslaughter verdict.

Standing alone these complaints would have no merit as they may properly be considered as trial tactics. However, when we look at the motivating force which prompted these decisions of trial counsel, it is apparent that "tactics" gave way to "conscience." In explanation of the agreement not to argue the case before the jury, the court-appointed attorney said:

I think an argument to the jury would have made me appear ridiculous in the light of evidence that was offered. . . .

I had enough confidence in the judgment of the jury to know that they could have drawn an inference, and I would have been a hypocrite and falsifier if I had gone before the jury and argued in the light of what Johns told me that that statement was accurate. . . .

Well, sir, I did not and I wouldn't be dishonest enough to do it in the light of Mr. Johns' statement to me. You can say what the law is and what the record discloses, but if I asked a client, an accused on defense, to explain some such statement as this and he gives me the explanation that Johns gave me, I consider it dishonest. You can talk about legal duty to client all you wish, but I consider it dishonest for me to get up before a jury and try to argue that the statement that came out from the Commonwealth was true when Johns had told me that it wasn't. The explanation that he gave me was very vague.

Immediately thereafter, the following occurred:

Q: That you could not conscientiously argue to the jury that he should be acquitted?
A: I definitely could not.
Q: Regardless of what the law is or what your duty to a client is?
A: You can talk about law and you can talk about my duty to clients, I felt it was my—that I couldn't conscientiously stand up there and argue that point in the light of what Johns had told me.

The attorney was then asked whether he ever considered requesting permission to withdraw from the case. He replied in the negative.

Effective Representation. No attorney should "frame" a factual defense in any case, civil or criminal, and it is not intimated by this opinion that the attorney should plant the seeds of falsehood in the mind of his client. In the instant case, however, the evidence adduced by the prosecution suggested some provocation for the act through the summary of the statement given by the defendant on the day following the killing. When the defendant was interviewed by his court-appointed attorney, the attorney stated that he had reason to doubt the accuracy of the defendant's statement. It was at this time that the attorney's conscience actuated his future conduct which continued throughout the trial. If this was the evidence presented by the prosecution, the defendant was entitled to the faithful and devoted services of his attorney uninhibited by the dictating conscience. The defendant could not be compelled to testify against himself, and if the prosecution saw fit to use the defendant's statement in aid of the prosecution, the attorney was duty bound to exert his best efforts in aid of his client. The failure to argue the case before the jury, while ordinarily only a trial tactic not subject to review, manifestly enters the field of incompetency when the reason assigned is the attorney's conscience. It is as improper as though the attorney had told the jury that his client had uttered a falsehood in making the statement. The right to an attorney embraces effective representation throughout all stages of the trial, and where the representation is of such low caliber as to amount to no representation, the guarantee of due process has been violated. *Powell v. State of Alabama,* 287 U.S. 45, 53 S.Ct. 55, 77 L.Ed. 158; *People v. DeSimone,* 9 Ill.2d 522, 138 N.E.2d 556.

The entire trial in the state court had the earmarks of an *ex parte* proceeding. If petitioner had been without the services of an attorney, but had remained mute, it is unlikely that he would have been worse off. The state argues that the defendant may have received a death sentence. Admitting this to be true, it affords no excuse for lack of effective representation.

Holding that the petitioner was not accorded a "fair trial" in the true sense of the word, because of the motivating forces which dictated the actions and decisions of his court-appointed counsel, we turn to the legal problem which has given this court grave concern. It is a general rule of law that a federal court cannot order the release of a state prisoner, grounded upon the lack of effective counsel in the state court proceeding, unless the incompetence and ineffectiveness of the attorney is so obvious that it becomes the duty of the trial judge or prosecutor (both state officers) to intervene and protect the rights of the accused. United States ex rel. *Darcy v. Handy*, 3 Cir., 203 F.2d 407, certiorari denied sub nom., *Maroney v. United States* ex rel. Darcy, 346 U.S. 865, 74 S.Ct. 103, 98 L.Ed. 375; *United States* ex rel. *Thompson v. Dye*, D.C.W.D.Pa., 103 F.Supp. 776, affirmed 3 Cir., 203 F. 2d 429, certiorari denied sub nom. *Thompson v. Dye*, 345 U.S. 960, 73 S.Ct. 946, 97 L.Ed. 1380; *Hudspeth v. McDonald*, 10 Cir., 120 F.2d 962, 968. With this general statement, this court is in accord.

As indicated, there is nothing apparent in this case which would require the trial judge or prosecutor to intervene. But the state of facts here presented indicates that the general rule should not be considered as inflexible. In *Massey v. Moore*, 348 U.S. 105, 75 S.Ct. 145, 99 L.Ed. 135, the Supreme Court indicated that, on the question of the mental condition of the accused at the time of trial, the presence or absence of affirmative misconduct on the part of the state at the trial was irrelevant. Cf. *Snider v. Smyth*, 4 Cir., 263 F.2d 372; *Betts v. Brady*, 316 U.S. 455, 473, 62 S.Ct. 1252, 86 L.Ed. 1595.

Conscience vs. Duty. If it be necessary to engraft an exception on the general rule, it would appear that one is appropriate here, for indeed it would be a dark day in the history of our judicial system if a conviction is permitted to stand where an attorney, furnished to an indigent defendant, candidly admits that his conscience prevented him from effectively representing his client according to the customary standards prescribed by attorneys and the courts.

Counsel for petitioner will prepare an appropriate order granting the writ of habeas corpus and remanding petitioner to the proper authorities of the State of Virginia for further proceedings on the charge of murder. Should the respondent elect to appeal from the order of this court, the effectiveness of the order shall be stayed pending appeal, provided that the appeal is promptly noted and perfected.

SUMMARY

The major thrust of this chapter is to flesh out the two-party adversary concept of America's legal system by detailing the duties and standards of behavior of the two legally trained major participants: the prosecutor and the defense counsel.

The prosecutor has the awesome duty of deciding whether or not to prosecute, determining the route of the accusation, and deciding whether to negotiate a guilty plea or go to trial. Defense counsel must effectively represent his client, the defendant; share differing responsibilities with his client for preparing a defense; advise his client candidly of all the aspects of the case, including possible outcomes and the rationale for pleading guilty if an advantageous plea can be arranged. From the initial investigation, through pretrial actions and the trial itself, to the post-conviction stage, each of these advocates must continue to serve his side in the search for truth on the issue of guilt or innocence.

DISCUSSION QUESTIONS

1. List five factors likely to support a prosecutor's decision not to prosecute.
2. What decisions regarding the conduct of his defense should be made by an accused after full consultation with his legal counsel? What decisions are the exclusive province of defense counsel after consultation with his client?
3. What kind of evidence should a prosecutor present to a grand jury in seeking a criminal indictment?
4. Discuss the implications of this situation: A defendant admits to his lawyer facts that establish guilt, but insists on his right to trial.
5. Outline the pretrial investigation a defense attorney pursues as a duty to his client.
6. In their closing arguments to a jury, what inferences from the evidence in the trial record may prosecutor or defense counsel develop?
7. What are the duties of defense counsel in the sentencing (post-verdict) stage of a trial? Of the prosecutor?
8. What provisions exist to provide indigent defendants with legal counsel?
9. Discuss the decision of the court in *Johns v. Smyth*, particularly the statement: "In a criminal case the client is entitled to a fair trial, but not a perfect one."

GLOSSARY

ADVOCACY. Defending, assisting, or pleading for another; to defend by argument.

ADVOCATE. One who renders legal advice and pleads the cause of another before a court or tribunal; a counselor; one who speaks in favor of another.

APPEAL.   Judicial review; a post-conviction step in judicial proceedings. After the decision of a trial court, the removal of the case (cause) to a higher court with authority to review the decision of the lower court for the purpose of obtaining a retrial.

BAIL.   Release of a defendant upon his written agreement to appear in court as required. Cash or other security may be required.

DISCOVERY.   Disclosure by the prosecution of certain evidence regarding a defendant in a pending trial. There is limited disclosure by the defense. Term is generally identified with defense pretrial request to prosecutor to disclose facts of the police case against defendant.

EXPERT WITNESS.   An individual, with reference to a particular subject, who possesses knowledge not acquired by ordinary persons; a man of science or a person possessing special or peculiar knowledge acquired from practice and experience.

GRAND JURY.   A certain number of persons selected according to law and sworn to the duty of receiving complaints and accusations of crime in criminal cases, to hear evidence presented by the "state," and to return indictments when they are satisfied a trial is warranted. The term "grand" developed because, at common law, the number of persons on this jury was set at not less than twelve nor more than twenty-three, while the ordinary *trial jury* (petit jury, as distinguished from grand jury) was a body of twelve persons.

GUILTY.   The result of a guilty verdict in a criminal prosecution (jury or judge); the result of judicial acceptance of a guilty plea; the opposite of innocence.

MOTION.   Application to court for a legal remedy.

PRELIMINARY HEARING.   A judicial hearing or examination of witnesses to determine whether or not a crime has been committed, and if the evidence presented by the prosecutor is sufficient to warrant the commitment, or bailing, of the accused pending trial.

PRESENTENCE REPORT.   A report by a probation officer of an investigation conducted at court direction into the social and criminal history and resources of a convicted defendant, and containing a recommendation to the sentencing judge concerning the best program of corrections for the offender.

Police Responsibility for Evidence: Standards

CHAPTER OBJECTIVES

1. Chapter 3 will discuss the now enlarged role of police in assisting the defense counsel throughout the procedure of pretrial discovery;
2. Disclose new national standards of work performance in criminal investigation that have been developed by the Police Task Force, National Advisory Commission on Criminal Justice Standards and Goals; and
3. Show that defense counsel can utilize these standards in the evaluation of local police work performance.

One of the major functions of police is to investigate reported crimes. The duties of police officers at the scene of a crime may include searching the crime scene and interviewing persons at the scene who witnessed the crime. The officer reporting the offense has the task of detailing the circumstances of the crime and arranging for the submission to an appropriate laboratory for examination any physical evidence discovered and collected during the scene search. Unless the case is closed or reassigned, the reporting officer has the further responsibility of making inquiries and taking other action which will identify the guilty person and accomplices, if any.

Dual Service Role of Police. For many years police agencies accepted this fundamental responsibility as serving the prosecution, and prevailing practices were oriented to the development of evidence for the state. However, the expansion of defendant's rights has placed the police in a service role to the defense counsel as well. This revision of role concepts has led to the development of standards which position the police as nonpartisan representatives of society acting in the interests of all concerned in the investigation of crime.

Standards for police behavior in criminal investigations clearly delineate this **dual service role of police.** The **standards** established by the fourteen-member Task Force on Police (an interdisciplinary group of practitioners and scholars from all areas of criminal justice) of the National Advisory Commission on Criminal Justice Standards and Goals (NACCJSG), published in *Report on Police*,[1] together with related standards shaped by task forces in other areas of criminal justice (courts, corrections, crime prevention), formulate for the first time *national* criminal justice standards. (The recommendations of each task force were processed through and approved by the parent or umbrella organization, the NACCJSG.)

Chief E. M. Davis of the Los Angeles Police Department, Chairman of the Task Force on Police, states in his preface to *Report on Police* that he and the members of his committee intended their report to be a practical document that would provide standards linked to the "real" world of American police service and represent the most up-to-date and proven experience in the police field; and that these standards would provide reasonable and practical answers to the many problems which daily confront working policemen.

CRIMINAL INVESTIGATION

Written investigative priorities should be established to ensure police agencies' best efforts. Guidelines for these priorities follow:

1.   Patrol officers, usually the first on the scene, should conduct thorough **preliminary investigations.** Investigative specialists should be assigned to serious or complex preliminary investigations.

2.   **Investigative priorities** are based upon the seriousness of the crime,

[1]National Advisory Commission on Criminal Justice Standards and Goals, **Report on Police** (Washington, D.C.: U.S. Government Printing Office, 1973).

time of reporting, available information about suspects, agency resources, and community attitudes.

3. Every police agency employing seventy-five or more personnel should assign full-time criminal investigators (for follow-up investigations). Agencies with fewer personnel should assign criminal investigation specialists only where specific needs are present:

a. **Specialization** within the criminal investigation unit should take place when necessary to improve overall efficiency within the agency.

b. Criminal investigation operations should be decentralized to the most effective command level; but unusual cases may be investigated by a centralized unit.

4. Quality investigation **control procedures** should include:

a. A follow-up report of each open investigation every ten days and command approval of every continuance of an investigation past thirty days.

b. Constant inspection and review of individual, team, and unit criminal investigation reports and investigator activity summaries; and

c. Team and unit performance measures based on arrests and dispositions, crimes cleared, property recovered, and caseload.

5. Every police agency with seventy-five or more personnel should consider the use of **case preparation technicians** to insure that all evidence that may lead to the conviction or acquittal of defendants is systematically prepared and presented for review by the prosecuting authority. The case preparation technician may handle:

a. Development of policies and procedures in cooperation with the prosecutor and court.

b. All police information on each case. This should be in a systematically prepared, written report that contains the following: copies of the incident report, follow-up reports, identification and laboratory reports, and any other reports necessitated by the investigation.

c. All case disposition information and notification records.

d. The establishment of complete case files.

e. Other case preparation duties, such as delivering case files to prosecutors; presenting subjects in custody for arraignment, or obtaining a warrant and disseminating warrant information; representing the agency at all pretrial hearings; notifying witnesses; documenting the final disposition of cases; and returning the case report file to the originating unit for retention.

6. Police agencies should **coordinate criminal investigations** with all other agency operations. This coordination should include:

a. Clearly defined procedures for the exchange of information between investigative specialists and between those specialists and
uniformed patrol officers;
b. Systematic rotation of generalists into investigative specialties;
and
c. Equitable publicity of the efforts of all agency elements.[2]

CRIMINAL CASE FOLLOW-UP

The system concept in criminal justice extends the criminal investigation
function of police far beyond case preparation—it also includes the **monitoring of cases and final disposition.** Because this is an emerging area
for police it has been limited to programs identified with major cases.
The follow-up of police investigations should lead to greater understanding by police of the many factors involved in the prosecutor's decision to charge or drop a case, the grand jury's decision not to indict,
a court's release of a defendant, or a jury's acquittal. Police practices
while conducting searches and seizures, preparing reports, or interviewing witnesses or interrogating suspects, can be evaluated regarding their
contribution to the dismissal of cases.

Recommendations of the Police Task Force of the National Advisory Commission on Criminal Justice Standards and Goals are summarized as follows:

1.   Every police agency should develop policies and procedures to follow up on the disposition of its criminal cases.

2.   Every police agency should identify criminal cases which require
special attention by the prosecuting agency, and require a **police representative** to attend personally all open judicial proceedings related to
these cases. A close personal liaison should be maintained with assigned
prosecutors.

3.   The police agency should review administratively all major criminal
cases prosecuting agencies decline to prosecute or later cause to be dismissed. That review should result in a referral of each such case to the
concerned officer's commanding officer for administrative action to
correct any police deficiencies which may have weakened the case.

4.   In some cases a referral should be made to the prosecuting attorney
for that agency's action to correct any deficiencies for which it may have
been responsible.

5.   Every police agency should encourage court and prosecutor evalua-

[2]**Ibid.**, pp. 233–34 (Standard 9.7—Criminal Investigation).

tion of investigations, case preparation, courtroom demeanor, and testimony of police officers and the police agency should be informed of those evaluations.

6. Every police agency should cooperate with other criminal justice agencies, particularly with the courts in making diversion, sentencing, probation, and parole determinations.[3]

POLICE LEGAL ADVISERS

The concept of in-house legal advice has arisen from the complexities of case and statute law and the multiple procedural safeguards protecting persons accused of crime. It has been fostered by the communication gap between police and prosecutor in criminal cases, and between police and city or county attorneys in civil matters.

Legal assistance to police should improve police compliance with law and upgrade police investigations, particularly in developing police procedures in regard to evidence and its use. Recommendations of the Police Task Force of NACCJSG contain the following major provisions:

1. Police agencies should make maximum use of the offices of city attorney or county attorney, the county prosecutor, and the state attorney general to acquire needed legal assistance. When necessary, the agency should employ a legal adviser.

2. **Legal assistance** may include:
   a. Legal counsel to the police executive in all phases of administration and operations;
   b. Liaison with the city or county attorney, the county prosecutor, the state attorney general, the United States attorney, the courts, and the local bar association;
   c. Review of general orders, training bulletins, and other directives to insure legal sufficiency;
   d. Case consultation with arresting officers and review of affidavits in support of arrest and search warrants in cooperation with the prosecutor's office;
   e. Advisory participation in operations where difficult legal problems can be anticipated;
   f. Attendance at major disturbances—and an on-call status for minor ones—to permit rapid consultation regarding legal aspects of the incident;

[3] Ibid., p. 86 (Standard 4.5—Criminal Case Follow-up).

g. Participation in training to insure continuing legal knowledge at all levels within the agency;

h. Drafting of procedural guides for the implementation of recent court decisions and newly enacted legislation;

i. Provision of legal counsel for ad hoc projects, grant proposal development, and special enforcement problems.

3. When **determining the need for a legal adviser** or a legal unit, the police agency should consider:

a. Whether the city or county attorney and the county prosecutor are located near police headquarters;

b. Whether the staffs of the city or county attorney and the county prosecutor are full-time or part-time, and whether they are permitted to engage in private practice;

c. Whether the city or county attorney and the county prosecutor have effective legislative programs;

d. Whether the county prosecutor's office can be consulted routinely on planned enforcement actions prior to arrests;

e. Whether assistant prosecutors discuss pending cases adequately with arresting officers prior to trial;

f. Whether the county prosecutor's office will draft affidavits for arrest and search warrants and give other legal assistance whenever needed;

g. Whether the city or county attorney's staff is willing to answer routine questions; how promptly they respond to requests for written opinions; and how detailed and complete such opinions are;

h. How willingly the city or county attorney files suits on behalf of the police agency, how vigorously he defends suits against the agency and its members, and how experienced his staff is in matters of criminal law and police liability;

i. The educational level of police agency employees, comprehensiveness of preservice training given officers, and the quantity and quality of agency in-service training.

4. There are several **constraints to legal assistance** for the police agency—the legal adviser should not prosecute criminal cases; decide what cases are to be prosecuted or what charges are to be brought, except by agreement with the prosecutor; be assigned tasks unrelated to the legal assistance function that would interfere with performance of that function; nor should he prosecute infractions of discipline before internal trial boards or serve as a member of any trial or arbitration board; and he may not accept any client who may be in conflict with his duties for the police agency.[4]

[4] **Ibid.**, pp. 280–81 (Standard 11.2—Legal Assistance).

THE CRIME SCENE AND PHYSICAL EVIDENCE

The increasing use of physical evidence by police criminal investigators in their dual role of servicing the prosecutor and, through pretrial discovery, the defendant and his legal counsel, requires the careful, comprehensive, and scientific examination of crime scenes. Dissatisfaction with the performance of rank-and-file police at crime scenes has led to the development of evidence technicians equipped with specialized equipment for gathering physical evidence.[5]

The Police Task Force of NACCJSG recommends the professionalization of this role of evidence technician and the establishment of local crime laboratories so that the physical evidence at crime scenes will be collected by a technician and forwarded to equally qualified laboratory technicians for examination, analysis, and interpretation. The essential elements of these two standards calling for evidence technicians and crime laboratories follow.

The Evidence Technician

1. Every state and every police agency should acknowledge the importance of efficient identification, collection, and preservation of **physical evidence;** its accurate and speedy analysis; and its proper presentation in criminal court proceedings. Every agency should insure the deployment of specially trained personnel to gather physical evidence 24 hours a day.

2. Police agencies should consider the use of specially trained regular patrol officers to devote a percentage of their regular duty time to the location, collection, and preservation of physical evidence.

3. Large agencies should use specially trained **evidence technicians** to locate, collect, and preserve physical evidence at crime scenes and to deliver such evidence to the appropriate laboratory facility.

4. All police agencies should have access to a formalized basic training course in evidence-gathering techniques to develop the agency's capacity to retrieve and use any physical evidence present at the scene of a criminal investigation. Every sworn officer should be responsible for evidence collection in cases where an evidence technician or a specially trained patrol officer is not available.

5. Whenever practicable the police agency should maintain a mobile

[5]Paul B. Weston, and Kenneth M. Wells, **Criminal Investigation: Basic Perspectives,** 2nd ed. (Englewood Cliffs, N.J.: Prentice-Hall, Inc., 1974), pp. 46–47.

evidence-collection van containing equipment for protecting and illuminating large crime scene areas and for storing and preserving physical evidence.

6.   Each police agency should be responsible for its own crime scene searches and should immediately insure that all crime scenes are thoroughly examined for physical evidence, and that all evidence collected is submitted to the appropriate laboratory facility for analysis.[6]

The Crime Laboratory

1.   Every state should have a consolidated criminal laboratory composed of local, regional, or state facilities capable of providing the most advanced **forensic science services** to police agencies.

2.   All police agencies should have access to at least one laboratory facility capable of timely and efficient processing of physical evidence.

3.   The laboratory facilities available should provide analysis for routine cases involving substances such as narcotics, alcohol, and urine; analysis and processing of most evidence within 24 hours of its delivery; immediate analysis of evidence, such as narcotics, where the detention or release of a subject depends upon the analysis; and qualitative field tests and quantitative follow-up tests of narcotics or dangerous drugs.

4.   The crime laboratory within a police agency should be a part of the organizational entity that includes other support services, and should be directed by an individual who reports only to the agency's chief executive or to a staff authority who reports directly to the chief executive.

5.   Every **crime laboratory technician** responsible for the completion of scientific analyses or testing should hold at least an earned baccalaureate degree in chemistry, criminalistics, or a closely related field from an accredited institution, and have a thorough working knowledge of laboratory procedures.

6.   The working staff must be sufficient to meet the demands of the laboratory caseload, and adequately trained and experienced.

7.   Salaries should be commensurate with the specialized duties and qualifications of each position so that well-qualified personnel are attracted to and retained in these positions.

8.   The police chief executive should insure that the police laboratory function receives appropriate fiscal support and that the adequacy of its facilities is considered in structuring the agency's annual budget.

---

[6]**Ibid.**, p. 295 (Standard 12.1—Evidence Technicians).

9. The **laboratory reporting system** must provide data relative to its involvement in:
   a. Reported crimes
   b. Investigated crimes
   c. Suspects identified or located
   d. Suspects cleared
   e. Suspects charged
   f. Prosecutions
   g. Acquittals
   h. Convictions[7]

SAFEKEEPING OF EVIDENCE

Police agencies must arrange for the safe storage of evidence, its retrieval from and return to storage as required by the nature and circumstances of individual cases, and the proper disposition of such evidence when no longer required. The requirements of the **chain of possession** call for documentation of this routine from the time of discovery through each change of custody to final disposition.

Evidence may have its own record-keeping program in many police agencies, but its storage facilities are generally joined with the storage facilities for other articles coming into the possession of police and being held until claimed by owners or other lawful disposition. Although police custodians of such property have always been security-conscious and alert for documentation of the disposition of evidence and other property, a theft of narcotics valued at over $7 million from the New York City Police Department Property Clerk's vault has led to new procedures in property protection for evidence and other stored property.

Police agencies desiring adequacy in this area must adjust local procedures and facilities to prevailing practices. The Police Task Force of NACCJSG has published recommendations for the safekeeping of all property in police custody. The major provisions of this standard follow.

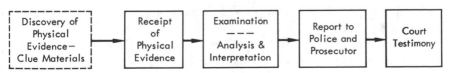

FIGURE 3. Forensic science services to police agency by a crime laboratory.

[7]*Ibid.*, pp. 299–300 (Standard 12.2—The Crime Laboratory).

1. *Records Management.* Each police agency must establish a system for the secure and efficient storage, classification, retrieval, and disposition of items of evidentiary or other value that come into the custody of the agency.

2. This will require the establishment of a filing systems that includes:
   a. A chronological record of each occasion when property is taken into police custody;
   b. A separate itemized list of all items of property that are taken into custody;
   c. A record that indicates the continuity of the property from its entry into the system to its final disposition. This record should include the name of each person accountable for each item of property at any given time.

3. Regular property inventories and property record audits should be conducted to insure the integrity of the system.

4. *Written Procedures.* The system should have written procedures governing the function of the property system. All components of a multicomponent property system should be governed by the same procedures.

5. *Duties of Personnel.* Civilian personnel may be assigned to all elements of the property system, thus releasing sworn officers for other police duties.

6. Personnel assigned to the property function are not to be involved in authorizing the booking, release, or disposition of property. Such authorization should be provided by the booking officer, the investigating officer, or another designated sworn employee.

7. The police agency should clearly designate the employees responsible for around-the-clock security of the property area and restrict entry of all other personnel into this area.

8. Personnel assigned to locate the owners of identifiable property should not be involved in the arrest or prosecution of the persons accused of crimes involving that property.

9. Procedures should be instituted to facilitate the authorized removal of property from the system as required and without delay.

10. All identifiable property should be returned as soon as practicable after the rightful owner is located. Prior to disposition, all such property should be checked against stolen property records and all firearms should be compared with records related to weapons to make certain that no "wants" or "holds" exist for such items.

11. When property is no longer needed for presentation in court, and the owner cannot be determined, it should be disposed of promptly.[8]

8Ibid., pp. 309–10 (Standard 12.3—The Property System).

POLICE INTELLIGENCE OPERATIONS

Collecting items of information concerning the nature of local crime and criminal behavior patterns and possible organizational or associational factors is within the criminal investigation function of police. In the course of police intelligence operations there are considerable surveillance activities, both visual and audio; extensive use of informants and undercover agents; the "turning" of criminals to cooperate with police and their development as accomplice-witnesses.

The scope of the activities of police assigned to intelligence work and the investigative function has varied from jurisdiction to jurisdiction. The publishing of a standard in this area by the Police Task Force of NACCJSG provides guidelines for the intelligence operations of police. The major elements of this standard follow.

1. The police agencies in every state should establish and maintain the capability to gather and evaluate information and to disseminate intelligence in a manner that protects every individual's right to privacy while it curtails organized crime and public disorder.

2. The state should establish a central gathering, analysis, and storage capability and an intelligence dissemination system.

3. The state system should disseminate specific intelligence to local agencies according to local needs and should disseminate general information throughout the state.

4. Local police agencies should actively participate in providing information and receiving intelligence from this system.

5. The number of local personnel assigned to this operation should be based on local conditions, but at least one person in each police agency should be designated to be responsible for liaison with the state intelligence system.

6. In smaller agencies the **intelligence specialist** should be required to take direct enforcement action only where limited agency resources make it absolutely necessary. In larger agencies the intelligence specialist should be required to take direct enforcement action only where a serious threat to life or property makes it absolutely necessary.

7. When the size of the intelligence operation permits, organized crime intelligence should be separate from civil disorder intelligence.

8. The intelligence operation should include an independent and well-secured reporting and record system.[9]

9 **Ibid.**, p. 250 (Standard 9.11—Intelligence Operations).

POLICE STANDARDS AND THE DEFENSE

The foregoing police standards offer a valid basis for the evaluation of police behavior in an investigation. The prosecutor, the court, and even more critically, the defense counsel can now probe police behavior against a background of performance standards aligned with the prevailing practices in "better" police organizations.

Areas of questioning can now range from whether the police witness followed the routine of his employing agency, and whether these prescribed procedures are in accordance with the authoritative standards developed by the Police Task Force and approved and published by the NACCJSG.

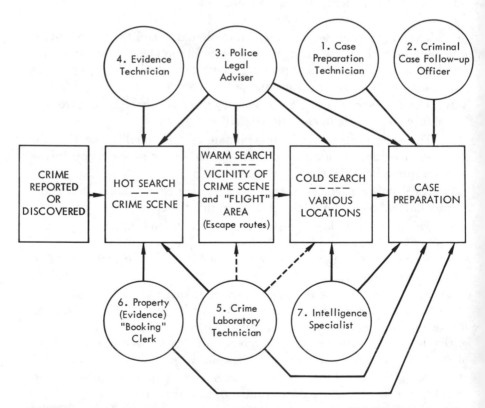

FIGURE 4.   Apprehension Process: impact areas of roles created by published standards of the National Advisory Commission on Criminal Justice Standards and Goals and related to criminal investigation. (Numbered as they appear in chapter.)

SUMMARY

New, *national* standards of work performance for police in the area of criminal investigation can place responsibility upon local police to improve any substandard practices.

Police criminal investigators have a dual service role in searching crime scenes, collecting physical evidence, and locating and interviewing witnesses. Through the court process of pretrial discovery many aspects of the police case must be disclosed to defense counsel; formerly, only the prosecutor had access to police case data. The Police Task Force of the National Advisory Commission on Criminal Justice Standards and Goals recommended and published standards in the first national formulation of guidelines for police behavior. These standards contain recommendations for routines concerned with criminal investigation; criminal case follow-up; legal assistance for police; searching for and collecting and preserving physical evidence; laboratory examinations of such evidence; the safekeeping of evidence and other property in police custody; and police intelligence operations.

These standards and the enlarged role of the police agency offer defense counsel new criteria for evaluating police behavior in a criminal investigation.

DISCUSSION QUESTIONS

1. What primary factor led to the role of police as nonpartisan investigators?

2. List and discuss the developing standards for criminal investigation.

3. What are the objectives of criminal case follow-up procedures?

4. What factors in local government would justify a police agency's need for a legal adviser or legal unit?

5. What are the advantages to a police agency of the development and use of evidence technicians in regard to physical evidence and its use in court? Of a professionally staffed and adequately equipped crime laboratory?

6. How does an effective system for property management of items of evidentiary and other value contribute to the admissibility of physical evidence?

7. Is it necessary to exercise the same care in collecting "intelligence" as in recording the statements of witnesses? Explain.

GLOSSARY

CRIMINALISTICS. Scientific discipline directed to the recognition, identification, individualization, and evaluation of physical evidence by the application of the natural sciences in matters of law and science.

DIVERSION. Finding alternatives to formal action within the criminal justice system.

FORENSIC SCIENCE. Application of scientific knowledge to the solution of crimes and in support of the investigation of crime. (See Criminalistics)

INTELLIGENCE (POLICE). Clandestine or secret collecting and evaluating of information about crime and criminals not normally available through overt investigative techniques.

PHYSICAL EVIDENCE. Things and traces (clue materials) found at crime scenes, upon suspects, or at places or upon persons otherwise related to a criminal investigation.

STANDARD. Desirable or ideal work performance level; work as expected by supervisors and associates; prevailing practices or authoritative recommendations to upgrade prevailing practices.

Witnesses and Testimonial Proof

CHAPTER OBJECTIVES

1. Chapter 4 will discuss testimony as distinguished from other evidence. It will also
2. Reveal the procedures for securing the attendance of witnesses in court, including explanations of subpoenas and writs of *habeas corpus;*
3. Examine the foundation that must be established to qualify witnesses and outline the circumstances of privileged communications; and finally,
4. Disclose the primary attack areas of cross-examination and the manner of impeaching witnesses.

Most evidence in criminal trials is testimonial. **Testimony** is a method for establishing disputed facts through the questioning of witnesses in open court. The witness' attendance in court allows personal scrutiny by the trier of fact. Testimony is the oral transmission of information from witness to jury.

Testimony has a trilogy of weaknesses: half-truths, lies, and silence. A witness can convince himself that he clearly observed a very nebulous or confused event or one that never happened. He may stretch his imagination to conform his testimony to any necessary story line. Sometimes, a lying witness may be really convinced he is telling the truth. The witness may be in the marginal area of consciousness, unwilling either to tell the truth or deliberately lie. A silent witness may conceal true facts within his personal knowledge.[1] Another weakness of testimonial proof may be exploited by cross-examination showing friendship, dislike, indebtedness, or animosity.

Perception, recall, and verbalization all militate against a witness' describing an observed event exactly as it happened. Generally, an observer sees the things he expects to see. The process of distortion also carries over into memory. The observer only remembers what he perceived minus what has been stamped out or obliterated by the decaying function of time—from the event to the statement or testimony of a witness. Putting memory into words in a courtroom lessens reliability because of the effect of the audience (jury, questioner, and spectators) on a witness. Fear, anger, and annoyance distort recall and verbalization. This effect is often heightened by the questioner's planned words and actions.[2]

Memory loss is probably the primary reason for the legal conclusion that **affirmative testimony is stronger than negative testimony.** The story of a credible witness about some observed happening is stronger than the story of an equally credible witness that nothing happened. The latter witness may have forgotten the event, but it is unlikely that any person would recall an event that did not happen.

In general, parties in a criminal case are allowed to call as many witnesses as necessary to establish their accusation or defense. Each side chooses the order in which it summons witnesses to give testimony.

In the interest of justice, any competent witness who appears to have personal knowledge of some relevant and material fact should be called to testify. The court, on its own motion or on the motion of any party, may call witnesses and question them as if they had been produced by a party to the action. The parties may object to the questions asked by the judge and the evidence offered as if such witnesses were called and examined by an adverse party. Such witnesses may be cross-examined by all parties.

Witnesses who are not parties to the action may be barred from hearing the testimony of other witnesses. They usually wait in the hall-

---

[1] Harry P. Kerr, **Opinion and Evidence: Cases for Argument and Discussion** (New York: Harcourt Brace Jovanovich, 1962), pp. 41–44.
[2] L. R. C. Howard, "Some Psychological Aspects of Oral Evidence," **The British Journal of Criminology**, 3, no. 4 (April 1963), 342–60.

way or a nearby room until called to testify. Witnesses who are neither parties to the action nor serving as legal counsel are excluded from the courtroom. This practice makes certain that no witness' testimony is influenced by the answers of other witnesses or the queries of an attorney or the court. This may not prevent collusion between witnesses, but it does make it hazardous. This procedure makes witnesses acting in concert about untrue facts more vulnerable to cross-examination.

ATTENDANCE OF WITNESSES

Citizens have a duty to appear and testify to such facts within their knowledge as may be necessary for the administration of justice. A criminal defendant has the right to be confronted with the witnesses against him at trial under the Sixth and Fourteenth Amendments. The right of confrontation prevents the use of depositions or *ex parte* affidavits against a defendant in place of personal examination and cross-examination of the witness.

The process used to compel appearance as a witness is the **subpoena** *ad testificandum*. A subpoena *duces tecum* compels the witness to bring specified books, documents, and records to court.

A properly served subpoena is a court order compelling the person named therein to be in court on a certain day. Fees and expenses are usually offered to persons residing a substantial distance away from the trial court. Special arrangements are made to secure the attendance of expert witnesses. Subpoenas are issued by the trial court, but either the prosecutor or defense counsel may secure subpoenas as necessary.

Witnesses who fail to respond to a subpoena may be cited and punished for contempt of court. Continued refusal to appear as a witness may result in the issuance of a body attachment or arrest warrant, ordering an appropriate court or peace officer to bring the reluctant witness to court. Out-of-state witnesses can be compelled to appear and testify.[3] Flight to avoid testifying as a witness in a felony trial is punishable as a federal offense.[4] The fugitive witness will be returned, when apprehended, to the federal judicial district in which the original crime was committed or is being tried. He may be prosecuted in federal court, and he may be served with a subpoena ordering him to appear and testify at the original trial.

When the testimony of a person in the custody of a law enforcement or correctional agency is material, his attendance at trial is ob-

---

[3]The Uniform Act to Serve the Attendance of Witnesses from Without the State in Criminal Cases (9 Uniform Laws Annotated 86) adopted by most states. (See Section 1334 **et seq.**, California Penal Code, for an example of the text of this act.)
[4]Title 18, United States Code, Section 1073.

tained by a court order or writ: *Habeas corpus ad testificandum*. The party calling the witness applies to the trial judge in writing saying that (1) the testimony to be given is material, and (2) the witness is detained in custody. If the trial judge concludes the application is in good order and good faith, he directs the person having custody of the prisoner-witness to bring him to court on a specific date to testify.

A witness is not considered "unavailable" for confrontation and cross-examination by the defendant unless the prosecutor has made a good faith and timely effort to obtain his presence at trial.[5]

Once in court, a witness who refuses to swear or affirm to tell the truth or to testify may be punished for contempt. When a witness refuses to answer a question, the court may rule that the question is both material and relevant and order the witness to answer. If the witness still refuses, he may be charged with contempt of court.

COMPETENCE

The competence of a witness and his credibility are closely related, but should not be confused. A witness' testimony must be based on his observation of the subject matter he is testifying about. In the proper case, a nonexpert may give opinion evidence, but during cross-examination opposing counsel can determine whether the witness' opportunity for observation was sufficient to afford a reasonable basis for the conclusion or opinion he expresses. A witness who has had a chance to observe should be considered competent to testify about what he observed, unless he is otherwise disqualified. The court rules upon a witness' **competence;** the **credibility** of a witness' testimony is evaluated by the jurors —or by the court in a trial without a jury. Competence is determined before evidence is given; credibility is evaluated after evidence is given. Briefly, a witness is competent if he is legally qualified to testify. He must have all the required characteristics, and none of the disabilities.

At common law, a potential witness who lacked religious belief was incompetent. Most states, by constitution or statute, no longer require a potential witness to believe in a supreme being or divine punishment. Instead of taking the oath, such witnesses affirm that they will tell the truth.[6]

Infamy was also a common law disqualification. Treason and felonies were designated many years ago as infamous crimes. After conviction for treason or felony a citizen lost the right to vote, to hold office, to serve on a jury, and to testify as a witness. Today, however, prior convictions of crime may reduce credibility but not competence.

[5]Barber v. Page, 390 U.S. 719 (1968).
[6]Rule 603, Federal Rules of Evidence.

Persons interested in the outcome of a case before the court were also excluded from the role of witness at common law. This exclusion even disqualified the defendant as a witness. Today, bias or interest may be shown to attack the credibility of a witness but not to prevent his testimony.

Mental incapacity can bar the testimony of a witness. A witness is ordinarily presumed to have the mental capacity to testify. However, his capacity may be challenged. The challenge may be based on the fact that the proffered witness is an infant or insane or intoxicated. The trial judge determines the competence of a child to testify. His decision is based on the child's comprehension of the obligation to tell the truth and his intellectual or physical capacity to observe and recall. The same general tests apply to the competence of an insane person. Intoxication may relate to the witness' condition at the time of the event he intends to testify about, or his condition at the time he is offered to testify. If the witness is intoxicated in court, his condition is pertinent to his competence as a witness. Intoxication at the time of the event has a bearing only on his credibility, unless the witness was too intoxicated to observe or recollect the event.

Policemen, attorneys in the case, jurors, and trial judges may all be competent to give evidence. If the evidence may be obtained through other witnesses, however, it is considered poor practice to call an attorney, juror, or judge in the case as a witness and it raises dangerous questions of due process. The Federal Rules of Evidence prevent the judge presiding at the trial, or a juror sitting in the trial, from testifying to evidence relevant to the issues of the trial.[7]

Parties to a crime and accomplices are competent to testify, although their participation in the offense or the advantages they might gain by giving testimony may affect their credibility. Although an accomplice is a competent witness, his testimony may be legally insufficient to convict the defendant unless it is corroborated by other admissible evidence.

A witness may be considered incompetent because of the confidentiality of privileged relationships such as husband and wife, or attorney and client.

PRIVILEGED COMMUNICATIONS

A witness may have a privilege not to testify, or one of the parties involved in the trial may have a privilege not to have the witness testify, when the matter sought to be disclosed is a communication made in confidence in the course of a husband and wife, lawyer and client,

[7]Rule 605–06.

clergyman and penitent or physician or psychotherapist and patient relationship.

The concept of privileged communications in Anglo-American criminal justice is based on the confidentiality of communications between husband and wife, attorney and client, priest and penitent, and physician and patient. Originally, privileged communications may have been based on the honor of a spouse, an attorney, a priest, or a physician. More recently, privileged communications have been protected for their inherent confidentiality. The privilege is based on the need to free a person from apprehension about matters he might communicate in the close relationship of marriage, while consulting a legal advisor, in the role of penitent, or as a patient receiving treatment. The success of the relationship requires that the communication be treated in confidence and not be disclosed. Confidentiality is an essential element of these relationships. Disclosure of any communication within these relationships is believed to threaten the foundations of community life, and is likely to do more harm to community life than the benefit that could be gained from dispensing with the confidential relationship.

Spouses, by common law and most statutes, are either partially or entirely incompetent to testify against each other. The basic reason for this rule is to promote the unity or confidential and close relationship between the **husband and wife,** because a different rule would tend to disrupt the home life of married couples. There is usually an exception to this rule when a crime is committed by one spouse against the other or against their children.

There is one jurisdiction which distinguishes a "marital privilege"[8] and a "confidential marital communication."[9] The marital privilege gives only the testifying spouse the privilege of not testifying against a spouse who is a party to the action, as well as not being called as a witness.[10] The spouse who is a party to the action does not hold the privilege under this part of the statute. When the communication between spouses has been made in confidence while they were husband and wife, both spouses have the privilege against disclosure and also preventing the disclosure by the other. In addition, neither spouse need be a party to the action in order to claim this privilege. This "confidential marital communication privilege" is sufficiently broad to prevent the testimony of an eavesdropper or the testimony of a third party to whom one of the spouses has revealed the confidential communication.[11] The usual exceptions apply, such as actions between spouses, or to communications made to enable anyone to commit a crime.

In the case of **attorney-client** privilege, a client would be unwilling

[8]California Evidence Code 970 **et seq.**
[9]California Evidence Code 980 **et seq.**
[10]California Evidence Code 971.
[11]California Evidence Code 980.

to communicate or cooperate with his own attorney. In criminal cases, this lack of confidentiality would destroy the adversary system of justice. The privilege is basically with the client, and though the attorney may claim the privilege it is only on behalf of the client. If the client waives the privilege, the attorney loses his right to claim the privilege.

However, there may be no attorney-client privilege: when the service of the attorney is sought to enable anyone to commit a crime or a fraud; when the communication is relevant to a breach of duty by the attorney to his client or the client to his attorney; or when the attorney has attested to a document relevant to the issues of the case.

In connection with **penitents and patients,** the penitent would be unable to fulfill his commitments to his God or his religion. Full disclosure by patients is essential to proper care and treatment, and would be impossible if disclosures were not confidential and could be the basis of, or used to aid, a criminal prosecution against a patient.

Marital communications are presumed to be confidential,[12] and at least one state, New Jersey, has enacted a legal presumption of confidentiality between lawyer and client. In California, all privileged communications claimed under the foregoing relationships are presumably confidential. The opponent of the claim of privilege has the burden of proving that the communication was not confidential.[13]

All too often, under common law, the privilege claimant was required to show the confidentiality of the communication. While this issue would be heard out of the presence of jurors, and often in chambers, it did compel many claimants to reveal the subject matter of the communication. These presumptions avoid the need for such disclosure.

The privilege of not revealing the content of a privileged communication is waived when any holder of the privilege, without coercion, discloses a significant part of the communication or has consented to such disclosure by others, or fails to claim the privilege when he has the standing and opportunity to claim it. However, one spouse's waiver of the privilege does not affect the right of the other spouse to institute a claim of privilege, and this is true of other joint holders of a privilege (two or more). The waiver of this right by any one joint holder of the privilege does not affect the right of another joint holder to claim the privilege.

THE PERSONAL KNOWLEDGE REQUIREMENT

Although each witness must affirm or swear to his willingness to testify truthfully, and can be heard only in the presence and subject to the ex-

---

[12]Blau v. United States, 340 U.S. 332 (1951).
[13]California Evidence Code, Section 917.

amination of all parties to an action, the major test for admitting testimony is personal knowledge. The testimony of a witness about a particular matter is inadmissible unless he has personal knowledge of the matter. When a party objects, such personal knowledge must be shown before the witness may testify. A witness who gives second-hand testimony under an exception to the hearsay rule (see Chapter 5, Hearsay Evidence), must have personal knowledge about the hearsay conduct or words. To a limited extent, expert witnesses are allowed to offer their opinion on fact situations which are not based on personal knowledge. However, the general requirement for both expert and nonexpert witnesses is personal knowledge. Did the witness perceive the event or incident about which he is willing to testify? Did he receive this knowledge through his senses (seeing, hearing, touching, smelling, or tasting)? If he did (and that may be shown by otherwise admissible evidence including the witness' own testimony) then his testimony satisfies this basic requirement of personal knowledge.

A witness with personal knowledge of an event or happening is generally assumed to recall it. A witness' faulty **recollection** may impair his recall of a perceived event or incident, but is more of a trade-off of problems than a part of the personal knowledge requirement. A witness may only claim that a certain item of testimony is true to his best recollection, but he implies he has knowledge about the matter. A witness often prefaces his recollection of a perceived event or incident with the words, "I think." Rulings over many years of courtroom use of this prefatory term make it synonymous with the words, "I believe." The testimony then given is viewed from this frame of reference: The witness is telling what he remembers.

The memory of a witness may be refreshed by questioning. Unfortunately, this is most often done by a hostile cross-examiner, but it may be done by the counsel who called the witness or by the trial judge. Sometimes, the testimony of one witness casts doubt about the recollection of another witness.

Any kind of reminder by association is a device which stimulates recollection. Police investigators often use open-end questions when interviewing witnesses to aid total recall: "And then what happened?" "What gave you that impression?" During pretrial conferences in the office of the prosecutor or defense counsel, witnesses are interviewed as a necessary step in preparing a case for trial. The memory of a witness may need refreshing at this time. A witness is often given the opportunity, in these pretrial conferences, to view a previous statement he made to police, or to review prior testimony or other data which may assist in total recall.

Record of Past Recollection. When recall of an observed event is less than perfect, counsel questioning a witness in court may hand a memorandum over to the witness for inspection to refresh the witness' memory. If the memorandum, upon inspection by the witness, does improve his recollection, he may testify from this revived recall of the fact involved.

Because such memorandum is not evidence, but only aids in eliciting testimony, it may not be proffered as tangible evidence by the party calling the witness. Counsel for the opposition, however, is entitled to inspect the memorandum handed to an in-court witness to search for grounds for objecting to its use. He may request it be made available for his reference during cross-examination. In some circumstances, he may ask that the memorandum be submitted to judge or jury for examination.

When recollection of the witness is not refreshed, the memorandum may be proffered as tangible evidence if the witness testifies that he has no present recollection of the event described, but does recognize the writing as made by him when the facts were still fresh in his mind. In effect, he testifies that the memorandum is a factual account of his past recollection. For a record of past recollection to be admissible, the witness must testify he knew the facts from personal knowledge and correctly recorded them when the facts were fresh in his memory.

In California, when a writing is handed to a witness to revive present recollection, all parties to the action must be given an opportunity to inspect it before any questions concerning it may be asked of the witness. The California Evidence Code also requires the production at the trial, at the request of the adverse party, of any writing used to refresh the memory of a witness—whether the witness used the writing to revive his recollection when testifying or before appearing in court. It does not matter when the writing was used to revive the witness' recollection. If the writing is not produced, the witness' testimony on the matter involved will be stricken from the court record. However, production may be excused and the testimony allowed to remain in the record if the writing is not in the possession or control of the witness or the party calling him, and cannot be procured by the witness or the party involved through the use of legal process or other means available to them. California discovery procedures (see Chapter 14) permit discovery of all written statements by a witness on the subject of his testimony so that the witness may be thoroughly cross-examined.

REASONABLE OPPORTUNITY FOR OBSERVATION

A witness can testify to an observable fact when he appears to have had a reasonable opportunity to observe it. If no reasonable opportunity existed within the scope of the witness' five senses, then he lacks personal knowledge and his testimony is inadmissible. The invalidation of proffered evidence for lack of personal knowledge is often confused with hearsay. This is understandable. Many witnesses seek to testify by claiming personal knowledge when they only know the fact involved from the reports of others. Although there are exceptions which permit this retelling of another's story, there is no exception to the doctrine of personal knowledge—no one can testify to a fact he did not observe.

There is a line of questioning which establishes the opportunity of a witness for observation:

Q: Where were you at approximately 11:00 P.M. on the 28th of July?
A: Home. 62 Cathcart Street.
Q: Did anything unusual occur at or about that time?
A: Yes.
Q: What?
A: I heard a lot of noise out front.
Q: What did you do?
A: I went to the window and looked out.
Q: What did you see?

This line of questioning places the witness in relation to the place of occurrence, orients his recall to the date and time of the event involved, and indicates he was attentive and had an opportunity to observe. It establishes a **foundation of place, time, and circumstances** for further questioning. Also, the noisy event which is the subject of the above series of questions must be within the scope of at least two senses, hearing and sight. Is it reasonable to assume that an average person would hear the noise of the event from his inside location? Is it possible for a person of average eyesight looking out of the same window to observe the location of the event?

EXAMINATION OF WITNESSES

In examining witnesses, a questioner will not be allowed to use questions assuming facts not proved, double (compound) questions, or queries that are argumentative or indefinite and uncertain. Cross-examination is the form of inquiry used to attack adverse witnesses. Trial judges will not permit witnesses to be abused beyond the reasonable techniques of cross-examination. Most courts permit some excesses in this area because it is often the role of the cross-examiner to discredit the witness if possible, to help the triers of fact determine the truth from conflicting testimony.

The questioning of a witness is controlled by the trial judge. He must see that questioning is effective for ascertaining the truth, that a witness is protected from undue harassment or embarrassment, and that a witness gives responsive answers to questions. The witness is expected to be **responsive to a question.** Unless he is restricted by the question's form, he may give more than a simple yes or no. Answers that are not responsive are stricken from the record on the motion of any party.

The examination of a witness generally proceeds along the following lines:

1. Direct examination, cross-examination, redirect examination, re-cross-examination, and continuing thereafter by redirect and recross-examination.

2. Each phase of the examination of a witness is usually concluded before the succeeding phase begins.

3. After direct and cross-examination, the court may allow additional testimony on new subject matter by the witness under examination if the interests of justice will be served by the new testimony. The adverse party may cross-examine upon this new subject.

4. The defendant in a criminal action may not, without his consent, be subject to direct examination by another party to the action.

EVIDENCE ON DIRECT EXAMINATION

The first questioning of a witness about a matter that is not within the scope of any previous examination of the witness is direct examination. This is a fundamental method of producing testimonial proof. It is the means by which a composite story is heard from the mouths of witnesses. It is the opportunity for the prosecutor or the defense counsel to ask questions designed to establish the existence or nonexistence of facts favorable or unfavorable to the party represented by the questioner.

The party calling the witness conducts the direct examination. The questioner is friendly, anxious to help the witness repeat the story he told during a pretrial interview or interviews. Of course, the witness is expected to tell his story in his own words as he best recalls it, but the questioner guides him to keep him from straying too far from facts relevant to the case at trial.

Questioners conducting a direct examination may use direct questions or the narrative form of inquiry. The direct question, in its most simple form, calls for a direct one-sentence answer. The narrative query offers the witness a chance to tell what happened at a certain time and place. The type of questions used will depend on the questioner's evaluation of the witness and his potential coherence in answering narrative questions. Direct questions are safe. Responses are not likely to deviate from the basic line of questioning.

Leading questions—phrased to suggest an answer—are not permitted. However, this type of question is permitted concerning noncontroversial data necessary as a prelude to the witness' testimony, or when necessary—because of the witness' youth, age, lost memory, or lack of intellectual capacity—to elicit the desired information.

The following illustrates an acceptable use of leading questions when the facts are not in controversy:

Q: Mrs. R———, were you home on the evening of July 28th?
A: Yes I was.
Q: At 10:30 or 11:00 o'clock that evening, did you have occasion to receive a phone call?
A: Yes, I did.

A prosecutor must be particularly adept at direct examination. He must create a clear visual picture of the crime and culprit through questions he asks witnesses and the answers he receives. The picture (or theory) of the crime must be sufficiently clear to convince each juror beyond a reasonable doubt that the crime was committed and the defendant committed it.

Direct examination is directive, but it is not suggestive of the desired or expected answer. Foundations of time, place and circumstances are a necessary prelude to the essential testimony. The best basis for asking clear questions and receiving relevant answers is a **pretrial conference with the witness.** This is not an attempt to coach the witness and there should be no feeling on the part of the attorney or witness that a discussion of the witness' testimony before the trial is a questionable practice. The purpose of the pretrial conference and discussion is to make certain that the attorney knows all the information this witness can testify to, and to advise the witness of the type of questions he should expect so the witness understands what information the attorney desires to obtain by the particular question asked.

Pretrial preparation by attorney and witness is the key to a well-presented case in chief, and if this part of the pretrial preparation is ignored or forgotten, some of the information available from a witness will be lost to the jury because the attorney does not know that the witness has it, or because the witness is unable to understand what information is sought by direct-examination questions.

CROSS-EXAMINATION AND ATTACK TECHNIQUES

Confrontation by Witnesses.   Cross-examination is the method by which a party to an action probes the knowledge, recollection, bias, and credibility of an adverse witness. Cross-examination is an absolute right and not merely a privilege. It is part of the constitutional mandate that an accused must be confronted by the witnesses against him. Testimony is not allowed to remain as evidence if the accused has not had the opportunity to fully cross-examine the witness giving the testimony.[14]

Ordinarily, a party may not cross-examine his own witness. However, the court may allow an exception if the witness is recalcitrant, unwilling, reluctant, uncandid, unfriendly and evasive, adverse, or hostile, or if the witness' testimony surprises the party who called him and is inconsistent with prior statements. The exception is not lightly granted by the court.

Cross-examination of a witness will be and should be thorough and probing and will not be unduly restricted by the court. It should be allowed to extend to anything that is relevant to show the improbability of the direct evidence and the credibility of the witness testifying.

A witness may be cross-examined about anything on which he has been directly examined. Cross-examination must be broadly related to the scope of the direct examination, but is not confined to a mere repetition of the testimony given on direct examination.

If a witness testifies about a portion of a transaction or conversation, the cross-examination may probe the entire transaction or conversation. All matters connected with the crime are within the scope of the cross-examination, and such searching questions may produce evidence which conflicts with other testimony produced by the opposing party.

Questions and subjects which are impeaching in nature, though not part of the direct examination, are within the province of cross-examiners, if they are relevant to credibility and not merely attempts to degrade the witness. The court will generally allow a wide latitude in this area of cross-examination.

More jurisdictions are allowing **impeachment of any witness** by any party, even the party calling the witness. The basis for this new direction is the premise that a party has no choice or selection of witnesses and thus should not be required to hold out any witness as worthy of belief.[15]

Inconsistent statements are important areas of attack by the cross-examiner. However, the inconsistent statements must concern relevant or material issues. Knowledge, accuracy, and recollection are also open subjects for inquiry on cross-examination. Knowing about sincerity, motive, bias, friendship, interest, and relation to parties helps the jurors

[14]Barber v. Page, 390 U.S. 719 (1968).
[15]United States v. Freeman, 302 F. 2d 347 (1962); 3 Wigmore Sec. 905. The statutes of Illinois, Massachusetts, New Mexico, and Vermont allow impeachment by any party under varying circumstances; the same result is reached in California, Kansas, and New Jersey—Rule 607, Federal Rules of Evidence.

evaluate the worth of the testimony given. Religious beliefs are not generally considered proper areas for cross-examination unless, of course, the religion is an issue in the case.

A prior conviction for a felony is also considered to be relevant to the credibility of any witness. In some jurisdictions this method of impeachment is limited by statute or court discretion to crimes which involve honesty or to recent, rather than remote, crimes. All require, at a minimum, that the prior crime be a felony. One jurisdiction admonishes the court to weigh the probability of the prior crime on the issue of credibility against the collateral prejudice which may be suffered by the defendant.[16]

When a witness is examined about a statement or other conduct inconsistent with any part of his testimony at the hearing, he need not usually be given any information about the statement or other conduct. Nor is it necessary in examining a witness concerning a writing to show, read or disclose to him any part of the writing.

Contradictory or Inconsistent Statements. A witness may be led— and to a certain degree—pushed, nudged, persuaded, and cajoled into positions **contradicting his previous testimony** or out-of-court statements. The techniques used by cross-examiners to obtain this desirable result are many and varied, but certain basic concepts govern most good cross-examinations. According to expert cross-examiners, there are three primary areas of attack: perception, memory, and candor. Each area has its special problems, but there is one universal technique used by conscientious cross-examiners and this is "fencing." The witness is led into the area of attack and surrounded with his own answers until he has no opening to escape through when the critical question is finally asked. If this is done thoroughly, and if the witness is vulnerable, the question will call for an answer which clearly shows the witness' lack of perception, or recollection, or that his previous testimony was somewhat less than the truth. And, if the questioner is extremely fortunate, it may show two or all three of the above. This type of questioning may even force the witness to make a statement directly inconsistent with other evidence or testimony.[17]

The ability of the cross-examiner to accomplish this result is directly related to the completeness of his previous investigation and pretrial preparation. This inquiry and diligence must provide him not only with the critical question but also with a knowledge of the horizons he must maintain to prevent the witness from explaining away a possible conflict or inconsistency. Unfortunately, many witnesses fail to realize

---

[16]People v. Beagle, 6 Cal. 3d 441 (1972); Rule 609, Federal Rules of Evidence.
[17]Paul B. Weston and Kenneth M. Wells, **The Administration of Justice**, 2nd ed. (Englewood Cliffs, N.J.: Prentice-Hall, Inc., 1973), Chapter 9.

that the cross-examiner will know about their expected testimony and the surrounding evidence. If a witness is lazy or lying and does not prepare himself to recall and testify to the facts he knows, or attempts to lie about them, he will find himself inside a "fence" and in danger of jeopardizing the case for the party who called him to testify.

SUMMARY

Subpoenas and *habeas corpus* proceedings compel the attendance of witnesses in court. Citizens have a duty to appear and testify, and defendants have a right to be confronted by witnesses against them. A witness must be competent, have personal knowledge of the event about which he is testifying, and show a reasonable opportunity for observation. Direct examination of witnesses is by the party calling them to court; cross-examination is by the opposing counsel and has certain "attack" areas intended to discredit the testimony of a witness and destroy the witness' credibility. Some proposed testimony may be within the scope of privileged communications and cannot be admitted because of the confidentiality of some relationships: husband and wife, attorney and client, clergyman and penitent, and physician or therapist and patient. As in court, the personal knowledge requirement of witnesses and their opportunity for observations is emphasized in this chapter.

DISCUSSION QUESTIONS

1. What is testimonial evidence?
2. What are the strengths and weaknesses of testimonial evidence?
3. Why are witnesses excluded from court unless they are testifying?
4. What methods may be used to obtain the presence of witnesses from inside or outside the state?
5. What factors bar a witness from testifying?
6. What matters may a witness testify to?
7. Explain the order of, and various methods of, examining witnesses.
8. How are witnesses attacked by the opposing attorney?

GLOSSARY

FOUNDATION (OF TESTIMONY). Establishing the fact that the opportunity of a witness to observe was sufficient to afford a reasonable basis for the proposed testimony.

IMPEACHMENT (OF WITNESS). Attacking the credibility of a witness.

INFAMY. Status of person convicted of crime such as treason and other major felonies. Infamous crimes are those that are scandalous or heinous; usually linked with severe punishment upon conviction.

HABEAS CORPUS. A name for writs seeking to bring a party in custody before a court or judge to examine into the lawfulness of imprisonment. Its sole function is to release from unlawful imprisonment. Technically habeas corpus *ad subjiendum.*

HABEAS CORPUS *ad testificandum.* Directed to a person having legal custody of a prisoner in a jail or prison and ordering him to bring a prisoner to court to testify. ("You have the body to testify.")

SUBPOENA. A process commanding the person named therein to appear before a court to testify as a witness.

SUBPOENA *duces tecum.* A process commanding a witness to bring to court a document or other record in his possession or control which is pertinent to trial issues.

5 Hearsay Evidence

CHAPTER OBJECTIVES

1. In Chapter 5, the concept of hearsay evidence will be defined, stressing the fact that

2. Hearsay evidence is excluded primarily because triers of fact have an inadequate opportunity to evaluate the truthfulness of hearsay declarants. But in the court's search for the truth and because of the inherent trustworthiness of certain kinds of hearsay evidence, the

3. Exceptions to the "hearsay rule" will be identified, with justifications cited for such exceptions. Finally,

4. Exceptions to the hearsay rule listed under the Federal Rules of Evidence will be offered for comparison.

Hearsay evidence is evidence of a statement that was made by someone other than the witness testifying at the hearing, and that is offered to prove the truth of the matter stated. Except as provided by law, hearsay evidence is inadmissible. This definition of hearsay evidence and the rule barring its admission are generally known and cited as **"the hearsay rule."**[1]

For purposes of the hearsay rule a "statement" is usually defined as an oral or written verbal expression, or nonverbal conduct intended as a substitute for oral or written expression.[2] Testimony describing assertive conduct, clearly meant as a communications medium, is hearsay; nonassertive conduct is not hearsay.

Hearsay evidence is testimony about someone else's "story," or a story out of another's mouth. The out-of-court originator of the story (known as the declarant) cannot be observed by the trier of fact for clues as to his willingness or capacity to tell the truth, which might be apparent if he were an in-court witness, nor can his veracity be tested by cross-examination. Observation and cross-examination are basic devices for evaluating the credibility of a witness.

The accuracy of any evidence once removed from the in-court witness' personal knowledge is less than perfect. Written statements can be tested for validity and genuineness. Oral statements are notorious for poor reporting. Memory and perception of meaning frustrate accurate reporting of oral statements: Is the statement related in the words of the declarant or is it what the witness interpreted those words to mean?

The controlling reason for rejecting hearsay when a party objects is that the objecting party has the right to prevent the trier of fact (juror or judge) from being improperly influenced by evidence which appears fair but which carries hazards that could be exposed or eliminated if the declarant were present to be cross-examined.

To be admitted, hearsay evidence must meet the conditions of the exceptions established by law. **Exceptions to the hearsay rule** may be found in statutes or in decisional law. Exceptions which permit hearsay evidence are operable only if the proffered evidence meets the other requirements of evidence generally, otherwise admissible hearsay might be excluded by some other rule of evidence such as the "privileged communications" or "best evidence" rule, or because the court decides its probative value is less than its prejudicial nature, or that it might confuse the issues or mislead the triers of fact.

The exceptions to the hearsay rule permit this type of evidence to be received in court only when it is necessary to diligent inquiry and the circumstances under which the evidence is developed will provide some guarantee of basic or inherent trustworthiness to substitute for the oath, cross-examination, and other tests of a witness' credibility. Usually the need for hearsay evidence is based on inability to locate and produce a witness, but the normal procedure for producing evidence

[1] California Evidence Code, Section 1200; Rule 801 (c), Federal Rules of Evidence.
[2] California Evidence Code, Section 225.

may be stymied in some other fashion. Exceptions to the hearsay rule are justified by circumstances pointing to trustworthiness; the statement itself, or the circumstances under which it was made, indicates the probability of its truth.

The exceptions to the hearsay rule are both a maze and a jungle for legal scholars. However, some simplification can be achieved by isolating the exceptions likely to be encountered in police investigations. These exceptions range from dying declarations through entries made in the regular course of business and spontaneous utterances and statements showing mental or physical condition, to extrajudicial admissions.

DYING DECLARATIONS

Evidence of a statement made by a dying person about the cause and circumstances of his death is admissible if the statement has been made upon his personal knowledge and under a sense and belief of immediately impending death.[3] It is thought that when a person knows he is going to die he will tell the truth because there is no longer a need or reason to lie and there is, perhaps, a religious reason to tell the truth.

In most states dying declarations are admissible only when the crime charged is the homicide of the hearsay-declarant—who is thus unable to appear in court and testify.

The declarant who is the real witness must have possessed the required qualifications to be accepted in court as a competent witness, if he were alive. Investigators should be alert for negative evidence about a dying declarant, just as they would for a live witness. Evidence tending to impeach the declarant might well be admissible under the same rules of evidence that would have applied to the declarant if he had testified in person. This is particularly true of prior statements by the declarant contradicting his dying declaration.

There are two key elements of a dying declaration: the victim's personal knowledge of the circumstances under which he received the likely-to-be-fatal injury, and his belief that death from the injury is imminent.

The **personal knowledge of a dying declarant** must be more than suspicion or conjecture. It should be shown that he knew, or had an opportunity to know the circumstances of his injury.

The declarant must have had a settled, hopeless **belief that his death was about to occur** without loss of time. Although the declarant must have had this settled and hopeless belief in a swift and certain death, his credibility is not impaired if he did not die shortly after his statement. The time lapse between statement and actual death may cause the

---

[3]California Evidence Code, Section 1242.

court to question the admissibility of a dying declaration because a lengthy time span will have a bearing on the issue of the victim's realization of impending death; but there is no requirement that the facts of life or death support the victim's expectation of a swift death.

The person taking a dying declaration statement must make sure the requirements of competence, personal knowledge, and settled and hopeless belief in impending death are satisfied by the form and content of the statement or by some act or circumstances which show the victim's belief in impending death. An affirmative response to the following questions should be sufficient to allow admission of the declaration: Do you remember what happened to you? Do you think you are going to die now?

The actual development of a dying declaration within the evidence structure of a criminal trial is probably the best illustration of the needs to be satisfied in the statement-taking. First, the preliminary facts are shown. Then the statement-taker is introduced and qualified as a witness. Finally, the statement itself is introduced.

SPONTANEOUS AND CONTEMPORANEOUS STATEMENTS

Closely aligned with the rationale for including dying declarations among the exceptions to the hearsay rule are the exceptions for spontaneous and contemporaneous statements. The inherent trustworthiness of a spontaneous statement is based on the declarant's lack of opportunity for reflection and deliberate fabrication. A contemporary statement clarifies the conduct of a declarant when the action and statement are linked and the action alone is equivocal or ambiguous. For instance, a prisoner staggered bleeding into the arms of a correctional officer. He pointed to another inmate and said "He cut me," then died. Testimony describing both the act and the statement was admissible against the accused.

These statements narrate, describe, or explain an act, condition, or event perceived by the declarant. They are made spontaneously while the declarant is under the stress of excitement brought on by these perceptions or while the declarant is engaged in some act and they help to explain, qualify or make understandable the conduct of the declarant.[4]

STATEMENTS OF MENTAL AND PHYSICAL STATE

Testimony about a declarant's statement of intent, plan, motive, design, mental feeling, pain, or bodily health may be admitted if it is offered to

[4]California Evidence Code, Section 1250.

(1) prove the **declarant's state of mind,** emotion, or physical sensation at the time of the statement or at any other time when it is itself an issue in the action; or (2) prove or explain the declarant's acts or conduct.[5]

In most states such evidence is admitted only when the previously existing mental or physical state is itself an issue in the criminal action and the evidence may not be used to prove any other fact. However, such statements are often circumstantial evidence of other facts important to the prosecution or defense of a criminal case. A mental state may be proved to have existed at the time of a crime which will serve to excuse the crime. The classic example is the claim of self-defense in homicide cases.

The record of the trial of Norman St. Martin for the murder of a fellow state prison inmate, Glen Howard Mason, contains testimony admitted under this exception. In this case, death was caused by stab or puncture wounds. The crime took place at a state prison. The "people" claimed that the defendant, Norman St. Martin, inflicted the death wounds on the deceased (Mason) maliciously, intentionally, and knowingly; the defense said it was a case of self-defense: yes, there had been a killing. The circumstances were substantially as detailed by the state's presentation of the evidence, but the defendant had been threatened by the victim and feared for his life when the victim approached in an apparent assault attempt, and the fatal blow was struck in fear and self-defense. The pertinent testimony on the **declarant's** (St. Martin) **state of mind** follows:

Prosecutor (Direct Examination of Witness)

Q: Can you tell us then, the best you can recall, what that conversation was between you and Mr. St. Martin?

A: Mr. St. Martin stated that these cats around the California institution were nothing, that they were just a bunch of jerks. Some of the people that he has done time with in institutions in the East were real cool cats; that in a place back East they did their own number. They didn't fool with another guy. They didn't stab some guy over nothing; that it meant something when they knocked a guy off. That they had the—they had the guts to do it face to face. They didn't do it in the back. At that time I asked him if that was how Mason had been stabbed, if he had done it face to face? His reply was that, "Mason saw who stabbed him." I asked him if he had stabbed with an upward swing, a jab, or a downward swing. He said, "Man, I don't know. I just did it. That's all."

Q: Recall any other conversation?

A: He asked—or I asked him—if he had got any hit or anything. He stated that Mason had made a motion towards his face and just got his eyelid, and that's why it happened.

[5]California Evidence Code, Section 1237.

Q: Did he say anything about Mr. Mason?

A: No, other than, "He scratches like a woman."

Q: Did he say anything else about Mr. Mason or what his role was there in the prison?

A: That he was a loudmouth, that he wouldn't let a man do his own number.

Defense Counsel (Cross-Examination of Witness):

Q: Now, as to this conversation that you stated you had with Mr. St. Martin, during this conversation, Mr. St. Martin seemed to be obsessed with the thought that persons were being stabbed in the back, isn't that correct?

A: I don't get your general—

Q: He made numerous references, didn't he, to being stabbed in the back, isn't that so? Persons being stabbed in the back?

A: In regard to how the general run of stabbings is done in institutions in California, yes.

Q: That's right. He seemed quite concerned about that, didn't he?

A: Yes.

Q: All right. Did he seem concerned about doing his own number, his own time?

A: Yes.

Q: What does that mean?

A: It means being left alone. Just completely left alone by their terminology where nobody bothers them.

Q: All right. And he further stated in this conversation to you, did he not, that somebody had been bothering him?

A: Yes.

Q: And did he say—did he make any mention as to how Mr. Mason had been bothering him?

A: Badmouthing him, I believe, is the way he put it.

Q: And what does that mean to you, badmouthing him?

A: It could mean a number of things.

Q: All right. By badmouthing, do you take that to mean saying things derogatory toward Mason—I mean toward Mr. St. Martin?

A: Could be. Yes.

Q: Could—? What else could badmouthing mean?

A: In some places, it could be a big noise, punk, anything of that type.

Q: Calling him things, is that right?

A: Could be. Correct. Yes.

Q: All right. As a matter of fact, didn't Mr. St. Martin state that Mr. Mason called him a punk?

A: He did, previously.

Q: What else did he say Mr. Mason had said about him, Mr. St. Martin?

A: I believe the only thing he said that he called—direct quote—would be that he called him a big noise, called him a punk. I believe that was all.

Q: And also perhaps that Mr. St. Martin didn't have the guts to do anything about anything?
A: I believe so, sir.

Although the direct examination of this witness did little more than suggest St. Martin's state of mind at the time of the attack, the contents of the cross-examination revealed the defendant's fearful state of mind.

WRITTEN STATEMENTS OF PAST RECOLLECTION

A written statement made when the fact recorded actually occurred, or within a short enough time thereafter to insure that the fact was fresh in the writer's memory, qualifies under an exception to the hearsay rule for the same reason that spontaneous and contemporary statements are admissible.

Recorded past recollections can usually be read into evidence by the recorder if they concern matters the witness cannot then recall fully and accurately, and if the statement is in a writing which:

1. Was made when the recorded fact actually occurred or was fresh in the witness' memory

2. Was made by the witness or under his direction, or by some other person to record the witness' statement at the time

3. Is offered after the witness testifies that the statement he made was true

4. Is offered after the writing is authenticated as an accurate record of the statement.[6]

PRIOR IDENTIFICATION

Prior identification of a suspect as the perpetrator of a crime, made by a witness while the crime or a related occurrence was fresh in his memory, is also considered contemporaneous with the crime. Evidence of prior identification is admissible under an exception to the hearsay rule, whether the witness admits or denies the prior identification.

The prior identification statement must identify a person who participated in a crime or other occurrence, and must be offered as evidence after the witness' testimony about the identification. If the identifying witness contradicts a prior identification statement, the prior statement may be used to discredit his testimony at the trial. If the witness re-

---

[6]California Evidence Code, Section 1237.

affirms the prior statement, it may be used as an earlier identification for its probative and rehabilitative value during the trial.[7]

BUSINESS RECORDS

In the United States today the definition of a business includes every kind of business, governmental activity, profession, occupation, calling, or operation of institutions, whether carried on for profit or not.[8] A business record may be admissible in criminal trials under an exception to the hearsay rule if it is in writing and meets the following requirements:

> 1. It was made in the regular course of business
> 2. It was made at or near the time of the act, condition, or event recorded
> 3. The custodian or some other qualified witness testifies to its identity and the mode of its preparation
> 4. The sources of its information and method and time of preparation indicate trustworthiness[9]

The indicia of trustworthiness are important to investigators. The special **reliability of business records** is that they are based on the first-hand observation of someone whose job it is to know the facts and record them. The recorder's business role must involve observing and recording the event, circumstances, occurrence, or incident reported, and the record must be based on his personal knowledge or come from someone with a business duty to report to the recorder. For instance, police accident reports are not admissible under this rule because they are based on the personal knowledge of participants and witnesses who have no business duty to report to the police. They are admitted into evidence to show the event happened, not how it happened.

Evidence concerning the absence of an entry in business records is acceptable under an exception to the hearsay rule to prove the non-occurrence of an act or event, or the nonexistence of a condition, when: (1) in the normal course of that business all such acts, events, or conditions are recorded at or near the time they occur or exist; (2) such records are preserved; and (3) the sources of information and the method and time of preparation of the records of that business are such that the absence of a record is a trustworthy indication that the act or

[7]Judy v. State, 218 Md. 168 (1958); State v. Simmons, 63 Wash. 2d 17 (1963); New Jersey Evidence Rule 63 (1) (c); New York Code of Criminal Procedure, Section 393-b; California Evidence Code, Section 1238.
[8]California Evidence Code, Section 1270.
[9]California Evidence Code, Section 1271.

event did not occur or that the condition did not exist.[10] Similarly, evidence concerning the absence of a public record or writing may be admissible under an exception to the hearsay rule when a public official, on demand, provides an authenticated certificate or its equivalent stating that he did not find a designated public record or writing after a diligent search.[11]

PUBLIC RECORDS

Official public records and writings made as a record of an act, event, or condition may be admissible under an exception to the hearsay rule when offered to prove the act, event, or condition. The records must be:

1. Made by a public employee acting within the scope of his duty
2. Made at or near the time of the act, event, or condition
3. Prepared by sources of information and at a time that indicates trustworthiness[12]

In certain public records, there are also specific indicia of trustworthiness because of the nature of the public records involved. These are such records as: The written finding of presumed death made by a federal employee authorized to make such findings pursuant to the Federal Missing Persons Act; official reports concerning birth, death, and marriage; and reports by a federal employee that a person is missing, captured, or the like.[13]

DECLARATIONS AGAINST INTEREST

A declaration against interest is believed to have inherent trustworthiness because a reasonable man in the same position as the declarant would not have made the statement unless he believed it to be true. Every attempt must be made to bring the declarant into court to testify and allow the functioning of oath, observation, and cross-examination to test the statement for credibility and accuracy. However, a declaration against interest is usually admissible under an exception to the hearsay rule when the declarant has knowledge of the subject in issue, is not available as an in-court witness, and the statement—when made—was: (1) so far contrary to the declarant's pecuniary or proprietary interest

[10]California Evidence Code, Section 1272.
[11]California Evidence Code, Section 1284.
[12]California Evidence Code, Section 1280.
[13]California Evidence Code, Sections 1282–83.

or (2) so far subjected him to the risk of civil or criminal liability or (3) so far tended to render invalid a claim by him against another, or (4) so far tended to create social disgrace, hatred, or ridicule for the declarant in the community that a reasonable man in his position would not have made the statement unless he believed it to be true.[14]

Declarations against interest are considered more reliable than hearsay evidence admissible under the various other exceptions on the assumption that a reasonable man does not state facts in conflict with his own interests. Many states limit this exception. However, the basic assumption in most states is that declarations are not made against interests described as pecuniary or financial, or proprietary or property. Declarations against penal interest—criminal liability—are less often accepted.

STATEMENTS OF CO-CONSPIRATORS

An essential element of the crime of **conspiracy** is joint action by two or more persons. Therefore, all of the participants in a criminal conspiracy are responsible for all of the acts done during the conspiracy. Because of this concept of joint responsibility, the testimony of one conspirator about statements made by another conspirator may be admissible as an exception to the hearsay rule. A conspirator who admits his guilt prior to trial often agrees to cooperate with the prosecutor and testify against his fellow conspirators at their trial. This witness may testify about a statement made by a specified defendant during the conspiracy in which he and this defendant participated and for which this defendant is now on trial. Such testimony is admitted solely on the issue of guilt or innocence of the specified defendant, and the prosecution must establish a foundation of sufficient evidence to sustain a judicial conclusion that the conspiracy existed and that this defendant participated in it.[15] When a person involved in a criminal conspiracy makes a written statement of guilt and implicates other conspirators, but refuses to testify against them at their trial, the written statement may be admissible in place of the testimony of the reluctant witness.

ADMISSIONS

Testimony concerning an admission by a person accused of crime may qualify under an exception to the hearsay rule if the admission is not

14California Evidence Code, Section 1230.
15California Evidence Code, Section 1223.

prohibited on constitutional grounds. An authorized or adoptive admission, authorized by the party against whom it will be used or endorsed by his conduct, may also be admissible.[16]

Under the Federal Rules of Evidence an admission by a party opponent is not hearsay when the statement is offered against a party and is:

> 1. His own statement, in either his individual or a representative capacity
>
> 2. A statement of which he has manifested his adoption or belief in its truth
>
> 3. A statement by a person authorized by him to make a statement concerning the subject
>
> 4. A statement by his agent or servant concerning a matter within the scope of his agency or employment, made during the existence of the relationship
>
> 5. A statement by a co-conspirator of a party during the course and in furtherance of the conspiracy.[17]

These admissions are excluded from the category of hearsay evidence because their admissibility is more the result of the adversary system than of the satisfaction of the condition of hearsay rule. No guarantee of trustworthiness is necessary in the case of an admission.

PRIOR STATEMENTS—WITNESSES

Witnesses who have not been unconditionally excused, and who have had a chance to explain or deny a contradictory statement, may be confronted with prior inconsistent statements to discredit testimony given at trial. When the credibility of a witness is attacked, such prior statements may be acceptable to show their content is consistent with the trial testimony of the witness.

Although the prior statements of witnesses are generally admissible under "exceptions to the hearsay rule," a problem comes up when the accused is the witness concerned. A defendant cannot be compelled to testify about his own guilt or innocence. A prior inconsistent statement may be admissible under an exception to the hearsay rule to impeach the defendant-witness, but only when the prior statement contradicts something he said under oath.

The Federal Rules of Evidence take a different direction concerning prior statements of witnesses:[18]

[16]California Evidence Code, Sections 1220–22.
[17]Rule 801(d) (2), Federal Rules of Evidence.
[18]Rule 801 (d) (1), Federal Rules of Evidence.

A statement is not hearsay if the declarant testifies at the trial or hearing and is subject to cross-examination concerning the statement and the statement is (a) inconsistent with his testimony, or (b) consistent with his testimony and is offered to rebut an express or implied charge against him of recent fabrication or improper influence or motive, or (c) one of identification of a person made after perceiving him.

The effect of this evidentiary change is to give such statements the status of substantive evidence, upon which a conviction may be based. In the U.S. Supreme Court case of *California v. Green*,[19] the California statute[20] which allowed such statements as substantive evidence was ruled constitutional and no violation of the confrontation clause. In that case the only witness to the crime (furnishing marijuana to a minor) made changes in his testimony from that given at a preliminary hearing and in a prior oral statement given to a police officer. The trial court, on the authority of the California statute, allowed the prosecution to introduce evidence of both the witness' testimony at the preliminary hearing and his oral (unsworn) statement to the police officer, both of which were inconsistent with his trial testimony. The witness' testimony at trial exculpated the defendant and the evidence of his prior statements (preliminary hearing and oral statement to the officer) incriminated the defendant. The trial court instructed the jury members that they could base a conviction on the evidence of the witness' prior statements if they believed them rather than his trial testimony. The key to the court's ruling was that the witness was on the witness stand at trial and subject to examination by both parties and personal observation by the jury.

EXCEPTIONS—FEDERAL RULES

The Federal Rules of Evidence also set out new language for old exceptions and new concepts concerning hearsay evidence in an extensive list of exceptions to the hearsay rule. Exceptions to the hearsay rule in this listing are divided into two categories: (1) those in which the availability of the declarant is immaterial, and (2) those in which the declarant is not available.

Exceptions which do not require the declarant to be available are:

1. *Present Sense Impression.* A statement describing or explaining an event or condition made while the declarant was perceiving the event or condition, or immediately thereafter.

2. *Excited Utterance.* A statement relating to a startling event or

[19]399 U.S. 149 (1970).
[20]California Evidence Code, Section 1235.

condition made while the declarant was under the stress of excitement caused by the event or condition.

3. *Then Existing Mental, Emotional, or Physical Condition.* A statement of the declarant's then existing state of mind, emotion, sensation, or physical condition (such as intent, plan, motive, design, mental feeling, pain, and bodily health), but not including a statement of memory or belief to prove the fact remembered or believed unless it relates to the execution, revocation, identification, or terms of declarant's will.

4. *Statements for Purposes of Medical Diagnosis or Treatment.* Statements made for purposes of medical diagnosis or treatment and describing medical history, or past or present symptoms, pain, or sensations, or the inception or general character of the cause or external source thereof insofar as reasonably pertinent to diagnosis or treatment.

5. *Recorded Recollection.* A memorandum or record concerning a matter about which a witness once had knowledge but now has insufficient recollection to enable him to testify fully and accurately, shown to have been made when the matter was fresh in his memory and to reflect that knowledge correctly. If admitted, the memorandum or record may be read into evidence but may not itself be received as an exhibit unless offered by an adverse party.

6. *Records of Regularly Conducted Activity.* A memorandum, report, record, or data compilation, in any form, of acts, events, conditions, opinions, or diagnoses made at or near the time by, or from information transmitted by, a person with knowledge, all in the course of a regularly conducted activity, as shown by the testimony of the custodian or other qualified witness, unless the sources of information or other circumstances indicate lack of trustworthiness.

7. *Absence of Entry in Records of Regularly Conducted Activity.* Evidence that a matter is not included in the memoranda, reports, records, or data compilations, in any form, of a regularly conducted activity, to prove the nonoccurrence or nonexistence of the matter, if the matter was of a kind of which a memorandum, report, record, or data compilation was regularly made and preserved, unless the sources of information or other circumstances indicate lack of trustworthiness.

8. *Public Records and Reports.* Records, reports, statements, or data compilations, in any form, of public offices or agencies, setting forth (a) the activities of the office or agency, or (b) matters observed pursuant to duty imposed by law, or (c) in civil cases and against the government in criminal cases, factual findings resulting from an investigation made pursuant to authority granted by law, unless the sources of information or other circumstances indicate lack of trustworthiness.

9. *Records of Vital Statistics.* Records or data compilations, in any

form, of births, fetal deaths, deaths, or marriages, if the report thereof was made to a public office pursuant to requirements of law.

10. *Absence of Public Record or Entry.* To prove the absence of a record, report, statement, or data compilation, in any form, or the non-occurrence or nonexistence of a matter of which a record, report, statement, or data compilation, in any form, was regularly made and preserved by a public office or agency, evidence in the form of a certification in accordance with Rule 902, or testimony, that diligent search failed to disclose the record, report, statement, or data compilation, or entry.

11. *Records of Religious Organizations.* Statements of births, marriages, divorces, deaths, legitimacy, ancestry, relationship by blood or marriage, or other similar facts of personal or family history, contained in a regularly kept record of a religious organization.

12. *Marriage, Baptismal, and Similar Certificates.* Statements of fact contained in a certificate that the maker performed a marriage or other ceremony or administered a sacrament, made by a clergyman, public official, or other person authorized by the rules or practices of a religious organization or by law to perform the act certified, and purporting to have been issued at the time of the act or within a reasonable time thereafter.

13. *Family Records.* Statements of fact concerning personal or family history contained in family Bibles, genealogies, charts, engravings on rings, inscriptions on family portraits, engravings on urns, crypts, or tombstones, or the like.

14. *Records of Documents Affecting an Interest in Property.* The record of a document purporting to establish or affect an interest in property, as proof of the content of the original recorded document and its execution and delivery by each person by whom it purports to have been executed, if the record is a record of a public office and an applicable statute authorized the recording of documents of that kind in that office.

15. *Statements in Documents Affecting an Interest in Property.* A statement contained in a document purporting to establish or affect an interest in property if the matter stated was relevant to the purpose of the document, unless dealings with the property since the document was made have been inconsistent with the truth of the statement or the purport of the document.

16. *Statements in Ancient Documents.* Statements in a document in existence twenty years or more whose authenticity is established.

17. *Market Reports, Commercial Publications.* Market quotations, tabulations, lists, directories, or other published compilations, generally

used and relied upon by the public or by persons in particular occupations.

18. *Learned Treatises.* To the extent called to the attention of an expert witness upon cross-examination or relied upon by him in direct examination, or pamphlets on a subject of history, medicine, or other science or art, established as a reliable authority by the testimony or admission of the witness or by other expert testimony or by judicial notice. If admitted, the statements may be read into evidence but may not be received as exhibits.

19. *Reputation Concerning Personal or Family History.* Reputation among members of his family by blood, adoption, or marriage, or among his associates, or in the community, concerning a person's birth, adoption, marriage, divorce, death, legitimacy, relationship by blood, adoption or marriage, ancestry, or other similar fact of his personal or family history.

20. *Reputation Concerning Boundaries of General History.* Reputation in a community, arising before the controversy, as to boundaries of or customs affecting lands in the community, and reputation as to events of general history important to the community or state or nation in which located.

21. *Reputation as to Character.* Reputation of a person's character among his associates or in the community.

22. *Judgment of Previous Conviction.* Evidence of a final judgment, entered after a trial or upon a plea of guilty (but not upon a plea of *nolo contendere*), adjudging a person guilty of a crime punishable by death or imprisonment in excess of one year, to prove any fact essential to sustain the judgment, but not including, when offered by the government in a criminal prosecution for purposes other than impeachment, judgments against persons other than the accused. The pendency of an appeal may be shown but does not affect admissibility.

23. *Judgment as to Personal, Family, or General History, or Boundaries.* Judgments as proof of matters of personal, family, or general history, or boundaries, essential to the judgment, if the same would be provable by evidence or reputation.

24. *Other Exceptions.* A statement not specifically covered by any of the foregoing exceptions but having comparable circumstantial guarantees of trustworthiness.[21]

The exceptions to the hearsay rule which require the **declarant to be unavailable** are situations in which the declarant

---

[21]Federal Rules of Evidence, Rule 803.

1. Is exempted by ruling of the judge on the ground of privilege from testifying concerning the subject matter of his statement; or

2. Persists in refusing to testify concerning the subject matter of his statement despite an order of the judge to do so; or

3. Testifies to a lack of memory of the subject of his statement; or

4. Is unable to be present or to testify at the hearing because of death or then existing physical or mental illness or infirmity; or

5. Is absent from the hearing and the proponent of his statement has been unable to procure his attendance by process or other reasonable means.

A declarant is not unavailable as a witness if his exemption, refusal, claim of lack of memory, inability, or absence is due to the procurement or wrongdoing of the proponent of his statement for the purpose of preventing the witness from attending or testifying.[22]

The following are not excluded by the hearsay rule if the declarant is unavailable as a witness:

1. *Former Testimony.*   Testimony given as a witness at another hearing of the same or a different proceeding, or in a deposition taken in compliance with law in the course of another proceeding, at the instance of or against a party with an opportunity to develop the testimony by direct, cross, or redirect examination, with motive and interest similar to those of the party against whom now offered.

2. *Statement of Recent Perception.*   A statement, not in response to the instigation of a person engaged in investigating, litigating, or settling a claim, which narrates, describes, or explains an event or condition recently perceived by the declarant, made in good faith, not in contemplation of pending or anticipated litigation in which he was interested, and while his recollection was clear.

3. *Statement Under Belief of Impending Death.*   A statement made by a declarant while believing that his death was imminent, concerning the cause or circumstances of what he believed to be his impending death.

4. *Statement Against Interest.*   A statement which was at the time of its making so far contrary to the declarant's pecuniary or proprietary interest, or so far tended to subject him to civil or criminal liability or to render invalid a claim by him against another or to make him an object of hatred, ridicule, or social disgrace, that a reasonable man in his position would not have made the statement unless he believed it to be true. A statement tending to expose the declarant to criminal liability and offered to exculpate the accused is not admissible unless corroborated.

22Rule 804 (a), Federal Rules of Evidence.

5. *Statement of Personal or Family History.* (a) A statement concerning the declarant's own birth, adoption, marriage, divorce, legitimacy, relationship by blood, adoption, or marriage, ancestry, or other similar fact of personal or family history, even though declarant had no means of acquiring personal knowledge of the matter stated; or (b) a statement concerning the foregoing matters, and death also, of another person, if the declarant was related to the other by blood, adoption, or marriage or was so intimately associated with the other's family as to be likely to have accurate information concerning the matter declared.

6. *Other Exceptions.* A statement not specifically covered by any of the foregoing exceptions but having comparable circumstantial guarantees of trustworthiness.[23]

HEARSAY WITHIN HEARSAY

There are other problems which arise in connection with hearsay. In the situation in which the hearsay declaration itself includes a further hearsay statement (hearsay within hearsay), the further hearsay should be admissible if it also conforms to the requirements of a hearsay exception. A hospital record which contains an entry of a patient's age based upon information furnished by his wife should be admissible as a regular hospital entry and the wife's statement qualifies as a statement of pedigree (if she is available) or as a statement made for the purpose of diagnosis or treatment. A dying declaration may incorporate a declaration against interest by another declarant.[24]

The opposing party may attack the credibility of the declarant just as if the declarant were a testifying witness.[25] Thus, character and conduct of declarant will be in issue as well as his prior conviction of crime when applicable. Inconsistent statements may also be introduced as impeachment even though there is no opportunity for the declarant to explain.[26]

Where the declarant is a witness, only prior inconsistent statements may be offered to impeach him. Where the declarant's statement is admitted, though hearsay, there is strong authority to allow both statements prior to and subsequent to the statement that was the subject of hearsay.[27]

[23]Rule 804(b), Federal Rules of Evidence.
[24]McCormack, Section 290, p. 611; Rule 805, Federal Rules of Evidence.
[25]Rule 806, Federal Rules of Evidence.
[26]Rule 613(b), Federal Rules of Evidence.
[27]McCormack 37, p. 69; 3 Wigmore, p. 1033; People v. Rosoto 58 Cal. 2d 304 (1962); Carver v. U.S. 164 U.S. 694 (1897); People v. Hines 287 N.Y. 93 (1940); California Evidence Code, Section 1202.

SUMMARY

The general rule of excluding hearsay evidence is presented as a lead to the special exceptions allowing for the admission of such evidence. The exclusion or acceptance of hearsay evidence is a complex of the personal knowledge requirements of testimonial evidence as opposed to the court's role to search for the truth of disputed issues and the inherent trustworthiness of certain types of hearsay evidence.

DISCUSSION QUESTIONS

1.   How valid is the assumption that jurors have an inadequate opportunity to discover the truthfulness of a hearsay-declarant?
2.   How would you define hearsay evidence?
3.   Under what circumstances will the admission of hearsay evidence increase the chances of discovering truth in a criminal trial?
4.   Proffered evidence, to be admissible under an exception to the hearsay rule, must meet the conditions of reliability and necessity. Explain.
5.   Which are more reliable, declarations against interest or spontaneous and contemporaneous utterances? Why?
6.   Why are prior statements of witnesses admissible as exceptions to the hearsay rule?
7.   Define "unavailability of a witness" under the Federal Rules of Evidence.

GLOSSARY

BEST EVIDENCE RULE.   The best evidence of the content of writing is the writing itself.

CONSPIRACY (CRIMINAL).   A combination of two or more persons for the purpose of committing by joint effort an unlawful act or using unlawful means for the commission of a lawful act.

DECLARANT.   A person who makes a declaration (statement).

NOLO CONTENDERE.   No contest; designation of a plea in a criminal action having the legal effect of a guilty plea but which cannot be used elsewhere as an admission.

PRIVILEGED COMMUNICATION.   A communication between persons in a confidential relationship who are under a special obligation of fidelity and secrecy, and which the law will not allow to be divulged (or inquired into) for the sake of public policy: husband and wife, attorney and client, etc.

6

Opinion Evidence

CHAPTER OBJECTIVES

1. In Chapter 6, opinion evidence will be described and defined, with its relationship to
2. Testimony given by a witness from personal observation or under an exception to the hearsay rule, and
3. Introduction into evidence of articles and exhibits.
4. The expertise factor as comparable to the personal knowledge requirement of lay witnesses will be developed, and
5. The in-court methodology of qualifying expert witnesses explored.

The ultimate issue in a criminal trial is the defendant's guilt or innocence. The trier of fact, juror or judge in non-jury trials, must reach a conclusion about this ultimate issue from the evidence produced in court. Witnesses are usually asked to confine their testimony about facts within their knowledge and are not allowed to express their opinions or conclusions because this would usurp the role of juror or judge.

There is a logical problem in distinguishing an observed and reported "fact" from an opinion or conclusion. The process of perceiving, recalling, and reporting involves a person's belief in what he observed and this is akin to an opinion or conclusion. Whether testimony is "fact" or opinion is a decision for the trial judge, subject to post-conviction review by appellate courts.

When a witness' opinion or conclusion is necessary to provide the triers of fact with data useful in their decision-making, such testimony may be admitted under an exception to the general rule.[1] Exceptions to the rule barring opinion evidence are broadly classified under four major headings:

> 1. Any witness—when necessary to summarize a total or collective event
>
> 2. Any witness—when questioned about a matter not amenable to the report-of-an-observer technique
>
> 3. Witnesses who possess a special knowledge through experience—when nonexpert testimony is necessary in an area of special knowledge related to the defendant, such as a particular business or occupation, or some point in issue
>
> 4. Witnesses qualified by education and experience as experts, when such expertise is necessary

Subject matter that is nonprofessional or is commonly known may not be the subject of **expert opinion.** An expert may state his opinion only on matters within his expertise. It would be improper for an expert to render an opinion as to whether a train stopped long enough to discharge passengers at a station. An "expert" could not express an opinion as to whether a suspect can be recognized by the flash of his pistol.

Neither a lay witness nor an expert will be allowed to testify to matters which call for a conclusion of law.

NONEXPERTS

Lay witnesses are divided into two general categories—the real nonexpert and the person with some special knowledge or qualification.

The nonexpert lay witness can express an opinion about areas of common knowledge, such as:

> 1. Drunkenness or sobriety
> 2. Emotional aspects of appearance and conduct
> 3. Age
> 4. Speed, distance, and size (from observation)

[1] Rule 701, Federal Rules of Evidence.

5. Identity based on physical characteristics and voice

A nonexpert witness, however, is not permitted to guess or speculate about what another person thought or intended. He may not give a supposed reason for another's action or observable attitude.

The lay witness with limited expertise may, after he is shown to have the qualifications or opportunity necessary for forming a valid opinion, be asked for his opinion in the area of his special knowledge or qualifications. These areas usually include: (1) value of the witness' services and property; (2) handwriting the witness can recognize; (3) sanity of an intimate acquaintance; and (4) character.

The scope of lay witness opinions permitted by law varies from one jurisdiction to another, but the words of California's Evidence Code sum up the general requirements for admitting this type of testimony: "If a witness is not testifying as an expert, his testimony in the form of an opinion is limited to such an opinion as is permitted by law, including but not limited to an opinion that is:

a. Rationally based on the perception of the witness; and
b. Helpful to a clear understanding of his testimony."[2]

Basis for Nonexpert Testimony. Of course, cross-examination about details of the observations that form the **basis for an opinion** is proper. Even on direct examination, the witness may be asked to give the reasons for his opinion and the data on which his opinion is based. Before allowing a witness to offer an opinion, the trial judge may require an examination concerning the matter used as a basis for the opinion, to determine whether some provision of law forbids the use of such a basis for the proffered opinion.[3]

The court may, and upon objection must, exclude opinion testimony that is based, in whole or in significant part, on matter that is not a proper basis for such an opinion. In such cases, the witness may, if there remains a proper basis for his opinion, then state his opinions after excluding from consideration the matter determined to be improper.[4]

EXPERTS—QUALIFICATIONS

An expert may give an opinion within his area of expertise as a means of enriching the triers of fact with his special knowledge. The expert helps the triers of fact to understand areas not within the common knowledge of nonexperts. The basic test of the **need for an expert** is

[2]California Evidence Code, Section 800.
[3]California Evidence Code, Section 802.
[4]California Evidence Code, Section 803.

whether his special expertise will be helpful to the jury in understanding the evidence or determining a fact in issue.[5] The experts' opinion is advisory, no more.

The jury must decide how much **credibility** to award an expert witness and how much weight to give his testimony in reaching a verdict, just as it is expected to evaluate all the evidence it receives. An expert witness may be asked about the compensation and expenses paid (or to be paid) to him, and whether he was appointed by the court or called by a party. This may help the jury evaluate the witness' credibility and decide how much weight to give to his testimony.[6]

If the triers of fact believe expert testimony is incorrect, they may disregard it. In California, the trial judge is required to instruct jurors about experts and their testimony. Such instruction must be made part of the judge's **charge to the jury** in any criminal proceeding during which an expert is allowed to express his opinion while testifying. These instructions are generally given as follows:

> A person is qualified to testify as an expert if he has special knowledge, skill, experience, training or education sufficient to qualify him as an expert on the subject to which his testimony relates. Duly qualified experts may give their opinions on questions in controversy at a trial. To assist you in deciding such questions, you may consider the opinion with the reasons cited, if any, by the expert who gives the opinion. You should give an expert opinion the weight to which you find it to be entitled, but you are not bound to accept it as conclusive. If you find any such opinion to be unreasonable, you may disregard it.

Experts must be qualified in court. That is, they must be questioned under oath so that the trial judge may rule on their competence as experts. Knowledge qualifies an expert. His knowledge is usually shown to be based on both experience and study, but the study need not be formal training or be marked by any significant educational achievement. However, in scientific areas related to academic discipline, it is desirable that the expert have at least a basic degree in his chosen field. Advanced degrees, teaching assignments, and publications support an expert's claim of special knowledge. The basic qualification required of an expert witness is that he satisfy the trial judge that he is an expert. He should be shown to have skill, experience, training, and education in the area of expertise he will testify about. If one of the parties objects that an expert is not qualified, his special knowledge must be shown before the witness may testify as an expert, but a witness' special knowledge may be shown by any admissible evidence, including his own testimony.[7]

[5]Rule 702, Federal Rules of Evidence.
[6]California Evidence Code, Section 722.
[7]California Evidence Code, Section 720.

Objections to the qualifications of an expert may be based on the credibility of his claims of expertise, as well as on the application of the proffered witness' special knowledge to his expected testimony. The objecting party may claim he is not an expert, or that he does not have the expert qualifications for the particular subject matter in issue at the trial.

Questions to develop the qualifications of an expert witness may proceed along the following lines:

Q: Your occupation, sir?
A: Physician and surgeon.
Q: Are you licensed to practice in this state?
A: I am.
Q: And when were you licensed, Doctor?
A: 1937, I believe.
Q: At the present time do you occupy any official position in this county?
A: I am one of the autopsy surgeons for the county coroner.
Q: How long have you held that position?
A: Over ten years.
Q: What are your educational qualifications, doctor?
A: I have a B.S. and an M.D. degree. The B.S. is from the University of California, and the M.D. is from St. Louis University.
Q: Now, doctor, what does your position as autopsy surgeon mean; what duties does your position as autopsy surgeon entail?
A: My duties are investigating causes of death and deceased persons that are brought to the coroner's office.
Q: And you develop, conduct autopsies and postmortem examinations, do you?
A: I do.
Q: Now, doctor, on the 22nd of June of this year, did you have occasion to perform an autopsy examination on the body of ———?
A: I did.

A more involved direct examination and aggressive cross-examination is likely when the expert is to testify in an uncommon area. The following transcript of a successful effort to qualify a psychologist as an interpreter of lie-detection tapes on the issue of the mental condition of a subject-defendant in a murder trial illustrates this.

DIRECT EXAMINATION

(By ———, counsel appearing in behalf of the defendant.)

Q: Your name is Hudson Jost?
A: Right.
Q: Where do you live, Mr. Jost?

A: Tempe, Arizona.

Q: And you are temporarily, or at least you came today, or came yesterday from Chicago?

A: Yes, that's right.

Q: Now, Mr. Jost, would you relate what your educational background is, sir?

A: My training was all at the University of Chicago. I had two years in a small college in the Midwest, went to the University of Chicago in 1933, received my Ph.D. there in 1940.

Q: What was your Ph.D. in, sir?

A: My Ph.D. is in the biological sciences with a major in psychology.

Q: And was your other educational background, was there anything in your other educational background concerning psychology?

A: Yes, my undergraduate major was psychology.

Q: And what has been your professional experience since 1940?

A: After 1940 I worked a year or so at the Institute for Juvenile Research. Then I was an instructor at the Gary Junior College. I then went to Antioch College, Yellow Spring, Ohio, as an assistant professor in psychology, also working at the Phells Research Institute. Then I went back to Chicago for a year as a research associate.

Q: Was that in the field of psychology?

A: That was in the field of psychology. Then I was associate professor in the Department of Psychiatry, University of Tennessee College of Medicine from 1945 to 1952. From 1952 to 1959 I was professor of psychology at the University of Georgia and head of the psychology department. In 1959 I went to Arizona State University as professor of psychology and chairman of the department.

Q: All right. Now, Dr. Jost, do you have any membership in any professional associations?

A: I'm a Fellow in Division Three of the American Psychological Association—this is a division of experimental psychology; in Division Six of the American Psychological Association, which is the division of physiological psychology. Fellow in the American Association for the Advancement of Science; member of the Arizona Psychological Association; and some others which I don't think are important at this time.

Q: And during the course of your professional career in psychology, have you had occasion to publish any works or studies in that field?

A: I have published between twenty-five and thirty articles in the area of psychology, primarily in the area of physiological psychology.

Q: And have you on any occasion prior to today testified in the courts of any state in the United States in the field of psychology?

A: Yes, I have testified in the courts of Georgia and Tennessee, in the area of electroencephalography, which is a branch of my work, and in Massachusetts in the area of the polygraph.

Q: You have previously then testified in courts concerning the polygraph?

A: Yes, that's true.

Q: Now, during the course of your professional career, have you made any special studies which would relate physical reactions to mental illness or disorder?

A: Yes, this has been one of the primary areas of all of my research. The area of physiological psychology is one: This is an attempt to understand the relationship between physiological reactivity and what we might call mental states or intelligence, or behavior would probably be a better word. And these studies have indicated that the physiological reactivity organism is related to the behavior of the organism. There is no question about this.

Q: In what specific fields in physiological psychology have you made special studies, Dr. Jost?

A: My area of interest has primarily been in the autonomic nervous system. This is the nervous system which is primarily related to emotional reactivity.

Q: When did you begin your studies in the field of physiological psychology?

A: This began around 1936 or 37, when I was searching for a problem for my dissertation. I was working at the University of Chicago. There were no commercial polygraphs available at that time. They weren't being manufactured. So it was necessary for us, Dr. Mandel Sherman and myself, to build our own polygraph similar to the ones that are available now except we used a photographic recording device rather than pens that are now being used.

THE COURT: Rather than what, Doctor?

THE WITNESS: The ink recordings now being used.

Q: And you began that work in that field in the, approximately, the late 30s?

A: In the late 30s.

Q: Now, I think you say that you have made special studies in the field relating to reaction on the polygraph to mental illnesses or disorders?

After several questions probing this expert's publications and research in this area, the counsel for the defense relinquished the witness for *voir dire* examination by the prosecutor—a necessary preliminary to any further questioning.

VOIR DIRE EXAMINATION

(By ———, counsel appearing in behalf of the prosecution.)

Q: Doctor, have you ever taken any formal courses in polygraph work of any kind?

A: No. I got into the field before there were any schools available for this.

Q: But since that, I understand that's true, you started out with your own home-made machine.

A: Yes.

Q: But have you taken this work in polygraph?

A: No, I haven't, I have taught at the schools, however. I taught at the Keeler School from 1952 to 1954, I believe I taught the psychology section at the Keeler School.

Q: How many tests have you run on polygraphs, approximately, would you
     have any idea?
A: Hundreds.
Q: And those would be for different purposes, would they not?
A: Oh, yes, they were all experimental runs.
Q: Did you do any tests for purposes of determining deception?
A: Only very indirectly. I don't consider myself qualified in this particular
     area.
Q: You don't feel that you are qualified to read polygrams—
A: Oh, yes.
Q: Just a minute. And determine therefrom whether or not there is a pat-
     tern of deception?
A: Oh, yes, I am able to do that, but I don't consider that my main respon-
     sibility.
Q: You say that most of your testing in the area of polygraph has been
     done in the area of research?
A: Right.
Q: Or in conjunction with your research?
A: Right.
Q: When you state that you tested—Well, I believe I will save that for
     cross-examination. That's all I have.

EXPERTS—OPINION TESTIMONY

Even after a witness has been qualified as an expert, his opinion testimony is limited. In California, **expert opinion testimony** is accepted if it
meets the following tests:

> 1.   The testimony is related to a subject that is sufficiently beyond
> common experience that the opinion of an expert would assist the trier
> of fact.
> 2.   The testimony is based on matter (including the expert's special
> knowledge, skill, experience, training, and education) perceived by, or
> personally known to, the witness, or made known to him at or before
> the hearing. The matter does not have to be admissible but it must be
> of a type that may reasonably be relied on by an expert in forming an
> opinion on the subject to which his testimony relates, and not matter
> an expert is precluded by law from using as a basis for his opinion.[8]

The many areas of expertise, and the wide range of subjects on
which an experts' opinion may be sought, may force the expert to rely
on reports, statements, and other data which might not be admissible at
trial. This is proper if he bases his opinion on data that would be relied
on by other experts in forming an opinion in the subject area involved.

[8]California Evidence Code, Section 801.

In criminal trials, expert testimony may embrace all the arts and sciences, but is usually given in the general areas of criminalistics, the medicolegal field, traffic accident reconstruction, engineering, finance, mathematics, and the behavioral sciences.

Older theory, case law, and statutes contained rules against allowing witnesses to express opinions on the ultimate issues. The reasoning behind this prohibition was to prevent the witness from usurping the province of the jury. Modern law and decision tend to abandon this restrictive rule and allow an otherwise properly admitted opinion to embrace an **ultimate issue** to be decided by the trier of fact. *McCormack*, Section 12, expressed the futility of prohibiting an otherwise proper opinion on an ultimate issue of the case. "Admissibility depends on the nature of the issue and the circumstances of the case." In an abortion case an opinion on the issue of whether the abortion was performed for the preservation of life was admissible: "there was no other practicable way of framing the questions if they were to serve the purpose of obtaining the benefit of the witnesses' expert knowledge as to matters on which enlightenment of the jury by the expert was proper."[9]

In **criminalistics,** the expert witness is expected to offer his opinion about the identifying characteristics of some item of physical evidence. His opinion must necessarily be based on his examination of the evidence and various physical and chemical tests he may have made. As a general rule, the criminalist must testify about the basis for his opinion before stating his beliefs or conclusions.

Criminalistics is synonymous with forensic science. The British criminalist, H. J. Walls, summarizes the growth and identifies the origin of forensic science in a few well-chosen though unusual words: "The pedigree of forensic science, as it is practiced today, is by forensic medicine out of police work."[10] Criminalistics has a related field of on-the-scene evidence technology. **Evidence technicians** or scenes-of-crime officers now process crime scenes for physical evidence such as weapons, fingerprints, and other traces. They often help to connect the evidence examined by criminalists with the crime scene and to offer testimony about the integrity of the scientific means used to collect the evidence.

Medicolegal experts also testify about the basis for their opinions. This area of forensic medicine covers opinions about injuries, wounds, suspected weapons, and death. Medicolegal opinions must be prefaced by testimony about the medicolegal examinations they are based on.

An expert in the area of **traffic accident reconstruction** may give his

---

[9]People v. Wilson, 25 Cal. 2d 343 (1944); Clifford-Jacobs v. Industrial Comm. 19 Ill. 2d 236 (1960); Dowling v. Shattuck, Inc. 91 N.H. 234 (1941); Schwieger v. Solbeck 191 Ore. 454 (1951); Kansas Code of Civil Procedure 60–456(4); New Jersey Evidence Rule 56(3); Rule 704, Federal Rules of Evidence, Section 805, California Evidence Code.

[10]H. J. Walls, **Forensic Science** (New York: Praeger, 1968), p. 1.

opinion after he is shown to have examined the accident scene and usually one or more of the vehicles involved.

Other experts may have no personal knowledge on which to base a
specific opinion. They may gain such knowledge by sitting in court and
listening to the testimony of witnesses. They may take the witness stand
and answer a **hypothetical question** based on facts which have become
part of the court record through the testimony of previous witnesses.

In the first instance, on direct examination, the expert witness is
asked whether he was in court and heard all of certain testimony given
by a specific witness or specified witnesses. The expert's "yes" answer
"places" the exact portion of previous in-court testimony which he will
use as a basis for his opinion. This gives the court and the triers of fact
a means of evaluating the expert's opinion for scope and credibility.

The hypothetical question sets out the exact limits of previous evidence on which the expert may base his opinion. In phrasing this question, the direct examiner uses only facts which are part of the trial
record. However, he need not use all of them. The hypothetical question
spells out or summarizes the facts forming the basis for the expert's
opinion.

An example of the testimony of an expert witness who has listened
to in-court evidence is contained in the testimony of Dr. Jost, qualified
as an expert in the field of polygraph tests and psychology:

Q: Now, Dr. Jost, did you receive from me a month or so ago a reproduc-
tion of three polygraph charts?

A: Right, I did.

Q: I want to show you—And did those polygraph charts purport to be
charts on a person named Barry Sigal?

A: Right.

Q: I want to show you Defendant's Exhibits D-1, which is a "Peak of Tension" Test, D-2, and D-3, which are "Relevant-Irrelevant" tests. This
is D-1 and D-2 and D-3.

A: Yes.

Q: And ask you if those appear to be the originals of the reproductions
which I sent you?

A: I'm sure they are, yes.

Q: Now, did I also send you, Dr. Jost—By the way, you were here during
my reading of the testimony of Sergeant K. E. Campbell?

A: Right.

Q: Did I send you, also, the material generally that I read here in front of
this jury?

A: Yes.

Q: The questions and answers and the critical questions as testified to by
Mr. Campbell?

A: Yes, I saw those.

Q: Did you make a study of these charts?

A: Yes, I did.

Q: Were you able to form any opinion from the charts and the material that I submitted to you, based upon Sergeant Campbell's testimony from the charts that you saw—of which those are the originals—and the material that I gave to you based on Sergeant Campbell's testimony relative to the mental condition of the individual whose reactions were recorded on that chart, on those charts?

In his response to this question, the witness gave his expert opinion that the defendant had a mental disorder, and then answered questions which justified his use of the polygraph charts to ascertain the characteristic physical reactions of the defendant (while being tested for deception by Sgt. Campbell) which led to his conclusion.

A: Yes, I spent quite a bit of time going over these in comparing them with charts which I had obtained on populations before, and these charts are very similar to those which were obtained on psychotic individuals.

An illustration of the hypothetical question is taken from a case, *People v. McCaughan*,[11] where the cause of death was in question, and the determination of whether death was a result of the defendant's act was a crucial issue. The prosecuting attorney, after the usual questions qualifying the witness as a physician-expert, asked the following hypothetical question:

Q: If a person is sitting on a chair, and her head is held back by the hair of her head so that her face is looking up towards the ceiling—also, her arms are being held, and another person is sitting on her lap—and then an amount of food is placed into the person's mouth, and she is resisting the—and then a towel is placed over her mouth and her nose is also being held for a period of time, and then the person slumps over and thereafter expires, and approximately four heaping tablespoons of food is found lodged in the trachea; now, Doctor, based upon this hypothetical question, what would be the cause of death, Doctor?

A: The cause of death would be due to asphyxia, caused by obstruction of the trachea with food.

When a hypothetical question is used in a trial, the trial judge, in his charge, will usually instruct the jury as follows:

In examining an expert witness, counsel may use a type of question known as a hypothetical question. The witness is asked to assume to be true a hypothetical state of facts, and to give an opinion based on that assumption.

[11] 49 Cal. 2d 409 (1957).

In accepting such a question, the court does not rule or necessarily find that all the assumed facts in this question have been proved. The court only determines that those assumed facts are within the probable or possible range of the evidence. It is for you, the jury, to ascertain from all the evidence whether or not the assumed facts in a hypothetical question have been proved. If you should find that any assumption in such a question has not been proved, you are to determine the effect of that failure of proof on the value and weight of the expert opinion.

EXPERTS—CROSS-EXAMINATION

Specific Attack Areas. Opposing counsel can probe the scientific principle and methodology involved in the experts' opinion during cross-examination. An expert witness may be cross-examined as any other witness is. He may also be fully cross-examined as to: (1) his qualifications, (2) the subject of his expert testimony, and (3) the matter his opinion is based on and the reasons for his opinion.[12]

A witness usually may not be cross-examined about the content or tenor of any scientific, technical, or professional text, treatise, journal, or similar publication that he has not referred to, considered, or relied on in forming his opinion, unless the publication has been admitted in evidence.[13]

A science book may be admitted as evidence during cross-examination to prove an opinion contained in the book, or to contradict the opinion of the witness, but only when the witness refers to it as an authority in his testimony. A standard cross-examination question is whether the witness considers a certain book to be a recognized and standard authoritative text on the subject of his opinion or any portion of it. When the witness admits a text is a standard work in the field, the cross-examiner directs the attention of the witness to an opinion in the text which contradicts the opinion of the expert. The trial judge will not allow this line of questioning to prove the textual opinion but will allow it as bearing on the weight the triers of fact should give to the expert's testimony.

If an expert witness is allowed to give an opinion based, in whole or in part, on the opinion or statement of another person, the other person may be called and cross-examined about the opinion or statement relied on by the first witness.[14]

General Attack Area: Bias or Interest. Experts may also be attacked on the basis of **interest or bias.** A cross-examiner can often

---

[12]California Evidence Code, Section 721.
[13]California Evidence Code, Section 721.
[14]California Evidence Code, Section 804.

destroy an expert witness by a line of questioning which will identify him as a paid witness. The state's criminalistics experts are vulnerable to questions designed to show that the criminalist is a salaried witness. Although a salary scheme seems to have more integrity than the fees of nonsalaried experts, the scheme has weaknesses when a cross-examiner probes whether the criminalist has ever testified for the defense, or against the police. This line of questioning puts the witness in a difficult situation. He works for the police or the prosecutor. He is an employee of a law enforcement agency. He is paid a salary, and he hardly ever testifies for a defendant. Some defense experts are vulnerable to the same type of attack. That is, that they have always testified for and been paid by the defense.

SUMMARY

Opinion evidence is admissible when the opinion or conclusion of an expert is necessary to provide the triers of fact with data necessary or useful to their decision-making role in a criminal trial. Lay or non-expert witnesses are limited in the scope of their opinions to areas of common knowledge or to areas in which they have acquired special knowledge. Expert witnesses are limited to the area in which they can show expertise through education and experience. The nonexpert with special knowledge or the expert witness must be qualified in court, under direct and cross-examination, in the area of proposed testimony. Opposing counsel can attack the qualifications of a nonexpert with special knowledge or an expert; he can also attack the subject of his testimony, and the basis for his opinion; and he can probe in an attempt to expose bias or interest. Hypothetical questions are a means to develop opinion evidence from expert witnesses. Trial judges will insert in their judicial instructions at the end of a trial in which opinion evidence is given by an expert that jurors should give to such testimony the weight they find it should be entitled.

DISCUSSION QUESTIONS

1. What is the difference between a "fact" and an "opinion"?
2. Who may give opinion evidence? When?
3. To what opinions may experts testify?
4. To what opinions may nonexperts testify?
5. How are experts "qualified" to testify?
6. What are the limits on expert testimony in your jurisdiction?

7. How may experts be attacked by opposing counsel?
8. Why are answers to hypothetical questions a weak type of evidence?

GLOSSARY

CRIMINALISTICS.   The application of science to the examination of physical
    evidence; linked to forensic science, the general application of science
    to the solution of crimes. Evidence technicians represent a sub-classifica-
    tion of this field.

EXPERTS.   Capable of being qualified in court as expert witnesses: men and
    women of science educated in art or science, or persons possessing spe-
    cial or unusual knowledge acquired from practical experience.

FORENSIC.   Related to courts of justice.

JUDICIAL INSTRUCTIONS.   A charge to the jury by trial judge; instructions as to
    the principles of law in a case and their application to the circumstances
    of the case being tried.

Voir Dire.   In-court preliminary examination of juror or witness when com-
    petency, interest, etc., is in dispute.

Case Studies: Testimonial Evidence

CHAPTER OBJECTIVES

1. The purpose of this chapter is to introduce students to case law through case study. In it
2. The case study method is used to review prior chapters;
3. The content of court opinions is reviewed to illustrate the application of the fundamentals of evidence to an issue in dispute;
4. Concurring and dissenting opinions are discussed to show differences of opinion by the reviewing judiciary; and
5. Identification is emphasized as a major area of testimonial evidence.

The case studies in this chapter concern testimonial evidence. Together, these five studies review in depth the giving of testimony by witnesses—the medium by which most proof is produced in court at criminal trials.

United States v. Wade is a landmark case that establishes the police lineup for identification of suspects by eyewitness as a "critical

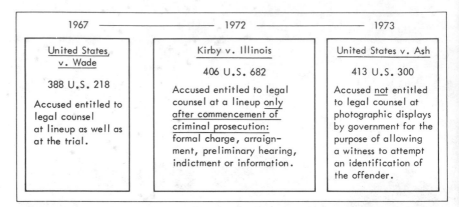

FIGURE 5. Clarification of the critical stage of the pretrial period—when the Sixth Amendment guarantee of "assistance" at trial assures legal aid for accused persons when confronted with both the intricacies of the law and the advocacy of the public prosecutor prior to trial.

stage" in the pretrial procedures against an accused person, during which an accused is entitled to legal assistance under the Sixth Amendment.

Kirby v. Illinois is a Supreme Court case following the *Wade* case and reflecting a significant change in the membership of the Court. It limits the decision of *Wade* to post-indictment lineups.

United States v. Ash followed *Kirby* and redefined the "critical stage of proceedings" requiring the presence of an attorney in the investigation or pretrial process.

Ramsey v. Virginia is a state case which focuses on the area of opinion evidence against the background of a case which progressed through trial court to appellate review.

People v. Bob is a California case concerned with hearsay evidence, another difficult-to-understand area of evidence for many people. This opinion reviews the "hearsay rule" and its potential for contributing to a miscarriage of justice unless carefully supervised by the judiciary.

CASE STUDY

United States v. Billy Joe Wade, 388 U.S. 218 (1967).

Opinion of the Court, delivered by Mr. Justice Brennan.*

The question here is whether courtroom identifications of an accused at trial are to be excluded from evidence because the accused was exhibited to the witnesses before trial at a post-indictment lineup con-

*Footnotes omitted. Headings added by authors for reader's convenience.

ducted for identification purposes without notice to and in the absence of the accused's appointed counsel.

Facts of Case. The federally insured bank in Eustace, Texas, was robbed on September 21, 1964. A man with a small strip of tape on each side of his face entered the bank, pointed a pistol at the female cashier and the vice president, the only persons in the bank at the time, and forced them to fill a pillowcase with the bank's money. The man then drove away with an accomplice who had been waiting in a stolen car outside the bank. On March 23, 1965, an indictment was returned against respondent, Wade, and two others for conspiring to rob the bank, and against Wade and the accomplice for the robbery itself. Wade was arrested on April 2, and counsel was appointed to represent him on April 26. Fifteen days later an FBI agent, without notice to Wade's lawyer, arranged to have the two bank employees observe a lineup made up of Wade and five or six other prisoners and conducted in a courtroom of the local county courthouse. Each person in the line wore strips of tape such as allegedly worn by the robber and upon direction each said something like "put the money in the bag," the words allegedly uttered by the robber. Both bank employees identified Wade in the lineup as the bank robber.

At trial, the two employees, when asked on direct examination if the robber was in the courtroom, pointed to Wade. The prior lineup identification was then elicited from both employees on cross-examination. At the close of testimony, Wade's counsel moved for a judgment of acquittal or, alternatively, to strike the bank officials' courtroom identifications on the ground that conduct of the lineup, without notice to and in the absence of his appointed counsel, violated his Fifth Amendment privilege against self-incrimination and his Sixth Amendment right to the assistance of counsel. The motion was denied, and Wade was convicted. The Court of Appeals for the Fifth Circuit reversed the conviction and ordered a new trial at which the in-court identification was to be excluded, holding that, though the lineup did not violate Wade's Fifth Amendment rights, "the lineup, held as it was, in the absence of counsel, already chosen to represent appellant, was a violation of his Sixth Amendment rights. . . ." 358 F2d 557, 560. We granted certiorari, 385 U.S. 811, 17 L. Ed. 2d 53, 87 S. Ct. 81, and set the case for oral argument with *Gilbert v. California,* 388 U.S. 263, 18 L. Ed. 2d 1178, 87 S. Ct. 1951, and *Stovall v. Denno,* 388 U.S. 293, 18 L. Ed. 2d 1199, 87 S. Ct. 1967, which present similar questions. We reverse the judgment of the Court of Appeals and remand to that court with direction to enter a new judgment vacating the conviction and remanding the case to the District Court for further proceedings consistent with this opinion.

I.

Privilege Against Self-Incrimination. Neither the lineup itself nor anything shown by this record that Wade was required to do in the lineup violated his privilege against self-incrimination. We have only recently reaffirmed that the privilege "protects an accused only from being compelled to testify against himself, or otherwise provide the State with evidence of a testimonial or communicative nature. . . ." *Schmerber v. California,* 384 U.S. 757, 761, 16 L. Ed. 2d 908, 914, 86 S. Ct. 1826. We there held that compelling a suspect to submit to a withdrawal of a sample of his blood for analysis for alcohol content and the admission in evidence of the analysis report were not compulsion to those ends. That holding was supported by the opinion in *Holt v. United States,* 218 U.S. 245, 54 L. Ed. 1021, 31 S. Ct. 2, in which case a question arose as to whether a blouse belonged to the defendant. A witness testified at trial that the defendant put on the blouse and it had fit him. The defendant argued that the admission of the testimony was error because compelling him to put on the blouse was a violation of his privilege. The Court rejected the claim as "an extravagant extension of the Fifth Amendment."

Mr. Justice Holmes saying for the Court:

> The prohibition of compelling a man in a criminal court to be witness against himself is a prohibition of the use of physical or moral compulsion to extort communications from him, not an exclusion of his body as evidence when it may be material. 218 U.S., at 252–253, 54 L. Ed. at 1029.

The Court in Holt, however, put aside any constitutional questions which might be involved in compelling an accused, as here, to exhibit himself before victims of or witnesses to an alleged crime; the Court stated, "we need not consider how far a court would go in compelling a man to exhibit himself." *Id.,* at 253, 54 L. Ed. at 1029.

We have no doubt that compelling the accused merely to exhibit his person for observation by a prosecution witness prior to trial involves no compulsion of the accused to give evidence having testimonial significance. It is compulsion of the accused to exhibit his physical characteristics, not compulsion to disclose any knowledge he might have. It is no different from compelling Schmerber to provide a blood sample or Holt to wear the blouse, and, as in those instances, is not within the cover of the privilege. Similarly, compelling Wade to speak within hearing distance of the witnesses, even to utter words purportedly uttered by the robber, was not compulsion to utter statements of a "testimonial" nature; he was required to use his voice as an identifying physical characteristic, not to speak his guilt. We held in Schmerber, *supra*, 384 U.S. at 761, 16 L. Ed. 2d at 914, that the distinction to be drawn under the Fifth Amendment privilege against self-incrimination is one between an accused's "communications" in whatever form, vocal or physical, and "compulsion which makes a suspect or accused the source of 'real or physical evidence,'" Schmerber, *supra*, 384 U.S. at 764, 16 L. Ed. 2d at 916. We recognized that "both federal and state courts have usually held that . . . [the privilege] offers no protection against compulsion to submit to fingerprinting, photography, or measurements, to write or speak for identification, to appear in court, to stand, to assume a stance, to walk, or to make a particular gesture." *Id.*, at 764, 16 L. Ed. 2d at 916. None of these activities becomes testimonial within the scope of the privilege because required of the accused in a pretrial lineup.

Moreover, it deserves emphasis that this case presents no question of the admissibility in evidence of anything Wade said or did at the lineup which implicates his privilege. The Government offered no such evidence as part of its case, and what came out about the lineup proceedings on Wade's cross-examination of the bank employees involved no violation of Wade's privilege.

II.

The fact that the lineup involved no violation of Wade's privilege against self-incrimination does not, however, dispose of his contention that the courtroom identifications should have been excluded because the lineup was conducted without notice to and in the absence of his counsel. Our rejection of the right to counsel claim in Schmerber rested on our conclusion in that case that "no issue of counsel's ability to assist petitioner in respect of any rights he did possess is presented." 384 U.S., at 766, 16 L. Ed. 2d at 917. In contrast, in this case it is urged that the assistance of counsel at the lineup was indispensable to protect Wade's most basic right as a criminal defendant—his right to a fair trial at which the witnesses against him might be meaningfully cross-examined.

Right to Counsel. The Framers of the Bill of Rights envisaged a broader role for counsel than under the practice then prevailing in England of merely advising his client in "matters of law," and eschewing any responsibility for "matters of fact." The constitutions in at least 11 of the 13 States expressly or impliedly abolished this distinction. *Powell v. Alabama*, 287 U.S. 45, 60–65, 77 L. Ed. 158, 166–68, 53 S. Ct. 55, 84 ALR 527; Note, 73 Yale L.J. 1000, 1030–33 (1964). "Though the colonial provisions about counsel were in accord on few things, they agreed on the necessity of abolishing the facts-law distinction; the colonists appreciated that if a defendant were forced to stand alone against the state, his case was foredoomed." 73 Yale L.J. *supra*, at 1033–34. This background is reflected in the scope given by our decisions to the Sixth Amendment's guarantee to an accused of the assistance of counsel for his defense. When the Bill of Rights was adopted, there were no organized police forces as we know them today. The accused confronted the prosecutor and the witness against him, and the evidence was marshalled, largely at the trial itself. In contrast, today's law enforcement machinery involves critical confrontations of the accused by the prosecution at pretrial proceedings where the results might well settle the accused's fate and reduce the trial itself to a mere formality. In recognition of these realities of modern criminal prosecution, our cases have construed the Sixth Amendment guarantee to apply to "critical" stages of the proceedings. The guarantee reads: "In all criminal prosecutions, the accused shall enjoy the right . . . to have the Assistance of Counsel *for his defence.*" (Emphasis supplied.) The plain wording of this guarantee thus encompasses counsel's assistance whenever necessary to assure a meaningful "defense."

Pretrial Period: Inherent Threat to Accused.   As early as *Powell v. Alabama, supra,* we recognized that the period from arraignment to trial was "perhaps the most critical period of the proceedings, . . ." *id.,* at 57, 77 L.Ed., at 164, 84 ALR 527, during which the accused "requires the guiding hand of counsel, . . ." *id.,* at 69, 77 L. Ed. 170, 84 ALR 527, if the guarantee is not to prove an empty right. That principle has since been applied to require the assistance of counsel at the type of arraignment—for example, that provided by Alabama—where certain rights might be sacrificed or lost: "What happens there may affect the whole trial. Available defenses may be irretrievably lost, if not then and there asserted. . . ." *Hamilton v. Alabama,* 368 U.S. 52, 54, 7 L. Ed. 2d 114, 116, 82 S. Ct. 157. See *White v. Maryland,* 373 U.S. 59, 10 L. Ed. 2d 193, 83 S. Ct. 1050. The principle was also applied in *Massiah v. United States,* 377 U.S. 201, 12 L. Ed. 2d 246, 84 S. Ct. 1199, where we held that incriminating statements of the defendant should have been excluded from evidence when it appeared that they were overheard by federal agents who, without notice to the defendant's lawyer, arranged a meeting between the defendant and an accomplice turned informant. We said, quoting a concurring opinion in *Spano v. New York,* 360 U.S. 315, 326, 3 L. Ed. 2d 1265, 1273, 79 S. Ct. 1202, that "anything less . . . might deny a defendant 'effective representation by counsel at the only stage when legal aid and advice would help him.' " 377 U.S., at 204, 12 L. Ed. 2d at 249.

In *Escobedo v. Illinois,* 378 U.S. 478, 12 L. Ed. 2d 977, 84 S. Ct.

1758, we drew upon the rationale of Hamilton and Massiah in holding that the right to counsel was guaranteed at the point where the accused, prior to arraignment, was subjected to secret interrogation despite repeated requests to see his lawyer. We again noted the necessity of counsel's presence if the accused was to have a fair opportunity to present a defense at the trial itself:

> The rule sought by the State here, however, would make the trial no more than an appeal from the interrogation; and the "right to use counsel at the formal trial [would be] a very hollow thing [if], for all practical purposes, the conviction is already assured by pretrial examination. . . . One can imagine a cynical prosecutor saying: 'Let them have the most illustrious counsel, now. They can't escape the noose. There is nothing that counsel can do for them at the trial.' " 378 U.S., at 487–88, 12 L. Ed. 2d at 984.

Finally in *Miranda v. Arizona,* 384 U.S. 436, 16 L. Ed. 2d 694, 86 S. Ct. 1602, 10 ALR3d 974, the rules established for custodial interrogation included the right to the presence of counsel. The result was rested on our finding that this and the other rules were necessary to safeguard the privilege against self-incrimination from being jeopardized by such interrogation.

Of course, nothing decided or said in the opinions in the cited cases links the right to counsel only to protection of Fifth Amendment rights. Rather those decisions "no more than reflect a constitutional principle established as long ago as *Powell v. Alabama. . . ." Massiah v. United States, supra,* 377 U.S., at 205, 12 L. Ed. 2d at 250. It is central to that principle that in addition to counsel's presence at trial, the accused is guaranteed that he need not stand alone against the State at any stage of the prosecution, formal or informal, in court or out, where counsel's absence might derogate from the accused's right to a fair trial. The security of that right is as much the aim of the right to counsel as it is of the other guarantees of the Sixth Amendment—the right of the accused to a speedy and public trial by an impartial jury, his right to be informed of the nature and cause of the accusation, and his right to be confronted with the witness against him and to have compulsory process for obtaining witnesses in his favor. The presence of counsel at such critical confrontations, as at the trial itself, operates to assure that the accused's interests will be protected consistently with our adversary theory of criminal prosecution. *Cf. Pointer v. Texas,* 380 U.S. 400, 13 L. Ed. 2d 923, 85 S. Ct. 1065.

In sum, the principle of *Powell v. Alabama* and succeeding cases requires that we scrutinize any pretrial confrontation of the accused to determine whether the presence of his counsel is necessary to preserve the defendant's basic right to a fair trial as affected by his right meaningfully to cross-examine the witnesses against him and to have effective assistance of counsel at the trial itself. It calls upon us to analyze whether potential substantial prejudice to defendant's rights inheres in the particular confrontation and the ability of counsel to help avoid that prejudice.

III.

Police Lineups. The Government characterizes the lineup as a mere preparatory step in the gathering of the prosecution's evidence, not different—for Sixth Amendment purposes—from various other preparatory steps, such as systematized or scientific analyzing of the accused's fingerprints, blood sample, clothing, hair, and the like. We think there are differences which preclude such stages being characterized as critical stages at which the accused has the right to the presence of his counsel. Knowledge of the techniques of science and technology is sufficiently available, and the variables in techniques few enough, that the accused has the opportunity for a meaningful confrontation of the Government's case at trial through the ordinary processes of cross-examination of the Government's expert witnesses and the presentation of the evidence of his own experts. The denial of a right to have his counsel present at such analyses does not therefore violate the Sixth Amendment; they are not critical stages since there is minimal risk that his counsel's absence at such stages might derogate from his right to a fair trial.

IV.

But the confrontation compelled by the State between the accused and the victim or witnesses to a crime to elicit identification evidence is peculiarly riddled with innumerable dangers and variable factors which might seriously, even crucially, derogate from a fair trial. The vagaries of eyewitness identification are well-known; the annals of criminal law are rife with instances of mistaken identification. Mr. Justice Frankfurter once said:

> What is the worth of identification testimony even when uncontradicted? The identification of strangers is proverbially untrustworthy. The hazards of such testimony are established by a formidable number of instances in the records of English and American trials. These instances are recent—not due to the brutalities of ancient criminal procedure. **The Case of Sacco and Vanzetti** 30 (1927).

A major factor contributing to the high incidence of miscarriage of justice from mistaken identification has been the degree of suggestion inherent in the manner in which the prosecution presents the suspect to witnesses for pretrial identification. A commentator has observed that "the influence of improper suggestion upon identifying witnesses probably accounts for more miscarriages of justice than any other single factor—perhaps it is responsible for more such errors than all other factors combined." WALL, EYE-WITNESS IDENTIFICATION IN CRIMINAL CASES 26. Suggestion can be created intentionally or unintentionally in many subtle ways. And the dangers for the suspect are particularly grave when the witness' opportunity for observation was insubstantial, and thus his susceptibility to suggestion the greatest. Moreover,

> it is a matter of common experience that, once a witness has picked out the accused at the lineup, he is not likely to go back on his word later on, so that in practice the issue of identity may (in the absence of other relevant evidence) for all practical purposes be determined there and then, before the trial. Williams and Hammelmann, **Identification Parades**, Part I (1963), Crim. L. Rev. 479, 482.

The pretrial confrontation for purpose of identification may take the form of a lineup, also known as an "identification parade" or "showup," as in the present case, or presentation of the suspect alone to the witness, as in *Stovall v. Denno*, 388 U.S. 293, 18 L. Ed. 2d 1199, 87 S. Ct. 1967, *supra*. It is obvious that risks of suggestion attend either form of confrontation and increase the dangers inhering in eyewitness identification. But as is the case with secret interrogations, there is serious difficulty in depicting what transpires at lineups and other forms of identification confrontations: "Privacy results in secrecy and this in turn results in a gap in our knowledge as to what in fact goes on. ..." *Miranda v. Arizona, supra*, 384 U.S. at 448, 16 L. Ed. 2d at 709, 10 ALR3d 974. For the same reasons, the defense can seldom reconstruct the manner and mode of lineup identification for judge or jury at trial. Those participating in a lineup with the accused may often be police officers; in any event, the participants' names are rarely recorded or divulged at trial. The impediments to an objective observation are increased when the victim is the witness. Lineups are prevalent in rape and robbery prosecutions and present a particular hazard that a victim's understandable outrage may excite vengeful or spiteful motives. In any event, neither witnesses nor lineup participants are apt to be alert for conditions prejudicial to the suspect. And if they were, it would likely be of scant benefit to the suspect since neither witnesses nor lineup participants are likely to be schooled in the detection of suggestive influences. Improper influences may go undetected by a suspect, guilty or not, who experiences the emotional tension which we might expect in one being confronted with potential accusers. Even when he does observe abuse, if he has a criminal record he may be reluctant to take the stand and open up the admission of prior convictions. Moreover, any protestations by the suspect of the fairness of the lineup made at trial are likely to be in vain; the jury's choice is between the accused's unsupported version and that of the police officers present. In short, the accused's inability effectively to reconstruct at trial any unfairness that occurred at the lineup may deprive him of his only opportunity meaningfully to attack the credibility of the witness' courtroom identification.

Conditions Prejudicial to Accused at Lineups. What facts have been disclosed in specific cases about the conduct of pretrial confrontations for identification illustrate both the potential for substantial prejudice to the accused at that stage and the need for its revelation at trial. A commentator provides some striking examples:

> In a Canadian case . . . the defendant had been picked out of a lineup of six men, of which he was the only Oriental. In other cases, a black-haired suspect was placed among a group of light-haired persons, tall suspects have been made to stand with short nonsuspects, and, in a case where the perpetrator of the crime was known to be a youth, a suspect under twenty was placed in a lineup with five other persons, all of whom were forty or over.

Similarly state reports, in the course of describing prior identifications admitted as evidence of guilt, reveal numerous instances of suggestive procedures, for example, that all in the lineup but the suspect were known to the identifying witness, that the other participants in a lineup were grossly dissimilar in appearance to the suspect, that only the suspect was required to wear distinctive clothing which the culprit allegedly wore, that the witness is told by the police that they have caught the culprit after which the defendant is brought before the witness alone or is viewed in jail, that the suspect is pointed out before or during a lineup, and that the participants in the lineup are asked to try on an article of clothing which fits only the suspect.

The potential for improper influence is illustrated by the circumstances, insofar as they appear, surrounding the prior identifications in the three cases we decide today. In the present case, the testimony of the identifying witnesses elicited on cross-examination revealed that those witnesses were taken to the courthouse and seated in the courtroom to await assembly of the lineup. The courtroom faced on a hallway observable to the witness through an open door. The cashier testified that she saw Wade "standing in the hall" within sight of an FBI agent. Five or six other prisoners later appeared in the hall. The vice president testified that he saw a person in the hall in the custody of the agent who "resembled the person that we identified as the one that had entered the bank."

The lineup in *Gilbert*, 388 U.S. 263, 18 L. Ed. 2d 1178, 87 S. Ct.

1951, *supra*, was conducted in an auditorium in which some 100 witnesses to several alleged state and federal robberies charged to Gilbert made wholesale identifications of Gilbert as the robber in each other's presence, a procedure said to be fraught with dangers of suggestion. And the vice of suggestion created by the identification of *Stovall, supra*, was the presentation to the witness of the suspect alone handcuffed to police officers. It is hard to imagine a situation more clearly conveying the suggestion to the witness that the one presented is believed guilty by the police. See Frankfurter, The Case of Sacco and Vanzetti 31 32.

The few cases that have surfaced therefore reveal the existence of a process attended with hazards of serious unfairness to the criminal accused and strongly suggest the plight of the more numerous defendants who are unable to ferret out suggestive influences in the secrecy of the confrontation. We do not assume that these risks are the result of police procedures intentionally designed to prejudice an accused. Rather we assume they derive from the dangers inherent in eyewitness identification and the suggestibility inherent in the context of the pretrial identification. Williams & Hammelmann in one of the most comprehensive studies of such forms of identification, said,

> The fact that the police themselves have, in a given case, little or no doubt that the man put up for identification has committed the offense, and that their chief preoccupation is with the problem of getting sufficient proof, because he has not "come clean," involves a danger that this persuasion may communicate itself even in a doubtful case to the witness in some way. . . . **Identification Parades**, Part I [1963] CRIM. L. REV. 479, 483.

Insofar as the accused's conviction may rest on a courtroom identification in fact the fruit of a suspect pretrial identification which the accused is helpless to subject to effective scrutiny at trial, the accused is deprived of that right of cross-examination which is an essential safeguard to his right to confront the witnesses against him. *Pointer v. Texas*, 380 U.S. 400, 13 L. Ed. 2d 923, 85 S. Ct. 1065. And even though cross-examination is a precious safeguard to a fair trial, it cannot be viewed as an absolute assurance of accuracy and reliability. Thus in the present context, where so many variables and pitfalls exist, the first line of defense must be the prevention of unfairness and the lessening of the hazards of eyewitness identification at the lineup itself. The trial which might determine the accused's fate may well not be that in the courtroom but that at the pretrial confrontation, with the State aligned against the accused, the witness the sole jury, and the accused unprotected aganist the overreaching, intentional or unintentional, and with little or no effective appeal from the judgment there rendered by the witness—"that's the man."

Post-indictment Lineup as Critical Stage: Right to Counsel.   Since it appears that there is grave potential for prejudice, intentional or not, in the pretrial lineup, which may not be capable of reconstruction at trial, and since presence of counsel itself can often avert prejudice and assure a meaningful confrontation at trial, there can be little doubt that for Wade the post-indictment lineup was a critical stage of the prosecution at which he was "as much entitled to such aid [of counsel] . . . as at the trial itself." *Powell v. Alabama, supra,* 287 U.S. 45, 57, 77 L. Ed. 158, 164, 53 S. Ct. 55, 84 ALR527. Thus both Wade and his counsel should have been notified of the impending lineup, and counsel's presence should have been a requisite to conduct of the lineup, absent an "intelligent waiver." See *Carnley v. Cochran,* 369 U.S. 506, 8 L. Ed. 2d 70, 82 S. Ct. 884. No substantial countervailing policy considerations have been advanced against the requirement of the presence of counsel. Concern is expressed that the requirement will forestall prompt identifications and result in obstruction of the confrontations. As for the first, we note that in the two cases in which the right to counsel is today held to apply, counsel had already been appointed and no argument is made in either case that notice to counsel would have prejudicially delayed the confrontations. Moreover, we leave open the question whether the presence of substitute counsel might not suffice where notification and presence of the suspect's own counsel would result in prejudicial delay. And to refuse to recognize the right to counsel for fear that counsel will obstruct the course of justice is contrary to the basic assumptions upon which this Court has operated in Sixth Amendment cases. We rejected similar logic in *Miranda v. Arizona* concerning presence of counsel during custodial interrogation, 384 U.S., at 480–81, 16 L. Ed. 2d at 727, 10 ALR3d 974:

> An attorney is merely exercising the good professional judgment he has been taught. This is not cause for considering the attorney a menace to law enforcement. He is merely carrying out what he is sworn to do under his oath—to protect to the extent of his ability the rights of his client. In fulfilling this responsibility the attorney plays a vital role in the administration of criminal justice under our Constitution.

In our view counsel can hardly impede legitimate law enforcement; on the contrary, for the reasons expressed, law enforcement may be assisted by preventing the infiltration of taint in the prosecution's identification evidence. That result cannot help the guilty avoid conviction but can only help assure that the right man has been brought to justice.

Legislative or other regulations, such as those of local police departments, which eliminate the risks of abuse and unintentional suggestion at lineup proceedings and the impediments to meaningful confrontation at trial may also remove the basis for regarding the stage as "critical." But neither Congress nor the federal authorities have seen fit to provide a solution. What we hold today "in no way creates a constitutional straightjacket which will handicap sound efforts at reform, nor is it intended to have this effect." *Miranda v. Arizona, supra,* 384 U.S. at 467, 16 L. Ed. 2d at 720, 10 ALR3d 974.

V.

Independent Origin of In-Court Identification. We come now to the question whether the denial of Wade's motion to strike the courtroom identification by the bank witnesses at trial because of the absence of his counsel at the lineup required, as the Court of Appeals held, the grant of a new trial at which such evidence is to be excluded. We do not think this disposition can be justified without first giving the Government the opportunity to establish by clear and convincing evidence that the in-court identifications were based upon observations of the suspect other than the lineup identification. See *Murphy v. Waterfront Commission,* 378 U.S. 52, 79, n. 18, 12 L. Ed. 2d 678, 695, 84 S. Ct. 1594. Where, as here, the admissibility of evidence of the lineup identification itself is not involved, a per se rule of exclusion of courtroom identification would be unjustified. See *Nardone v. United States,* 308 U.S. 338, 341, 84 L. Ed. 307, 311, 60 S. Ct. 266. A rule limited solely to the exclusion of testimony concerning identification at the lineup itself, without regard to admissibility of the courtroom identification, would render the right to counsel an empty one. The lineup is most often used, as in the present case, to crystallize the witnesses' identification of the defendant for future reference. We have already noted that the lineup identification will have that effect. The State may then rest upon the witnesses' unequivocal courtroom identification, and not mention the pretrial identification as part of the State's case at trial. Counsel is then in the predicament in which Wade's counsel found himself—realizing that possible unfairness at the lineup may be the sole means of attack upon the unequivocal courtroom identification, and having to probe in the dark in an attempt to discover and reveal unfairness, while bolstering the government witness' courtroom identification by bringing out and dwelling upon his prior identification. Since counsel's presence at the lineup would equip him to attack not only the lineup identification but the courtroom identification as well, limiting the impact of violation of the right to counsel to exclusion of evidence only of identification at the lineup itself disregards a critical element of that right.

We think it follows that the proper test to be applied in these situations is that quoted in *Wong Sun v. United States,* 371 U.S. 471, 488, 9 L. Ed. 2d 441, 455, 83 S. Ct. 407,

Whether, granting establishment of the primary illegality, the evidence to which instant objection is made has been come at by exploitation of that illegality or instead by means sufficiently distinguishable to be purged of the primary taint. MAGUIRE, EVIDENCE OF GUILT 221 (1959). See also **Hoffa v. United States**, 385 U.S. 293, 309, 17 L. Ed. 2d 374, 386, 87 S. Ct. 408.

Application of this test in the present context requires consideration of various factors; for example, the prior opportunity to observe the alleged criminal act, the existence of any discrepancy between any pre-lineup description and the defendant's actual description, any identification prior to lineup of another person, the identification by picture of the defendant prior to the lineup, failure to identify the defendant on a prior occasion, and the lapse of time between the alleged act and the lineup identification. It is also relevant to consider those facts which, despite the absence of counsel, are disclosed concerning the conduct of the lineup.

We doubt that the Court of Appeals applied the proper test for exclusion of the in-court identification of the two witnesses. The court stated that "it cannot be said with any certainty that they would have recognized appellant at the time of trial if this intervening lineup had not occurred," and that the testimony of the two witnesses "may well have been colored by the illegal procedure [and] was prejudicial." 358 F2d, at 560. Moreover, the court was persuaded, in part, by the "compulsory verbal responses made by Wade at the instance of the Special Agent." *Ibid.* This implies the erroneous holding that Wade's privilege against self-incrimination was violated so that the denial of counsel required exclusion.

On the record now before us we cannot make the determination whether the in-court identifications had an independent origin. This was not an issue at trial, although there is some evidence relevant to a determination. That inquiry is most properly made in the District Court. We therefore think the appropriate procedure to be followed is to vacate the conviction pending a hearing to determine whether the in-court identifications had an independent source, or whether, in any event, the introduction of the evidence was harmless error, *Chapman v. California*, 386 U.S. 18, 17 L. Ed. 2d 705, 87 S. Ct. 824, and for the District Court to reinstate the conviction or order a new trial, as may be proper. See *United States v. Shotwell Mfg.*, 355 U.S. 233, 245–46, 2 L. Ed. 2d 234, 242, 78 S. Ct. 245.

The judgment of the Court of Appeals is vacated and the case is remanded to that court with direction to enter a new judgment vacating the conviction and remanding the case to the District Court for further proceedings consistent with this opinion.

It is so ordered.

Separate Opinions*

Four separate opinions were filed in this case. One is a concurring opinion, the others dissent in part and concur in part.

Opinion of Mr. Justice Clark, concurring.

With reference to the lineup point involved in this case I cannot, for the life of me, see why a lineup is not a critical stage of the prosecution. Identification of the suspect—a prerequisite to establishment of guilt—occurs at this stage, and with *Miranda v. Arizona*, 384 U.S. 436, 16 L. Ed. 2d 694, 86 S. Ct. 1602, 10 ALR3d 974 (1966), on the books, the requirement of the presence of counsel arises, unless waived by the suspect. I dissented in *Miranda* but I am bound by it now, as we all are. *Schmerber v. California*, 384 U.S. 757, 16 L. Ed. 2d 908, 86 S. Ct. 1826 (1966), precludes petitioner's claim of self-incrimination. I therefore join the opinion of the Court.

Opinion of Mr. Justice Black, dissenting in part and concurring in part.

On March 23, 1965, respondent Wade was indicted for robbing a bank; on April 2, he was arrested; and on April 26, the court appointed a lawyer to represent him. Fifteen days later, while Wade was still in custody, an FBI agent took him and several other prisoners into a room at the courthouse, directed each to participate in a lineup wearing strips of tape on his face and to speak the words used by the robber at the bank. This was all done in order to let the bank employee witnesses look at Wade for identification purposes. Wade's lawyer was not notified of or present at the lineup to protect his client's interests. At Wade's trial, two bank employees identified him in the courtroom. Wade objected to this testimony, when, on cross-examination, his counsel elicited from these witnesses the fact that they had seen Wade in the lineup. He contended that by forcing him to participate in the lineup, wear strips of tape on his face, and repeat the words used by the robber, all without counsel, the Government had (1) compelled him to be a witness against himself in violation of the Fifth Amendment, and (2) deprived him of the assistance of counsel for his defense in violation of the Sixth Amendment.

The Court in Part I of its opinion rejects Wade's Fifth Amendment contention. From that I dissent. In Parts II–IV of its opinion, the Court sustains Wade's claim of denial of right to counsel in the out-of-court lineup, and in that I concur. In Part V, the Court remands the case to

*Footnotes omitted. Headings added by authors for reader's convenience.

the District Court to consider whether the courtroom identification of Wade was the fruit of the illegal lineup, and, if it was, to grant him a new trial unless the court concludes that the courtroom identification was harmless error. I would reverse the Court of Appeals' reversal of Wade's conviction, but I would not remand for further proceedings since the prosecution did not use the out-of-court lineup identification against Wade at his trial, I believe the conviction should be affirmed.

In rejecting Wade's claim that his privilege against self-incrimination was violated by compelling him to appear in the lineup wearing the tape and uttering the words given him by the police, the Court relies on the recent holding in **Schmerber v. California**, 384 U.S. 757, 16 L. Ed. 2d 908, 86 S. Ct. 1826. In that case the Court held that taking blood from a man's body against his will in order to convict him of a crime did not compel him to be a witness against himself. I dissented from that holding, 384 U.S., at 773, 16 L. Ed. 2d at 921, and still dissent. The Court's reason for its holding was that the sample of Schmerber's blood taken in order to convict him was neither "testimonial" nor "communicative" evidence. I think it was both. It seems quite plain to me that the Fifth Amendment's Self-incrimination Clause was designed to bar the Government from forcing any person to supply proof of his own crime, precisely what Schmerber was forced to do when he was forced to supply his blood. The Government simply took his blood against his will and over his counsel's protest for the purpose of convicting him of crime. So here, having Wade in its custody awaiting trial to see if he could or would be convicted of crime, the Government forced him to stand in a lineup, wear strips on his face, and speak certain words, in order to make it possible for government witnesses to identify him as a criminal. Had Wade been compelled to utter these or any other words in open court, it is plain that he would have been entitled to a new trial because of having been compelled to be a witness against himself. Being forced by the Government to help convict himself and to supply evidence against himself by talking outside the courtroom is equally violative of his constitutional right not to be compelled to be a witness against himself. Consequently, because of this violation of the Fifth Amendment, and not because of my own personal view that the Government's conduct was "unfair," "prejudicial," or "improper," I would prohibit the prosecution's use of lineup identification at trial.

II.

Right to Counsel.   I agree with the Court, in large part because of the reasons it gives, that failure to notify Wade's counsel that Wade was to be put in a lineup by government officers and to be forced to talk and wear tape on his face denied Wade the right to counsel in violation of the Sixth Amendment. Once again, my reason for this conclusion is solely the Sixth Amendment's guarantee that "the accused shall enjoy the right . . . to have the Assistance of Counsel for his defense." As this Court's opinion points out, "the plain wording of this guarantee thus encompasses counsel's assistance whenever necessary to assure a meaningful 'defense.' " And I agree with the Court that a lineup is a "critical stage" of the criminal proceedings against an accused, because it is a stage at which the Government makes use of his custody to obtain crucial evidence against him. Besides counsel's presence at the lineup being necessary to protect the defendant's specific constitutional rights to confrontation and the assistance of counsel at the trial itself, the assistance of counsel at the lineup is also necessary to protect the defendant's in-custody assertion of his privilege against self-incrimination, *Miranda v. Arizona*, 384 U.S. 436, 16 L. Ed. 2d 694, 86 S. Ct. 1602, 10 ALR 3d 974, for contrary to the Court, I believe that counsel may advise the defendant not to participate in the lineup or to participate only under certain conditions.

I agree with the Court that counsel's presence at the lineup is necessary to protect the accused's right to a "fair trial," only if by "fair trial" the Court means a trial in accordance with the "Law of the Land" as specifically set out in the Constitution. But there are implications in the Court's opinion that by a "fair trial" the Court means a trial which a majority of this Court deems to be "fair" and that a lineup is a "critical stage" only because the Court, now assessing the "innumerable dangers" which inhere in it, thinks it is such. That these implications are justified is evidenced by the Court's suggestion that "legislative or other regulations . . . which eliminate the risks of abuse . . . at lineup proceedings . . . may also remove the basis for regarding the stage as 'critical.' " And it is clear from the Court's opinion in *Gilbert v. California*, 388 U.S. 263, 18 L. Ed. 2d 1178, 87 S. Ct. 1951, that it is willing to make the Sixth Amendment's guarantee of right to counsel dependent on the Court's own view of whether a particular stage of the proceedings—though "critical" in the sense of the prosecution's gathering of evidence—is "critical" to the Court's own view of a "fair trial." I am wholly unwilling to make the specific constitutional right of counsel dependent on judges' vague and transitory notions of fairness and their equally transitory, though thought to be empirical, assessment of the "risk that . . . counsel's absence . . . might derogate from . . . [a defendant's] right to a fair trial." *Ante*, at 1158. See *Pointer v. Texas*, 380 U.S. 400, 412, 13 L. Ed. 2d 923, 931, 85 S. Ct. 1065 (concurring opinion of Goldberg, J.).

III.

Independent Origin of In-Court Identification. I would reverse Wade's conviction without further ado had the prosecution at trial made use of his lineup identification either in place of courtroom identification or to bolster in a harmful manner crucial courtroom identification. But the prosecution here did neither of these things. After prosecution witnesses under oath identified Wade in the courtroom, it was the defense, and not the prosecution, which brought out the prior lineup identification. While stating that "a per se rule of exclusion of courtroom identification would be unjustified," the Court, nevertheless, remands this case for "a hearing to determine whether the in-court identifications had an independent source," or were the tainted fruits of the invalidly conducted lineup. From this holding I dissent.

In the first place, even if this Court has power to establish such a rule of evidence, I think the rule fashioned by the Court is unsound. The "tainted fruit" determination required by the Court involves more than considerable difficulty. I think it is practically impossible. How is a witness capable of probing the recesses of his mind to draw a sharp line between a courtroom identification due exclusively to an earlier lineup and a courtroom identification due to memory not based on the lineup? What kind of "clear and convincing evidence" can the prosecution offer to prove upon what particular events memories resulting in an in-court identification rest? How long will trials be delayed while judges turn psychologists to probe the subconscious minds of witnesses? All these questions are posed but not answered by the Court's opinion. In my view, the Fifth and Sixth Amendments are satisfied if the prosecution is precluded from using lineup identification as either an alternative to or corroboration of courtroom identification. If the prosecution does neither and its witnesses under oath identify the defendant in the courtroom, then I can find no justification for stopping the trial in midstream to hold a lengthy "tainted fruit" hearing. The fact of and circumstances surrounding a prior lineup identification might be used by the defense to impeach the credibility of the in-court identifications, but not to exclude them completely.

But more important, there is no constitutional provision upon which I can rely that directly or by implication gives this Court power to establish what amounts to a constitutional rule of evidence to govern, not only the Federal Government, but the States in their trial of state crimes under state laws in state courts. See *Gilbert v. California*, 388 U.S. 263, 18 L. Ed. 2d 1178, 87 S. Ct. 1951, *supra*. The Constitution deliberately reposed in the States very broad power to create and to try crimes according to their own rules and policies. *Spencer v. Texas*, 385 U.S. 554, 17 L. Ed. 2d 606, 87 S. Ct. 648. Before being deprived of this power, the least that they can ask is that we should be able to point to a federal constitutional provision that either by express language or by necessary implication grants us the power to fashion this novel rule of evidence to govern their criminal trials. *Cf. Berger v. New York*, 388

U.S. 70, 18 L. Ed. 2d 1040, (Black, J., dissenting). Neither *Nardone v. United States*, 308 U.S. 338, 84 L. Ed. 307, 60 S. Ct. 266, nor *Wong Sun v. United States*, 371 U.S. 471, 9 L. Ed. 2d 441, 83 S. Ct. 407, both federal cases and both decided "in other contexts," supports what the Court demands of the States today.

Perhaps the Court presumes to write this constitutional rule of evidence on the basis of the Fourteenth Amendment's Due Process Clause. This is not the time or place to consider that claim. Suffice it for me to say briefly that I find no such authority in the Due Process Clause. It undoubtedly provides that a person must be tried in accordance with the "Law of the Land." Consequently, it violates due process to try a person in a way prohibited by the Fourth, Fifth, or Sixth Amendments of our written Constitution. But I have never been able to subscribe to the dogma that the Due Process Clause empowers this Court to declare any law, including a rule of evidence, unconstitutional which it believes is contrary to tradition, decency, fundamental justice, or any of the other wide-meaning words used by judges to claim power under the Due Process Clause. See e. g., *Rochin v. California*, 342 U.S. 165, 96 L. Ed. 183, 72 S. Ct. 205, 25 ALR2d 1396. I have an abiding idea that if the Framers had wanted to let judges write the Constitution on any such day-to-day beliefs of theirs, they would have said so instead of so carefully defining their grants and prohibitions in a written constitution. With no more authority than the Due Process Clause I am wholly unwilling to tell the state or federal courts that the United States Constitution forbids them to allow courtroom identification without the prosecution's first proving that the identification does not rest in whole or in part on an illegal lineup. Should I do so, I would feel that we are deciding what the Constitution is, not from what it says, but from what we think it would have been wise for the Framers to put in it. That to me would be "judicial activism" at its worst. I would leave the States and Federal Government free to decide their own rules of evidence. That, I believe, is their constitutional prerogative.

I would affirm Wade's conviction.

Opinion of Mr. Justice White, whom Mr. Justice Harlan and Mr. Justice Stewart join, dissenting in part and concurring in part.

The Court has again propounded a broad constitutional rule barring use of a wide spectrum of relevant and probative evidence, solely because a step in its ascertainment or discovery occurs outside the presence of defense counsel. This was the approach of the Court in *Miranda v. Arizona*, 384 U.S. 436, 16 L. Ed. 2d 694, 86 S. Ct. 1602, 10 ALR3d 974. I objected then to what I though was an uncritical and doctrinaire approach without satisfactory factual foundation. I have much the same view of the present ruling and therefore dissent from the judgment and from Parts II, IV, and V of the Court's opinion.

New Per Se *Rule.*   The Court's opinion is far-reaching. It proceeds first by creating a new per se rule of constitutional law: a criminal suspect cannot be subjected to a pretrial identification process in the absence of his counsel without violating the Sixth Amendment. If he is, the State may not buttress a later courtroom identification of the witness by any reference to the previous identification. Furthermore, the courtroom identification is not admissible at all unless the State can establish by clear and convincing proof that the testimony is not the fruit of the earlier identification made in the absence of defendant's counsel—admittedly a heavy burden for the State and probably an impossible one. To all intents and purposes, courtroom identifications are barred if pretrial identifications have occurred without counsel being present.

The rule applies to any lineup, to any other techniques employed to produce an identification and a fortiori to a face-to-face encounter between the witness and the suspect alone regardless of when the identification occurs, in time or place, and whether before or after indictment or information. It matters not how well the witness knows the suspect, whether the witness is the suspect's mother, brother, or long-time associate, and no matter how long or well the witness observed the perpetrator at the scene of the crime. The kidnap victim who has lived for days with his abductor is in the same category as the witness who has had only a fleeting glimpse of the criminal. Neither may identify the suspect without defendant's counsel being present. The same strictures apply regardless of the number of other witnesses who positively identify the defendant and regardless of the corroborative evidence showing that it was the defendant who had committed the crime.

Improper Police Procedures.   The premise for the Court's rule is not the general unreliability of eyewitness identifications nor the difficulties inherent in observation, recall, and recognition. The Court assumes a narrower evil as the basis for its rule—improper police suggestion which contributes to erroneous identifications. The Court apparently believes that improper police procedures are so widespread that a broad prophylactic rule must be laid down, requiring the presence of counsel at all pretrial identifications, in order to detect recurring instances of police misconduct. I do not share this pervasive distrust of all official investigations. None of the materials the Court relies upon supports it. Certainly, I would bow to solid fact, but the Court quite obviously does not have before it any reliable, comprehensive survey of current police practices on which to base its new rule. Until it does, the Court should avoid excluding relevant evidence from state criminal trials. *Cf. Washington v. Texas,* 388 U.S. 14, 18 L. Ed. 2d 1019, 87 S. Ct. 1920.

The Court goes beyond assuming that a great majority of the country's police departments are following improper practices at pretrial identifications. To find the lineup a "critical" stage of the proceeding and to exclude identifications made in the absence of counsel, the Court must also assume that police "suggestion," if it occurs at all, leads to erroneous rather than accurate identifications and that reprehensible police conduct will have an unavoidably and largely undiscoverable impact on the trial. This in turn assumes that there is now no adequate source from which defense counsel can learn about the circumstances of the pretrial identification in order to place before the jury all of the considerations which should enter into an appraisal of courtroom identification evidence. But these are treacherous and unsupported assumptions, resting as they do on the notion that the defendant will not be aware, that the police and the witness will forget or prevaricate, that defense counsel will be unable to bring out the truth and that neither jury, judge, nor appellate court is a sufficient safeguard against unacceptable police conduct occurring at a pretrial identification procedure. I am unable to share the Court's view of the willingness of the police and the ordinary citizen-witness to dissemble, either with respect to the identification of the defendant or with respect to the circumstances surrounding a pretrial identification.

There are several striking aspects to the Court's holding. First, the rule does not bar courtroom identifications where there have been no previous identifications in the presence of the police, although when identified in the courtroom, the defendant is known to be in custody and charged with the commission of a crime. Second, the Court seems to say that if suitable legislative standards were adopted for the conduct of pretrial identifications, thereby lessening the hazards in such confrontations, it would not insist on the presence of counsel. But if this is true, why does not the Court simply fashion what it deems to be constitutionally acceptable procedures for the authorities to follow? Certainly the Court is correct in suggesting that the new rule will be wholly inapplicable where police departments themselves have established suitable safeguards.

Third, courtroom identification may be barred, absent counsel at a prior identification, regardless of the extent of counsel's information concerning the circumstances of the previous confrontation between witness and defendant—apparently even if there were recordings or sound-movies of the events as they occurred. But if the rule is premised on the defendant's right to have his counsel know, there seems little basis for not accepting other means to inform. A disinterested observer, recordings, photographs—any one of them would seem adequate to furnish the basis for a meaningful cross-examination of the eyewitness who identifies the defendant in the courtroom.

I share the Court's view that the criminal trial, at the very least, should aim at truthful factfinding, including accurate eyewitness identifications. I doubt, however, on the basis of our present information, that the tragic mistakes which have occurred in criminal trials are as much the product of improper police conduct as they are the consequence of the difficulties inherent in eyewitness testimony and in resolving evidentiary conflicts by court or jury. I doubt that the Court's new rule will obviate these difficulties, or that the situation will be measurably improved by inserting defense counsel into the investigative processes of police departments everywhere.

But, it may be asked, what possible state interest militates against requiring the presence of defense counsel at lineups? After all, the argument goes, he *may* do some good, he *may* upgrade the quality of identification evidence in state courts and he can scarcely do any harm. Even if true, this is a feeble foundation for fastening an ironclad constitutional rule upon state criminal procedures. Absent some reliably established constitutional violation, the processes by which the States enforce their criminal laws are their own prerogative. The States *do* have an interest in conducting their own affairs, an interest which cannot be displaced simply by saying that there are no valid arguments with respect to the merits of a federal rule emanating from this Court.

Concern for Prompt and Efficient Law Enforcement. Beyond this, however, requiring counsel at pretrial identifications as an invariable rule trenches on other valid state interests. One of them is its concern with the prompt and efficient enforcement of its criminal laws. Identifications frequently take place after arrest but before an indictment is returned or an information is filed. The police may have arrested a suspect on probable cause but may still have the wrong man. Both the suspect and the State have every interest in a prompt identification at that stage, the suspect in order to secure his immediate release and the State because prompt and early identification enhances *accurate* identification and because it must know whether it is on the right investigative track. Unavoidably, however, the absolute rule requiring the presence of counsel will cause significant delay and it may very well result in no pretrial identification at all. Counsel must be appointed and a time arranged convenient for him and the witnesses. Meanwhile, it may be necessary to file charges against the suspect who may then be released on bail, in the federal system very often on his own recognizance, with neither the State nor the defendant having the benefit of a properly conducted identification procedure.

Nor do I think the witnesses themselves can be ignored. They will now be required to be present at the convenience of counsel rather than their own. Many may be much less willing to participate if the identification stage is transformed into an adversary proceeding not under the control of a judge. Others may fear for their own safety if their identity is known at an early date, especially when there is no way of knowing until the lineup occurs whether or not the police really have the right man.

Finally, I think the Court's new rule is vulnerable in terms of its own impeachable purpose of increasing the reliability of identification testimony.

Obligation of Law Enforcement Officers, Role of Defense Counsel. Law enforcement officers have the obligation to convict the guilty and to make sure they do not convict the innocent. They must be dedicated to making the criminal trial a procedure for the ascertainment of the true facts surrounding the commission of the crime. To this extent, our so-called adversary system is not adversary at all; nor should it be. But defense counsel has no comparable obligation to ascertain or present the truth. Our system assigns him a different mission. He must be and is interested in preventing the conviction of the innocent, but, absent a voluntary plea of guilty, we also insist that he defend his client whether he is innocent or guilty. The State has the obligation to present the evidence. Defense counsel need present nothing, even if he knows what the truth is. He need not furnish any witnesses to the police, or reveal any confidences of his client, or furnish any other information to help the prosecution's case. If he can confuse a witness, even a truthful one, or make him appear at a disadvantage, unsure or indecisive, that will be his normal course. Our interest in not convicting the innocent permits counsel to put the State to its proof, to put the State's case in the worst possible light, regardless of what he thinks or knows to be the truth. Undoubtedly there are some limits which defense counsel must observe but more often than not, defense counsel will cross-examine a prosecution witness, and impeach him if he can, even if he thinks the witness is telling the truth, just as he will attempt to destroy a witness who he thinks is lying. In this respect, as part of our modified adversary system and as part of the duty imposed on the most honorable defense counsel, we countenance or require conduct which in many instances has little, if any, relation to the search for truth.

I would not extend this system, at least as it presently operates, to police investigations and would not require counsel's presence at pretrial identification procedures. Counsel's interest is in not having his client placed at the scene of the crime, regardless of his whereabouts. Some counsel may advise their clients to refuse to make any movements or to speak any words in a lineup or even appear in one. To that extent the impact on truthful factfinding is quite obvious. Others will not only observe what occurs and develop possibilities for later cross-examination but will hover over witnesses and begin their cross-examination then, menacing truthful factfinding as thoroughly as the Court fears the police now do. Certainly there is an implicit invitation to counsel to suggest rules for the lineup and to manage and produce it as best he can. I therefore doubt that the Court's new rule, at least absent some clearly defined limits on counsel's role, will measurably contribute to more reliable pretrial identifications. My fears are that it will have precisely the opposite result. It may well produce fewer convictions, but that is hardly a proper measure of its long-run acceptability. In my view, the State is entitled to investigate and develop its case outside the presence of defense counsel. This includes the right to have private conversations with identification witnesses, just as defense counsel may have his own consultations with these and other witnesses without having the prosecutor present.

Whether today's judgment would be an acceptable exercise of supervisory power over federal courts is another question. But as a constitutional matter, the judgment in this case is erroneous and although I concur in Parts I and III of the Court's opinion I respectfully register this dissent.

Opinion of Mr. Justice Fortas, with whom the Chief Justice and Mr. Justice Douglas join, concurring in part and dissenting in part.

Privilege Against Self-Incrimination. I agree with the Court that the exhibition of the person of the accused at a lineup is not itself a violation of the privilege against self-incrimination. In itself, it is no more subject to constitutional objection than the exhibition of the person of the accused in the courtroom for identification purposes. It is an incident of the State's power to arrest, and a reasonable and justifiable aspect of the State's custody resulting from arrest. It does not require that the accused take affirmative, volitional action, but only that, having been duly arrested he may be seen for identification purposes. It is, however, a "critical stage" in the prosecution, and I agree with the Court that the opportunity to have counsel present must be made available.

In my view, however, the accused may not be compelled in a lineup to speak the words uttered by the person who committed the crime. I am confident that it could not be compelled in court. It cannot be compelled in a lineup. It is more than passive, mute assistance to the eyes of the victim or of witnesses. It is the kind of volitional act—the kind of forced cooperation by the accused—which is within the historical perimeter of the privilege against compelled self-incrimination.

Our history and tradition teach and command that an accused may stand mute. The privilege means just that; not less than that. According to the Court, an accused may be jailed—indefinitely—until he is willing to say, for an identifying audience, whatever was said in the course of the commission of the crime. Presumably this would include, "Your money or your life"—or perhaps, words of assault in a rape case. This is intolerable under our constitutional system.

I completely agree that the accused must be advised of and given the right of counsel before a lineup—and I join in that part of the Court's opinion: but this is an empty right unless we mean to insist upon the accused's fundamental constitutional immunities. One of these is that the accused may not be compelled to speak. To compel him to speak would violate the privilege against self-incrimination, which is incorporated in the Fifth Amendment.

This great privilege is not merely a shield for the accused. It is also a prescription of technique designed to guide the State's investigation. History teaches us that self-accusation is an unreliable instrument of detection, apt to inculpate the innocent-but-weak and to enable the guilty to escape. But this is not the end of the story. The privilege historically goes to the roots of democratic and religious principle. It prevents the debasement of the citizen which would result from compelling him to "accuse" himself before the power of the state. The roots of the privilege are deeper than the rack and the screw used to extort confessions. They go to the nature of a free man and to his relationship to the state.

An accused cannot be compelled to utter the words spoken by the criminal in the course of the crime. I thoroughly disagree with the Court's statement that such compulsion does not violate the Fifth Amendment. The Court relies upon **Schmerber v. California**, 384 U.S. 757, 16 L. Ed. 2d 908, 86 S. Ct. 1826 (1966), to support this. I dissented in Schmerber, but if it were controlling here, I should, of course, acknowledge its binding effect unless we were prepared to overrule it. But Schmerber, which authorized the forced extraction of blood from the veins of an unwilling human being, did not compel the person actively to cooperate—to accuse himself by a volitional act which differs only in degree from compelling him to act out the crime, which, I assume, would be rebuffed by the Court. It is the latter feature which places the compelled utterance by the accused squarely within the history and noble purpose of the Fifth Amendments' commandment.

To permit Schmerber to apply in any respect beyond its holding is, in my opinion, indefensible. To permit its insidious doctrine to extend beyond the invasion of the body, which it permits, to compulsion of the will of a man, is to deny and defy a precious part of our historical faith and to discard one of the most profoundly cherished instruments by which we have established the freedom and dignity of the individual. We should not so alter the balance between the rights of the individual and of the state, achieved over centuries of conflict.

While the Court holds that the accused must be advised of and given the right to counsel at the lineup, it makes the privilege meaningless in this important respect. Unless counsel has been waived or, being present, has not objected to the accused's utterance of words used in the course of committing the crime, to compel such an utterance is constitutional error.

Accordingly, while I join the Court in requiring vacating of the judgment below for a determination as to whether the identification of respondent was based upon factors independent of the lineup, I would do so not only because of the failure to offer counsel before the lineup but also because of the violation of respondent's Fifth Amendment rights.

CASE STUDY

Thomas Kirby v. Illinois, 406 U.S. 682 (1972).

Mr. Justice Stewart announced the judgment of the court.* Justices Berger, Blackmun, Rehnquist concurring; Justices Brennan, Douglas, Marshall, and White dissenting.

Wade-Gilbert Per Se *Exclusionary Rule.* In *United States v. Wade*, 388 U.S. 218, 18 L. Ed. 2d 1149, 87 S. Ct. 1926, and *Gilbert v. California*, 388 U.S. 263, 18 L. Ed. 2d 1178, 87 S. Ct. 1951, this Court held "that a post-indictment pretrial lineup at which the accused is exhibited to identifying witnesses is a critical stage of the criminal prosecution; that police conduct of such a lineup without notice to and in the absence of his counsel denies the accused his Sixth [and Fourteenth] Amendment right to counsel and calls in question the admissibility at trial of the in-court identifications of the accused by witnesses who attended the lineup." *Gilbert v. California, supra,* at 272, 18 L. Ed. 2d at 1186. Those cases further held that no "in-court identifications" are admissible in evidence if their "source" is a lineup conducted in violation of this constitutional standard. "Only a per se exclusionary rule as to such testimony can be an effective sanction," the Court said, "to assure that law enforcement authorities will respect the accused's constitutional right to the presence of his counsel at the critical lineup." *Id.,* at 273, 18 L. Ed. 2d at 1186. In the present case we are asked to extend the *Wade-Gilbert* per se exclusionary rule to identification testimony based upon a police station showup that took place *before* the defendant had been indicted or otherwise formally charged with any criminal offense.

Facts of Case. On February 21, 1968, a man named Willie Shard reported to the Chicago police that the previous day two men had robbed him on a Chicago street of a wallet containing, among other

*Footnotes omitted. Headings added by authors for reader's convenience.

things, traveler's checks and a Social Security card. On February 22, two police officers stopped the petitioner and a companion, Ralph Bean, on West Madison Street in Chicago. When asked for identification, the petitioner produced a wallet that contained three traveler's checks and a Social Security card, all bearing the name of Willie Shard. Papers with Shard's name on them were also found in Bean's possession. When asked to explain his possession of Shard's property, the petitioner first said that the traveler's checks were "play money," and then told the officers that he had won them in a crap game. The officers then arrested the petitioner and Bean and took them to a police station.

Only after arriving at the police station, and checking the records there, did the arresting officers learn of the Shard robbery. A police car was then dispatched to Shard's place of employment, where it picked up Shard and brought him to the police station. Immediately upon entering the room in the police station where the petitioner and Bean were seated at a table, Shard positively identified them as the men who had robbed him two days earlier. No lawyer was present in the room, and neither the petitioner nor Bean had asked for legal assistance, or been advised of any right to the presence of counsel.

More than six weeks later, the petitioner and Bean were indicted for the robbery of Willie Shard. Upon arraignment, counsel was appointed to represent them, and they pleaded not guilty. A pretrial motion to suppress Shard's identification testimony was denied, and at the trial Shard testified as a witness for the prosecution. In his testimony he described his identification of the two men at the police station on February 22, and identified them again in the courtroom as the men who had robbed him on February 20. He was cross-examined at length regarding the circumstances of his identification of the two defendants. *Cf. Pointer v. Texas*, 380 U.S. 400, 13 L. Ed. 2d 923, 85 S. Ct. 1065. The jury found both defendants guilty, and the petitioner's conviction was affirmed on appeal. *People v. Kirby*, 121 Ill. App. 2d 323, 257 N.E.2d 589. The Illinois appellate court held that the admission of Shard's testimony was not error, relying upon an earlier decision of the Illinois Supreme Court, *People v. Palmer*, 41 Ill. 2d 571, 244 N.E.2d 173, holding that the Wade-Gilbert per se exclusionary rule is not applicable to pre-indictment confrontations.

We granted certiorari, limited to this question.

Privilege Against Self-Incrimination. We note at the outset that the constitutional privilege against compulsory self-incrimination is in no way implicated here. The Court emphatically rejected the claimed applicability of that constitutional guarantee in Wade itself:

Neither the lineup itself nor anything shown by this record that Wade was required to do in the lineup violated his privilege against self-incrimination.

> We have only recently reaffirmed that the privilege "protects an accused only from being compelled to testify against himself, or otherwise provide the State with evidence of a testimonial or communicative nature. . . ."
>
> We have no doubt that compelling the accused merely to exhibit his person for observation by a prosecution witness prior to trial involves no compulsion of the accused to give evidence having testimonial significance. It is compulsion of the accused to exhibit his physical characteristics, not compulsion to disclose any knowledge he might have. . . .

It follows that the doctrine of *Miranda v. Arizona,* 384 U.S. 436, 16 L. Ed. 2d 694, 86 S. Ct. 1602, 10 A.L.R. 3d 974, has no applicability whatever to the issue before us; for the Miranda decision was based exclusively upon the Fifth and Fourteenth Amendment privilege against compulsory self-incrimination, upon the theory that custodial *interrogation* is inherently coercive.

Right to Counsel. The *Wade-Gilbert* exclusionary rule, by contrast, stems from a quite different constitutional guarantee—the guarantee of the right to counsel contained in the Sixth and Fourteenth Amendments. Unless all semblance of principled constitutional adjudication is to be abandoned, therefore, it is to the decisions construing that guarantee that we must look in determining the present controversy.

In a line of constitutional cases in this Court stemming back to the Court's landmark opinion in *Powell v. Alabama,* 287 U.S. 45, 77 L. Ed. 158, 53 S. Ct. 55, 84 A.L.R. 527, it has been firmly established that a person's Sixth and Fourteenth Amendment right to counsel attaches only at or after the time that adversary judicial proceedings have been initiated against him. (Citations.)

This is not to say that a defendant in a criminal case has a constitutional right to counsel only at the trial itself. The Powell case makes clear that the right attaches at the time of arraignment, and the Court has recently held that it exists also at the time of a preliminary hearing. *Coleman v. Alabama, supra.* But the point is that, while members of the Court have differed as to existence of the right to counsel in the contexts of some of the above cases, *all* of those cases have involved points of time at or after the initiation of adversary judicial criminal proceedings—whether by way of formal charge, preliminary hearing, indictment, information, or arraignment.

The only seeming deviation from this long line of constitutional decisions was *Escobedo v. Illinois,* 378 U.S. 478, 12 L. Ed. 2d 977, 84 S. Ct. 1758. But *Escobedo* is not apposite here for two distinct reasons. First, the Court in retrospect perceived that the "prime purpose" of *Escobedo* was not to vindicate the constitutional right to counsel as such, but, like *Miranda,* "to guarantee full effectuation of the privilege against self-incrimination. . . ." *Johnson v. New Jersey*, 384 U.S. 719, 729, 16 L. Ed. 2d 882, 890, 86 S. Ct. 1772. Secondly, and perhaps even more important for purely practical purposes, the Court has limited the holding of *Escobedo* to its own facts, *Johnson v. New Jersey, supra,* at 733–734, 16 L. Ed. 2d at 892, and those facts are not remotely akin to the facts of the case before us.

Commencement of Criminal Prosecution. The initiation of judicial criminal proceedings is far from a mere formalism. It is the starting point of our whole system of adversary criminal justice. For it is only then that the government has committed itself to prosecute, and only then that the adverse positions of government and defendant have solidified. It is then that a defendant finds himself faced with the prosecutorial forces of organized society, and immersed in the intricacies of substantive and procedural criminal law. It is this point, therefore, that marks the commencement of the "criminal prosecutions" to which alone the explicit guarantees of the Sixth Amendment are applicable. See *Powell v. Alabama*, 287 U.S., at 66–71, 77 L. Ed., at 169–171, 84 A.L.R. 527; *Massiah v. United States*, 377 U.S. 201, 12 L. Ed. 2d 246, 84 S. Ct. 1199; *Spano v. New York*, 360 U.S. 315, 324, 3 L. Ed. 2d 1265, 1272, 79 S. Ct. 1202 (Douglas, J., concurring).

In this case we are asked to import into a routine police investiga tion an absolute constitutional guarantee historically and rationally ap plicable only after the onset of formal prosecutorial proceedings. We decline to do so. Less than a year after *Wade* and *Gilbert* were decided, the Court explained the rule of those decisions as follows: "The rationale of those cases was that an accused is entitled to counsel at any 'critical stage of the *prosecution,*' and that a post-indictment lineup is such a 'critical stage.' " (Emphasis supplied). *Simmons v. United States*, 390 U.S. 377, 382–383, 19 L. Ed. 2d 1247, 1252, 88 S. Ct. 967. We decline to depart from that rationale today by imposing a per se exclusionary rule upon testimony concerning an identification that took place long before the commencement of any prosecution whatever.

What has been said is not to suggest that there may not be occasions during the course of a criminal investigation when the police do abuse identification procedures. Such abuses are not beyond the reach of the Constitution. As the Court pointed out in *Wade* itself, it is always necessary to "scrutinize *any* pretrial confrontation." . . . 388 U.S. at 227, 18 L. Ed. 2d at 1157. The Due Process Clause of the Fifth and Fourteenth Amendments forbids a lineup that is unnecessarily suggestive and conducive to irreparable mistaken identification. *Stovall v. Denno*, 388 U.S. 293, 18 L. Ed. 2d 1199, 87 S. Ct. 1967; *Foster v. California*, 394 U.S. 440, 22 L. Ed. 2d 402, 89 S. Ct. 1127. When a person has not been formally charged with a criminal offense, *Stovall* strikes the appropriate constitutional balance between the right of a suspect to be protected from prejudicial procedures and the interest of society in the prompt and purposeful investigation of an unsolved crime.

The judgment is affirmed.

Mr. Justice Brennan, with whom Mr. Justice Douglas and Mr. Justice Marshall join, dissenting.*

Wade-Gilbert Per Se *Exclusionary Rule.* After petitioner and Ralph Bean were arrested, police officers brought Willie Shard, the robbery victim, to a room in a police station where petitioner and Bean were seated at a table with two other police officers. Shard testified at trial that the officers who brought him to the room asked him if petitioner and Bean were the robbers and that he indicated they were. The prosecutor asked him, "And you positively identified them at the police station, is that correct?" Shard answered, "Yes." Consequently, the question in this case is whether, under *Gilbert v. California*, 388 U.S. 263, 18 L. Ed. 2d 1178, 87 S. Ct. 1951 (1967), it was constitutional error to admit Shard's testimony that he identified petitioner at the pretrial stationhouse showup when that showup was conducted by the police without advising petitioner that he might have counsel present. *Gilbert* held, in the context of a post-indictment lineup, that "only a per se exclusionary rule as to such testimony can be an effective sanction to assure that law enforcement authorities will respect the accused's constitutional right to the presence of his counsel at the critical lineup." *Id.*, at 273, 18 L. Ed. 2d at 1186. I would apply Gilbert and the principles of its companion case, *United States v. Wade*, 388 U.S. 218, 18 L. Ed. 2d 1149, 87 S. Ct. 1926 (1967), and reverse.

In *Wade*, after concluding that the lineup conducted in that case did not violate the accused's right against self-incrimination. *id.*, at 221–223, 18 L. Ed. 2d at 1153–1155, the Court addressed the argument "that the assistance of counsel at the lineup was indispensable to protect Wade's most basic right as a criminal defendant—his right to a fair trial at which the witnesses against him might be meaningfully cross-examined," *id.*, at 223–224, 18 L. Ed. 2d at 1155. The Court began by emphasizing that the Sixth Amendment guarantee "encompasses counsel's assistance whenever necessary to assure a meaningful 'defense.'" *Id.*, at 225, 18 L. Ed. 2d at 1156. After reviewing *Powell v. Alabama*, 287 U.S. 45, 77 L. Ed. 158, 53 S. Ct. 55, 84 A.L.R. 527 (1932); *Hamilton v. Alabama*, 368 U.S. 52, 7 L. Ed. 2d 114, 82 S. Ct. 157 (1961); and *Massiah v. United States*, 377 U.S. 201, 12 L. Ed. 2d 246, 84 S. Ct. 1199

*Extracts only; footnotes omitted. Headings added by authors for reader's convenience.

(1964), the Court, 388 U.S., at 225, 18 L. Ed. 2d at 1156, focused upon two cases that involved the right against self-incrimination:

> In **Escobedo v. Illinois**, 378 U.S. 478, [12 L. Ed. 2d 977, 84 S. Ct. 1758], we drew upon the rationale of **Hamilton** and **Massiah** in holding that the right to counsel was guaranteed at the point where the accused, prior to arraignment, was subjected to secret interrogation despite repeated requests to see his lawyer. We again noted the necessity of counsel's presence if the accused was to have a fair opportunity to present a defense at the trial itself. . . . **United States v. Wade**, 388 US, at 225–226, 18 L Ed 2d at 1156.

> In **Miranda v. Arizona**, 384 U. S. 436 [16 L. Ed. 2d 694, 86 S. Ct. 1602, 10 A.L.R.3d 974], the rules established for custodial interrogation included the right to the presence of counsel. The result was rested on our finding that this and the other rules were necessary to safeguard the privilege against self-incrimination from being jeopardized by such interrogation." **Id.**, at 226, 18 L. Ed. 2d at 1157.

The Court then pointed out that

> nothing decided or said in the opinions in [**Escobedo** and **Miranda**] links the right to counsel only to protection of Fifth Amendment rights." **Ibid.**

To the contrary, the Court said, those decisions simply reflected the constitutional

> principle that in addition to counsel's presence at trial, the accused is guaranteed that he need not stand alone against the State at any stage of the prosecution, formal or informal, in court or out, where counsel's absence might derogate from the accused's right to a fair trial. The security of that right is as much the aim of the right to counsel as it is of the other guarantees of the Sixth Amendment. . . . **Id.**, at 226–227, 18 L. Ed. 2d at 1157.

This analysis led to the Court's formulation of the controlling principle for pretrial confrontations:

> In sum, the principle of **Powell v. Alabama** and succeeding cases requires that we scrutinize **any** pretrial confrontation of the accused to determine whether the presence of his counsel is necessary to preserve the defendant's basic right to a fair trial as affected by his right meaningfully to cross-examine the witnesses against him and to have effective assistance of counsel at the trial itself. It calls upon us to analyze whether potential substantial prejudice to defendant's rights inheres in the particular confrontation and the ability of counsel to help avoid that prejudice. **Id.**, at 227, 18, L. Ed. 2d at 1157

It was that constitutional principle that the Court applied in Wade to pretrial confrontations for identification purposes. The Court first met the Government's contention that a confrontation for identification is "a mere preparatory step in the gathering of the prosecution's evidence," much like the scientific examination of fingerprints and blood samples. The Court responded that in the latter instances "the accused has the opportunity for a meaningful confrontation of the Government's case at trial through the ordinary processes of cross-examination of the Government's expert witnesses and the presentation of the evidence of his own experts." The accused thus has no right to have counsel present at such examinations: "they are not critical stages since there is minimal risk that his counsel's absence at such stages might derogate from his right to a fair trial." *Id.*, at 227–228, 18 L. Ed. 2d at 1158.

In-Court Identification. In contrast, the Court said, "the confrontation compelled by the State between the accused and the victim or witnesses to a crime to elicit identification evidence is peculiarly riddled with innumerable dangers and variable factors which might seriously, even crucially, derogate from a fair trial." *Id.*, at 228, 18 L. Ed. 2d at 1158. Most importantly, "the accused's inability effectively to reconstruct at trial any unfairness that occurred at the lineup may deprive him of his only opportunity meaningfully to attack the credibility of the witness' courtroom identification." *Id.*, at 231–232, 18 L. Ed. 2d at 1160. The Court's analysis of pretrial confrontations for identification purposes produced the following conclusion:

> Insofar as the accused's conviction may rest on a courtroom identification in fact the fruit of a suspect pretrial identification which the accused is helpless to subject to effective scrutiny at trial, the accused is deprived of that right of cross-examination which is an essential safeguard to his right to confront the witnesses against him. **Pointer v. Texas**, 380 U.S. 400, [13 L. Ed. 2d 923, 85 S. Ct. 1065]. And even though cross-examination is a precious safeguard to a fair trial, it cannot be viewed as an absolute assurance of accuracy and reliability. Thus in the present context, where so many variables and pitfalls exist, the first line of defense must be the prevention of unfairness and the lessening of the hazards of eyewitness identification at the lineup itself. The trial which might determine the accused's fate may well not be that in the courtroom but that at the pretrial confrontation, with the State aligned against the accused, the witness the sole jury, and the accused unprotected against the overreaching, intentional or unintentional, and with little or no effective appeal from the judgment there rendered by the witness—"that's the man." **Id.**, at 235–236, 18 L. Ed. 2d at 1162.

Post-Arrest vs. Post-Charge Lineups. The Court then applied that conclusion to the specific facts of the case.

Since it appears that there is grave potential for prejudice, intentional or not, in the pretrial lineup, which may not be capable of reconstruction at trial, and since presence of counsel itself can often avert prejudice and assure a meaningful confrontation at trial, there can be little doubt that for Wade the post-indictment lineup was a critical stage of the prosecution at which he was "as much entitled to such aid [of counsel] . . . as at the trial itself." **Id.**, at 236–237, 18 L. Ed. 2d at 1162, 1163.

"The initiation of adversary judicial criminal proceedings," ante, at 689, 32 L. Ed. 2d at 417, is completley irrelevant to whether counsel is necessary at a pretrial confrontation for identification in order to safeguard the accused's constitutional rights to confrontation and the effective assistance of counsel at his trial.

In view of *Wade*, it is plain, and the plurality today does not attempt to dispute it, that there inhere in a confrontation for identification conducted after arrest the identical hazards to a fair trial that inhere in such a confrontation conducted "after the onset of formal prosecutorial proceedings." *Id.*, at 690, 32 L. Ed. 2d 418. The plurality apparently considers an arrest, which for present purposes we must assume to be based upon probable cause, to be nothing more than part of "a routine police investigation," *ibid.*, and thus not "the starting point of our whole system of adversary criminal justice," *id.*, at 689, 32 L. Ed. 2d at 418. An arrest, according to the plurality, does not face the accused "with the prosecutorial forces of organized society," nor immerse him "in the intricacies of substantive and procedural criminal law." Those consequences ensue, says the plurality, only with "the initiation of judicial criminal proceedings," "for it is only then that the government has committed itself to prosecute, and only then that the adverse positions of government and defendant have solidified." *Ibid.* If these propositions do not amount to "mere formalism," *ibid.*, it is difficult to know how to characterize them. An arrest evidences the belief of the police that the perpetrator of a crime has been caught. A post-arrest confrontation for identification is not "a mere preparatory step in the gathering of the prosecution's evidence." *Wade, supra*, at 227, 18 L. Ed. 2d at 1157. A primary, and frequently sole, purpose of the confrontation for identification at that stage is to accumulate proof to buttress the conclusion of the police that they have the offender in hand. The plurality offers no reason, and I can think of none, for concluding that a post-arrest confrontation for identification, unlike a post-charge confrontation, is not among those "critical confrontations of the accused by the prosecution at pretrial proceedings where the results might well settle the accused's fate and reduce the trial itself to a mere formality." *Id.*, at 224, 18 L. Ed. 2d at 1156.

CASE STUDY

United States v. Charles J. Ash, Jr., 413 U.S. 300 (1973).

Mr. Justice Blackmun delivered the opinion of the Court.*

In this case the Court is called upon to decide whether the Sixth Amendment grants an accused the right to have counsel present whenever the Government conducts a post-indictment photographic display, containing a picture of the accused, for the purpose of allowing a witness to attempt an identification of the offender. The United States Court of Appeals for the District of Columbia Circuit, sitting *en banc*, held, by a 5-to-4 vote, that the accused possesses this right to counsel. 149 U.S. App. D.C. 1, 461 F2d 92 (1972). The court's holding is inconsistent with decisions of the courts of appeals of nine other circuits. We granted certiorari to resolve the conflict and to decide this important constitutional question. 407 U.S. 909, 32 L. Ed. 2d 682, 92 S. Ct. 2436 (1972). We reverse and remand.

I

Facts of Case. On the morning of August 26, 1965, a man with a stocking mask entered a bank in Washington, D.C., and began waving a pistol. He ordered an employee to hang up the telephone and instructed all others present not to move. Seconds later a second man, also wearing a stocking mask, entered the bank, scooped up money from tellers' drawers into a bag, and left. The gunman followed, and both men escaped through an alley. The robbery lasted three or four minutes.

A Government informer, Clarence McFarland, told authorities that he had discussed the robbery with Charles J. Ash, Jr., the respondent here. Acting on this information, an FBI agent, in February 1966, showed five black-and-white mug shots, of Negro males of generally the same age, height, and weight, one of which was of Ash, to four witnesses. All four made uncertain identifications of Ash's picture. At this time Ash was not in custody and had not been charged. On April 1, 1966, an indictment was returned charging Ash and a co-defendant, John L. Bailey, in five counts related to this bank robbery, in violation of D.C. Code § 22–2901 and 18 U.S.C. § 2113(a).

Trial was finally set for May 1968, almost three years after the

---

*Extracts only; footnotes omitted. Headings added by authors for reader's convenience.

crime. In preparing for trial, the prosecutor decided to use a photographic display to determine whether the witnesses he planned to call would be able to make in-court identifications. Shortly before the trial, an FBI agent and the prosecutor showed five color photographs to the four witnesses who previously had tentatively identified the black-and-white photograph of Ash. Three of the witnesses selected the picture of Ash, but one was unable to make any selection. None of the witnesses selected the picture of Bailey which was in the group. This post-indictment identification provides the basis for respondent Ash's claim that he was denied the right to counsel at a "critical stage" of the prosecution.

No motion for severance was made, and Ash and Bailey were tried jointly. The trial judge held a hearing on the suggestive nature of the pretrial photographic displays. The judge did not make a clear ruling on suggestive nature, but held that the Government had demonstrated by "clear and convincing" evidence that in-court identifications would be "based on observation of the suspect other than the intervening observation."

At trial, the three witnesses who had been inside the bank identified Ash as the gunman, but they were unwilling to state that they were certain of their identifications. None of these made an in-court identification of Bailey. The fourth witness, who had been in a car outside the bank and had seen the fleeing robbers after they had removed their masks, made positive in-court identifications of both Ash and Bailey. Bailey's counsel then sought to impeach this in-court identification by calling the FBI agent who had shown the color photographs to the witnesses immediately before trial. Bailey's counsel demonstrated that the witness who had identified Bailey in court had failed to identify a color photograph of Bailey. During the course of the examination, Bailey's counsel also, before the jury, brought out the fact that this witness had selected another man as one of the robbers. At this point the prosecutor became concerned that the jury might believe that the witness had selected a third person when, in fact, the witness had selected a photograph of Ash. After a conference at the bench, the trial judge ruled that all five color photographs would be admitted into evidence. The Court of Appeals held that this constituted the introduction at the prosecutor's request and over the objection of defense counsel.

McFarland testified as a Government witness. He said he had discussed plans for the robbery with Ash before the event and, later, had discussed the results of the robbery with Ash in the presence of Bailey. McFarland was shown to possess an extensive criminal record and a history as an informer.

The jury convicted Ash on all counts. It was unable to reach a verdict on the charges against Bailey, and his motion for acquittal was granted. Ash received concurrent sentences on the several counts, the two longest being 80 months to 12 years.

The five-member majority of the Court of Appeals held that Ash's right to counsel, guaranteed by the Sixth Amendment, was violated when his attorney was not given the opportunity to be present at the photographic displays conducted in May 1968 before the trial. The majority relied on this Court's lineup cases, *United States v. Wade*, 388 U.S. 218, 18 L. Ed. 2d 1149, 87 S. Ct. 1926 (1967), and *Gilbert v. California*, 388 U.S. 263, 18 L. Ed. 2d 1178, 87 S. Ct. 1951 (1967), and on *Stovall v. Denno*, 388 U.S. 293, 18 L. Ed. 2d 1199, 87 S. Ct. 1967 (1967).

The majority did not reach the issue of suggestiveness; their opinion implies, however, that they would order a remand for additional findings by the District Court. 149 U.S. App. D.C., at 7; 461 F2d, at 98. The majority refrained from deciding whether the in-court identifications could have independent bases, 149 U.S. App. D.C., at 14–15 and nn 20, 21; 461 F2d, at 105–106 and nn 20, 21, but expressed doubt that the identifications at the trial had independent origins.

Dissenting opinions, joined by four judges, disagreed with the decision of the majority that the photographic identification was a "critical stage" requiring counsel, and criticized the majority's suggestion that the in-court identifications were tainted by defects in the photographic identifications. 149 U.S. App. D.C., at 14–43; 461 F2d, at 106–134.

II

Right to Counsel. The Court of Appeals relied exclusively on that portion of the Sixth Amendment providing, "In all criminal prosecutions, the accused shall enjoy the right ... to have the Assistance of Counsel for his defence." The right to counsel in Anglo-American law has a rich historical heritage, and this Court has regularly drawn on that history in construing the counsel guarantee of the Sixth Amendment. We reexamine that history in an effort to determine the relationship between the purposes of the Sixth Amendment guarantee and the risks of a photographic identification.

In *Powell v. Alabama*, 287 U.S. 45, 60–66, 77 L. Ed. 158, 53 S. Ct. 55, 84 A.L.R. 527 (1932), the court discussed the English common law rule that severely limited the right of a person accused of a felony to consult with counsel at trial. The Court examined colonial constitutions and statutes and noted that "in at least twelve of the thirteen colonies the rule of the English common law, in the respect now under consideration, had been definitely rejected and the right to counsel fully recognized in all criminal prosecutions, save that in one or two instances the right was limited to capital offenses or to the more serious crimes." 287 U.S., at 64–65, 77 L. Ed. 158, 84 A.L.R. 527. The Sixth Amendment counsel guarantee, thus, was derived from colonial statutes and constitutional provisions designed to reject the English common law rule.

Apparently several concerns contributed to this rejection at the very time when countless other aspects of the common law were being imported. One consideration was the inherent irrationality of the English limitation. Since the rule was limited to felony proceedings, the result, absurd and illogical, was that an accused misdemeanant could rely fully on counsel, but the accused felon, in theory at least, could consult counsel only on legal questions that the accused proposed to the court. See *Powell v. Alabama*, 287 U.S. at 60, 77 L. Ed. 158, 84 A.L.R. 527. English writers were appropriately critical of this inconsistency.

A concern of more lasting importance was the recognition and awareness that an unaided layman had little skill in arguing the law or in coping with an intricate procedural system. The function of counsel as a guide through complex legal technicalities long has been recognized by this Court. Mr. Justice Sutherland's well-known observations in Powell bear repeating here:

> Even the intelligent and educated layman has small and sometimes no skill in the science of law. If charged with crime, he is incapable, generally, of determining for himself whether the indictment is good or bad. He is unfamiliar with the rules of evidence. Left without the aid of counsel he may be put on trial without a proper charge, and convicted upon incompetent evidence, or evidence irrelevant to the issue or otherwise inadmissible. He lacks both the skill and knowledge adequately to prepare his defense, even though he have a perfect one. He requires the guiding hand of counsel at every step in the proceedings against him. Without it, though he be not guilty, he faces the danger of conviction because he does not know how to establish his innocence. 287 U.S., at 69, 77 L. Ed. 158, 84 A.L.R. 527.

The Court frequently has interpreted the Sixth Amendment to assure that the "guiding hand of counsel" is available to those in need of its assistance. See, for example, *Gideon v. Wainwright*, 372 U.S. 335, 344–345, 9 L. Ed. 2d 799, 83 S. Ct. 792, 93, A.L.R.2d 733 (1963), and *Argersinger v. Hamlin*, 407 U.S. 25, 31, 32 L. Ed. 2d 530, 92 S. Ct. 2006 (1972).

Another factor contributing to the colonial recognition of the accused's right to counsel was the adoption of the institution of the public prosecutor from the Continental inquisitorial system. One commentator has explained the effect of this development:

> Early in the eighteenth century the American System of judicial administration adopted an institution which was (and to some extent still is) unknown in England: while rejecting the fundamental juristic concepts upon which continental Europe's inquisitorial system of criminal procedure is predicated, the

colonies borrowed one of its institutions, the public prosecutor, and grafted it upon the body of English (accusatorial) procedure embodied in the common law. Presumably, this innovation was brought about by the lack of lawyers, particularly in the newly settled regions, and by the increasing distances between the colonial capitals on the eastern seaboard and the ever-receding western frontier. Its result was that, at a time when virtually all but treason trials in England were still in the nature of suits between private parties, the accused in the colonies faced a government official whose specific function it was to prosecute, and who was incomparably more familiar than the accused with the problems of procedure, the idiosyncrasies of juries, and, last but not least, the personnel of the court. F. Heller, The Sixth Amendment 20–21 (1951).

Thus an additional motivation for the American rule was a desire to minimize the imbalance in the adversary system that otherwise resulted with the creation of a professional prosecuting official. Mr. Justice Black, writing for the Court in *Johnson v. Zerbst*, 304, U.S. 458, 462–463, 82 L. Ed. 1461, 58 S. Ct. 1019, 146 A.L.R. 357 (1938), spoke of this equalizing effect of the Sixth Amendment's counsel guarantee:

It embodies a realistic recognition of the obvious truth that the average defendant does not have the professional legal skill to protect himself when brought before a tribunal with power to take his life or liberty, wherein the prosecution is presented by an experienced and learned counsel.

This historical background suggests that the core purpose of the counsel guarantee was to assure "Assistance" at trial, when the accused was confronted with both the intricacies of the law and the advocacy of the public prosecutor. Later developments have led this Court to recognize that "Assistance" would be less than meaningful if it were limited to the formal trial itself.

This extension of the right to counsel to events before trial has resulted from changing patterns of criminal procedure and investigation that have tended to generate pretrial events that might appropriately be considered to be parts of the trial itself. At these newly emerging and significant events, the accused was confronted, just as at trial, by the procedural system, or by his expert adversary, or by both. In *Wade*, the Court explained the process of expanding the counsel guarantee to these confrontations:

When the Bill of Rights was adopted, there were no organized police forces as we know them today. The accused confronted the prosecutor and the witnesses against him, and the evidence was marshalled, largely at the trial itself. In contrast, today's law enforcement machinery involves critical confrontations of the accused by the prosecution at pretrial proceedings where the results might well settle the accused's fate and reduce the trial itself to a mere formality. In recognition of these realities of modern criminal prosecution, our cases have construed the Sixth Amendment guarantee to apply to "critical" stages of the proceedings. 388 U.S., at 224, 18 L. Ed. 2d 1149.

The Court consistently has applied an historical interpretation of the guarantee, and has expanded the constitutional right to counsel only when new contexts appear presenting the same dangers that gave birth initially to the right itself.

Critical Stage of Pretrial Proceedings. Recent cases demonstrate the historical method of this expansion. In *Hamilton v. Alabama*, 368 U.S. 52, 7 L. Ed. 2d 114, 82 S. Ct. 157 (1961), and in *White v. Maryland*, 373 U.S. 59, 10 L. Ed. 2d 193, 83 S. Ct. 1050 (1963), the accused was confronted with the procedural system and was required, with definite consequences, to enter a plea. In *Massiah v. United States*, 377 U.S. 201, 12 L. Ed. 2d 246, 84 S. Ct. 1199 (1964), the accused was confronted by prosecuting authorities who obtained, by ruse and in the absence of defense counsel, incriminating statements. In *Coleman v. Alabama*, 399 U.S. 1, 26 L. Ed. 2d 387, 90 S. Ct. 1999 (1970), the accused was confronted by his adversary at a "critical stage" preliminary hearing at which the uncounseled accused could not hope to obtain so much benefit as could his skilled adversary.

The analogy between the unrepresented accused at the pretrial confrontation and the unrepresented defendant at trial, implicit in the cases mentioned above, was explicitly drawn in *Wade:*

> The trial which might determine the accused's fate may well not be that in the courtroom but that at the pretrial confrontation, with the State aligned against the accused, the witness the sole jury, and the accused unprotected against the overreaching, intentional or unintentional, and with little or no effective appeal from the judgment there rendered by the witness—"that's the man." 388 U.S., at 235–236, 18 L. Ed. 2d 1149.

Throughout this expansion of the counsel guarantee to trial-like confrontations, the function of the lawyer has remained essentially the same as his function at trial. In all cases considered by the Court, counsel has continued to act as a spokesman for, or advisor to, the accused. The accused's right to the "Assistance of Counsel" has meant just that, namely, the right of the accused to have counsel acting as his assistant. In *Hamilton* and *White*, for example, the Court envisioned the lawyer as advising the accused on available defenses in order to allow him to plead intelligently. 368 U.S., at 54–55, 7 L. Ed. 2d 114; 373 U.S., at 60, 10 L. Ed. 2d 193. In *Massiah* counsel could have advised his client on the benefits of the Fifth Amendment and could have sheltered him from the overreaching of the prosecution. 377 U.S., at 205, 12 L. Ed. 2d 246.

Cf. Miranda v. Arizona, 384 U.S. 436, 466, 16 L. Ed. 2d 694, 86 S. Ct. 1602, 10 A.L.R.3d 974 (1966). In *Coleman* the skill of the lawyer in examining witnesses, probing for evidence, and making legal arguments was relied upon by the Court to demonstrate that, in the light of the purpose of the preliminary hearing under Alabama law, the accused required "Assistance" at that hearing. 399 U.S. at 9, 26 L. Ed. 2d 387.

The function of counsel in rendering "Assistance" continued at the lineup under consideration in Wade and its companion cases. Although the accused was not confronted there with legal questions, the lineup offered opportunities for prosecuting authorities to take advantage of the accused. Counsel was seen by the Court as being more sensitive to, and aware of, suggestive influences than the accused himself, and as better able to reconstruct the events at trial. Counsel present at lineup would be able to remove disabilities of the accused in precisely the same fashion that counsel compensated for the disabilities of the layman at trial. Thus the Court mentioned that the accused's memory might be dimmed by "emotional tension," that the accused's credibility at trial would be diminished by his status as defendant, and that the accused might be unable to present his version effectively without giving up his privilege against compulsory self-incrimination. 388 U.S., at 230–231, 18 L. Ed. 2d 1149. It was in order to compensate for these deficiencies that the Court found the need for the assistance of counsel.

Test: Right to Counsel.   This review of the history and expansion of the Sixth Amendment counsel guarantee demonstrates that the test utilized by the Court has called for examination of the event in order to determine whether the accused required aid in coping with legal problems or assistance in meeting his adversary. Against the background of this traditional test, we now consider the opinion of the Court of Appeals.

Although the Court of Appeals' majority recognized the argument that "a major purpose behind the right to counsel is to protect the defendant from errors that he himself might make if he appeared in court alone," the court concluded that "other forms of prejudice," mentioned and recognized in *Wade*, could also give rise to a right to counsel. 149 U.S. App. D.C., at 10, 461 F2d, at 101. These forms of prejudice were felt by the court to flow from the possibilities for mistaken identification inherent in the photographic display.

We conclude that the dangers of mistaken identification, mentioned in Wade, were removed from context by the Court of Appeals and were incorrectly utilized as a sufficient basis for requiring counsel. Although Wade did discuss possibilities for suggestion and the difficulty for reconstructing suggestivity, this discussion occurred only after the Court had concluded that the lineup constituted a trial-like confrontation, requiring the "Assistance of Counsel" to preserve the adversary process by compensating for advantages of the prosecuting authorities.

The above discussion of *Wade* has shown that the traditional Sixth Amendment test easily allowed extension of counsel to a lineup. The similarity to trial was apparent, and counsel was needed to render "Assistance" in counterbalancing any "overreaching" by the prosecution.

After the Court in *Wade* held that a lineup constituted a trial-like confrontation requiring counsel, a more difficult issue remained in the case for consideration. The same changes in law enforcement that led to lineups and pretrial hearings also generated other events at which the accused was confronted by the prosecution. The Government had argued in *Wade* that if counsel was required at a lineup, the same forceful considerations would mandate counsel at other preparatory steps in the "gathering of the prosecution's evidence," such as, for particular example, the taking of fingerprints or blood samples. 388 U.S., at 227, 18 L. Ed. 2d 1149.

The Court concluded that there were differences. Rather than distinguishing these situations from the lineup in terms of the need for counsel to assure an equal confrontation at the time, the Court recognized that there were times when the subsequent trial would cure a one-sided confrontation between prosecuting authorities and the uncounseled defendant. In other words, such stages were not "critical." Referring to fingerprints, hair, clothing, and other blood samples, the Court explained:

> Knowledge of the techniques of science and technology is sufficiently available, and the variables in techniques few enough, that the accused has the opportunity for a meaningful confrontation of the Government's case at trial through the ordinary processes of cross-examination of the Government's expert witnesses and the presentation of the evidence of his own experts. 388 U.S., at 227–228, 18 L. Ed. 2d 1149.

Counsel at Trial Can Substitute for Counsel at Pretrial Confrontation. The structure of *Wade*, viewed in light of the careful limitation of the Court's language to "confrontations," makes it clear that lack of scientific precision and inability to reconstruct an event are not the tests for requiring counsel in the first instance. These are, instead, the tests to determine whether confrontation with counsel at trial can serve as a substitute for counsel at the pretrial confrontation. If accurate reconstruction is possible, the risks inherent in any confrontation still remain, but the opportunity to cure defects at trial causes the confrontation to cease to be "critical." The opinion of the Court even indicated that changes in procedure might cause a lineup to cease to be a "critical" confrontation:

Legislative or other regulations, such as those of local police departments, which eliminate the risks of abuse and unintentional suggestion at lineup proceedings and the impediments to meaningful confrontation at trial may also remove the basis for regarding the stage as "critical." 388 U.S., at 239, 18 L. Ed. 2d 1149.

See, however, 388 U.S., at 262, 18 L. Ed. 2d 1149, note.

The Court of Appeals considered its analysis complete after it decided that a photographic display lacks scientific precision and ease of accurate reconstruction at trial. That analysis, under *Wade*, however, merely carries one to the point where one must establish that the trial itself can provide no substitute for counsel if a pretrial confrontation is conducted in the absence of counsel. Judge Friendly, writing for the Second Circuit in *United States v. Bennett*, 409 F2d 888 (1969), recognized that the "criticality" test of Wade, if applied outside the confrontation context, would result in drastic expansion of the right to counsel:

> None of the classical analyses of the assistance to be given by counsel, Justice Sutherland's in **Powell v. Alabama** . . . and Justice Black's in **Johnson v. Zerbst** . . . and **Gideon v. Wainwright** . . . suggests that counsel must be present when the prosecution is interrogating witnesses in the defendant's absence even when, as here, the defendant is under arrest; counsel is rather to be provided to prevent the defendant himself from falling into traps devised by a lawyer on the other side and to see to it that all available defenses are proffered. Many other aspects of the prosecution's interviews with a victim or a witness to a crime afford just as much opportunity for undue suggestion as the display of photographs; so, too, do the defense's interviews, notably with alibi witnesses. 409 F2d, at 899–900.

We now undertake the threshhold analysis that must be addressed.

Right to Counsel at Photographic Identification. A substantial departure from the historical test would be necessary if the Sixth Amendment were interpreted to give Ash a right to counsel at the photographic identification in this case. Since the accused himself is not present at the time of the photographic display, and asserts no right to be present, Brief for the Respondent 40, no possibility arises that the accused might be misled by his lack of familiarity with the law or overpowered by his professional adversary. Similarly, the counsel guarantee would not be used to produce equality in a trial-like adversary confrontation. Rather, the guarantee was used by the Court of Appeals to produce confrontation at an event that previously was not analogous to an adversary trial.

Even if we were willing to view the counsel guarantee in broad terms as a generalized protection of the adversary process, we would be unwilling to go so far as to extend the right to a portion of the prosecutor's trial-preparation interviews with witnesses. Although photography is relatively new, the interviewing of witnesses before trial is a procedure that predates the Sixth Amendment. In England in the 16th and 17th centuries counsel regularly interviewed witnesses before trial. The traditional counterbalance in the American adversary system for these interviews arises from the equal ability of defense counsel to seek and interview witnesses himself.

That adversary mechanism remains as effective for a photographic display as for other parts of pretrial interviews. No greater limitations are placed on defense counsel in constructing displays, seeking witnesses, and conducting photographic identifications than those applicable to the prosecution. Selection of the picture of a person other than the accused, or the inability of a witness to make any selection, will be useful to the defense in precisely the same manner that the selection of a picture of the defendant would be useful to the prosecution. In this very case, for example, the initial tender of the photographic display was by Bailey's counsel, who sought to demonstrate that the witness had failed to make a photographic identification. Although we do not suggest that equality of access to photographs removes all potential for abuse, it does remove any inequality in the adversary process itself and thereby fully satisfies the historical spirit of the Sixth Amendment's counsel guarantee.

The argument has been advanced that requiring counsel might compel the police to observe more scientific procedures or might encourage them to utilize displays. This Court has recognized that improved procedures can minimize the dangers of suggestions. *Simmons v. United States*, 390 U.S. 377, 386, n 6, 19 L. Ed. 2d 1247, 88 S. Ct. 967 (1968). Commentators have also proposed more accurate techniques.

Pretrial photographic identifications, however, are hardly unique in offering possibilities for the actions of the prosecutor unfairly to prejudice the accused. Evidence favorable to the accused may be withheld; testimony of witnesses may be manipulated; the results of laboratory tests may be contrived. In many ways the prosecutor, by accident or by design, may improperly subvert the trial. The primary safeguard against abuses of this kind is the ethical responsibility of the prosecutor, who, as so often has been said, may "strike hard blows" but not "foul ones." *Berger v. United States*, 295 U.S. 78, 88, 79 L. Ed. 1314, 55 S. Ct. 629 (1935); *Brady v. Maryland*, 373 U.S. 83, 87–88, 10 L. Ed. 2d 215, 83 S. Ct. 1194 (1963). If that safeguard fails, review remains available under due process standards. See *Giglio v. United States*, 405 U.S. 150, 31 L. Ed. 2d 104, 92 S. Ct. 763 (1972); *Mooney v. Holohan*, 294 U.S. 103, 112, 79 L. Ed. 791, 55 S. Ct. 340, 98 A.L.R. 406 (1935); *Miller v. Pate*, 386 U.S. 1, 17 L. Ed. 2d 690, 87 S. Ct. 785 (1967); *Chambers v. Mississippi*, 410 U.S. 284, 35 L. Ed. 2d 297, 93 S. Ct. 1038 (1973).

These same safeguards apply to misuse of photographs. See *Simmons v. United States*, 390 U.S., at 384, 19 L. Ed. 2d 1247.

We are not persuaded that the risks inherent in the use of photographic displays are so pernicious that an extraordinary system of safeguards is required.

Holding: No Right to Counsel at Photographic Identifications. We hold, then, that the Sixth Amendment does not grant the right to counsel at photographic displays conducted by the Government for the purpose of allowing a witness to attempt an identification of the offender. This holding requires reversal of the judgment of the Court of Appeals. Although respondent Ash has urged us to examine this photographic display under the due process standard enunciated in *Simmons v. United States*, 390 U.S., at 384, 19 L. Ed. 2d 1247, the Court of Appeals, expressing the view that additional findings would be necessary, refused to decide the issue. 149 U.S. App. D.C., at 7, 461 F2d, at 98. We decline to consider this question on this record in the first instance. It remains open, of course, on the Court of Appeals' remand to the District Court.

Reversed and remanded.

Mr. Justice Brennan, dissenting:*

Lineups for Identification vs. Photographic Identification. On April 1, 1966, an indictment was returned charging respondent and a co-defendant in five counts relating to the robbery of the American Security and Trust Company. Trial was finally set for May 8, 1968, almost three years after the crime and more than two years after the return of the indictment. During the entire two-year period between indictment and trial, although one of the witnesses expressly sought an opportunity to see respondent in person, the Government never attempted to arrange a corporeal lineup for the purposes of identification. Rather, *less than 24 hours before trial,* the FBI agent, accompanied by the prosecutor, showed five color photographs to the witnesses, three of whom identified the picture of respondent.

At trial, all four witnesses made in-court identifications of respondent, but only one of these witnesses was "positive" of her identification. The fact that three of the witnesses had previously identified respondent from the color photographs, and the photographs themselves, were also admitted into evidence. The only other evidence implicating respondent in the crime was the testimony of the Government informant. On the basis of this evidence, respondent was convicted on all counts of the indictment.

---

*Extracts only; footnotes omitted.

On appeal, the United States Court of Appeals for the District of Columbia Circuit, sitting *en banc*, reversed respondent's conviction. 461 F2d 92 (1972). Noting that "the dangers of mistaken identification from uncounseled lineup identifications . . . are applicable in large measure to photographic as well as corporeal identifications," the Court of Appeals reasoned that this Court's decisions in *Wade, Gilbert*, and *Stovall*, compelled the conclusion that a pretrial photographic identification, like a lineup, is a "critical" stage of the prosecution at which the accused is constitutionally entitled to the attendance of counsel. Accordingly, the Court of Appeals held that respondent was denied his Sixth Amendment right to "the Assistance of Counsel for his defense" when his attorney was not given an opportunity to attend the display of the color photographs on the very eve of trial. In my view, both the reasoning and conclusion of the Court of Appeals were unimpeachably correct, and I would therefore affirm.

Prior Lineup Cases. In June 1967, this Court decided a trilogy of "lineup" cases which brought into sharp focus the problems of pretrial identification. See *United States v. Wade, supra; Gilbert v. California, supra; Stovall v. Denno, supra.* In essence, those decisions held (1) that a pretrial lineup is a "critical stage" in the criminal process at which the accused is constitutionally entitled to the presence of counsel; (2) that evidence of an identification of the accused at such an uncounseled lineup is per se inadmissible; and (3) that evidence of a subsequent in-court identification of the accused is likewise inadmissible unless the Government can demonstrate by clear and convincing evidence that the in-court identification was based upon observations of the accused independent of the prior uncounseled lineup identification. The considerations relied upon by the Court in reaching these conclusions are clearly applicable to photographic as well as corporeal identifications. Those considerations bear repeating here in some detail, for they touch upon the very heart of our criminal justice system—the right of an accused to a fair trial, including the effective "Assistance of Counsel for his defense."

At the outset, the Court noted that "identification evidence is peculiarly riddled with innumerable dangers and variable factors which might seriously, even crucially, derogate from a fair trial." *United States v. Wade, supra,* at 228, 18 L. Ed. 2d 1149. Indeed, "the vagaries of eyewitness identification are well-known; the annals of criminal law are rife with instances of mistaken identification." *Ibid.* Apart from "the dangers inherent in eyewitness identification," such as unreliable memory or perception, the Court pointed out that "a major factor contributing to the high incidence of miscarriage of justice from mistaken identification has been the degree of suggestion inherent in the manner in which the prosecution presents the suspect to witnesses for pretrial identification." *Ibid.* The Court recognized that the dangers of suggestion are not necessarily due to "police procedures intentionally designed to prejudice an accused." *Id.*, at 235, 18 L. Ed. 2d 1149. On the contrary, "suggestion can be created intentionally or unintentionally in many subtle ways." *Id.*, at 229, 18 L. Ed. 2d 1149. And " 'The fact that the police themselves have, in a given case, little or no doubt that the man put up for identification has committed the offense . . . involves a danger that this persuasion may communicate itself even in a doubtful case to the witness in some way. . . .' " *Id.*, at 235, 18 L. Ed. 2d 1149, quoting Williams and Hammelmann, Identification Parades, Part I [1963] Crim. L. Rev. 479, 483.

The Court also expressed concern over the possibility that a mistaken identification at a pretrial lineup might itself be conclusive on the question of identity, thereby resulting in the conviction of an innocent man. The Court observed that " 'once a witness has picked out the accused at the lineup, he is not likely to go back on his word later on, so that in practice the issue of identity may (in the absence of other relevant evidence) for all practical purposes be determined there and then, before the trial.' " *United States v. Wade, supra,* at 229, 18 L. Ed. 2d 1149, quoting Williams and Hammelmann, *supra,* at 482.

Moreover, "the defense can seldom reconstruct the manner and mode of lineup identification for judge or jury at trial." *Wade v. United States, supra,* at 230, 18 L. Ed. 2d 1149. For "as is the case with secret interrogations, there is serious difficulty in depicting what transpires at lineups. . . ." *Ibid.* Although the accused is present at such corporeal identifications, he is hardly in a position to detect many of the more subtle "improper influences" that might infect the identification. In addition, the Court emphasized that "neither witnesses nor lineup participants are apt to be alert for conditions prejudicial to the suspect. And if they were, it would be of scant benefit to the suspect since neither witnesses nor lineup participants are likely to be schooled in the detection of suggestive influences." *Id.*, at 230, 18 L. Ed. 2d 1149. As a result, "even though cross-examination is a precious safeguard to a fair trial, it cannot [in this context] be viewed as an absolute assurance of accuracy and reliability." *Id.*, at 235, 18 L. Ed. 2d 1149.

With these considerations in mind, the Court reasoned that "the accused's inability effectively to reconstruct at trial any unfairness that occurred at the lineup may deprive him of his only opportunity meaningfully to attack the credibility of the witness' courtroom identification." *Id.*, at 231–232, 18 L. Ed. 2d 1149. And "insofar as the accused's conviction may rest on a courtroom identification in fact the fruit of a suspect pretrial identification which the accused is helpless to subject to effective scrutiny at trial, the accused is deprived of that right of cross-examination which is an essential safeguard to his right to confront the witnesses against him." *Id.*, at 235, 18 L. Ed. 2d 1149. Thus, noting that "presence of counsel [at the lineup] can often avert prejudice and assure a meaningful confrontation at trial," the Court concluded that a pretrial corporeal identification is "a critical stage of the prosecution at which [the accused is] 'as much entitled to such aid [of counsel] . . . as at the trial itself.' " *Id.*, at 236, 237, 18 L. Ed. 2d 1149, quoting *Powell v. Alabama*, 287 U.S. 45, 57, 77 L. Ed. 158, 53 S. Ct. 55, 84 A.L.R. 527 (1932).

Photographic Identification: Conditions Prejudicial to Accused. As the Court of Appeals recognized, "the dangers of mistaken identification . . . set forth in Wade are applicable in large measure to photographic as well as corporeal identifications." 461 F2d, at 100. To the extent that misidentification may be attributable to a witness' faulty memory or perception, or inadequate opportunity for detailed observation during the crime, the risks are obviously as great at a photographic display as at a lineup. But "because of the inherent limitations of photography, which presents its subject in two dimensions rather than the three dimensions of reality, . . . a photographic identification, even when properly obtained, is clearly inferior to a properly obtained corporeal identification." P. Wall, Eyewitness Identification in Criminal Cases 70 (1965). Indeed, noting "the hazards of initial identification by photograph," we have expressly recognized that "a corporeal identification . . . is normally more accurate" than a photographic identification. *Simmons v. United States*, 390 U.S. 377, 384, 386 n 6, 19 L. Ed. 2d 1247, 88 S. Ct. 967 (1968). Thus, in this sense at least, the dangers of misidentification are even greater at a photographic display than at a lineup.

Moreover, as in the lineup situation, the possibilities for impermissible suggestion in the context of a photographic display are manifold. See *Simmons v. United States, supra*, at 383, 19 L. Ed. 2d 1247. Such suggestion, intentional or unintentional, may derive from three possible sources. First, the photographs themselves might tend to suggest which of the pictures is that of the suspect. For example, differences in age, pose, or other physical characteristics of the persons represented, and variations in the mounting, background, lighting or markings of the photographs all might have the effect of singling out the accused.

Second, impermissible suggestion may inhere in the manner in which the photographs are displayed to the witness. The danger of misidentification is, of course, "increased if the police display to the witness . . . the pictures of several persons among which the photograph of a single such individual recurs or is in some way emphasized." *Simmons v. United States, supra*, at 383, 19 L. Ed. 2d 1247. And if the photographs are arranged in an asymmetrical pattern, or if they are displayed in a time sequence that tends to emphasize a particular photograph, "any identification of the photograph which stands out from the rest is no more reliable than an identification of a single photograph, exhibited alone." P. Wall, *supra*, at 81.

Third, gestures or comments of the prosecutor at the time of the display may lead to an otherwise uncertain witness to select the "correct" photograph. For example, the prosecutor might "indicate to the witness that [he has] other evidence that one of the persons pictured committed the crime," and might even point to a particular photograph and ask whether the person pictured "looks familiar." More subtly, the prosecutor's inflection, facial expressions, physical motions and myriad other almost imperceptible means of communication might tend, intentionally or unintentionally, to compromise the witness' objectivity. Thus, as is the case with lineups, "improper photographic identification procedures, . . . by exerting a suggestive influence upon the witnesses, can often lead to an erroneous identification. . . ." P. Wall, *supra*, at 89. And "regardless of how the initial misidentification comes about, the witness thereafter is apt to retain in his memory the image of the photograph rather than of the person actually seen. . . ." *Simmons v. United States, supra*, at 383–384, 19 L. Ed. 2d 1247. As a result, " 'the issue of identity may (in the absence of other relevant evidence) for all practical purposes be determined there and then, before the trial.' " *United States v. Wade, supra*, at 229, 18 L. Ed. 2d 1149, quoting Williams and Hammelmann, *supra*, at 482.

Moreover, as with lineups, the defense can "seldom reconstruct" at trial the mode and manner of photographic identification. It is true, of course, that the photographs used at the pretrial display might be preserved for examination at trial. But "it may also be said that a photograph can preserve the record of a lineup; yet this does not justify a lineup without counsel." 461 F2d, at 100–101. *Cf. United States v. Wade, supra*, at 239 and n 30, 18 L. Ed. 2d 1149. Indeed, in reality, preservation of the photographs affords little protection to the unrepresented accused. For although retention of the photographs may mitigate the dangers of misidentification due to the suggestiveness of the photographs themselves, it cannot in any sense reveal to defense counsel the more subtle, and therefore more dangerous. suggestiveness that might derive from the manner in which the photographs were displayed or any accompanying comments or gestures. Moreover, the accused cannot rely upon the witnesses themselves to expose these latter sources of suggestion, for the witnesses are not "apt to be alert for conditions prejudicial to the suspect. And if they were, it would be of scant benefit to the suspect" since the witnesses are hardly "likely to be schooled in the detection of suggestive influences." *United States v. Wade, supra*, at 230, 18 L. Ed. 2d 1149.

Finally, and *unlike the lineup situation*, the accused himself is not even present at the photographic identification, thereby reducing the likelihood that irregularities in the procedures will ever come to light. Indeed, in *Wade*, the Government itself observed:

> When the defendant is present—as he is during a lineup—he may personally observe the circumstances, report them to his attorney, and (if he chooses to take the stand) testify about them at trial. . . . In the absence of an accused, on the other hand, there is no one present to verify the fairness of the interview or to report any irregularities. If the prosecution were tempted to engage in "sloppy or biased or fraudulent" conduct, . . . it would be far more likely to do so when the accused is absent than when he is himself being "used."

Thus, the difficulties of reconstructing at trial an uncounseled photographic display are at least equal to, and possibly greater than, those involved in reconstructing an uncounseled lineup. And, as the Government argued in *Wade*, in terms of the need for counsel, "there is no meaningful difference between a witness' pretrial identification from photographs and a similar identification made at a lineup." For in both situations, "the accused's inability effectively to reconstruct at trial any unfairness that occurred at the [pretrial identification] may deprive him of his only opportunity meaningfully to attack the credibility of the witness' courtroom identification." *United States v. Wade, supra,* at 231–232, 18 L. Ed. 2d 1149. As a result, both photographic and corporeal identification creates grave dangers that an innocent defendant might be convicted simply because of his inability to expose a tainted identification. This being so, considerations of logic, consistency and, indeed, fairness compel the conclusion that a pretrial photographic identification, is a "critical stage of the prosecution at which [the accused is] 'as much entitled to such aid [of counsel] . . . as at the trial itself.'" *United States v. Wade, supra,* at 237, 18 L. Ed. 2d 1149, quoting *Powell v. Alabama, supra,* at 57, 77 L. Ed. 158, 84 A.L.R. 527.

Critical Stage of Prosecution and Right to Counsel. Ironically, the Court does not seriously challenge the proposition that presence of counsel at a pretrial photographic display is essential to preserve the accused's right to a fair trial on the issue of identification. Rather, in what I can only characterize a triumph of form over substance, the Court seeks to justify its result by engrafting a wholly unprecedented— and wholly unsupportable—limitation on the Sixth Amendment right of "the accused . . . to have the Assistance of Counsel for his defense." Although apparently conceding that the right to counsel attaches, not only at the trial itself, but at all "critical stages" of the prosecution, the Court holds today that, in order to be deemed "critical," the particular "stage of the prosecution" under consideration must, at the very least, involve the physical "presence of the accused," at a "trial-like confrontation" with the Government, at which the accused requires the "guiding hand of counsel." A pretrial photographic identification does not, of course, meet these criteria.

In support of this rather crabbed view of the Sixth Amendment, the Court cites our decisions in *Coleman v. Alabama*, 399 U.S. 1, 26 L. Ed. 2d 387, 90 S. Ct. 1999 (1970), *Massiah v. United States*, 377 U.S. 201, 12 L. Ed. 2d 246, 84 S. Ct. 1199 (1964), *White v. Maryland*, 373 U.S. 59, 10 L. Ed. 2d 193, 83 S. Ct. 1050 (1963), and *Hamilton v. Alabama*, 368 U.S. 52, 7 L. Ed. 2d 114, 82 S. Ct. 157 (1961). Admittedly, each of these decisions guaranteed the assistance of counsel in pretrial proceedings at least arguably involving the physical "presence of the accused," at a "trial-like confrontation" with the Government, at which the accused required the "guiding hand of counsel." Moreover, as the Court points out, these decisions are consistent with the view that the Sixth Amendment "embodies a realistic recognition of the obvious truth that the average defendant does not have the professional legal skill to protect himself when brought before a tribunal with power to take his life or liberty, wherein the prosecution is presented by an experienced and learned counsel." *Johnson v. Zerbst*, 304 U.S. 458, 462–463, 82 L. Ed. 1461, 58 S. Ct. 1019, 146 A.L.R. 357 (1938). But, contrary to the Court's assumption, this is merely one *facet* of the Sixth Amendment guarantee, and the decisions relied upon by the Court represent, not the boundaries of the right to counsel, but mere applications of a far broader and more reasoned understanding of the Sixth Amendment than that espoused today.

The fundamental premise underlying *all* of this Court's decisions holding the right to counsel applicable at "critical" pretrial proceedings, is that a "stage" of the prosecution must be deemed "critical" for the purposes of the Sixth Amendment if it is one at which the presence of counsel is necessary "to protect the fairness of *the trial itself.*" *Schneckloth v. Bustamonte*, 412 U.S. 218, 36 L. Ed. 2d 854, 93 S. Ct. 2041 (1973) (emphasis added). Thus, in *Hamilton v. Alabama, supra*, for example, we made clear that an arraignment under Alabama law is a "critical stage" of the prosecution, not only because the accused at such an arraignment requires "the guiding hand of counsel," but, more broadly, because "what happens there may affect the whole trial." *Id.*, at 54, 7 L. Ed. 2d 114. Indeed, to exclude counsel from a pretrial proceeding at which his presence might be necessary to assure the fairness of the subsequent trial would, in practical effect, render the Sixth Amendment guarantee virtually meaningless, for it would "deny a defendant 'effective representation by counsel at the only stage when legal aid and advice would help him.'" *Massiah v. United States, supra*, at 204, 12 L. Ed. 2d 246, quoting *Spano v. New York*, 360 U.S. 315, 326, 3 L. Ed. 2d

1265, 79 S. Ct. 1202 (1959) (Douglas J., concurring); see *Escobedo v. Illinois*, 378, U.S. 478, 484–485, 12 L. Ed. 2d 977, 84 S. Ct. 1758 (1964).

This established conception of the Sixth Amendment guarantee is, of course, in no sense dependent upon the physical "presence of the accused," at a "trial-like confrontation" with the Government, at which the accused requires the "guiding hand of counsel." On the contrary, in *Powell v. Alabama*, 287 U.S. 45, 77 L. Ed. 158, 53 S. Ct. 55, 84 A.L.R. 527 (1932), the seminal decision in this area, we explicitly held the right to counsel applicable at a stage of the pretrial proceedings involving *none* of the three criteria set forth by the Court today. In *Powell*, the defendants in a State felony prosecution were not appointed counsel until the very eve of trial. This Court held, in no uncertain terms, that such an appointment could not satisfy the demands of the Sixth Amendment, for " 'it is vain . . . to guarantee [the accused] counsel without giving the latter any opportunity to acquaint himself with the facts or law of the case.' " *Id.*, at 59, 77 L. Ed. 158, 84 A.L.R. 527. In other words, *Powell* made clear that, in order to preserve the accused's right to a fair trial and to "effective and substantial" assistance of counsel at that trial, the Sixth Amendment guarantee necessarily encompasses a reasonable period of time before trial during which counsel might prepare the defense. Yet it can hardly be said that this preparatory period of research and investigation involves the physical "presence of the accused," at a "trial-like confrontation" with the Government, at which the accused requires the "guiding hand of counsel."

Moreover, despite the Court's efforts to re-write *Wade* so as to suggest a precedential basis for its own analysis, the rationale of Wade lends no support whatever to today's decision. In *Wade*, after concluding that compelled participation in a lineup does not violate the accused's right against self-incrimination, the Court addressed the argument "that the assistance of counsel at the lineup was indispensable to protect *Wade's* most basic right as a criminal defendant—his right to a fair trial at which the witnesses against him might be meaningfully cross-examined." *United States v. Wade, supra*, at 223–224, 18 L. Ed. 2d 1149. The Court then surveyed the history of the Sixth Amendment, and specifically concluded that that Amendment guarantees "counsel's assistance *whenever* necessary to assure a meaningful 'defense.' " *Id.*, at 225, 18 L. Ed. 2d 1149 (emphasis added). Then, after examining this Court's prior decisions concerning the applicability of the counsel guarantee, the Court stressed once again that a pretrial proceeding is a "critical stage" of the prosecution if "the presence of counsel is necessary to preserve the defendant's basic right to a fair trial as affected by his right meaningfully to cross-examine the witnesses against him and to have effective assistance of counsel at the trial itself." *Id.*, at 227, 18 L. Ed. 2d 1149.

The Court next addressed the Government's contention that a lineup is "a mere preparatory step in the gathering of the prosecution's evidence, not different—for Sixth Amendment purposes—from various other preparatory steps, such as systematized or scientific analyzing of the accused's fingerprints, blood sample, clothing, hair, and the like." *Id.*, at 227, 18 L. Ed. 2d 1149. If the Court in *Wade* had even the remotest intention of embracing the wooden interpretation of the Sixth Amendment ascribed to it today, it could have rejected the Government's contention simply by pointing out the obvious fact that such "systematized or scientific analyzing" does not in any sense involve the physical "presence of the accused" at a "trial-like confrontation" with the Government, at which the accused requires the "guiding hand of counsel." But the Court offered not even the slightest hint of such an approach. Instead, the Court reasoned that, in light of the scientific nature of such analyses,

> the accused has the opportunity for a meaningful confrontation of the Government's case at trial through the ordinary processes of cross-examination of the Government's expert witness and the presentation of the evidence of his own experts. The denial of a right to have his counsel present at such analyses does not therefore violate the Sixth Amendment; **they are not critical stages since there is minimal risk that his counsel's absence at such stages might derogate from his right to a fair trial.**" Id., at 227–228, 18 L. Ed. 2d 1149 (emphasis added).

Finally, after discussing the dangers of misidentification arising out of lineup procedures and the difficulty of reconstructuring the lineup at trial, the Court noted that "insofar as the accused's conviction may rest on a courtroom identification in fact the fruit of a suspect pretrial identification which the accused is helpless to subject to effective scrutiny at trial, the accused is deprived of that right of cross-examination which is an essential safeguard to his right to confront the witnesses against him." *Id.*, at 235 18 L. Ed. 2d 1149. The Court therefore concluded that "since it appears that there is a grave potential for prejudice, intentional or not, in the pretrial lineup, which may not be capable of reconstruction at trial, and since presence of counsel itself can often avert prejudice and assure a meaningful confrontation at trial, there can be little doubt that for Wade the post-indictment lineup was a critical stage of the prosecution at which he was 'as much entitled to such aid [of counsel] . . . as at the trial itself.' " *Id.*, at 236–237, 18 L. Ed. 2d 1149.

Thus, contrary to the suggestion of the Court, the conclusion in *Wade* that a pretrial lineup is a "critical stage" of the prosecution did not in any sense turn on the fact that a lineup involves the physical "presence of the accused" at a "trial-like confrontation" with the Government. And that conclusion most certainly did not turn on the notion that presence of counsel was necessary so that counsel could offer legal advice or "guidance" to the accused at the lineup. On the contrary, Wade envisioned counsel's function at the lineup to be primarily that of a trained observer, able to detect the existence of any suggestive influences and capable of understanding the legal implications of the events that transpire. Having witnessed the proceedings, counsel would then be in a position effectively to reconstruct at trial any unfairness that occurred at the lineup, thereby preserving the accused's fundamental right to a fair trial on the issue of identification.

Lineups vs. Photographic Identification. There is something ironic about the Court's conclusion today that a pretrial lineup identification is a "critical stage" of the prosecution because counsel's presence can help to compensate for the accused's deficiencies as an observer, but that a pretrial photographic identification is not a "critical stage" of the prosecution because the accused is not able to observe at all. In my view, there simply is no meaningful difference, in terms of the need for attendance of counsel, between corporeal and photographic identifications. And applying established and well-reasoned Sixth Amendment principles, I can only conclude that a pretrial photographic display, like a pretrial lineup, is a "critical stage" of the prosecution at which the accused is constitutionally entitled to the presence of counsel.

CASE STUDY

Ramsey v. Commonwealth of Virginia, 200 Va. 245, 105 SE 2d 155 (1958).*

Facts of Case. On July 2, 1957, Harry Lucas Ramsey was found guilty by a jury and sentenced to confinement in the penitentiary for one year on an indictment charging that on February 13, 1957, he did wilfully, maliciously and feloniously set fire to or burn his dwelling house with goods and chattels therein, which were insured at the time against loss or damage by fire, with intent to injure the insurer. ¶ 18–158, Code 1950. Ramsey's motion to set aside the verdict was overruled and judgment was entered thereon.

The evidence may be summarized as follows:

Ramsey purchased an old building for $250. With the assistance of his father and neighbors it was dismantled and reconstructed on property, approximately four miles north of Buena Vista on State Highway No. 706, which he had acquired. Additional materials purchased and used in reconstructing the frame dwelling, which consisted of four

---

*Headings added by authors for reader's convenience.

rooms and rested on unmortared cinder block pillars, amounted to $292.

On January 4, 1957, Ramsey applied to Earl Starkey, an insurance agent in Buena Vista, for fire coverage in the sum of $4,000. After describing the premises, Ramsey was informed by Starkey that he could not write insurance in that amount but he "might" write it for $3,000. Whereupon Ramsey stated: "Well, I have over $2,000 in material in this dwelling." Ramsey paid the required premium. The next day Starkey inspected the dwelling and wrote Ramsey advising that $1,000 was the maximum coverage he would be willing to write and refunded the premium paid. Ramsey then contacted another agent in Buena Vista, a Mrs. Paxton, who issued a standard fire insurance policy for $2,500 on the dwelling and $500 on personal property contained therein, effective January 5, 1957. This policy was in force when the dwelling and its contents were destroyed by fire.

Deputy Sheriff Elmo Cooper testified that a two and one-half ton International truck with the rear portion resting on cinder blocks had been parked with the front end facing east or toward the dwelling and approximately 15 feet from it for several months prior to the fire, and that sometime between the afternoon preceding the day of the fire and the next morning the position of the truck had been reversed so that the front end of the truck faced west or away from the house. Robert Hall, who assisted Ramsey in moving the truck stated the land sloped and the change was made to place the rear end of the truck higher than the front end in order to prevent grease from running out the rear end.

At about 6:45 P.M. on February 13, 1957 Ramsey and his family left their home and drove to East Lexington Church which is a distance of six and one-half miles. There was a fire burning in a stove at the time of departure. Upon arrival Ramsey parked his vehicle and his family entered the church. He walked to East Lexington Grocery Store which is near the church. While there he called Pete's Taxi at 7:25 P.M. and inquired as to the round trip fare to Mountain View School which is near his residence. A taxi cab operated by Robert E. Fox soon thereafter picked up accused and drove him to the vicinity of his home. Ramsey told Fox he wanted to be back at the church by 7:55 P.M. so that no one at the church would realize that he was gone. He also stated to Fox: "I have a deal cooked up but I don't have to tell you what it is."

Ramsey left the taxi cab in the vicinity of Mountain View Church, at a point about 75 yards from his home and he headed in that direction. The evidence is silent as to whether or not he entered his dwelling. Fox proceeded a short distance in order to turn his vehicle around. After a lapse of between two and three minutes Ramsey re-entered the taxi cab about where he left it at approximately 7:45 P.M., arrived at East Lexington Church at about 7:55 P.M. and took a seat in the church where he remained until he was notified around 9:45 P.M. that his dwelling was on fire. Fox stated that it was a cold dark night; that he did not observe any lights in the direction of Ramsey's dwelling; that Ramsey was not indulging in intoxicants; that he did not smell the odor of kerosene or gasoline about him; that he showed no signs of exertion or excitement, and that Ramsey just wanted to "go and come."

The fire was first seen by neighbors at 9:30 P.M. Flames were coming out from under the eaves, but the walls were standing. Responding to a call, the Buena Vista fire department arrived at the scene about 9:50 P.M. at which time the building was completely destroyed.

Several days after the fire, Ramsey contacted Fox, the cab driver, and requested Fox not to mention to members of his church that he had driven him down to the vicinity of his home on the evening of the fire, for it would put him in a bad light with them.

The size of the dwelling was approximately 18 feet across the front and 24 feet deep. It had a metal roof and a unlined cinder block chimney near the center which fell during the fire. Between 30 and 40 feet from a corner of the house there was a power line pole. On it was a small transformer and a power line connected which led toward the destroyed dwelling house. It was touching the ground short of where the residence formerly stood. There was no authorized electrical service going into the house.

Included among the articles found in the debris were a cast iron cook stove, a cast iron heater, evidence of electrical appliances, a gasoline power saw, several small metal cans and a five gallon can, bits of wire similar to extension cord wire, a small clamp identified as the type used to make electrical connections, and an old model fuse box.

Several witnesses testified in behalf of the accused, but he elected not to take the stand.

Hypothetical Question. In addition to challenging the sufficiency of the evidence to support a conviction, Ramsey contends the lower court erred in permitting the Commonwealth to propound a hypothetical question to Augustus S. Hydrick, Special Agent for National Board of Fire Underwriters.

The hypothetical question follows:

Assuming that a person is occupying a dwelling as described in the evidence in this case, assuming that there is no direct evidence of exterior wiring into the dwelling and no meter or fuse box connected to wiring from the transformer to the dwelling, assuming further that on Tuesday, February 12, 1957, a two and one-half ton truck of the occupant was parked close to the dwelling with the cab of the truck facing the dwelling and on Wednesday, February 13, 1957, the truck was turned around and moved so that it was approximately 30 feet away from the dwelling with the cab facing away from the dwelling, assuming further that the occupant had invested less than $600 in material in the dwelling when he applied for a $4,000 fire insurance policy thereon and represented to the fire insurance agent that he had over $2,000 in material invested therein, assuming further that the occupant of the dwelling left it unoccupied on the 13th day of February, 1957, with a small fire in the heater located in the front room being the only fire in the dwelling at or approximately 6:30 p.m., assuming further that the occupant returned by taxi to the dwelling at or approximately 7:45 p.m., assuming further that the occupant made no complaint or report of any unusual fire when leaving the dwelling by the same taxi at or about 7:50 p.m., assuming further there is no evidence of exterior fires adjoining the building, assuming further there was no physical evidence in the debris of **any** objects calculated to produce spontaneous combustion, assuming further there was no direct evidence of defective heaters or flues in the dwelling, assuming further that the occupant when returning to the dwelling from church by the same taxi between 7:30 and 8 o'clock p.m. advised the taxi driver if he got back to church before 8 o'clock no one would know he had gone, assuming further that the occupant several days after the fire sought out and told the taxi driver if anyone questioned him about the trip to forget it and deny taking him, assuming further that the dwelling was completely destroyed by fire originating sometime between 9 and 9:30 p.m. on February 13, 1957, based on the assumptions in this hypothetical question and on your knowledge and experience as a Special Agent for the National Board of Fire Underwriters do you have an opinion as to the origin of such a fire, and if so, please state your opinion to the Court and jury?"

Over the objection of accused, Hydrick was permitted to answer the question. After a very lengthy response in which he stated his reasons for the opinion reached, he concluded by saying:

Considering the accidental causes, which we felt were eliminated as the cause of this fire, coupled with experience and the unusual circumstances that transpired shortly prior to this fire, several days before, the night of the fire and two or three days after the fire, and when all matters were considered together I reached the conclusion that we had an incendiary fire.

Ultimate Issue.   Ramsey argues that the question and answer were improper and constituted prejudicial error because the province of the jury was invaded as to the ultimate facts in issue. He maintains it was for the jury to decide whether or not the fire was of incendiary origin along with who was the guilty agent, and not for an expert witness to determine.

In *Southern Railway Co. v. Mauzy*, 98 Va. 692, 694, 37 SE 285, 286, the admissibility of opinions of witnesses was discussed. There we said:

No principle of law is better settled than that the opinions of witnesses are, in general, inadmissible; that witnesses can testify to facts only, and not to opinions or conclusions based upon the facts **Hanriot v. Sherwood**, 82 Va. 1; **Hammond v. Wood**, [Woodman] 41 Me. 177 (66 Am.Dec. 219). To this general rule there are exceptions. The case at bar, however, does not come within their influence. In the valuable note to the case last cited (66 Am.Dec. 228), it is said, with abundant authority in its support, that "the competency of expert testimony in a particular case depends upon the question as to whether or not any peculiar knowledge, science, skill or art, not possessed by ordinary persons, is necessary to the determination of the matter at issue; . . . that expert testimony is admissible as to matters within the experience or knowledge of persons of ordinary information, as to which the jury are competent to draw their own inferences from the facts given in evidence before them, without extraneous aid other than the instruction of the court upon questions of law." See also 20 Am.Jur., Evidence, ¶ 781, p. 651.

In 20 Am.Jur., Evidence, § 782, pp. 653, 654, it is stated:

In many cases it is asserted as a broad general rule, often assumed to be an inflexible rule of law, that while an expert may be permitted to express his opinion, or even his belief, he cannot give his opinion upon the precise or ultimate fact in issue before the jury, which must be determined by them. In other words, while a jury is entitled to the aid of experts in determining the existence or nonexistence of facts not within common knowledge, an expert witness must not take the place of the jury and declare his belief as to an ultimate fact. . . .

It is said in Wharton's Criminal Evidence, 11th Ed., Vol. 2, § 956, pp. 1680, 1681:

. . . In an arson case, a witness cannot, as a general rule, testify concerning his opinion as to whether the fire was or was not of incendiary origin, that being a question for the jury to determine, and upon which they can usually form their own opinion without any need of expert advice. However, exceptional cases may arise which would justify the admission of expert opinion testimony on such a question as an aid to the jury in arriving at their determination. . . .

Another expression of the rule is stated in Curtis, The Law of Arson, Evidence; Opinions, § 422, pp. 441, 442:

One who observes a fire, even though he is an experienced fireman, will not be permitted to express his opinion as to its cause or origin. Nor should the court admit the opinion of one who makes a subsequent investigation of the fire, although he may qualify as an expert. He should detail the facts coming to his attention and permit the jurors to draw their own conclusions as to the cause. . . . See **People's v. Grutz**, 212 N.Y. 72, 105 NE 843, LRA 1915D, 229.

Mitchell v. Commonwealth, 141 Va. 541, 365, 127 SE 368, 375, involves the prosecution of a bank officer for making entries with intent to conceal the true state of his account. There we made the following observation:

> It is assigned as error that the trial court, over the objection of the accused, permitted a witness for the commonwealth to be asked and to answer the following question: "Will you state whether or not the effect of such entries made upon the books of the bank would be to conceal the true state of the account of John Mitchell, Jr., in the bank?" To which the witness replied, "Yes." The question was a leading one put to a witness not shown to be an expert. But whether expert or not, it called for the opinion of the witness upon what was practically the very issue to be tried by the jury, and not to what was disclosed by the books of the bank. He was asked as to the "effect" of such entries. This was a question to be determined by the jury from the evidence in the case and not from the opinion of an adverse witness. In **Thorton v. Commonwealth**, 113 Va. 736, 73 SE 581, the case was reversed solely on the ground that a very similar question was allowed to be asked an expert witness. **Redman v. Community Hotel Corp.**, 138 W.Va. 456, 76 SE 2d 759.

In the recent case of *Newton v. City of Richmond*, 198 Va. 869, 875, 96 SE 2d 775, 780, accused was convicted in the court below for operating his vehicle while under the influence of intoxicants. In reversing and remanding the case for a new trial, Mr. Justice Miller, speaking for the court, said *inter alia:*

> No specific objection was made to that part of Dr. Kaye's testimony which says that in his opinion the person whose blood he analyzed was intoxicated "to a degree where he was not fit to operate an automobile." Yet upon a retrial he should not be allowed to express his opinion upon accused's **fitness "to operate an automobile."** To do so goes beyond giving expert testimony as to degrees of intoxication and invades the province of the jury.

The hypothetical question propounded to Hydrick and his response thereto were highly prejudicial to accused and constituted reversible error. It invaded the province of the jury as to the ultimate issues to be decided. Those issues were (1) whether or not the fire was of incendiary origin, and (2) whether or not Ramsey was the criminal agent. While Hydrick's answer told the jury in his opinion the fire was of incendiary origin, yet the form of the question and the answer to it unquestionably point to Ramsey as the guilty agent. Under the facts in this case the jury was able to form a correct opinion without the aid of expert testimony, and such testimony was not necessary or proper to explain or elucidate the subject under investigation.

For the reasons stated, the judgment of conviction is reversed, the verdict set aside, and a new trial awarded if the Commonwealth be so advised.

Reversed and remanded.

CASE STUDY

People v. Bob, 29 Cal. 321, 175 P. 2d 12 (1946).*

Facts of Case.   Defendant Bob had been adjudged guilty of the crime of murder of the first degree and sentenced to pay the extreme penalty. His appeal is automatically before this court by virtue of the provisions of section 1239 of the Penal Code.

After his arrest Bob told the officers freely of the circumstances leading to the homicide, and at the trial he repeated his story on the witness stand.

It appears that in the early evening of November 16, 1945, Bob and an acquaintance named Johnson met in a pool hall in Stockton and decided to go out "hustling," which in the vernacular means "to roll a drunk, strong-arm somebody." According to the testimony of Bob, they walked by the Elks Club, where Johnson went in a doorway and picked up a piece of iron pipe. The two then continued walking until they noticed a Japanese man across the street talking to a boy. Johnson intruded upon this conversation and found that the Japanese, George S. Yoshioka, who had served in the United States Army, was inquiring where he could find some girls. Johnson stated that he knew where girls were to be found. He and Yoshioka and Bob walked down the street. They paused near a hotel on South Center Street, and then rounded the corner of the building into a vacant lot. Bob stayed a few feet away. Johnson and Yoshioka talked awhile and then Johnson suddenly hit Yoshioka on the head with the iron pipe, repeating the blows until unconsciousness resulted. Bob went through Yoshioka's pockets and extracted a wallet. Johnson took Yoshioka's wrist watch.

Bob and Johnson then went to the hotel room of Johnson's wife, where Johnson proceeded to clean up and prepared to flee the state. The sum of $37, found in the wallet, was divided equally by the two men. Johnson also found a $50 bill which he did not mention to Bob. Bob went back into the street, met one Simmons, and told him of the crime. He and Simmons returned to Yoshioka and Simmons took Yoshioka's shoes. Soon thereafter Yoshioka's body was observed by a passer-by, and the police were notified. Yoshioka passed away in the hospital without regaining consciousness, the cause of death being a fractured skull. The bloodstained pipe was found on the ground near the spot where Yoshioka's head had rested, but its rusty surface gave forth no fingerprints.

*Headings added by authors for reader's convenience.

Johnson was taken into custody in Texas and returned to California. On December 1, 1945, in the early morning, Bob was arrested for "causing trouble" in a cafe, and was booked as a suspect vagrant. When the police took him to the fingerprinting desk, he there saw Johnson. This led to his voluntary confession of complicity in the robbery and murder of Yoshioka. He was questioned by an assistant district attorney in the presence of police officers and a court reporter, and the entire conversation was reduced to writing. Johnson was then brought in, and in the presence of the same officers and of Bob, his statement was taken in the same manner. It differed from the statement of Bob in this: That whereas Bob accused Johnson of being the man who picked up the pipe, lured the Japanese to the lot, and struck the fatal blows. Johnson claimed that he was the bystander and that it was Bob who procured the pipe, talked and walked with the victim, and then killed him. At the close of the questioning of Johnson, Bob stated that it was Johnson who used the pipe. A colloquy then ensued between Johnson and Bob, wherein each made accusations against the other. This was also reduced to writing and together with Johnson's statement was read in evidence.

Hearsay Evidence. The two men were tried separately. On the trial of Bob his confession to the police was introduced in evidence. Johnson's statement contained the assertion that Bob struck the lethal blow. As above stated, that was denied by Bob. The balance of the statement was in accordance with Bob's confession and he did not deny it. Under those circumstances Johnson's statement was clearly hearsay evidence and was admissible under any exception to the hearsay rule. (*People v. Simmons*, 28 Cal.2d 699 [172 P.2d 18].) The error in the admission of that evidence, especially the part to the effect that defendant struck the deadly blow is conceded by the prosecution, hence it has waived any claim to the sufficiency of defendant's objection to the evidence in the court below.

> If the adverse party does not oppose the consideration of a question for want of an objection in the trial court, the point will often be considered waived, on the ground that the appellate court is not bound on its own motion to invoke the rule requiring objection to be made in the court below. (4 C.J.S., Appeal & Error, § 245.)

Moreover, under all the circumstances defendant's objection was sufficient. The record shows that when Johnson's statement was offered, defendant's counsel stated: "We object to any statement made by Johnson." Later defendant's counsel stated:

> I believe **that Johnson could be brought here as a witness** and I renew my objection to this statement **inasmuch as he can be produced, and should be**

produced, to make his own statement before the jury rather than relying upon his statement that was made some time ago, and his statement having been transcribed, the best evidence is from the lips of the witness, **let the jury see him and determine from his attitude** before the jury whether or not he is speaking the truth. This is certainly secondary evidence. [Emphasis added.]

The court stressed the point (justifying its ruling of admissibility) after both objections, and on other occasions, that *if the statement was made in the presence of defendant it would be admissible.* After the court made such remarks following the last mentioned objection, defendant's counsel stated:

This [referring to Johnson's statement made out of court] is not a judicial proceeding. It's an ex parte affair, and **we have a right to have him produced**, and that evidence certainly might be of very much greater advantage to the jury **in determining whether he is speaking the truth** than merely the recital of a statement that's been reduced to writing by somebody else. [Emphasis added.]

Hearsay Rule. The proper ground of objection to the evidence would have been that it was hearsay, and ordinarily that ground should be specified in the objection, but it is manifest that although the word "hearsay" was not used in giving the grounds of the objections, the whole tenor of them was plainly directed to that ground. The essence of the hearsay rule is that the witness is not in court and subject to cross-examination and is not available for the jury to judge his credibility. Those were the very things urged by defendant's counsel. That the court understood that the objection was grounded in hearsay is evidenced by its remarks about the presence of defendant when the statements were made. It is many times erroneously assumed that the mere presence of the other party when a statement is made will erase its hearsay character. The presence of the other party is ordinarily no test. It becomes important only when the statement is offered for the purpose of showing an admission of guilt by defendant. It is apparent from the remarks of the court that even if hearsay (using that word) had been specified as the ground of the objection the trial court would have overruled it. It is true that the particularly mischievous part of Johnson's statement (that Bob rather than he struck the blow) was not pointed out by defendant's objection but it is clear from the attitude and expressed view of the court that it would have overruled even a specific objection.

In the light of the rules applicable to the necessity of making objections to evidence in the trial court to save the point on appeal, the objections made should be held to state sufficiently the ground of the objection and the part of the evidence to which objection was made.

Notwithstanding the rule that the specific ground for an objection must be given and the particular portion of evidence which is inadmissible must be pointed out where other parts are admissible, "technicalities should be liberally viewed when urged against a defendant in a criminal case. And the mere fact that the objection could have been made in better form will not justify a refusal to consider it, where the intention of the defendant could not be misunderstood. So also if it is evident from the discussion over an objection between the court and counsel that another ground of objection perfectly obvious from the nature of the question, would have been overruled if made, this ground will be considered on appeal." (8 Cal.Jur. 503.) See *People v. Boggess*, 194 Cal. 212 [228 P. 448]; *People v. Shattuck*, 109 Cal. 673 [42 P. 315]; *People v. Yee Fook Din*, 106 Cal. 163 [39 P. 530]; *People v. Darby*, 64 Cal.App.2d 25 [148 P.2d 28]; *People v. Converse*, 28 Cal.App. 687 [153 P. 734].) It is said in *People v. Yee Fook Din, supra*, at page 166: "Appellant could certainly have made his objections in better form, and could thus have brought here a record presenting his point in a clearer light; but *technicalities should be liberally viewed when urged against a defendant in a criminal case.*" [Emphasis added.] It is aptly said in *People v. Converse, supra*, at page 691, where the objection of immaterial matter rather than *hearsay* was held sufficient:

> It will not do to say that the ruling complained of was free from error because counsel for the defendant did not see fit to object specially upon the ground that the question called for testimony which in addition to being immaterial was incompetent because hearsay. Objections to questions calling for inadmissible testimony are designed and are required for the purpose of directing the attention of the trial court and of opposing counsel to the particular vice of the testimony sought to be elicited by the question; and it is the general rule that the efficacy of an objection is dependent upon the precision with which it is made. In the present case, however, **upon its face the character of the question must have fully apprized the trial court of the hearsay nature of the testimony called for; and it is evident by the discussion of the objection indulged in between court and counsel that an objection upon the ground of hearsay would have been overruled** upon the theory that, not withstanding its hearsay character, such testimony was admissible upon redirect examination as a material and undisclosed portion of a conversation called for and narrated upon cross-examination. Obviously therefore it would have been useless to have specified incompetency as an additional ground of objection; and this perhaps was one of the reasons why counsel for defendant failed to do so. [Emphasis added.]

In *People v. Boggess, supra*, at page 232, it is said:

> While it is true ordinarily that an objection to evidence must be sufficiently specific to inform the court of the scope of the objection, nevertheless, where

the record shows, as it does in the instant case, that all the parties, including the court, must have understood the purpose of the objection, it will not be said that the objection failed of its purpose." Such is equally true in the case at bar. The court said in **People v. Darby, supra,** at page 33: "We do not feel inclined to deprive defendant of his right to demand that he be tried with competent evidence because of the oversight of his counsel in the midst of a difficult trial to remember that he should add the word, hearsay, to the statement of his objection.

Viewing what transpired in the trial court at the time the Johnson statement was offered in evidence in the light of the foregoing authorities, there is little foundation for the contention that no proper objection was made to the portion of the Johnson statement which was denied by the defendant, on the specific ground that said statement was not admissible as an accusatory statement because of such denial, and that the trial court was not required to segregate the portions of the statement which might have been excluded, and was never given an opportunity or called upon to rule on the question presented for the first time on appeal. While the objection could have been more specific, we think it was sufficient to call to the attention of the trial court the inadmissible character of the portion of Johnson's statement which was denied by defendant, and the trial court should have excluded that portion of said statement. The fact that defendant admitted the truth of a portion of Johnson's statement did not render the entire statement admissible in the face of the objection.

At the time of the crime here involved, defendant was only nineteen years of age. From the evidence here adduced (other than the objectionable evidence) it seems more probable that Johnson, who participated with defendant in the commission of the crime, struck the blows which caused the death of Yoshioka. Johnson was tried separately and a jury, after finding him guilty of murder of the first degree, fixed his punishment at life imprisonment. Johnson was several years older than the defendant, and it could be inferred that he was the mastermind in conspiring to commit as well as execute the commission of the crime. It cannot be doubted that the error in admitting in evidence the hearsay statement of Johnson was prejudicial to defendant in view of the fact that Johnson's punishment was fixed at life imprisonment and the defendant's punishment was fixed at death. In fact the vital issue, and the only one over which there could be any controversy, was whether defendant should be imprisoned for life or suffer the death penalty. His participation in the commission of the crime was admitted by him. And since the murder was committed in the perpetration of a robbery, it cannot be denied that it was murder of the first degree. But the jury might well have fixed defendant's punishment at life imprisonment had the hearsay declaration of Johnson not been admitted in evidence. This declaration placed before the jury the only statement that defendant struck the blows which caused Yoshioka's death. Since the only other evidence shows that it was Johnson and not defendant who struck the fatal blows, and Johnson's punishment was fixed at only life imprisonment, we are unable to escape the conclusion that the admission in evidence of the hearsay statement of Johnson was error, that such error was prejudicial and that defendant should be granted a new trial.

The Legislature of California has taken extraordinary precaution to safeguard the rights of those upon whom the death penalty is imposed by the trial court, by providing for an automatic appeal to the Supreme Court of this state in all such cases (Pen. Code, § 1239) and enjoining upon this court an examination of the record and the preparation of a formal opinion and decision from which it should appear that no miscarriage of justice has resulted. In view of this declared policy, and the fact known to this court that many capital cases are defended by counsel appointed by the court who may be inexperienced in the handling of criminal cases, it would seem appropriate for this court to take a liberal view of the technical rules applicable to criminal cases generally (see *People v. Yee Fook Din, supra,* 166) and examine the record with the view of determining whether or not in the light of all that transpired at the trial of the case a miscarriage of justice has resulted.

The judgment and order denying a new trial are reversed.

Justices Gibson, C. J., Traynor, J., and Schauer, J., concurred.

Opinion of Mr. Justice Shenk, dissenting; Mr. Justice Edmonds and Mr. Justice Spence joined in the dissenting opinion.

The judgement of reversal is placed on the tenuous ground that there was prejudicial error in admitting in evidence those portions of Johnson's lengthy statement which contained declarations accusing defendant of wielding the lethal weapon because at the conclusion of Johnson's statement Bob denied being the leading actor in this atrocious drama participated in by both men. The circumstances attending the felonious killing were freely related and admitted by Bob except as noted. Thus the sole ground for discovery of error is the introduction in evidence of the denied accusations by Johnson made in the presence of Bob that the latter procured and wielded the weapon.

Objections. The two men were tried separately. On the trial of Bob his confession to the police was introduced in evidence. Johnson's statement made in the presence of Bob was also read, together with the colloquy between the two men. No ground of objection to the admission of the statement was at first specified. Counsel merely stated, "We object to any statement made by Johnson." The court then asked the witness (who reported the conversations), "Well, was it in the presence of the defendant?", and, upon receiving an affirmative reply, stated, "Very well. The objection is overruled." (See Code Civ. Proc., § 1870, subd. 3.) After the reading of the Johnson statement was commenced defense counsel interposed an objection upon the ground that Johnson should be brought in as a witness and that the reading of his prior and transcribed statement was not the best evidence. In overruling the objection on this ground the court said: "Any statement he [Johnson] made that was not made in the presence of this defendant would certainly not be admissible. This is a statement, a conversation, in the presence of the defendant in which the defendant took part. . . ."

On oral argument in this court Bob's counsel again contended that the Johnson statement was inadmissible on the ground that Johnson was in the county jail and could have been called as a witness.

There is no indication in the record that any declaration of Johnson was objected to on the ground that it was denied by Bob. (See *People v. Simmons*, 28 Cal.2d 699 [172 P.2d 18], and cases therein cited; 8 Cal. Jur., p. 102, § 196; 20 Am.Jur., p. 483, § 570.) Most of Johnson's declarations were admissible even over any objection by reason of not having been denied. Bob's statement disclosed participation with Johnson in the commission of the crime. He corroborated most of the incriminatory accusations made against him by Johnson and some of them he expressly admitted. The possibility of the rejection of a portion of the Johnson statement because it contained the accusations that Bob enticed the victim and struck the fatal blow, which Bob denied, was not brought to the attention of the trial court. There was no objection on that ground, no motion to strike, and no request for an instruction that the jury disregard the accusations which Bob denied, namely, the declarations that Bob lured the victim and wielded the lethal weapon. The trial court was not required on its own motion to segregate the portions of the statement which might have been excluded by appropriate objection from the clearly admissible portions. The trial court was never given the opportunity or called upon to rule on the question now presented for the first time on appeal.

The question whether some portion of the Johnson statement might have been excluded, had timely objection been made, is not a question for consideration on this appeal. It is the law that a reviewing court will not consider an objection to the admission of evidence unless the ground of the objection has been specified in the trial court. (*People v. Schafer*, 161 Cal. 573, 578–79 [119 P. 920]; *People v. Farmer*, 77 Cal. 1, 7 [18 P. 800]; *People v. Duran*, 57 Cal.App.2d 363, 370 [134 P.2d 305]; *People v. Wignall*, 125 Cal.App. 465, 474–75 [13 P.2d 995]; *People v. Jones*, 12 Cal.App. 129, 132 [106 P. 724]; 8 Cal.Jur. p. 503, § 517.) Therefore, despite the concession of the attorney general to the contrary, there was no error in the trial court's ruling on the admission of the statement.

By his own confession Bob was a participant in an atrocious murder committed in the course of robbery of the victim. This could only be murder of the first degree (Pen. Code § 189). The record conclusively establishes Bob's guilt as to that degree of murder. His guilt is established regardless of which of the two men struck the fatal blow. (*People v. Whitson*, 25 Cal.2d 593 [154 P.2d 867]; *People v. Gomez*, 209 Cal. 296, 298–99 [286 P. 998]; *People v. Arnold*, 199 Cal. 471 [250 P. 168]; *People v. Matthew*, 194 Cal. 273, 278–79 [228 P. 424]; *People v. Bringhurst*, 192 Cal. 748 [221 P. 897]; 4 Cal.Jur. 10-Yr. Supp. p. 557, § 39.)

No extenuating circumstance is shown. Bob admitted that he and Johnson started out with the intention to "roll" someone, that he knew Johnson had the pipe, and that he "figured" Johnson would use it. Each declared that no other person was involved in the affair. Regardless of which did the actual killing, they were the only persons responsible for the perpetration of the crime. Assuming that Johnson completed the killing Bob took part in it and in the robbery of the fatally wounded victim which ensued. Not only that but a short time afterward Bob returned to the scene and although the victim was still alive witnessed without remonstrance the taking of the murdered man's shoes by Simmons.

On the evidence the jury would not have been justified in returning any verdict other than that of murder of the first degree.

The jury was properly instructed with reference to its duties and responsibilities and to its right, in its discretion, to relieve this defendant of the extreme penalty. This the jury chose not to do. The fact that the confederate Johnson was so relieved on a separate trial and before another jury does not establish a miscarriage of justice in Bob's case. It is impossible to say what prejudices, because of the innocent victim's Japanese ancestry, may have crept into the jury box in Johnson's case to influence a verdict of imprisonment for life in that case. It is a matter of common report that at the time of the trial and because of the hostilities between our country and Japan this prejudice was so pronounced that juries in other cases rendered verdicts of not guilty for no apparent reason or excuse except that the victims were of the Japanese race. The innocent victim in this case was an ex-serviceman who had been wounded in active service in France as a member of the Armed Forces of the United States. It is obvious that no prejudice against him because of his race had any influence on the jury's action in the present case.

The judgment should be affirmed.

SUMMARY

United States v. Wade established the post-indictment police lineup as a critical stage of the pretrial confrontation between the accused and the prosecution at which the accused is entitled to legal counsel. Police conduct of post-indictment lineups without notice to and in the absence of counsel for the accused jeopardizes the admissibility at trial of the in-court identifications of the accused by witnesses who attended the line-up. *Kirby v. Illinois* held that the foregoing doctrine (Wade-Gilbert *Per Se* Exclusionary Rule) was not applicable to pre-indictment lineups. A person's Sixth and Fourteenth Amendment right to counsel attaches only at or after the time that adversary judicial proceedings have been initiated against him. *United States v. Ash* further explored this area of pretrial identification evidence and procedural safeguards, but ruled that the Sixth Amendment does not grant the accused the right to counsel at photographic identifications.

Dissenting opinions in the foregoing cases held that an accused should be entitled to counsel at pre-arrest lineups rather than just post-charge lineups, and at photographic identifications as well as at lineups, because conditions prejudicial to the accused existed and lack of legal counsel was likely to jeopardize the accused's right to a fair trial.

Ramsey v. Virginia and *People v. Bob* reveal the intricacies of the hearsay rule in their reviewing of exceptions to this rule in relation to opinion evidence, hypothetical questions, and a co-defendant's statement.

DISCUSSION QUESTIONS

1. How would you define a "critical stage" of pretrial procedures?
2. What criteria are established for evaluating police lineups in the opinion of the court in *United States v. Wade?*
3. How does the opinion of Mr. Justice Black in *United States v. Wade* differ from the opinion of the court?
4. How does the opinion of Mr. Justice Black in *United States v. Wade* differ from the opinion of Mr. Justice Fortas?
5. Why was the hypothetical question in *Ramsey v. Commonwealth* considered prejudiced?
6. Why was the admission in evidence of the Johnson hearsay statement prejudicial to the defendant in the case of *People v. Bob?*
7. How does the dissenting opinion in *People v. Bob* disagree with the opinion of the court?

8.   Compare the successive cases of *Wade, Kirby*, and *Ash*, and explain the differences in the rights of defendants at lineups.
9.   Is an accused person entitled to legal counsel at a photographic display shown to a witness for the purpose of identification?

GLOSSARY

CITATION.   Reference to an authority; U.S. Supreme Court decisions give the case name, the volume and page numbers (*U.S. Reports*), and the year in which the case was decided.

CORPOREAL.   Of or pertaining to the human body.

INTER ALIA.   Among other items or things; used when the complete wording of a law is not given.

PER SE.   By itself.

Articles
and
Exhibits of
Evidence

8

CHAPTER OBJECTIVES

1. Chapter 8 deals with articles and exhibits of evidence. Real evidence is defined, with a focus on

2. Physical evidence and its utility in court. Associative evidence is also explored, as is the concept of the transfer of things and traces from or to a crime scene or suspect; also examined are the

3. Role of nontestimonial evidence in the identification of persons; and the

4. Nature of documentary evidence, including explanations of the best evidence and parol evidence rules. Finally, there is a discussion of how otherwise

5. Mute articles or exhibits of evidence can communicate when viewed in court and are linked to testimonial evidence.

Real, demonstrative, objective or autopsic evidence consists of tangible items submitted as exhibits or articles for inspection which can be personally scrutinized by the judge or jury. Submission of tangible evidence by either party to a criminal proceeding calls for a belief or conclusion, but the fact-finder is not asked to believe that certain facts are true on the sole basis of any witness' testimony. The triers of fact can use their own sense of observation and perception in evaluating the exhibits and articles of evidence submitted to them. Testimonial evidence is necessary, however, to introduce and identify the exhibit or article, and to relate its connection with the issue.

Exhibits and articles of evidence may be either persons or things that can be produced in court and seen. They are exhibitive or demonstrative. Decisions about admitting this type of evidence are made by the trial judge. Persons or articles shown to the triers of fact should be connected with the crime in issue. Their admissibility depends on the circumstances under which they are proffered.

Tangible evidence may be admitted to illustrate the crime or the transaction on which the charge of crime is based. Tangible evidence includes (1) the fruits of crime, such as the stolen property in theft cases; (2) the instrumentalities or agencies of crime, such as burglar's tools or an assailant's weapon; (3) contraband, such as drugs and illegal weapons; and (4) other articles of evidential value.

PHYSICAL EVIDENCE

Physical evidence is a term developed by police investigators and criminalists to describe a tangible "**thing**"—in solid, liquid or gaseous form —or a "**trace**" which can be scientifically examined in a laboratory. In the application of scientific techniques to the problems of crime and criminals, the term "physical evidence" is used to describe articles of evidence which can be the subject of scientific inspection.

This term covers the kind of evidence likely to be found at the scene of a crime, or on or about a suspect, which can be collected by investigators, evidence technicians, field criminalists, or medicolegal experts. "Things" collected as possible items of evidence by police and their technicians include weapons, imprints, and impressions, while "traces" may be dust and dirt, microscopic particles of hair and fibres, or paint transfers. Medicolegal experts may isolate traces of a poison as physical evidence, recover identity clues by scraping the fingernails of a victim, or develop evidence in homicide cases in which the photographic evidence of wounds and the suspect weapon are often joined as physical evidence—an exhibit and an article.

ASSOCIATIVE EVIDENCE

Associative evidence is a nonlegal term for physical evidence which has been examined by an expert criminalist and which may be used for evidence through comparison. The theory of association is inherent in the concept of transfer evidence: Some thing or trace is both left at the crime scene and carried away from it by the criminal. Associative evidence is developed when expert examination reveals a relationship between (1) physical evidence found at the crime scene, and (2) apparently similar evidence located on the person of the suspect, his clothing, home, or automobile. A bullet recovered from a homicide victim is found to match a bullet fired from a weapon found on an arrestee at the time of arrest. A unique shoeprint found at a crime scene, adequately identified as the footprint of the crime's perpetrator, is shown to match the prints of shoes owned by the defendant. A strangely shaped bludgeon is suspected of causing the multiple wounds in a murder case, and a hammer with a strangely shaped head is found in the trunk of a suspect's car upon arrest. Autopsy surgeons say this weapon caused the victim's wounds.

A major objective of the science of **criminalistics** is the identification of physical evidence. An item of evidence is placed in a certain class or "set" and then its uniqueness is developed. The goal is to identify qualities that set the item apart from other items within the class or set —to "individualize" it within reasonable limits of probability. Once physical evidence is thus individualized, other suspect materials can be tested for the traditional "match"—identification. This aspect of criminalistics has contributed to the growing use of associative evidence in criminal trials.

Quite frequently, the associative items of evidence are sufficiently similar to give the result of the comparison analysis sound probative force—particularly when it is the expressed opinion of the expert that a "match" has been discovered.

Associative evidence, when properly demonstrated as an exhibit (alone or supplemented by the opinion of an expert), is beyond the realm of opinion evidence and emerges as a new concept in the truly physical demonstrative field.

BODY EXAMINATION EVIDENCE

Nontestimonial evidence related to the person of a suspect or accused person can be classified in two broad groups: **identifying and incriminating.**

There is a unique quality of identification in body evidence. An eyewitness who views suspects in a police lineup is examining real evidence—the person and appearance of the individuals in the lineup. A suspect or prisoner may be asked to speak for identification, and the resulting sounds can also be categorized as real evidence. The physiological process of speaking is an observable, physical, and quite distinctive characteristic. Handwriting samples can be compared with suspect hand-writing for the purpose of identification. Blood may serve to identify a body abnormality such as alcohol in the blood. Hair, nail scrapings, the residue of firearms use, and similar physical evidence may also help in identification after processing by criminalists in police laboratories.

The main problems in searching for and retrieving body evidence involve discovering the evidence and preventing its destruction. Body evidence is frequently concealed in the human body. Such evidence has been recovered from the mouths of suspects, from the rectums of prisoners, and an attempt has been made to retrieve contraband from the stomach of an arrested person.[1]

It might appear that a suspect or prisoner would be protected from these intrusions by the Fifth Amendment's guarantee against self-incrimination, but body evidence has been defined as nontestimonial.[2] The privilege against self-incrimination does not protect the suspect or defendant from being compelled, in appropriate circumstances, (1) to submit to fingerprinting, photography or measurements; (2) to write or speak for identification; (3) to appear in court; (4) to stand, to assume a stance, to walk, or to make a particular gesture.[3]

EYEWITNESS EVIDENCE OF IDENTIFICATION

Identification by eyewitnesses to a crime involves using the body of the person viewed as an item of evidence. This is real evidence in use, and direct evidence of prime importance when it places the defendant at the crime scene.

Every precaution should be taken by investigators not to ruin the legal significance of eyewitness identification by substandard pretrial investigative techniques. Among these precautions are: (1) recognizing that the post indictment **police lineup** is a "critical stage" of the pretrial procedure against a person accused of crime. (2) not letting eyewitnesses view **photographs** of suspects that a reviewing court might consider "suggestive."

The cases that developed these guidelines for police were *United States v. Wade*, and *Kirby v. Illinois*.[4] The Kirby case limited the requirements in *Wade* to lineups after the indictment against the defendant has been filed in court. Thus, a pre-indictment lineup was not deemed by the Supreme Court in *Kirby* as a critical stage of the proceedings. In a

---

[1]Rochin v. California, 342 U.S. 165 (1952).
[2]Schmerber v. California, 384 U.S. 757 (1966).
[3]United States v. Wade, 388 U.S. 218 (1967).
[4]388 U.S. 218 (1967); 406 U.S. 682 (1972).

later case, *United States v. Ash,*[5] the court redefined the term *critical stage of the proceedings* by saying that it pertains "when there is a physical confrontation with the accused at which he requires aid in coping with legal problems or help in meeting his adversaries." Using this definition, the court in *Ash* approved the viewing of photographs of the defendant and others for the purpose of identification by witnesses after the indictment was filed in court against the defendant.

After the *Wade* decision, police procedures provided for **defense counsel at lineups** so that attorneys could observe the lineup and identification procedures in each case in which the defendant refused to waive such attendance. During the period between *Wade, Kirby,* and *Ash,* defense attorneys, by their presence, comments, suggestions, and protests of prejudicial lineup procedures, served to update and improve those procedures to the point that a court attack based upon the "unfair" lineup was virtually precluded. If the effect of *Kirby* and *Ash* is to again keep defense attorneys out of the lineup procedure, police and prosecutors should expect in-court attacks on "unfair" lineup proceedings to increase significantly.

Unless the right to an attorney in a post-indictment lineup is intelligently waived, the prisoner and his counsel must be given proper notice about a forthcoming lineup, and counsel must be present at the lineup. When the attorney is present he can effectively reconstruct or prevent any unfairness that may occur at the lineup and use any unfairness as a basis for attacking the credibility of the eyewitness identification.

As in the visual scanning of a lineup of five to seven "suspects," witnesses attempting to make auditory **identifications** must scan the voice samples of all participants in the lineup and select the voice they believe they heard at the time of the crime.

The court said in the *Wade* decision that during a proper lineup, the prisoner could be required to exhibit his physical characteristics and wear a selected article of clothing. In these procedures, the court found no compulsion to disclose any knowledge the prisoner possessed. This was no different from the taking of a blood sample[6] or wearing a blouse.[7]

Similarly, compelling Wade to speak within earshot of the eyewitnesses as they viewed the lineup, even requiring him to speak the words the witnesses said they had heard spoken during the robbery by the robber, was not considered compulsion to testify. Wade was not asked to speak about his guilt or innocence, but simply to speak, because the human voice is an identifiable physical characteristic. This constitutes **nontestimonial identification evidence.**

[5]United States v. Ash, 413 U.S., 300 (1973).
[6]Schmerber v. California, 384 U.S. 757 (1966).
[7]Holt v. U.S. 218 U.S. 245 (1910).

Therefore, real evidence such as articles of clothing, the defendant's physical characteristics, and the human voice may be used as evidence of identity when coupled with testimonial evidence.

The body of the defendant in court is the best source for eyewitness identification. The in-court identification is not a suggestive process. It is similar to the examination of any article of evidence for identification. It is also a "matching" from memory, a comparison of the defendant's general appearance or other means of ready identification with a recollected image.

IDENTIFICATION: BLOOD, HANDWRITING, AND FINGERPRINTS

Blood samples, handwriting, and fingerprints are major items of body evidence. Court decisions about body intrusions in these evidence areas have established guidelines for collecting this type of evidence, and for comparing and analyzing body fluids and characteristics for the purpose of identification. In 1957, blood taken from an unconscious person injured in a traffic accident blazed the path for court approval of minor and reasonable intrusions on the body.[8] The rule categorizing body characteristics as nontestimonial followed in 1966.[9] In 1967, handwriting samples as distinguished from the content of writings were defined as identifying physical characteristics.[10]

BLOOD SAMPLES

The U.S. Supreme Court decision in *Breithaupt v. Abram*[11] demonstrates judicial willingness to permit reasonable body intrusions to develop evidence that a person has ingested a certain amount of alcohol. Breithaupt was injured when the car he was driving collided with another vehicle. The occupants of the other car in the accident were killed. Breithaupt survived. While he was unconscious from his injuries and receiving emergency medical care in a nearby hospital, at the request of police investigating the accident, the attending physician took a blood sample and turned it over to the police for analysis to determine whether Breithaupt was intoxicated. Laboratory tests revealed .17 percent alcohol in Breithaupt's blood. He was convicted of manslaughter at a trial in which evidence about the blood sample was admitted over defense objection. It was argued on appeal that Breithaupt's constitutional rights

[8]Breithaupt v. Abram, 352 U.S. 432 (1957).
[9]Schmerber v. California, 384 U.S. 757 (1966).
[10]Gilbert v. California, 388 U.S. 263 (1967).
[11]352 U.S. 432 (1957).

had been violated because an unconscious man could not give consent and waive his privilege against self-incrimination, and that the actual taking of a blood sample was a brutal and offensive procedure that violated the defendant's rights to due process. The court said blood was a nontestimonial body substance and not within the Fifth Amendment's protection against self-incrimination. The court also held there was nothing brutal or offensive in the taking of a blood sample by a physician or medical technician noting that many persons willingly submitted to such tests with proper medical precautions, as a matter of course, and said that the taking of the blood without consent while Breithaupt was unconscious did not violate his constitutional rights.

The court's acceptance of blood samples to show that someone is likely to have been intoxicated, and its willingness to permit the bodily intrusion involved, was firmly established in *Schmerber v. California*.[12] Schmerber was arrested for driving a vehicle while under the influence of intoxicating liquor. He was asked to cooperate in testing his possible blood-alcohol content. He refused on advice of his attorney, and a blood sample was extracted by a physician at a hospital. He was convicted and appealed. The appeal argued a trilogy of constitutional violations: (1) self-incrimination, (2) right to counsel, and (3) search and seizure.

The court's decision rejected Schmerber's claim of protection under the Fifth Amendment. The privilege against self-incrimination concerns the communications of an accused person, according to the court. The extraction of a body fluid for chemical analysis or the body fluid itself were neither compelled testimony nor enforced communication by Schmerber. In studying the requirements of the Sixth Amendment under these circumstances, the court concluded that because the privilege against self-incrimination did not exist, there was little point in providing legal counsel to advise Schmerber at this time. The court's opinion said Schmerber was entitled to the protection of the Fourth Amendment proviso against unreasonable searches, but held that there was no violation, that the search was reasonable on these grounds:

1. There was probable cause for arresting Schmerber and charging him with driving a vehicle while under the influence of intoxicating liquor. (There was testimony at trial about the smell of alcohol on Schmerber's breath and the condition of his eyes—bloodshot, watery, glassy.)
2. The bodily intrusion could not be delayed while application was made to court for a search warrant, because of the oxidation of alcohol in the human body with the passage of time.
3. There was no objection to the test on the grounds of fear, health, or religion.
4. The search was performed in a reasonable manner.

[12]384 U.S. 757 (1966).

HANDWRITING EXEMPLARS

The request by police for handwriting samples from a person accused of crime is not viewed as a critical stage of the pretrial proceedings because any threat to a fair trial can be brought out and corrected at trial. Unlike the lineup, there is nothing suggestive to witnesses, and numerous additional handwriting samples can be made for comparison analysis. The high court's opinion in *Gilbert v. California*[13] states this principle as follows:

> **First.** The taking of the exemplars did not violate petitioner's Fifth Amendment privilege against self-incrimination. The privilege reaches only compulsion of an accused's communications, whatever form they might take, and the compulsion of responses which are also communications, for example, compliance with a subpoena to produce one's papers, and not compulsion which makes a suspect or accused the source of real or physical evidence. (**Schmerber v. California**, 384 U.S. 757). One's voice and handwriting are, of course, means of communication. It by no means follows, however, that every compulsion of an accused to use his voice or write compels a communication within the cover of the privilege. A mere handwriting exemplar, in contrast to the content of what is written, like the voice or body itself, is an identifying physical characteristic outside its protection. (**United States v. Wade**, 388 U.S. 218). No claim is made that the content of the exemplars was testimonial or communicative matter.
>
> **Second.** The taking of the exemplars was not a critical stage of the criminal proceedings entitling petitioner to the assistance of counsel. Putting aside the fact that the exemplars were taken before the indictment and appointment of counsel, there is minimal risk that the absence of counsel might derogate from his right to a fair trial. If, for some reason, an unrepresentative exemplar is taken, this can be brought out and corrected through the adversary process at trial since the accused can make an unlimited number of additional exemplars for analysis and comparison by government and defense handwriting experts. Thus, the accused has the opportunity for a meaningful confrontation of the state's case at trial through the ordinary processes of cross-examination of the state's expert (handwriting) witnesses and the presentation of the evidence of his own experts (handwriting).

A person's handwriting is a means of communication, but when the identifying physical characteristics of the handwriting are of primary importance, rather than the content of the writing, forcing a person to write does not violate the privilege against self-incrimination. Handwriting exemplars are nontestimonial, identifying physical characteristics outside the protection of the Fifth Amendment.

[13]388 U.S. 263 (1967).

FINGERPRINTING

Fingerprint impressions are classic evidence of identity often found at crime scenes in some form, latent, partial, plastic and so forth. Fingerprints used for comparison, unless taken from police records, must be taken by procedures that qualify as reasonable under the provisions of the Fourth Amendment. Otherwise, evidence based on the impressions will be inadmissible at trial. Most fingerprint impressions compared with fingerprints found at crime scenes are part of police records, the impressions having been taken for the purpose of identification at the time of arrest. When fingerprints are not available for comparison, the safeguards of the Fourth Amendment apply to any intrusion to secure them.

Because fingerprinting discloses many unique characteristics useful in identification common to criminal investigation, the taking of fingerprints can be classified as a search for identification evidence. In *Davis v. Mississippi*,[14] the U.S. Supreme Court held that detention for the sole purpose of obtaining fingerprints made such evidence invalid because it was secured in the course of an unreasonable search. However, the court's opinion implied police could make such an intrusion lawful by: (1) seeking prior court approval, and (2) restricting the request to a convenient fingerprinting session unaccompanied by any form of interrogation.

DOCUMENTARY EVIDENCE

A "**writing**" means handwriting, typewriting, printing, photostating, photographing, and every other means of recording upon any tangible thing, any form of communication or representation, including letters, words, pictures, sounds or symbols, or combinations thereof.[15]

A handwriting must be authenticated before it may be received in evidence, or before secondary evidence of its content may be received in evidence. If a portion of the writing material to the dispute has been altered, or appears to have been altered after the writing was made, the person offering the writing must account for the alteration, or the appearance of being altered. He may do this by showing that: (1) the alteration was made by someone else without his consent; (2) it was made with the consent of parties affected by it; or (3) that it was otherwise properly or innocently made; or (4) that the alteration did not change the meaning or language of the instrument.[16]

[14]394 U.S. 721 (1969).
[15]California Evidence Code, Section 250.
[16]California Evidence Code, Section 1401–2.

Authentication requires the production of evidence which will show the writing is what it is supposed to be. If it is offered as genuine, there must be proof of its integrity. If it is offered as a forgery, there must be proof it is a forged writing. The evidence necessary for authentication depends on the circumstances under which the document is presented. Some documents are self-authenticating while others require proof of signing of the signature or of a comparison of signatures.

A writing may be authenticated by evidence that: (1) the opposing party has at some time admitted its authenticity, or that (2) the opposing party has acted as though the document were authentic.

Writings more than thirty years old can be authenticated by comparison with writings of known equal age, generally respected and acted on as genuine by persons with an interest in knowing whether the suspect writing is genuine. Authentication can also be made by evidence that the writing was received in response to a communication sent to the claimed author, or that it refers to or states matters unlikely to be known by anyone other than the alleged author. Authenticity may also be shown by acknowledgements and seals of public agencies or officials.[17] A writing may be authenticated by the testimony of anyone who saw the writing executed, including a witness who signed it. When the testimony of someone who signed the writing is required and he cannot recollect the execution of the writing, or denies it, other evidence may be presented to authenticate the document.

A writing may also be authenticated by evidence that the handwriting is genuine. Opinions about the genuineness of the handwriting may be accepted from qualified nonexpert or expert witnesses who have (1) seen the supposed writer write; or (2) seen a writing purporting to be in the handwriting of the supposed writer on which the supposed writer has acted; or (3) received letters in the due course of mail purporting to be from the supposed writer in response to letters they have duly addressed and mailed to the supposed writer; or (4) obtained personal knowledge of the handwriting of the supposed writer by other means.

THE BEST EVIDENCE RULE

The best evidence rule applies only to **writings**. In proving the content of a writing, the writing itself is the best evidence of its content. Copies of writings or testimonial evidence of their content are admissible only after an in-court showing that the writing itself cannot be obtained and brought to court.

Secondary evidence, written or oral, may be admissible when:

[17]California Evidence Code, Sections 1411–14, 1419, 1420–21, 1450, and 1455.

1. The writing is lost or has been destroyed without fraudulent intent on the part of the person proffering the evidence (the proponent).

2. The writing is not reasonably procurable by the proponent by use of the court's process or by other available means.

3. The opponent had control of the writing and was expressly or impliedly notified, by the pleadings or otherwise, that the writing would be needed at the hearing, and on request at the hearing the opponent has failed to produce the writing.

4. The writing is a record of other writing in the custody of a public entity.

5. The writing has been recorded in the public records and, by statute, the record or an attested or certified copy of it is sufficient.

6. The writing is not closely related to the controlling issues and it would be inexpedient to require its production.

7. The writing consists of numerous accounts or other writings that cannot be examined in court without great loss of time, and the evidence sought from them is only the general result of the whole. (The court, in its discretion, may require that such accounts or other writings be produced for inspection by the adverse party.)

The usual procedure for handling this aspect of documentary evidence requires the production of a copy of a writing. If a copy cannot be produced, the proponent is often required to show that despite due diligence he has failed to locate a copy of the writing or, if he has located a copy, that he is unable to produce it in court. Then, other secondary evidence can be utilized for authentication.[18]

PAROL EVIDENCE RULE

The evidence about the terms and content of a written contract is the writing that has been made and signed by the contracting parties. This is documentary evidence. This integration of the history of negotiating a contract with the written end-product has led to development of the parol evidence rule: When an agreement is placed in writing, the court will reject oral testimony about arrangements made or things said which would tend to substitute the unwritten for the written contract which has been agreed upon and signed, to the possible prejudice of one of the contracting parties.

However, a written contract can be attacked by any evidence for fraud and illegality. Investigators may need this type of evidence in "shylocking" investigations, that is, loans at usurious interest rates. These contracts, when written, often do not reveal the amount of interest in the contract, which may be little more than a promissory note for the amount of the loan plus the interest, usually discounted when the loan was made.

[18]Rules 1003–08, Federal Rules of Evidence; **McCormick**, Sections 200–207.

VIEWING THE CRIME SCENE

The court decides whether or not to take a jury to view a crime scene. The court's decision will not be reversed unless it is clearly shown that the court abused its discretion.

Usually a request to view the crime scene will be denied if an adequate representation of the scene by photographs, diagrams, maps, or clear testimony is available.

Neither the judge nor individual members of the jury are allowed to view the scene independently. If the judge or a juror does so, it is grounds for a mistrial. All evidence received by the triers of fact must be received in court or by direction of the judge if he rules the crime scene should be viewed.

If the crime scene is viewed as a part of the admissible evidence during the trial, the jurors should not try demonstrating tests or experiments except under the direction of the court with the concurrence of counsel.

MAPS AND DIAGRAMS

Maps and diagrams are admissible as evidence when they are reasonably necessary to understand the testimony of witnesses and when a foundation of accuracy is laid by the person who prepared the map.

Under some circumstances, an inaccurate sketch will be admissible if it is reasonably related and explanatory of the testimony of the witness who drew it and used it to illustrate his testimony.

Maps are generally used to illustrate testimony relating to the scene of a crime. However, drawings and sketches may be admissible when the subject matter is anatomy, shape or location of a wound, kinds of marks on an item of evidence, graphs, and the like.

Admission of this evidence rests in the discretion of the trial judge and his decision will be reversed only where a clear abuse of discretion is shown.[19]

PHOTOGRAPHS

To be admissible, a photograph must be relevant, accurately taken, and a correct representation of the subject portrayed. The admissibility of photographs is discretionary with the court.

[19]Silvey v. Harm, 120 Cal. App. 561 (1932).

Photographs of a victim of crime are regularly admitted, even when they are gruesome and likely to prejudice the triers of fact. There must be some nonprejudicial basis, however, for their introduction, such as illustrating a wound, a part of the crime scene, a particular position of the victim, or some other relevant and material fact. The trial court must decide whether the probative value of the photograph outweighs the probable prejudicial effect.[20]

The court may refuse admission to prejudicial photographs when other evidence and testimony clear and uncontradicted on the disputed issue is available.

EXPERIMENTS AND DEMONSTRATIONS

Some experts are termed demonstrative experts because they supplement their testimony with exhibits or demonstrations. This is particularly true of witnesses skilled in examining questioned documents. The exhibits of these experts, usually consisting of photographic enlargement of similarities or differences in the suspect handwriting, is demonstrative evidence. The fact-finders look at the exhibits in order to understand the rationale for the expert's opinion.

A demonstration must be "in kind" in its relationship to the testimony of the witness, that is it must support his testimony. In-court demonstrations must be simple and easily understood. Out-of-court demonstrations must be explained with coherence and unity. It is vital that the triers of fact understand the demonstration if it is to be a basis for fact-finding.[21]

An excellent in-court demonstration was given during a murder trial in which the fatal wound was inflicted with a knife. The murder weapon, a long and slender knife, had been admitted as evidence during the prosecution's case in chief. The following portions of the testimony in this case accompanied the demonstration that was part of the core testimony associated with the defendant's claim of self-defense:

Direct Examination of Defendant:

(Defense counsel laid a foundation for the following line of questioning by questions establishing defendant's identity and recall of the event.)

Q: Well, at that time, what happened?
A: Well, I seen a knife when he flashed it. He made a motion toward me, and I grabbed it.

[20]People v. Love, 53 Cal. 2nd 843 (1960).
[21]People v. Adamson 27 Cal. 2d 478 (1946).

Q: What kind of a motion did he make toward you?
A: Come down from over his head.
Q: And where had his hand been prior to the time he came down toward you with the knife in his hand?
A: Up by the pillow.
Q: Did you get a good look at the knife?
A: No, I didn't.
Q: What occurred then when he made a motion toward you with the knife?
A: I grabbed his hand by the wrist when he came down and I pulled him toward me against the wall and then I came back over to him, and that is when the knife hit him.
Q: You grabbed the hand that had the knife?
A: Yes.

(Thereupon the witness left the stand and approached the area in back of counsel table, before the jury stand).

Q: Which hand held the knife?
A: In his right hand.
Q: If I am Mr. Morris and I have the knife in my right hand, and I strike toward you, what did you do?
A: Well, I was—I reached up and grabbed him by the wrist, right here.
Q: And then what did you do?
A: Reached around toward the wall and leaned on the wall and pulled him.
Q: And then what happened?
A: Grabbed him by the wrist and turned it, and that is when the knife hit him.
Q: What happened when you turned the knife into him?
A: He let go of the knife.
Q: What did you do?
A: I pulled it back out.

Expert witnesses may describe and give the results of out-of-court experiments conducted under conditions corresponding to the scene of the crime. **Ballistics evidence** is usually based upon an out-of-court experiment reproducing the firing of a firearm in a laboratory test, with the recovered test bullet as the evidence admitted as the result of the out-of-court experimenting.

A nonexpert witness, as well as an expert, can conduct simple experiments such as firing shots to estimate the range of a shooting event. When it is necessary to know the distance at which an assailant shot his victim, tests with guns of calibre and barrel length similar to the weapon used in a shooting have been fired at clean and nonyielding surfaces. Tests from various ranges show a pattern matching the victim's wound or wounds at some specific distance. The resulting evidence can be used to estimate the distance from gun to victim.

Demonstrations and experiments, in or out of court, tie together exhibits and articles of evidence and join them with the testimony of witnesses. They are effective combinations of compelling evidence.

SUMMARY

Real evidence is a tangible item presented in court as an exhibit or article of evidence. Physical evidence consists of things and traces that link a suspect to a crime scene, or vice versa. Body evidence is nontestimonial despite its theme of identification. Documentary evidence is concerned with writings and has its own special rules (authentication, best evidence, and parol evidence). Maps, diagrams, and photographs are admissible when trial judges believe they are relevant, necessary, and an accurate representation of the subject illustrated. Testimonial evidence is used to introduce real or documentary evidence, to report examinations of physical evidence, and to explain various exhibits of items of evidence or related demonstrations; and is a means by which opinion evidence may be admissible.

DISCUSSION QUESTIONS

1. How is testimony related to demonstrative evidence?
2. What is associative evidence? What is its value?
3. What are some problems of identity evidence?
4. What evidence may be taken from the body of the suspect?
5. What is the best evidence rule?
6. What may be demonstrated in court?
7. What are the major aspects of the "parol evidence rule"?
8. What are the basic requirements for the admissibility of photographs as evidence?

GLOSSARY

AUTOPSIC (EVIDENCE).   Evidence as a result of viewing an object or thing.

BALLISTICS.   Science of the motion of projectiles; firearms identification; the scientific examination of evidence found at crime scenes and connected with firearms; firearms, spent bullets, empty cartridge or shell cases, and cartridges and shells.

EXEMPLAR (HANDWRITING).   A specimen (of handwriting); an example; a model.

LATENT (FINGERPRINT).   Not visible to ordinary visual examination; must be searched for with special skill and equipment. A latent fingerprint can be developed by evidence technicians and preserved as evidence.

PLASTIC (FINGERPRINT).   A finger impression made in a pliable (plastic) substance.

Direct vs. Circumstantial Evidence

CHAPTER OBJECTIVES

1. In this chapter, the important differences between direct and circumstantial (indirect) evidence will be listed and explained, and the

2. Role of circumstantial evidence will be explored as corroboration of direct evidence.

3. The essential requirements of a "chain" of circumstantial evidence in circumstantial-evidence-only cases will be outlined, and

4. Reasoning from evidence—inferences and presumptions—will be described.

Triers of fact may base their decisions on either or both of two classes of **evidence: direct and circumstantial.**

Direct evidence means evidence that directly proves a fact, without any inference or presumption, and which in itself, if true, conclusively establishes that fact.

Direct evidence of a person's conduct consists of testimony by a witness who, at the time in question, and with his physical senses, perceived the person's conduct, or some portion of it, and recalls what he perceived. Direct evidence applies to the fact to be proved immediately and directly by witnesses testifying about matters they know personally without the need of any intervening fact or process of deduction. The value of the evidence rests on the truth of the fact asserted by the witness. The direct evidence of one witness who is entitled to full credit is sufficient for proof of any fact, except when additional evidence is required by a special circumstance such as the rule requiring that an accomplice's testimony be corroborated.

All other evidence is circumstantial. The basic clarity of the standard definition of direct evidence has created the "all other" terminology to define circumstantial evidence, and probably explains the use of the term "indirect" as a synonym for circumstantial.

The two classes of evidence are often described as direct and indirect evidence. Circumstantial evidence, however, is a more appropriate term. This class of evidence is, in fact, based on analysis and interpretation of circumstances and facts. Circumstantial evidence is evidence of things, of facts and circumstances, of a succession of events, all of which must be investigated and interpreted. Circumstantial evidence is the "language of things," when interpreted and explained; and the tale of an isolated fact, when its relations and significance to a disputed fact are clearly shown.[1]

When the question of guilt or innocence rests substantially on circumstantial evidence, each essential fact contributing to the classic "chain of circumstances" must be proven beyond a reasonable doubt; and the total measure of proven circumstances must be not only consistent with a hypothesis of guilt but inconsistent with any hypothesis of innocence.

INFERENCES

An inference is a deduction drawn by a process of logical reasoning; it is not evidence but the result of **reasoning from evidence**. An inference is supported by evidence when it can be described as a conclusion which can be logically and reasonably drawn from the impact of the evidence on the trier of fact. The scope or limits of the inference to be drawn may be limited by the nature of the evidence and the reasonableness of the possible inference. When an inference can be made it is up to the trier of fact to make it by reasonable and logical deduction of some fact from

[1]Albert S. Osborn, ed., **Questioned Document Problems**, 2d ed. (Albany, N.Y.: Boyd Printing Co., 1946), pp. 21, 107.

another fact or group of facts that have been found or otherwise established in the criminal action.

The usual objection to the introduction of an item of circumstantial evidence is lack of relevancy, that—even if true—the inference for which the evidence is offered does not necessarily follow as a logical conclusion. The evidence will usually be admitted if it is shown that the proffered evidence will establish a fact for which the desired inference is a probable or natural explanation or is more probable than other explanations. The odds must be that the inference claimed is the true proposition, or that the proffered evidence makes probable the existence of the fact in dispute. Of course, an item of evidence may be rejected on grounds of legal relevancy. The trial judge may, after weighing values against dangers, rule it out as misleading, confusing, or too remote.

PRESUMPTIONS

A presumption is a rule of law by which a judge attaches to one evidentiary fact certain procedural consequences such as the duty of the opposition to produce contrary evidence. A presumption is a deduction which the law requires a trier of facts to make. A conclusive presumption is a rule of law determining that only one inference can or must be drawn from certain evidence. A rebuttable presumption determines the inference to be drawn only in the absence of evidence to the contrary. It is dangerous to completely rely on rebuttable presumptions instead of gathering and producing positive evidence about these issues. There are presumptions of legitimacy, of continuance of things once proved to exist, of death, of death in bigamy cases, survivorship in the death of two or more persons in a common disaster, foreign law, and ownership from possession. More important in criminal investigations and prosecutions are the rebuttable presumptions of innocence; sanity and capacity; identity, from a name; chastity, honesty; intent, from voluntary acts; malice, from intentional acts; and guilt, from preparations, flight, attempt to escape, withholding evidence, or false statements.

THE ROLE OF CIRCUMSTANTIAL EVIDENCE IN CORROBORATING DIRECT EVIDENCE

As each item of circumstantial evidence is proffered, it must withstand the objections of the opposing party. Preliminary facts may have to be established to show a fair inference can be drawn from the proffered evidence, either alone or when connected with other evidence. Counsel seeking admission of such evidence may be forced to show legal sufficiency. He may have to show that the "chain" of proof is sufficient to establish, *prima facie*, the fact in issue, guilt or innocence.

The direct evidence of witnesses can be and sometimes needs to be corroborated by circumstantial evidence, for instance, testimony of a witness who observed the defendant a short distance from the scene, before or after the crime. This is direct evidence of the observation, but only inferential evidence of the defendant's presence at the scene or of his guilt. In one murder case, the accused was seen throwing away some then unknown articles. This was direct evidence that the articles found in that spot were thrown away by the accused. The articles were a bloodstained hammer and a jacket. To connect the accused with the crime charged, the recovered articles had to be "circumstantially" connected with the scene of the crime at the time of the crime (as loot or debris) or with the dead victim (as blood or weapon). The recovered articles did "circumstantially" connect with the time and place of the crime, and "circumstantially" as well as directly with the defendant. The weapon was shown to be the murder weapon by testimony of the autopsy surgeon, and a criminalist testified that numerous dog hairs found on the jacket were similar to dog hairs taken from the defendant's dog.

Physical evidence, after being examined and tested in a criminalistics laboratory, may serve as the base for an expert's opinion. This type of evidence is associative, connecting the accused with the crime scene in some manner and indicating his presence at the scene. Fingerprints, footprints, and like traces along with the testimony of the identification technician or the criminalist are examples of this type of evidence.

Testimony that places a suspect near a crime scene, and scientific evidence of traces and things found at crime scenes, corroborate the direct evidence of eyewitnesses. Without the direct evidence of eyewitnesses, such evidence will only contribute to the "chain" of inferential evidence.

The investigation of the tragic death of 14-year-old Stephanie Bryan[2] illustrates the web of direct and circumstantial evidence which may ensnare a defendant:

> Stephanie Bryan, a shy 14-year-old honor student at Willard Junior High School in Berkeley, California, disappeared on April 28, while walking home from school along Ashby Avenue. Stephanie was carrying several books, including a French textbook and a purse which contained a wallet and a pair of glasses. She was wearing, among other garments, a navy blue cardigan sweater over a white slip-on sweater, a blue cotton skirt, several petticoats, nylon panties and a brassiere. About 4:15 p.m. on the day Stephanie disappeared, several motorists saw a man struggling with a young girl in a car that had stopped suddenly at the side of Tunnel Road in Contra Costa County, near the Broad-

2People v. Abbott, 47 Cal. 2d 362 (1956).

way Tunnel, a few miles north of the Claremont Hotel. The girl appeared to be very frightened and was screaming. She was in the back seat of the car, and the man, who was leaning over the front seat, was beating her and pulling her down and away from the rear window. She was wearing a navy blue cardigan garment over something white.

On May 2, four days after Stephanie's disappearance, her French textbook was found beside Franklin Canyon Road in Contra Costa County. Except for the fact that its cover was slightly dampened by dew, the book was clean and dry, although it had rained in the area on April 29 and 30.

Nothing further was learned about Stephanie's disappearance until July 15, when her purse and wallet were found in Alameda at the home of defendant, Abbott. His wife discovered the articles in a cardboard box in the basement and, after reading the identification cards that were in the wallet, she went upstairs and excitedly asked her husband and others who were present if Stephanie Bryan was not the name of the girl whose disappearance had been reported in the newspapers. Abbott said that the purse probably belonged to some friend of Mrs. Abbott. A guest suggested that the police be called, and this was done. The police searched Abbott's home the following day, and found Stephanie's glasses, brassiere, and the rest of her books buried in the basement under eight inches of sand.

At the time of these events, Abbott was twenty-seven years old and attending the University of California at Berkeley. He was a regular customer at a doughnut shop located less than a block from the school Stephanie attended. This shop was frequented by pupils from that school, and Stephanie occasionally made purchases there. When questioned by the police, Abbott said that on April 28, the day of Stephanie's disappearance, he left his home in Alameda in the morning and drove to a mountain cabin in Trinity County that was owned by his wife's family. He said that he arrived at the cabin sometime after 8:30 that evening and remained there until May 1. Abbott described in detail the route he said he had taken from his home in Alameda to the cabin in Trinity County.

On July 20, a search party discovered Stephanie's body in a shallow grave about three hundred feet from the cabin in Trinity County. Her panties, which had been "cut or torn" through the left side and the crotch, were knotted around her neck. The rest of the clothing Stephanie was wearing on the day of her disappearance was on her body, except for her brassiere, which, as we have seen, was found in Abbott's basement.

Because of extensive decomposition, it was impossible to determine by a physical examination whether Stephanie had been sexually attacked. Her body had been buried in a state of rigor mortis, and the victim's arms and hands were raised in front of her face. There were multiple compound fractures of the skull and two holes about two inches in diameter through the skull. The head injuries were the principal cause of Stephanie's death. Particles of soil had become enmeshed in her cardigan sweater, and it could be inferred that the soil was wet when she was buried. It had rained and snowed near the cabin for several days prior to April 30, but there had been very little rain in the area during May, June, or July.

A search of Abbott's car led to the discovery of two hairs which were indistinguishable from Stephanie's and six hairs which were very similar to hers. Eighteen fibers matching those in four of her garments were also found. There was blood deep in the floor mat in the back of the car, but no blood on the surface, indicating that the mat had been washed.

The cardboard box in which Stephanie's purse and wallet were found (in the basement of Abbott's residence) contained old clothes which Abbott usually wore at the mountain cabin. His boots were encrusted with red mud which was the same as a sample of soil taken from Stephanie's grave at a point nine inches below the surface. Several fragments of bloodstained cleansing tissue, which had been carried by a pack rat from the grave site to a nearby nest, were of the type used by Abbott.

At the trial, Abbott testified that he was not in Berkeley on April 28, that he started for the cabin from his home about 10:45 a.m. and, en route, stopped at a restaurant about 3:00 p.m., where he was served by a 25- or 30-year-old waitress with dusty blonde hair. He testified that he also stopped at the Wildwood Inn for a drink about 8:30 p.m., and that he then drove two miles to the mountain cabin, built a fire, and went to bed.

Abbott's account of his activities on April 28 was in conflict not only with the evidence connecting him with Stephanie's disappearance and death set forth above but with other testimony as well. He was seen at the state controller's office in Oakland at 1:30 p.m. and at the beauty shop where his wife worked about 2:30 p.m. A witness testified that he saw Abbott at the doughnut shop on the afternoon in question and that he saw him leave about 3:20 p.m. and enter his car, a Chevrolet sedan. Five persons testified that they witnessed the struggle between a man and a young girl on Tunnel Road near the Broadway Tunnel. One of them identified Abbott as the man in the car. Another stated that a picture of Abbott published in a newspaper resembled the man. A third said that the man was about thirty years of age and had a receding hairline like Abbott's. The other two witnesses described the car in which the incident occurred as similar to Abbott's. Tunnel Road leads to the Orinda Crossroads, and from this point, several roads lead to Highway 40, which may be used to reach the area in Trinity County in which the mountain cabin (owned by the family of Mrs. Abbott) is located.

Abbott was seen near the cabin on the morning of April 29, and he was at Wildwood Inn, a nearby tavern, from 2:00 p.m. until midnight of that day. Abbott's brother and sister-in-law joined him at the cabin about 3:00 a.m. on April 30. They all left at the same time on the afternoon of May 1, Abbott driving alone in his car. Their return route took them over Franklin Canyon Road where Stephanie's French textbook was discovered about 7:30 a.m. the next morning. During this portion of the trip, Abbott's car was behind the one in which his brother and sister-in-law were riding. Abbott arrived home about 8 or 9 o'clock that evening.

On May 2, Abbott returned to the area in Contra Costa County through which he had traveled the day before on his way home from the mountain cabin. The records of an oil company showed that he had purchased gasoline at a station located near the place where Stephanie's book had been found earlier that morning. Abbott admitted being in the vicinity between 11:00 a.m. and 1 p.m., and said he had gone there to purchase used tires. He was unable to name or describe any place where he had stopped to look at tires, and he did not purchase any. The area is about twelve miles north of the campus of the university where Abbott had classes scheduled at 10, 11, and 1 o'clock.

THE CHAIN OF CIRCUMSTANTIAL EVIDENCE

Circumstantial evidence in cases in which there is no direct evidence to identify the defendant as the guilty person must be clear, convincing, and conclusive, excluding all rational doubt of guilt. This inferential relationship of various and related items of evidence can be as convincing in its nature and substance as direct evidence from a credible witness. When the facts and circumstances disclosed by each item of circumstantial evidence form an evidence structure which excludes any reasonable inference of innocence, a clear and strong conclusion as to guilt can be achieved.

A strong circumstantial-evidence case will contain evidence that the accused had the "motive" or "disposition" to commit the crime, the possession of the means to commit it, and was present at the scene at or about the time of the crime. Evidence of "motive" may be shown in a number of ways. The accused can be revealed as a person who "profited" from the crime (fraud, fire, murder of unwanted spouse), or as a person who was jealous, revengeful, or had a sexual motivation. Evidence of the means to commit a specific crime may be shown by:

(1) possession or ownership of the murder weapon; (2) possession of contraband in cases of the sale of contraband; and (3) possession of access tools necessary for the commission of the crime (burglary and safe burglaries).

Evidence of opportunity—presence at the crime scene—may be shown by:

(1) paint transfers connected with the scene of the crime; (2) bloodstains of victim on the accused; (3) debris on the accused traceable to the crime scene; (4) admissions of presence; (5) possession of loot traceable to the crime scene; and (6) absence of an alibi.

Similar acts by a defendant in the past may support an inference about the defendant at the time of a criminal trial. Evidence about past crimes cannot be admitted just to show a person with a criminal record is more likely to be guilty of the crime charged than an individual without a prior criminal history. Such evidence can be admitted, however, to show: (1) motive, (2) intent, (3) identity, (4) absence of mistake, and (5) a common scheme or plan.

Motive

Evidence that the defendant had attempted on other occasions to have intercourse with the victim is admissible to establish a motive for the subsequent murder.[3] When the motive for the charged crime is concealment of a prior crime, evidence of the prior crime is admissible.[4]

Intent

Evidence that the accused shot the victim on a prior occasion is admissible in a trial based on a second shooting of the same victim to show an intent to murder.[5] However, not every case of specific intent will allow the admission of prior unlawful acts.[6]

Identity

When an identification by police witness was questioned by the defense, the fact that the defendant had previously been arrested for robbery by the same police witness was admissible.[7]

Absence of Accident or Mistake

Evidence about prior sales of obscene material to minors was admissible to show that the defendant's sale to a minor in the case charged was no accident or mistake.[8]

Common Scheme or Plan

Evidence about other thefts may be admissible where these acts show a similarity in pattern, a *modus operandi*, to the crime presently charged.[9] In a prosecution for assault and robbery, evidence was admissible about a prior robbery during which, by threats, the defendant obtained the name and address of the present victim.[10]

A 1956 illegal gambling case shows how valuable circumstantial evidence can be.[11] Sam Goldstein was charged, in a two-count information, of unlawfully keeping a place for taking wagers on horse races, and unlawfully accepting such bets. Goldstein was observed conducting the

---

3People v. Malguist, 26 Ill. 2d 22, 185 NE 2d 825.
4Ables v. State, 201 Tenn. 491; 300 SW 2d 890.
5Moss v. State, 364 SW 2d 389 (Tex.).
6People v. Kelly, 66 Cal. 2d 232, 424 P. 2d 947.
7San Fratello v. State, 154 So. 2d 327 (Fla.).
8State v. Locks, 94 Ariz. 134, 382 P. 2d 241.
9Pabst v. State, 169 So. 2d 329 (Fla.).
10State v. Yoshino, 45 Hawaii 206, 364 P. 2d 638.
11People v. Goldstein, 139 Cal. App. 2d 146, 293 P. 2d 495 (1956).

typical operation of a bookmaker. When he was arrested, the arresting officers seized betting records in a search incidental to the arrest. Goldstein was convicted on both counts and appealed.

The court's opinion in this case sums up the evidence and its likely impact on the jury as follows:

> The evidence points convincingly to the guilt of defendant. Within a period of two and one-quarter hours on February 16, 1955, eight to ten persons went into defendant's newsstand, did not stop in the front room but went into the rear room. Defendant immediately followed each one into that room. He returned to the front room ten or fifteen seconds later, each time putting his pen into his shirt pocket. The other person immediately left the premises. No one of the eight to ten persons made a purchase. The only window in the rear room was covered by a green shade. Shortly after 2:00 p.m. that day the offiicers found six betting markers with a series of letters written on them, all in defendant's handwriting, in the rear room. All the betting markers, with one exception, were written with ink; the one exception was written partly with ink and partly with a pencil. When asked what they were, defendant replied they were a form of double bookkeeping for tax evasion purposes, and when asked to explain, said, "I can't; you will have to talk to my lawyer." The officers found a newspaper of February 16, 1955, open to the entries "at the current tracks" in the rear room. The betting markers showed bets on horses running at Santa Anita and Hialeah on February 16, 1955.

> The fact that all the evidence was circumstantial does not lessen its weight, for circumstantial evidence is as adequate to convict as direct evidence. That the officers did not observe any activity in the rear room, did not know who any of the persons were who went into that room, that the six papers were not dated, that neither "owe sheets" nor a "scratch sheet" were found on the premises, that no one saw anyone place a bet, and that Officer Marshall supposed a code of the kind indicated by the six papers could be applied "to a business operation, or purchases, and so forth," do not weaken the force of the evidence on which the verdict rests.

> The offense charged in Count 1 was complete when it was shown that the accused occupied a place with paraphernalia for the purpose of registering bets on February 16, 1955. The offense denounced is the occupancy of the place with the necessary equipment for registering bets, not the actual taking of bets. The evidence to the effect that the notations on the slips of paper, admittedly in the handwriting of defendant, were records of bets on horses which ran on February 16, 1955, together with the other circumstances related, established that defendant registered bets on that day. There is no doubt the jury was justified in concluding that defendant was guilty as charged in both counts.

SUMMARY

Evidence that directly proves a fact without the need for any intervening fact or deduction is direct evidence; all other evidence is circumstantial (indirect). Circumstantial evidence has utility in coorborating direct evidence, particularly when physical evidence is linked with testimony of its finding and examination. When circumstantial evidence is clear, convincing, and conclusive it can be used alone to exclude all rational doubt of guilt. Circumstantial evidence can be used to show a motive for a crime, the necessary intent, identity of defendant, absence of mistake or accident, and the existence of a common scheme or plan.

DISCUSSION QUESTIONS

1. What are the similarities and differences between inferences and presumptions?
2. Is the opinion of an expert concerning associative evidence circumstantial or direct evidence?
3. What is the role of circumstantial evidence in corroborating direct evidence?
4. How much circumstantial evidence is needed in cases without direct evidence to identify the defendant as the person responsible for the alleged crime?
5. When can evidence of past crimes be admitted as circumstantial evidence?
6. What is the role of circumstantial evidence in revealing the accused's presence at the crime scene? In demonstrating an accused had possession of the means to commit the alleged crime?

GLOSSARY

MODUS OPERANDI (M.O.).   Method of operation; used in the identification of criminals by their crime techniques or habitual criminal conduct.

Case Studies—Nontestimonial Evidence

CHAPTER OBJECTIVES

1. The material in Chapter 10 presents more case studies for the purpose of reviewing evidence in action and applying rules to circumstances in specific cases. Within the chapter,

2. Distinction is made between limited protective searches and searches incident to arrest; also we examine the concept that all custodial arrests are alike in their justification for searches incident to arrest.

3. The exclusionary rule is defined and described as a judicial technique to deter police from violating the constitutional rights of individuals; and the rules delineating both

4. Stop and frisk and seizure and search are summarized. In addition, the exclusionary rule is again discussed, this time relating to its power to bar the admissibility of evidence secured in the course of an unreasonable search.

The case studies in this chapter are concerned with things, articles, and objects of evidence; lawful searches; and the right to privacy.

Terry v. Ohio is a landmark "arrest" case because it spells out the difference between a "stop" and an "arrest" and the circumstances that justify making a "stop." At the same time, it is a landmark case on search and seizure because it defines the concept of a "frisk," a superficial search for weapons. This is a "protective search" by a police officer who has "stopped" a suspicious person.

Adams v. Williams extends the principles of *Terry v. Ohio* to police officers acting on an informant's tip rather than on personal observation.

United States v. Robinson rules that the limitations placed upon police by *Terry v. Ohio* on protective searches conducted in investigatory stop situations based on less than probable causes are not to be carried over to searches made incident to lawful custodial arrests.

Gustafson v. Florida establishes the full search of the person of a suspect made incident to a lawful custodial arrest as within the authority of the arresting officer, despite the fact that petitioner was arrested for the offense of driving his automobile without a valid operator's license.

Chimel v. California limits the scope of a warrantless search incidental to a valid arrest to the area within the immediate control of the prisoner at the time of the arrest, and in which he might gain possession of a weapon or of destructible evidence.

Warden v. Hayden is a landmark case in the search-and-seizure area because in this case the court accepted "hot pursuit" of a fleeing criminal suspect as justification for entering and searching premises without a warrant. It is also a classic because it brings what has been termed "mere evidence" into the category of things that may be seized during a lawful search—adding mere evidence to contraband and the fruits and instrumentalities of crime.

These six cases emphasize lawful searching procedures and the type of physical evidence that may be found during an investigation and used as evidence during the offender's trial.

CASE STUDY

Terry v. Ohio, 392 U.S. 1 (1968).

Opinion of the Court, delivered by Mr. Chief Justice Warren.*

This case presents serious questions concerning the role of the Fourth Amendment in the confrontation on the street between the citizen and the policeman investigating suspicious circumstances.

*Footnotes omitted. Headings added by authors for reader's convenience.

Facts of Case. Petitioner Terry was convicted of carrying a concealed weapon and sentenced to the statutorily prescribed term of one to three years in the penitentiary. Following the denial of a pretrial motion to suppress, the prosecution introduced in evidence two revolvers and a number of bullets seized from Terry and a co-defendant, Richard Chilton, by Cleveland Police Detective Martin McFadden. At the hearing on the motion to suppress this evidence, Officer McFadden testified that while he was patrolling in plain clothes in downtown Cleveland at approximately 2:30 in the afternoon of October 31, 1963, his attention was attracted by two men, Chilton and Terry, standing on the corner of Huron Road and Euclid Avenue. He had never seen the two men before, and he was unable to say precisely what first drew his eyes to them. However, he testified that he had been a policeman for 39 years and a detective for 35 and that he had been assigned to patrol this vicinity of downtown Cleveland for shoplifters and pickpockets for 30 years. He explained that he had developed routine habits of observation over the years and that he would "stand and watch people or walk and watch people at many intervals of the day." He added: "Now, in this case when I looked over they didn't look right to me at the time."

His interest aroused, Officer McFadden took up a post of observation in the entrance to a store 300 to 400 feet away from the two men. "I get more purpose to watch them when I seen their movements," he testified. He saw one of the men leave the other one and walk southwest on Huron Road, past some stores. The man paused for a moment and looked in a store window, then walked on a short distance, turned around and walked back toward the corner, pausing once again to look in the same store window. He rejoined his companion at the corner, and the two conferred briefly. Then the second man went through the same series of motions, strolling down Huron Road, looking in the same window, walking on a short distance, turning back, peering in the store window again, and returning to confer with the first man at the corner. The two men repeated this ritual alternately between five and six times apiece—in all roughly a dozen trips. At one point, while the two were standing together on the corner, a third man approached them and engaged them briefly in conversation. This man then left the two others and walked west on Euclid Avenue. Chilton and Terry resumed their measured pacing, peering, and conferring. After this had gone on for 10 to 12 minutes, the two men walked off together, heading west on Euclid Avenue, following the path taken earlier by the third man.

By this time Officer McFadden had become thoroughly suspicious. He testified that after observing their elaborately casual and oft-repeated reconnaissance of the store window on Huron Road, he suspected the two men of "casing a job, a stick-up," and that he considered it his duty as a police officer to investigate further. He added that he feared "they may have a gun." Thus, Officer McFadden followed Chilton and Terry and saw them stop in front of Zucker's store to talk to the same man who had conferred with them earlier on the street corner. Deciding that the situation was ripe for direct action, Officer McFadden approached the three men, identified himself as a police officer and asked for their names. At this point his knowledge was confined to what he had observed. He was not acquainted with any of the three men by name or by sight, and he had received no information concerning them from any other source. When the men "mumbled something" in response to his inquiries, Officer McFadden grabbed petitioner Terry, spun him around so that they were facing the other two, with Terry between McFadden and the others, and patted down the outside of his clothing. In the left breast pocket of Terry's overcoat Officer McFadden felt a pistol. He reached inside the overcoat pocket, but was unable to remove the gun. At this point, keeping Terry between himself and the others, the officer ordered all three men to enter Zucker's store. As they went in, he removed Terry's overcoat completely, removed a .38-caliber revolver from the pocket and ordered all three men to face the wall with their hands raised. Officer McFadden proceeded to pat down the outer clothing of Chilton and the third man, Katz. He discovered another revolver in the outer pocket of Chilton's overcoat, but no weapons were found on Katz. The officer testified that he only patted the men down to see whether they had weapons, and that he did not put his hands beneath the outer garments of either Terry or Chilton until he felt their guns. So far as appears from the record, he never placed his hands beneath Katz's outer garments. Officer McFadden seized Chilton's gun, asked the proprietor of the store to call a police wagon, and took all three men to the station, where Chilton and Terry were formally charged with carrying concealed weapons.

On the motion to suppress the guns the prosecution took the position that they had been seized following a search incident to a lawful arrest. The trial court rejected this theory, stating that it "would be stretching the facts beyond reasonable comprehension" to find that Officer McFadden had had probable cause to arrest the men before he patted them down for weapons. However, the court denied the defendants' motion on the ground that Officer McFadden, on the basis of his experience, "had reasonable cause to believe . . . that the defendants were conducting themselves suspiciously, and some interrogation should be made of their action." Purely for his own protection, the court held, the officer had the right to pat down the outer clothing of these men, who he had reasonable cause to believe might be armed. The court distinguished between an investigatory "stop" and an arrest, and between a "frisk" of the outer clothing for weapons and a full-blown search for evidence of crime. The frisk, it held, was essential to the proper performance of the officer's investigatory duties, for without it, "the answer to the police officer may be a bullet, and a loaded pistol discovered during the frisk is admissible."

After the court denied their motion to suppress, Chilton and Terry waived jury trial and pleaded not guilty. The court adjudged them guilty, and the Court of Appeals for the Eighth Judicial District, Cuyahoga County, affirmed. *State v. Terry*, 5 Ohio App. 2d 122, 214 NE 2d 114 (1966). The Supreme Court of Ohio dismissed their appeal on the ground that no "substantial constitutional question" was involved. We granted certiorari, 387 U.S. 929, 18 L. Ed. 2d 989, 87 S. Ct. 2050 (1967), to determine whether the admission of the revolvers in evidence violated petitioner's rights under the Fourth Amendment, made applicable to the States by the Fourteenth. *Mapp v. Ohio*, 367 U.S. 643, 6 L. Ed. 2d. 1081, 81 S. Ct. 1684, 84 ALR2d 933 (1961). We affirm the conviction.

I.

The Fourth Amendment provides that "the right of the people to be secure in their persons, houses, papers, and effects, against unreasonable searches and seizures, shall not be violated. . . ." This inestimable right of personal security belongs as much to the citizen on the streets of our cities as to the homeowner closeted in his study to dispose of his secret affairs. For, as this Court has always recognized,

> No right is held more sacred, or is more carefully guarded, by the common law, than the right of every individual to the possession and control of his own person, free from all restraint or interference of others, unless by clear and unquestionable authority of law. **Union Pac. R. Co. v. Botsford**, 141 U.S. 250, 251, 35 L. Ed. 734, 737, 11 S. Ct. 1000 (1891).

Fourth Amendment Protects People, Not Places. We have recently held that "the Fourth Amendment protects people, not places," *Katz v. United States*, 389 U.S. 347, 351, 19 L. Ed. 2d 576, 582, 88 S. Ct. 507 (1967), and wherever an individual may harbor a reasonable "expectation of privacy," *id.*, at 361, 19 L. Ed. 2d at 588 (Mr. Justice Harlan, concurring), he is entitled to be free from unreasonable governmental intrusion. Of course, the specific content and incidents of this right must be shaped by the context in which it is asserted. For "what the Constitution forbids is not all searches and seizures, but unreasonable searches and seizures." *Elkins v. United States*, 364 U.S. 206, 222, 4 L. Ed. 2d 1669, 1680, 80 S. Ct. 1437 (1960). Unquestionably petitioner was entitled to the protection of the Fourth Amendment as he walked down the street in Cleveland. *Beck v. Ohio*, 379 U.S. 89, 13 L. Ed. 2d

142, 85 S. Ct. 223 (1964); *Rios v. United States,* 364 U.S. 253, 4 L. Ed. 2d 1688, 80 S. Ct. 1431 (1960); *Henry v. United States,* 361 U.S. 98, 4 L. Ed. 2d 134, 80 S. Ct. 168 (1959); *United States v. Di Re,* 332 U.S. 581, 92 L. Ed. 210, 68 S. Ct. 222 (1948); *Carroll v. United States,* 267 U.S. 132, 69 L. Ed. 543, 45 S. Ct. 280, 39 ALR 790 (1925). The question is whether in all the circumstances of this on-the-street encounter, his right to personal security was violated by an unreasonable search and seizure.

We would be less than candid if we did not acknowledge that this question thrusts to the fore difficult and troublesome issues regarding a sensitive area of police activity—issues which have never before been squarely presented to this Court. Reflective of the tension involved are the practical and constitutional arguments pressed with great vigor on both sides of the public debate over the power of the police to "stop and frisk"—as it is sometimes euphemistically termed—suspicious persons.

Stop and Frisk of Suspicious Persons by Police. On the other hand, it is frequently argued that in dealing with the rapidly unfolding and often dangerous situations on city streets the police are in need of an escalating set of flexible responses, graduated in relation to the amount of information they possess. For this purpose it is argued that distinctions should be made between a "stop" and an "arrest" (or a "seizure" of a person), and between a "frisk" and a "search." Thus, it is argued, the police should be allowed to "stop" a person and detain him briefly for questioning upon suspicion that he may be connected with criminal activity. Upon suspicion that the person may be armed, the police should have the power to "frisk" him for weapons. If the "stop" and the "frisk" give rise to probable cause to believe that the suspect has committed a crime, then the police should be empowered to make a formal "arrest," and a full incident "search" of the person. This scheme is justified in part upon the notion that a "stop" and a "frisk" amount to a mere "minor inconvenience and petty indignity," which can properly be imposed upon the citizen in the interest of effective law enforcement on the basis of a police officer's suspicion.

On the other side the argument is made that the authority of the police must be strictly circumscribed by the law of arrest and search as it has developed to date in the traditional jurisprudence of the Fourth Amendment. It is contended with some force that there is not—and cannot be—a variety of police activity which does not depend solely upon the voluntary cooperation of the citizen and yet which stops short of an arrest based upon probable cause to make such an arrest. The heart of the Fourth Amendment, the argument runs, is a severe requirement of specific justification for any intrusion upon protected personal security, coupled with a highly developed system of judicial controls to enforce upon the agents of the State the commands of the Constitution. Acquiescence by the courts in the compulsion inherent in the field interrogation practices at issue here, it is urged, would constitute an abdication of judicial control over, and indeed an encouragement of, substantial interference with liberty and personal security by police officers whose judgment is necessarily colored by their primary involvement in "the often competitive enterprise of ferreting out crime." *Johnson v. United States*, 333 U.S. 10, 14, 92 L. Ed. 436, 440, 68 S. Ct. 367 (1948). This, it is argued, can only serve to exacerbate police-community tensions in the crowded centers of our nation's cities.

Exclusionary Rule. In this context we approach the issues in this case mindful of the limitations of the judicial function in controlling the myriad daily situations in which policemen and citizens confront each other on the street. The State has characterized the issue here as "the right of a police officer . . . to make an on-the-street stop, interrogate and pat down for weapons (known in street vernacular as "stop and frisk)." But this is only partly accurate. For the issue is not the abstract propriety of the police conduct, but the admissibility against petitioner of the evidence uncovered by the search and seizure. Ever since its inception, the rule excluding evidence seized in violation of the Fourth Amendment has been recognized as a principal mode of discouraging lawless police conduct. See *Weeks v. United States*, 232 U.S. 383, 391–93, 58 L. Ed. 652, 655, 656, 34 S. Ct. 341, LRA 1915B 834 (1914). Thus its major thrust is a deterrent one, see *Linkletter v. Walker*, 381 U.S. 618, 629–35, 14 L. Ed. 2d 601, 608–12, 85 S. Ct. 1731 (1965), and experience has taught that it is the only effective deterrent to police misconduct in the criminal context, and that without it the constitutional guarantee against unreasonable searches and seizures would be a mere "form of words." *Mapp v. Ohio*, 367 U.S. 643, 655, 6 L. Ed. 2d 1081, 1090, 81 S. Ct. 1684, 84 ALR2d 933 (1961). The rule also serves another vital function—"the imperative of judicial integrity." *Elkins v. United States*, 364 U.S. 206, 222, 4 L. Ed. 2d 1669, 1680, 80 S. Ct. 1437 (1960). Courts which sit under our Constitution cannot and will not be made party to lawless invasions of the constitutional rights of citizens by permitting unhindered governmental use of the fruits of such invasions. Thus in our system evidentiary rulings provide the context in which the judicial process of inclusion and exclusion approves some conduct as comporting with constitutional guarantees and disapproves other actions by state agents. A ruling admitting evidence in a criminal trial, we recognize, has the necessary effect of legitimizing the conduct which produced the evidence, while an application of the exclusionary rule witholds the constitutional imprimatur.

The exclusionary rule has its limitations, however, as a tool of judicial control. It cannot properly be invoked to exclude the products of legitimate police investigative techniques on the ground that much conduct which is closely similar involves unwarranted intrusions upon constitutional protections. Moreover, in some contexts the rule is ineffective as a deterrent. Street encounters between citizens and police officers are incredibly rich in diversity. They range from wholly friendly exchanges of pleasantries or mutually useful information to hostile confrontations of armed men involving arrests, or injuries, or loss of life. Moreover, hostile confrontations are not all of a piece. Some of them begin in a friendly enough manner, only to take a different turn upon the injection of some unexpected element into the conversation. Encounters are initiated by the police for a wide variety of purposes, some of which are wholly unrelated to a desire to prosecute for crime. Doubtless some police "field interrogation" conduct violates the Fourth Amendment. But a stern refusal by this Court to condone such activity does not necessarily render it responsive to the exclusionary rule. Regardless of how effective the rule may be where obtaining convictions is an important objective of the police, it is powerless to deter invasions of constitutionally guaranteed rights where the police either have no interest in prosecuting or are willing to forgo successful prosecution in the interest of serving some other goal.

Proper adjudication of cases in which the exclusionary rule is invoked demands a constant awareness of these limitations. The wholesale harassment by certain elements of the police community, of which minority groups, particularly Negroes, frequently complain, will not be stopped by the exclusion of any evidence from any criminal trial. Yet a rigid and unthinking application of the exclusionary rule, in futile protest against practices which it can never be used effectively to control, may exact a high toll in human injury and frustration of efforts to prevent crime. No judicial opinion can comprehend the protean variety of the street encounter, and we can only judge the facts of the case before us. Nothing we say today is to be taken as indicating approval of police conduct outside the legitimate investigative sphere. Under our decision, courts still retain their traditional responsibility to guard against police conduct which is overbearing or harassing, or which trenches upon personal security without the objective evidentiary justification which the Constitution requires. When such conduct is identified, it must be condemned by the judiciary and its fruits must be excluded from evidence in criminal trials. And, of course, our approval of legitimate and restrained investigative conduct undertaken on the basis of ample factual justification should in no way discourage the employment of other remedies than the exclusionary rule to curtail abuses for which that sanction may prove inappropriate.

Having thus roughly sketched the perimeters of the constitutional debate over the limits on police investigative conduct in general and the background against which this case presents itself, we turn our attention to the quite narrow question posed by the facts before us: whether it is always unreasonable for a policeman to seize a person and subject him to a limited search for weapons unless there is probable cause for an arrest. Given the narrowness of this question, we have no occasion to canvass in detail the constitutional limitations upon the scope of a policeman's power when he confronts a citizen without probable cause to arrest him.

II.

Relevance of Fourth Amendment to Stop and Frisk by Police. Our first task is to establish at what point in this encounter the Fourth Amendment becomes relevant. That is, we must decide whether and when Officer McFadden "seized" Terry and whether and when he conducted a "search." There is some suggestion in the use of such terms as "stop" and "frisk" that such police conduct is outside the purview of the Fourth Amendment because neither action rises to the level of a "search" or "seizure" within the meaning of the Constitution. We emphatically reject this notion. It is quite plain that the Fourth Amendment governs "seizures" of the person which do not eventuate in a trip to the station house and prosecution for crime—"arrests" in traditional terminology. It must be recognized that whenever a police officer accosts an individual and restrains his freedom to walk away, he has "seized" that person. And it is nothing less than sheer torture of the English language to suggest that a careful exploration of the outer surfaces of a person's clothing all over his or her body in an attempt to find weapons is not a "search." Moreover, it is simply fantastic to urge that such a procedure performed in public by a policeman while the citizen stands helpless, perhaps facing a wall with his hands raised, is a "petty indignity." It is a serious intrusion upon the sanctity of the person, which may inflict great indignity and arouse strong resentment, and it is not to be undertaken lightly.

The danger in the logic which proceeds upon distinctions between a "stop" and an "arrest," or "seizure" of the person, and between a "frisk" and a "search" is twofold. It seeks to isolate from constitutional scrutiny the initial stages of the contact between the policeman and the citizen. And by suggesting a rigid all-or-nothing model of justification and regulation under the Amendment, it obscures the utility of limitations upon the scope, as well as the initiation, of police action as a means of constitutional regulation. This Court has held in the past that a search which is reasonable at its inception may violate the Fourth

Amendment by virtue of its intolerable intensity and scope. *Kremen v. United States,* 353 U.S. 346, 1 L. Ed. 2d 876, 77 S. Ct. 828 (1957); *Go-Bart Importing Co. v. United States,* 282 U.S. 344, 356–58, 75 L. Ed. 374, 381–83, 51 S. Ct. 153 (1931); see *United States v. Di Re,* 332 U.S. 581, 586–87, 92 L. Ed. 210, 216, 68 S. Ct. 222 (1948). The scope of the search must be "strictly tied to and justified by" the circumstances which rendered its initiation permissible. *Warden v. Hayden,* 387 U.S. 294, 310, 18 L. Ed. 2d 782, 794, 87 S. Ct. 1642 (1967) (Mr. Justice Fortas, concurring); see, e.g., *Preston v. United States,* 376 U.S. 364, 367–68, 11 L. Ed. 2d 777, 780, 781, 84 S. Ct. 881 (1964); *Agnello v. United States,* 269 U.S. 20, 30–31, 70 L. Ed. 145, 148, 46 S. Ct. 4, 51 ALR 409 (1925).

The distinctions of classical "stop-and-frisk" theory thus serve to divert attention from the central inquiry under the Fourth Amendment— the reasonableness in all the circumstances of the particular governmental invasion of a citizen's personal security. "Search" and "seizure" are not talismans. We therefore reject the notions that the Fourth Amendment does not come into play at all as a limitation upon police conduct if the officers stop short of something called a "technical arrest" or a "full-blown search."

In this case there can be no question, then, that Officer McFadden "seized" petitioner and subjected him to a "search" when he took hold of him and patted down the outer surfaces of his clothing. We must decide whether at that point it was reasonable for Officer McFadden to have interfered with petitioner's personal security as he did. And in determining whether the seizure and search were "unreasonable" our inquiry is a dual one—whether the officer's action was justified at its inception, and whether it was reasonably related in scope to the circumstances which justified the interference in the first place.

III.

Search Warrants. If this case involved police conduct subject to the Warrant Clause of the Fourth Amendment, we would have to ascertain whether "probable cause" existed to justify the search and seizure which took place. However, that is not the case. We do not retreat from our holdings that the police must, whenever practicable, obtain advance judicial approval of searches and seizures through the warrant procedure, see e. g., *Katz v. United States,* 389 U.S. 347, 19 L. Ed. 2d 576, 88 S. Ct. 507 (1967); *Beck v. Ohio,* 379 U.S. 89, 96, 13 L. Ed. 2d 142, 147, 85 S. Ct. 223 (1964); *Chapman v. United States,* 365 U.S. 610, 5 L. Ed. 2d 828, 81 S. Ct. 776 (1961), or that in most instances failure to comply with the warrant requirement can only be executed by exigent circumstances, see, *e.g., Warden v. Hayden,* 387 U.S. 294, 18

L. Ed. 2d 782, 87 S. Ct. 1642 (1967) (hot pursuit); cf. *Preston v. United States*, 376 U.S. 364, 367–68, 11 L. Ed. 2d 777, 780, 781, 84 S. Ct. 881 (1964). But we deal here with an entire rubric of police conduct—necessarily swift action predicated upon the on-the-spot observations of the officer on the beat—which historically has not been, and as a practical matter could not be, subjected to the warrant procedure. Instead, the conduct involved in this case must be tested by the Fourth Amendment's general proscription against unreasonable searches and seizures.

Reasonableness of Search: Belief of Man of Reasonable Caution. Nonetheless, the notions which underlie both the warrant procedure and the requirement of probable cause remain fully relevant in this context. In order to assess the reasonableness of Officer McFadden's conduct as a general proposition, it is necessary "first to focus upon the governmental interest which allegedly justifies official intrusion upon the constitutionally protected interests of the private citizen," for there is "no ready test for determining reasonableness other than by balancing the need to search [or seize] against the invasion which the search [or seizure] entails." *Camara v. Municipal Court*, 387 U.S. 523, 534–35, 536–37, 18 L. Ed. 2d 930, 938–40, 87 S. Ct. 1727 (1967). And in justifying the particular intrusion the police officer must be able to point to specific and articulable facts which, taken together and with rational inferences from those facts, reasonably warrant that intrusion. The scheme of the Fourth Amendment becomes meaningful only when it is assured that at some point the conduct of those charged with enforcing the laws can be subjected to the more detached, neutral scrutiny of a judge who must evaluate the reasonableness of a particular search or seizure in light of the particular circumstances. And in making that assessment it is imperative that the facts be judged against an objective standard: would the facts available to the officer at the moment of the seizure or the search "warrant a man of reasonable caution in the belief" that the action taken was appropriate? Cf. *Carroll v. United States*, 267 U.S. 132, 69 L. Ed. 543, 45 S. Ct. 280, 39 ALR 790 (1925); *Beck v. Ohio*, 379 U.S. 89, 96–97, 13 L. Ed. 2d 142, 147, 148, 85 S. Ct. 223 (1964). Anything less would invite intrusions upon constitutionally guaranteed rights based on nothing more substantial than inarticulate hunches, a result this Court has consistently refused to sanction. See, *e.g.*, *Beck v. Ohio, supra*; *Rios v. United States*, 364 U.S. 253, 4 L. Ed. 2d 1688, 80 S. Ct. 1431 (1960); *Henry v. United States*, 361 U.S. 98, 4 L. Ed. 2d 134, 80 S. Ct. 168 (1959). And simple "'good faith on the part of the arresting officer is not enough.' . . . If subjective good faith alone were the test, the protections of the Fourth Amendment would evaporate, and the people would be 'secure in their persons, houses, papers, and effects,' only in the discretion of the police." *Beck v. Ohio, supra*, at 97, 13 L. Ed. 2d at 148.

Police Investigative Function. Applying these principles to this case, we consider first the nature and extent of the governmental interests involved. One general interest is of course that of effective crime prevention and detection; it is this interest which underlies the recognition that a police officer may in appropriate circumstances and in an appropriate manner approach a person for purpose of investigating possibly criminal behavior even though there is no probable cause to make an arrest. It was this legitimate investigative function Officer McFadden was discharging when he decided to approach petitioner and his companions. He had observed Terry, Chilton, and Katz go through a series of acts, each of them perhaps innocent in itself, but which taken together warranted further investigation. There is nothing unusual in two men standing together on a street corner, perhaps waiting for someone. Nor is there anything suspicious about people in such circumstances strolling up and down the street, singly or in pairs. Store windows, moreover, are made to be looked in. But the story is quite different where, as here, two men hover about a street corner for an extended period of time, at the end of which it becomes apparent that they are not waiting for anyone or anything; where these men pace alternately along an identical route, pausing to stare in the same store window roughly 24 times; where each completion of this route is followed immediately by a conference between the two men on the corner; where they are joined in one of these conferences by a third man who leaves swiftly; and where the two men finally follow the third and rejoin him a couple of blocks away. It would have been poor police work indeed for an officer of 30 years' experience in the detection of thievery from stores in this same neighborhood to have failed to investigate this behavior further.

Police Intrusion on Personal Security. The crux of this case, however, is not the propriety of Officer McFadden's taking steps to investigate petitioner's suspicious behavior, but rather, whether there was justification for McFadden's invasion of Terry's personal security by searching him for weapons in the course of that investigation. We are now concerned with more than the governmental interest in investigaing crime; in addition, there is the more immediate interest of the police officer in taking steps to assure himself that the person with whom he is dealing is not armed with a weapon that could unexpectedly and fatally be used against him. Certainly it would be unreasonable to require that police officers take unnecessary risks in the performance of their duties. American criminals have a long tradition of armed violence, and every year in this country many law enforcement officers are killed in the line of duty, and thousands more are wounded. Virtually all of these deaths and a substantial portion of the injuries are inflicted with guns and knives.

In view of these facts, we cannot blind ourselves to the need for law enforcement officers to protect themselves and other prospective victims of violence in situations where they may lack probable cause for an arrest. When an officer is justified in believing that the individual whose suspicious behavior he is investigating at close range is armed and presently dangerous to the officer or to others, it would appear to be clearly unreasonable to deny the officer the power to take necessary measures to determine whether the person is in fact carrying a weapon and to neutralize the threat of physical harm.

We must still consider, however, the nature and quality of the intrusion on individual rights which must be accepted if police are to be conceded the right to search for weapons in situations where probable cause to arrest for crime is lacking. Even a limited search of the outer clothing for weapons constitutes a severe, though brief, intrusion upon cherished personal security, and it must surely be an annoying, frightening, and perhaps humiliating experience. Petitioner contends that such an intrusion is permissible only incident to a lawful arrest, either for a crime involving the possession of weapons or for a crime the commission of which led the officer to investigate in the first place. However, this argument must be closely examined.

Petitioner does not argue that a police officer should refrain from making any investigation of suspicious circumstances until such time as he has probable cause to make an arrest; nor does he deny that police officers in properly discharging their investigative function may find themselves confronting persons who might well be armed and dangerous. Moreover, he does not say that an officer is always unjustified in searching a suspect to discover weapons. Rather, he says it is unreasonable for the policeman to take that step until such time as the situation evolves to a point where there is probable cause to make an arrest. When that point has been reached, petitioner would concede the officer's right to conduct a search of the suspect for weapons, fruits or instrumentalities of the crime, or "mere" evidence, incident to the arrest.

There are two weaknesses in this line of reasoning, however. First, it fails to take account of traditional limitations upon the scope of searches, and thus recognizes no distinction in purpose, character, and extent between a search incident to an arrest and a limited search for weapons. The former, although justified in part by the acknowledged necessity to protect the arresting officer from assault with a concealed weapon, *Preston v. United States* 376 U.S. 364, 367, 11 L. Ed. 2d 777, 780, 84 S. Ct. 881 (1964), is also justified on other grounds, ibid., and can therefore involve a relatively extensive exploration of the person. A search for weapons in the absence of probable cause to arrest, however, must, like any other search, be strictly circumscribed by the exigencies which justify its initiation. *Warden v. Hayden*, 387 U.S. 294, 310, 18 L. Ed. 2d 782, 794, 87 S. Ct. 1642 (1967) (Mr. Justice Fortas, concurring). Thus it must be limited to that which is necessary for the discovery of weapons which might be used to harm the officer or others nearby, and may realistically be characterized as something less than a "full" search, even though it remains a serious intrusion.

Limited Protective Search for Weapons. A second, and related, objection to petitioner's argument is that it assumes that the law of arrest has already worked out the balance between the particular interests involved here—the neutralization of danger to the policeman in the investigative circumstance and the sanctity of the individual. But this is not so. An arrest is a wholly different kind of intrusion upon individual freedom from a limited search for weapons, and the interests each is designed to serve are likewise quite different. An arrest is the initial stage of a criminal prosecution. It is intended to vindicate society's interest in having its laws obeyed, and it is inevitably accompanied by future interference with the individual's freedom of movement, whether or not trial or conviction ultimately follows. The protective search for weapons, on the other hand, constitutes a brief, though far from inconsiderable, intrusion upon the sanctity of the person. It does not follow that because an officer may lawfully arrest a person only when he is apprised of facts sufficient to warrant a belief that the person has committed or is committing a crime, the officer is equally unjustified, absent that kind of evidence, in making any intrusions short of an arrest. Moreover, a perfectly reasonable apprehension of danger may arise long before the officer is possessed of adequate information to justify taking a person into custody for the purpose of prosecuting him for a crime. Petitioner's reliance on cases which have worked out standards of reasonableness with regard to "seizures" constituting arrests and searches incident thereto is thus misplaced. It assumes that the interests sought to be vindicated and the invasions of personal security may be equated in the two cases, and thereby ignores a vital aspect of the analysis of the reasonableness of particular types of conduct under the Fourth Amendment. See *Camara v. Municipal Court,* *supra.*

Belief of Reasonably Prudent Man; Police Expertise. Our evaluation of the proper balance that has to be struck in this type of case leads us to conclude that there must be narrowly drawn authority to permit a reasonable search for weapons for the protection of the police officer, where he has reason to believe that he is dealing with an armed and dangerous individual, regardless of whether he has probable cause to arrest the individual for a crime. The officer need not be absolutely certain that the individual is armed; the issue is whether a reasonably prudent man in the circumstances would be warranted in the belief that his safety or that of others was in danger.

Cf. Beck v. Ohio, 379 U.S. 89, 91, 13 L. Ed. 2d 142, 145, 85 S. Ct. 223 (1964); *Brinegar v. United States,* 338 U.S. 160, 174–76, 93 L. Ed. 1879, 1889–91, 69 S. Ct. 1302 (1949); *Stacey v. Emery,* 97 U.S. 642, 645, 24 L. Ed. 1035, 1036 (1878). And in determining whether the officer acted reasonably in such circumstances, due weight must be given, not to his inchoate and unparticularized suspicion or "hunch," but to the specific reasonable inferences which he is entitled to draw from the facts in light of his experience. *Cf. Brinegar v. United States, supra.*

IV.

Reasonableness of Seizure and Search. We must now examine the conduct of Officer McFadden in this case to determine whether his search and seizure of petitioner were reasonable, both at their inception and as conducted. He had observed Terry, together with Chilton and another man, acting in a manner he took to be preface to a "stick-up." We think on the facts and circumstances Officer McFadden detailed before the trial judge a reasonably prudent man would have been warranted in believing petitioner was armed and thus presented a threat to the officer's safety while he was investigating his suspicious behavior. The actions of Terry and Chilton were consistent with McFadden's hypothesis that these men were contemplating a daylight robbery—which, it is reasonable to assume would be likely to involve the use of weapons—and nothing in their conduct from the time he first noticed them until the time he confronted them and identified himself as a police officer gave him sufficient reason to negate that hypothesis. Although the trio had departed the original scene, there was nothing to indicate abandonment of an intent to commit a robbery at some point. Thus, when Officer McFadden approached the three men gathered before the display window at Zucker's store he had observed enough to make it quite reasonable to fear that they were armed; and nothing in their response to his hailing them, identifying himself as a police officer, and asking their names served to dispel that reasonable belief. We cannot say his decision at that point to seize Terry and pat his clothing for weapons was the product of a volatile or inventive imagination, or was undertaken simply as an act of harassment; the record evidences the tempered act of a policeman who in the course of an investigation had to make a quick decision as to how to protect himself and others from possible danger, and took limited steps to do so.

The manner in which the seizure and search were conducted is, of course, as vital a part of the inquiry as whether they were warranted at all. The Fourth Amendment proceeds as much by limitations upon the scope of governmental action as by imposing preconditions upon its initiation. Compare *Katz v. United States*, 389 U.S. 347, 354–56, 19 L. Ed. 2d 576, 583–85, 88 S. Ct. 507 (1967). The entire deterrent purpose of the rule excluding evidence seized in violation of the Fourth Amendment rests on the assumption that "limitations upon the fruit to be gathered tend to limit the quest itself." *United States v. Poller*, 43 F2d 911, 914 (CA2d Cir. 1930); see *e.g., Linkletter v. Walker*, 381 U.S. 618, 629–35, 14 L. Ed. 2d 601, 608–12, 85 S. Ct. 1731 (1965); *Mapp v. Ohio*, 367 U.S. 643, 6 L. Ed. 2d 1081, 81 S. Ct. 1684, 84 ALR2d 933 (1961); *Elkins v. United States*, 364 U.S. 206, 216–21, 4 L. Ed. 2d 1669, 1676–79, 80 S. Ct. 1437 (1960). Thus evidence may not be introduced if it was discovered by means of a seizure and search which were not reasonably related in scope to the justification for their initiation. *Warden v. Hayden*, 387 U.S. 294, 310, 18 L. Ed. 2d 782, 793, 87 S. Ct. 1642 (1967) (Mr. Justice Fortas, concurring).

We need not develop at length in this case, however, the limitations which the Fourth Amendment places upon a protective seizure and search for weapons. These limitations will have to be developed in the concrete factual circumstances of individual cases. See *Sibron v. New York*, 392 U.S. 40, 20 L. Ed. 2d 917, 88 S. Ct. 1889. Suffice it to note that such a search, unlike a search without a warrant incident to a lawful arrest, is not justified by any need to prevent the disappearance or destruction of evidence of crime. See *Preston v. United States*, 376 U.S. 364, 367, 11 L. Ed. 2d 777, 780, 84 S. Ct. 881 (1964). The sole justification of the search in the present situation is the protection of the police officer and others nearby, and it must therefore be confined in scope to an intrusion reasonably designed to discover guns, knives, clubs, or other hidden instruments for the assault of the police officer.

Scope of Search. The scope of the search in this case presents no serious problem in light of these standards. Officer McFadden patted down the outer clothing of petitioner and his two companions. He did not place his hands in their pockets or under the outer surface of their garments until he had felt weapons, and then he merely reached for and removed the guns. He never did invade Katz's person beyond the outer surfaces of his clothes, since he discovered nothing in his pat-down which might have been a weapon. Officer McFadden confined his search strictly to what was minimally necessary to learn whether the men were armed and to disarm them once he discovered the weapons. He did not conduct a general exploratory search for whatever evidence of criminal activity he might find.

V.

Holding. We conclude that the revolver seized from Terry was properly admitted in evidence against him. At the time he seized petitioner and searched him for weapons, Officer McFadden had reasonable grounds to believe that petitioner was armed and dangerous, and it was necessary for the protection of himself and others to take swift measures to discover the true facts and neutralize the threat of harm if it materialized. The policeman carefully restricted his search to what was appropriate to the discovery of the particular items which he sought. Each case of this sort will, of course, have to be decided on its own facts. We merely hold today that where a police officer observes unusual conduct which leads him reasonably to conclude in light of his experience that criminal activity may be afoot and that the persons with whom he is dealing may be armed and presently dangerous, where in the course of investigating this behavior he identifies himself as a policeman and makes reasonable inquiries, and where nothing in the initial stages of the encounter serves to dispel his reasonable fear for his own or others' safety, he is entitled for the protection of himself and others in the area to conduct a carefully limited search of the outer clothing of such persons in an attempt to discover weapons which might be used to assault him. Such a search is a reasonable search under the Fourth Amendment, and any weapons seized may properly be introduced in evidence against the person from whom they were taken.

Separate Opinions

Mr. Justice Black concurs in the judgment and the opinion except where the opinion quotes from and relies upon this Court's opinion in *Katz v. United States* and the concurring opinion in *Warden v. Hayden.*

Two concurring and one dissenting opinion express the viewpoints of Justices Harlan, White, and Douglas.

Opinion of Mr. Justice Harlan, concurring.

While I unreservedly agree with the Court's ultimate holding in this case, I am constrained to fill in a few gaps, as I see them, in its opinion. I do this because what is said by this Court today will serve as initial guidelines for law enforcement authorities and courts throughout the land as this important new field of law develops.

A police officer's right to make an on-the-street "stop" and an accompanying "frisk" for weapons is of course bounded by the protections afforded by the Fourth and Fourteenth Amendments. The Court holds, and I agree, that while the right does not depend upon the possession by the officer of a valid warrant, nor upon the existence of probable cause, such activities must be reasonable under the circumstances as the officer credibly relates them in court. Since the question in this and most cases is whether evidence produced by a frisk is admissible, the problem is to determine what makes a frisk reasonable.

If the State of Ohio were to provide that police officers could, on articulable suspicion less than probable cause, forcibly frisk and disarm persons thought to be carrying concealed weapons, I would have little doubt that action taken pursuant to such authority could be constitutionally reasonable. Concealed weapons create an immediate and severe danger to the public, and though that danger might not warrant routine general weapons checks, it could well warrant action on less than a "probability." I mention this line of analysis because I think it vital to point out that it cannot be applied in this case. On the record before us Ohio has not clothed its policemen with routine authority to frisk and disarm on suspicion; in the absence of state authority, policemen have no more right to "pat down" the outer clothing of passers-by, or of persons to whom they address casual questions, than does any other citizen. Consequently, the Ohio courts did not rest the constitutionality of this frisk upon any general authority in Officer McFadden to take reasonable steps to protect the citizenry, including himself, from dangerous weapons.

The state courts held, instead, that when an officer is lawfully confronting a possibly hostile person in the line of duty he has a right, springing only from the necessity of the situation and not from any broader right to disarm, to frisk for his own protection. This holding, with which I agree and with which I think the Court agrees, offers the only satisfactory basis I can think of for affirming this conviction. The holding has, however, two logical corollaries that I do not think the Court has fully expressed.

Reasonableness of Forcible Stop by Police.   In the first place, if the frisk is justified in order to protect the officer during an encounter with a citizen, the officer must first have constitutional grounds to insist on an encounter, to make a *forcible* stop. Any person, including a policeman, is at liberty to avoid a person he considers dangerous. If and when a policeman has a right instead to disarm such a person for his own protection, he must first have a right not to avoid him but to be in his presence. That right must be more than the liberty (again, possessed by every citizen) to address questions to other persons, for ordinarily the person addressed has an equal right to ignore his interrogator and walk away; he certainly need not submit to a frisk for the questioner's protection. I would make it perfectly clear that the right to frisk in this case depends upon the reasonableness of a forcible stop to investigate a suspected crime.

Where such a stop is reasonable, however, the right to frisk must be immediate and automatic if the reason for the stop is, as here, an articulable suspicion of a crime of violence. Just as a full search incident to a lawful arrest requires no additional justification, a limited frisk incident to a lawful stop must often be rapid and routine. There is no reason why an officer, rightfully but forcibly confronting a person suspected of a serious crime, should have to ask one question and take the risk that the answer might be a bullet.

The facts of this case are illustrative of a proper stop and an incident frisk. Officer McFadden had no probable cause to arrest Terry for anything, but he had observed circumstances that would reasonably lead an experienced, prudent policeman to suspect that Terry was about to engage in burglary or robbery. His justifiable suspicion afforded a proper constitutional basis for accosting Terry, restraining his liberty of movement briefly, and addressing questions to him, and Officer McFadden did so. When he did, he had no reason whatever to suppose that Terry might be armed, apart from the fact that he suspected him of planning a violent crime. McFadden asked Terry his name, to which Terry "mumbled something." Whereupon McFadden, without asking Terry to speak louder and without giving him any chance to explain his presence or his actions, forcibly frisked him.

I would affirm this conviction for what I believe to be the same reasons the court relies on. I would, however, make explicit what I think is implicit in affirmance on the present facts. Officer McFadden's right to interrupt Terry's freedom of movement and invade his privacy arose only because circumstances warranted forcing an encounter with Terry in an effort to prevent or investigate a crime. Once that forced encounter was justified, however, the officer's right to take suitable measures for his own safety followed automatically.

Upon the foregoing premises, I join the opinion of the Court.

Opinion of Mr. Justice White, concurring.

I join the opinion of the Court, reserving judgment, however, on some of the Court's general remarks about the scope and purpose of the exclusionary rule which the Court has fashioned in the process of enforcing the Fourth Amendment.

Also, although the Court puts the matter aside in the context of this case, I think an additional word is in order concerning the matter of interrogation during an investigative stop. There is nothing in the Constitution which prevents a policeman from addressing questions to anyone on the streets. Absent special circumstances, the person approached may not be detained or frisked but may refuse to cooperate and go on his way. However, given the proper circumstances, such as those in this case, it seems to me the person may be briefly detained against his will while pertinent questions are directed to him. Of course, the person stopped is not obliged to answer, answers may not be compelled, and refusal to answer furnishes no basis for an arrest, although it may alert the officer to the need for continued observation. In my view, it is temporary detention, warranted by the circumstances, which chiefly justifies the protective frisk for weapons. Perhaps the frisk itself, where proper, will have beneficial results whether questions are asked or not. If weapons are found, an arrest will follow. If none are found, the frisk may nevertheless serve preventive ends because of its unmistakable message that suspicion has been aroused. But if the investigative stop is sustainable at all, constitutional rights are not necessarily violated if pertinent questions are asked and the person is restrained briefly in the process.

Opinion of Mr. Justice Douglas, dissenting.

I agree that petitioner was "seized" within the meaning of the Fourth Amendment. I also agree that frisking petitioner and his companions for guns was a "search." But it is a mystery how that "search" and that "seizure" can be constitutional by Fourth Amendment standards, unless there was "probable cause" to believe that (1) a crime had been committed or (2) a crime was in the process of being committed or (3) a crime was about to be committed.

Probable Cause. The opinion of the Court disclaims the existence of "probable cause." If loitering were in issue and that was the offense charged, there would be "probable cause" shown. But the crime here is carrying concealed weapons; and there is no basis for concluding that the officer had "probable cause" for believing that crime was being committed. Had a warrant been sought, a magistrate would, therefore, have been unauthorized to issue one, for he can act only if there is a showing of "probable cause." We hold today that the police have greater authority to make a "seizure" and conduct a "search" than a judge has to authorize such action. We have said precisely the opposite over and over again.

In other words, police officers up to today have been permitted to effect arrests or searches without warrants only when the facts within their personal knowledge would satisfy the constitutional standard of *probable cause.* At the time of their "seizure" without a warrant they must possess facts concerning the person arrested that would have satisfied a magistrate that "probable cause" was indeed present. The term "probable cause" rings a bell of certainty that is not sounded by phrases such as "reasonable suspicion." Moreover, the meaning of "probable cause" is deeply imbedded in our constitutional history. As we stated in *Henry v. United States*, 361 U.S. 98, 100–02, 4 L. Ed. 2d 134, 137–38, 80 S. Ct. 168.

> The requirement of probable cause has roots that are deep in our history. The general warrant, in which the name of the person to be arrested was left

blank, and the writs of assistance, against which James Otis inveighed, both perpetuated the oppressive practice of allowing the police to arrest and search on suspicion. Police control took the place of judicial control, since no showing of "probable cause" before a magistrate was required.

That philosophy [rebelling against these practices] later was reflected in the Fourth Amendment. And as the early American decisions both before and immediately after its adoption show, common rumor or report, suspicion, or even "strong reason to suspect" was not adequate to support a warrant for arrest. And that principle has survived to this day. . . .

It is important, we think, that this requirement [of probable cause] be strictly enforced, for the standard set by the Constitution protects both the officer and the citizen. If the officer acts with probable cause, he is protected even though it turns out that the citizen is innocent. . . . And while a search without a warrant is, within limits, permissible if incident to a lawful arrest, if an arrest without a warrant is to support an incidental search, it must be made with probable cause. . . . This immunity of officers cannot fairly be enlarged without jeopardizing the privacy or security of the citizen.

The infringement on personal liberty of any "seizure" of a person can only be "reasonable" under the Fourth Amendment if we require the police to possess "probable cause" before they seize him. Only that line draws a meaningful distinction between an officer's mere inkling and the presence of facts within the officer's personal knowledge which would convince a reasonable man that the person seized has committed, is committing, or is about to commit a particular crime.

In dealing with probable cause, . . . as the very name implies, we deal with probabilities. These are not technical; they are the factual and practical considerations of everyday life on which reasonable and prudent men, not legal technicians, act. **Brinegar v. United States**, 338 U.S. 160, 175, 93 L. Ed. 1879, 1890, 69 S. Ct. 1302.

To give the police greater power than a magistrate is to take a long step down the totalitarian path. Perhaps such a step is desirable to cope with modern forms of lawlessness. But if it is taken, it should be the deliberate choice of the people through a constitutional amendment. Until the Fourth Amendment, which is closely allied with the Fifth, is rewritten, the person and the effects of the individual are beyond the reach of all government agencies until there are reasonable grounds to believe (probable cause) that a criminal venture has been launched or is about to be launched.

Extension of Power of Police. There have been powerful hydraulic pressures throughout our history that bear heavily on the Court to water down constitutional guarantees and give the police the upper hand. That hydraulic pressure has probably never been greater than it is today.

Yet if the individual is no longer to be sovereign, if the police can pick him up whenever they do not like the cut of his jib, if they can "seize" and "search" him in their discretion, we enter a new regime. The decision to enter it should be made only after a full debate by the people of this country.

CASE STUDY

Frederick E. Adams v. Robert Williams,* 407 U.S. 143 (1972).

Mr. Justice Rehnquist delivered the opinion of the Court.

Facts of Case.   Respondent Robert Williams was convicted in a Connecticut state court of illegal possession of a handgun found during a "stop and frisk,"as well as possession of heroin that was found during a full search incident to his weapons arrest. After respondent's conviction was affirmed by the Supreme Court of Connecticut, 157 Conn. 114, 249 A. 2d 245 (1968), this Court denied certiorari. 395 U.S. 927 (1969). Williams' petition for federal habeas corpus relief was denied by the District Court and by a divided panel of the Second Circuit, 436 F. 2d 30 (1970), but on rehearing *en banc* the Court of Appeals granted relief. 441 F. 2d 394 (1971). That court held that evidence introduced at Williams' trial had been obtained by an unlawful search of his person and car, and thus the state court judgments of conviction should be set aside. Since we conclude that the policeman's actions here conformed to the standards this Court laid down in *Terry v. Ohio*, 392 U.S. 1 (1968), we reverse.

Police Sgt. John Connolly was alone early in the morning on car patrol duty in a high crime area of Bridgeport, Connecticut. At approximately 2:15 A.M. a person known to Sgt. Connolly approached his cruiser and informed him that an individual seated in a nearby vehicle was carrying narcotics and had a gun at his waist.

After calling for assistance on his car radio, Sgt. Connolly approached the vehicle to investigate the informant's report. Connolly tapped on the car window and asked the occupant, Robert Williams, to open the door. When Williams rolled down the window instead, the sergeant reached into the car and removed a fully loaded revolver from Williams' waistband. The gun had not been visible to Connolly from outside the car, but it was in precisely the place indicated by the informant. Williams was then arrested by Connolly for unlawful possession of the pistol. A search incident to that arrest was conducted after other officers arrived. They found substantial quantities of heroin on Williams'

---

*Footnotes omitted. Headings added by authors for reader's convenience.

person and in the car, and they found a machete and a second revolver hidden in the automobile.

Respondent contends that the initial seizure of his pistol, upon which rested the later search and seizure of other weapons and narcotics, was not justified by the informant's tip to Sgt. Connolly. He claims that absent a more reliable informant, or some corroboration of the tip, the policeman's actions were unreasonable under the standards set forth in *Terry v. Ohio, supra.*

Reasonable Investigatory Stop. In *Terry* this Court recognized that "a police officer may in appropriate circumstances and in an appropriate manner approach a person for the purpose of investigating possible criminal behavior even though there is no probable cause to make an arrest." 392 U.S., at 22. The Fourth Amendment does not require a policeman who lacks the precise level of information necessary for probable cause to arrest to simply shrug his shoulders and allow a crime to occur or a criminal to escape. On the contrary, *Terry* recognizes that it may be the essence of good police work to adopt an intermediate response. See *id.*, at 23. A brief stop of a suspicious individual, in order to determine his identity or to maintain the status quo momentarily while obtaining more information, may be most reasonable in light of the facts known to the officer at the time. *Id.*, at 21–22; see *Gaines v. Craven*, 448 F. 2d 1236 (CA9 1971); *United States v. Unverzagt*, 424 F. 2d 396 (CA8 1970).

Limited Protective Search for Weapons. The Court recognized in *Terry* that the policeman making a reasonable investigatory stop should not be denied the opportunity to protect himself from attack by a hostile suspect. "When an officer is justified in believing that the individual whose suspicious behavior he is investigating at close range is armed and presently dangerous to the officer or to others," he may conduct a limited protective search for concealed weapons. *Id.*, at 24. The purpose of this limited search is not to discover evidence of crime, but to allow the officer to pursue his investigation without fear of violence, and thus the frisk for weapons might be equally necessary and reasonable whether or not carrying a concealed weapon violated any applicable state law. So long as the officer is entitled to make a forcible stop and has reason to believe that the suspect is armed and dangerous, he may conduct a weapons search limited in scope to this protective purpose. *Id.*, at 30.

Applying these principles to the present case we believe that Sgt. Connolly acted justifiably in responding to his informant's tip. The informant was known to him personally and had provided him with information in the past. This is a stronger case than obtains in the case of an anonymous telephone tip. The informant here came forward personally to give information that was immediately verifiable at the scene. Indeed, under Connecticut law, the informant herself might have been subject to immediate arrest for making a false complaint had Sgt. Connolly's investigation proven the tip incorrect. Thus, while the Court's decisions indicate that this informant's unverified tip may have been insufficient for a narcotics arrest or search warrant, see, *e. g.*, *Spinelli v. United States*, 393 U.S. 410 (1969); *Aguilar v. Texas*, 378 U.S. 108 (1964), the information carried enough indicia of reliability to justify the officer's forcible stop of Williams.

Officer's Personal Observation vs. Information from Informant. In reaching this conclusion, we reject respondent's argument that reasonable cause for a stop and frisk can only be based on the officer's personal observation, rather than on information supplied by another person. Informants' tips, like all other clues and evidence coming to a policeman on the scene, may vary greatly in their value and reliability. One simple rule will not cover every situation. Some tips, completely lacking in indicia of reliability, would either warrant no police response or require further investigation before a forcible stop of a suspect would be authorized. But in some situations—for example, when the victim of a street crime seeks immediate police aid and gives a description of his assailant, or when a credible informant warns of a specific impending crime—the subtleties of the hearsay rule should not thwart an appropriate police response.

While properly investigating the activity of a person who was reported to be carrying narcotics and a concealed weapon and who was sitting alone in a car in a high crime area at 2:15 in the morning. Sgt. Connolly had ample reason to fear for his safety. When Williams rolled down his window, rather than complying with the policeman's request to step out of the car so that his movements could more easily be seen, the revolver allegedly at Williams' waist became an even greater threat. Under these circumstances the policeman's action in reaching to the spot where the gun was thought to be hidden constituted a limited intrusion designed to insure his safety, and we conclude that it was reasonable. The loaded gun seized as a result of this intrusion was therefore admissible at Williams' trial. *Terry v. Ohio, supra*, at 30.

Probable Cause. Once Sgt. Connolly had found the gun precisely where the informant had predicted, probable cause existed to arrest Williams for unlawful possession of the weapon. Probable cause to arrest depends "upon whether, at the moment the arrest was made . . . the facts and circumstances within [the arresting officers'] knowledge and of which they had reasonably trustworthy information were sufficient to warrant a prudent man in believing that the [suspect] had committed or was committing an offense." *Beck v. Ohio*, 379 U.S. 89,

91 (1964). In the present case the policeman found Williams in possession of a gun in precisely the place predicted by the informant. This tended to corroborate the reliability of the informant's further report of narcotics, and together with the surrounding circumstances certainly suggested no lawful explanation for possession of the gun. Probable cause does not require the same type of specific evidence of each element of the offense as would be needed to support a conviction. See *Draper v. United States*, 358 U.S. 307, 311–312 (1959). Rather, the court will evaluate generally the circumstances at the time of the arrest to decide if the officer had probable cause for his action:

> In dealing with probable cause, however, as the very name implies, we deal with probabilities. These are not technical; they are the factual and practical considerations of everyday life on which reasonable and prudent men, not legal technicians, act. **Brinegar v. United States**, 338 U.S. 160, 175 (1949).

See also *id.*, at 177. Under the circumstances surrounding Williams' possession of the gun seized by Sgt. Connolly, the arrest on the weapons charge was supported by probable cause, and the search of his person and of the car incident to that arrest was lawful. See *Brinegar v. United States, supra*; *Carroll v. United States*, 267 U.S. 132 (1925). The fruits of the search were therefore properly admitted at Williams' trial, and the Court of Appeals erred in reaching a contrary conclusion.

Reversed.

CASE STUDY

Ted Steven Chimel v. California, 395 U.S. 752 (1969).

Mr. Justice Stewart delivered the opinion of the Court.*

This case raises basic questions concerning the permissible scope under the Fourth Amendment of a search incident to a lawful arrest.

Facts of Case. The relevant facts are essentially undisputed. Late in the afternoon of September 13, 1965, three police officers arrived at the Santa Ana, California, home of the petitioner with a warrant authorizing his arrest for the burglary of a coin shop. The officers knocked on the door, identified themselves to the petitioner's wife, and asked if they might come inside. She ushered them into the house, where they waited 10 or 15 minutes until the petitioner returned home from work. When the petitioner entered the house, one of the officers

*Extracts only, footnotes omitted. Headings added by authors for reader's convenience.

handed him the arrest warrant and asked for permission to "look a-round." The petitioner objected, but was advised that "on the basis of the lawful arrest," the officers would nonetheless conduct a search. No search warrant had been issued.

Accompanied by the petitioner's wife, the officers then looked through the entire three-bedroom house, including the attic, the garage, and a small workshop. In some rooms the search was relatively cursory. In the master bedroom and sewing room, however, the officers directed the petitioner's wife to open drawers and "to physically move contents of the drawers from side to side so that [they] might view any items that would have come from [the] burglary." After completing the search, they seized numerous items—primarily coins, but also several medals, tokens and a few other objects. The entire search took between 45 minutes and an hour.

At the petitioner's subsequent state trial on two charges of bur-glary, the items taken from his house were admitted into evidence against him, over his objection that they had been unconstitutionally seized. He was convicted, and the judgments of conviction were affirmed by both the California Court of Appeal, 61 Cal. Rptr. 714, and the California Supreme Court, 68 Cal. 2d 436, 439 P2d 333. Both courts accepted the petitioner's contention that the arrest warrant was invalid because the supporting affidavit was set out in conclusory terms, but held that since the arresting officers had procured the warrant "in good faith," and since in any event they had had sufficient information to constitute probable cause for the petitioner's arrest, that arrest had been lawful. From this conclusion the appellate courts went on to hold that the search of the petitioner's home had been justified, despite the absence of a search warrant, on the ground that it had been incident to a valid arrest. We granted certiorari in order to consider the petitioner's substantial constitutional claims. 393 U.S. 958, 21 L. Ed. 2d 372, 89 S. Ct. 404.

Without deciding the question, we proceed on the hypothesis that the California courts were correct in holding that the arrest of the petitioner was valid under the Constitution. This brings us directly to the question whether the warrantless search of the petitioner's entire house can be constitutionally justified as incident to that arrest. The decisions of this Court bearing upon that question have been far from consistent, as even the most cursory review makes evident.

Warrantless Search Incident to Lawful Arrest. Approval of a warrantless search incident to a lawful arrest seems first to have been articulated by the Court in 1914 as dictum in *Weeks v. United States*, 232 U.S. 383, 58 L. Ed. 652, 34 S. Ct. 341, L.R.A. 1915B 834, in which the Court stated:

What then is the present case? Before answering that inquiry specifically, it may be well by a process of exclusion to state what it is not. It is not an assertion of the right on the part of the Government, always recognized under English and American law, to search the person of the accused when legally arrested to discover and seize the fruits or evidences of crime. **Id.**, at 392, 58 L. Ed. at 655, L.R.A. 1915B 834.

That statement made no reference to any right to search the *place* where an arrest occurs, but was limited to a right to search the "person." Eleven years later the case of *Carroll v. United States*, 267 U.S. 132, 69 L. Ed. 543, 45 S. Ct. 280, 39 A.L.R. 790, brought the following embellishment of the Weeks statement:

When a man is legally arrested for an offense, whatever is found upon his person **or in his control** which it is unlawful for him to have and which may be used to prove the offense may be seized and held as evidence in the prosecution. **Id.**, at 158, 69 L. Ed. at 553, 39 A.L.R. 790. (Emphasis added.)

Still, that assertion too was far from a claim that the "place" where one is arrested may be searched so long as the arrest is valid. Without explanation, however, the principle emerged in expanded form a few months later in *Agnello v. United States*, 269 U.S. 20, 70 L. Ed. 145, 46 S. Ct. 4, 51 A.L.R. 409—although still by way of dictum:

The right without a search warrant contemporaneously to search persons lawfully arrested while committing crime and to search the place where the arrest is made in order to find and seize things connected with the crime as its fruits or as the means by which it was committed, as well as weapons and other things to effect an escape from custody, is not to be doubted. (Citations.)

And in *Marron v. United States*, 275 U.S. 192, 72 L. Ed. 231, 48 S. Ct. 74, two years later, the dictum of Agnello appeared to be the foundation of the Court's decision. In that case federal agents had secured a search warrant authorizing the seizure of liquor and certain articles used in its manufacture. When they arrived at the premises to be searched, they saw "that the place was used for retailing and drinking intoxicating liquors." *Id.*, at 194, 72 L. Ed. at 236. They proceeded to arrest the person in charge and to execute the warrant. In searching a closet for the items listed in the warrant they came across an incriminating ledger, concededly not covered by the warrant, which they also seized. The Court upheld the seizure of the ledger by holding that since the agents had made a lawful arrest, "[t]hey had a right without a warrant contemporaneously to search the place in order to find and seize the things used to carry on the criminal enterprise." *Id.*, at 199, 72 L. Ed. at 238.

That the *Marron* opinion did not mean all that it seemed to say became evident, however, a few years later in *Go-Bart Importing Co. v. United States,* 282 U.S. 344, 75 L. Ed. 374, 51 S. Ct. 153, and *United States v. Lefkowitz,* 285 U.S. 452, 76 L. Ed. 877, 52 S. Ct. 420, 82 A.L.R. 775. In each of those cases the opinion of the Court was written by Mr. Justice Butler, the author of the opinion in *Marron.* In *Go-Bart,* agents had searched the office of persons whom they had lawfully arrested, and had taken several papers from a desk, a safe, and other parts of the office. The Court noted that no crime had been committed in the agents' presence, and that although the agent in charge "had an abundance of information and time to swear out a valid [search] warrant, he failed to do so." 282 U.S., at 358, 75 L. Ed. at 383. In holding the search and seizure unlawful, the Court stated:

> Plainly the case before us is essentially different from **Marron v. United States,** 275 U.S. 192 [72 L. Ed. 231, 48 S. Ct. 74]. There, officers executing a valid search warrant for intoxicating liquors found and arrested one Birdsall who in pursuance of a conspiracy was actually engaged in running a saloon. As an incident to the arrest they seized a ledger in a closet where the liquor or some of it was kept and some bills beside the cash register. These things were visible and accessible and in the offender's immediate custody. There was no threat of force or general search or rummaging of the place. 282 U.S., at 358, 75 L. Ed. at 383.

This limited characterization of *Marron* was reiterated in *Lefkowitz,* a case in which the Court held unlawful a search of desk drawers and a cabinet despite the fact that the search had accompanied a lawful arrest. 285 U.S., at 465, 76 L. Ed. at 882, 82 A.L.R. 775.

The limiting views expressed in *Go-Bart* and *Lefkowitz* were thrown to the winds, however, in *Harris v. United States,* 331 U.S. 145, 91 L. Ed. 1399, 67 S. Ct. 1098, decided in 1947. In that case, officers had obtained a warrant for Harris' arrest on the basis of his alleged involvement with the cashing and interstate transportation of a forged check. He was arrested in the living room of his four-room apartment, and in an attempt to recover two canceled checks thought to have been used in effecting the forgery, the officers undertook a thorough search of the entire apartment. Inside a desk drawer they found a sealed envelope marked "George Harris, personal papers." The envelope, which was then torn open, was found to contain altered Selective Service documents, and those documents were used to secure Harris' conviction for violating the Selective Training and Service Act of 1940. The Court rejected Harris' Fourth Amendment claim, sustaining the search as "incident to arrest." *Id.,* at 151, 91 L. Ed. at 1406.

Search Warrants. Only a year after Harris, however, the pendulum swung again. In *Trupiano v. United States*, 334 U.S. 699, 92 L. Ed. 1663, 68 S. Ct. 1229, agents raided the site of an illicit distillery, saw one of several conspirators operating the still, and arrested him, contemporaneously "seiz[ing] the illicit distillery." *Id.*, at 702, 92 L. Ed. at 1667. The Court held that the arrest and others made subsequently had been valid, but that the unexplained failure of the agents to procure a search warrant—in spite of the fact that they had had more than enough time before the raid to do so—rendered the search unlawful. The opinion stated:

> It is a cardinal rule that, in seizing goods and articles, law enforcement agents must secure and use search warrants wherever reasonably practicable. . . . This rule rests upon the desirability of having magistrates rather than police officers determine when searches and seizures are permissible and what limitations should be placed upon such activities. . . . To provide the necessary security against unreasonable intrusions upon the private lives of individuals, the framers of the Fourth Amendment required adherence to judicial processes wherever possible. And subsequent history has confirmed the wisdom of that requirement. . . .
>
> A search or seizure without a warrant as an incident to a lawful arrest has always been considered to be a strictly limited right. It grows out of the inherent necessities of the situation at the time of the arrest. But there must be something more in the way of necessity than merely a lawful arrest. *Id.*, at 705, 708, 92 L. Ed. at 1669, 1671.

In 1950, two years after *Trupiano*, came **United States v. Rabinowitz**, 339 U.S. 56, 94 L. Ed. 653, 70 S. Ct. 430, the decision upon which California primarily relies in the case now before us. In *Rabinowitz*, federal authorities had been informed that the defendant was dealing in stamps bearing forged overprints. On the basis of that information they secured a warrant for his arrest, which they executed at his one-room business office. At the time of his arrest, the officers "searched the desk, safe, and file cabinets in the office for about an hour and a half," *id*, at 59, 94 L. Ed. at 656, and seized 573 stamps with forged overprints. The stamps were admitted into evidence at the defendant's trial, and this Court affirmed his conviction, rejecting the contention that the warrantless search had been unlawful. The Court held that the search in its entirety fell within the principle giving law enforcement authorities "the right 'to search the place where the arrest is made in order to find and seize things connected with the crime. . . .' " *Id.*, at 61, 94 L. Ed. at 658. Harris was regarded as "ample authority" for that conclusion. *Id.*, at 63, 94 L. Ed. at 658. The opinion rejected the rule of *Trupiano* that "in seizing goods and articles, law enforcement agents must secure and use search warrants wherever reasonably practicable." The test, said the Court, "is not whether it is reasonable to procure a search warrant, but whether the search was reasonable." *Id.*, at 66, 94 L. Ed. at 660.

Rabinowitz has come to stand for the proposition, inter alia, that a warrantless search "incident to a lawful arrest" may generally extend to the area that is considered to be in the "possession" or under the "control" of the person arrested. And it was on the basis of that proposition that the California courts upheld the search of the petitioner's entire house in this case. That doctrine, however, at least in the broad sense in which it was applied by the California courts in this case, can withstand neither historical nor rational analysis.

Even limited to its own facts, the *Rabinowitz* decision was, as we have seen, hardly founded on an unimpeachable line of authority. As Mr. Justice Frankfurter commented in dissent in that case, the "hint" contained in *Weeks* was, without persuasive justification, "loosely turned into dictum and finally elevated to a decision." 339 U.S., at 75, 94 L. Ed. at 665. And the approach taken in cases such as *Go-Bart, Lefkowitz,* and *Trupiano* was essentially disregarded by the *Rabinowitz* Court.

Fourth Amendment: Right to Privacy. Nor is the rationale by which the State seeks here to sustain the search of the petitioner's house supported by a reasoned view of the background and purpose of the Fourth Amendment. Mr. Justice Frankfurter wisely pointed out in his *Rabinowitz* dissent that the Amendment's proscription of "unreasonable searches and seizures" must be read in light of "the history that gave rise to the words"—a history of "abuses so deeply felt by the Colonies as to be one of the potent causes of the Revolution. . . ." 339 U.S., at 69, 94 L. Ed. at 662. The Amendment was in large part a reaction to the general warrants and warrantless searches that had so alienated the colonists and had helped speed the movement for independence. In the scheme of the Amendment, therefore, the requirement that "no Warrants shall issue, but upon probable cause," plays a crucial part. As the Court put it in *McDonald v. United States,* 335 U.S. 451, 93 L. Ed. 153, 69 S. Ct. 191:

> We are not dealing with formalities. The presence of a search warrant serves a high function. Absent some grave emergency, the Fourth Amendment has interposed a magistrate between the citizen and the police. This was done not to shield criminals nor to make the home a safe haven for illegal activities. It was done so that an objective mind might weigh the need to invade that privacy in order to enforce the law. The right of privacy was deemed too precious to entrust to the discretion of those whose job is the detection of crime and the arrest of criminals. . . . And so the Constitution requires a magistrate to pass on the desires of the police before they violate the privacy of the home. We cannot be true to that constitutional requirement and excuse the absence of a search warrant without a showing by those who seek exemp-

tion from the constitutional mandate that the exigencies of the situation made that course imperative. **Id.,** at 455–456, 93 L. Ed. at 158.

Even in the *Agnello* case the Court relied upon the rule that "belief, however well founded, that an article sought is concealed in a dwelling house furnishes no justification for a search of that place without a warrant. And such searches are held unlawful notwithstanding facts unquestionably showing probable cause." 269 U.S., at 33, 70 L. Ed. at 149, 51 A.L.R. 409. Clearly, the general requirement that a search warrant be obtained is not lightly to be dispensed with, and "the burden is on those seeking [an] exemption [from the requirement] to show the need for it. . . ." *United States v. Jeffers,* 342 U.S. 48, 51, 96 L. Ed. 59, 64, 72 S. Ct. 93.

Scope of Search. Only last Term in *Terry v. Ohio,* 392 U.S. 1, 20 L. Ed. 2d 889, 88 S. Ct. 1868, we emphasized that "the police must, whenever practicable, obtain advance judicial approval of searches and seizures through the warrant procedure," *id.,* at 20, 20 L. Ed. 2d at 905, and that "the scope of [a] search must be 'strictly tied to and justified by' the circumstances which rendered its initiation permissible." *Id.,* at 19, 20 L. Ed. 2d at 904. The search undertaken by the officer in that "stop and frisk" case was sustained under that test, because it was no more than a "protective . . . search for weapons." *Id.,* at 29, 20 L. Ed. 2d at 910. But in a companion case, *Sibron v. New York,* 392 U.S. 40, 20 L. Ed. 2d 917, 88 S. Ct. 1889, we applied the same standard to another set of facts and reached a contrary result, holding that a policeman's action in thrusting his hand into a suspect's pocket had been neither motivated by nor limited to the objective of protection. Rather, the search had been made in order to find narcotics, which were in fact found.

Area in Immediate Control of Arrestee. A similar analysis underlies the "search incident to arrest" principle, and marks its proper extent. When an arrest is made, it is reasonable for the arresting officer to search the person arrested in order to remove any weapons that the latter might seek to use in order to resist arrest or effect his escape. Otherwise the officer's safety might well be endangered, and the arrest itself frustrated. In addition, it is entirely reasonable for the arresting officer to search for and seize any evidence on the arrestee's person in order to prevent its concealment or destruction. And the area into which an arrestee might reach in order to grab a weapon or evidentiary items must, of course, be governed by a like rule. A gun on a table or in a drawer in front of one who is arrested can be as dangerous to the arresting officer as one concealed in the clothing of the person arrested. There is ample justification, therefore, for a search of the arrestee's person and the area "within his immediate control"—construing that phrase to mean the area from within which he might gain possession of a weapon or destructible evidence.

There is no comparable justification, however, for routinely searching any room other than that in which an arrest occurs—or, for that matter, for searching through all the desk drawers or other closed or concealed areas in that room itself. Such searches, in the absence of well-recognized exceptions, may be made only under the authority of a search warrant. The "adherence to judicial processes" mandated by the Fourth Amendment requires no less.

This is the principle that underlay our decision in *Preston v. United States*, 376 U.S. 364, 11 L. Ed. 2d 777, 84 S. Ct. 881. In that case three men had been arrested in a parked car, which had later been towed to a garage and searched by police. We held the search to have been unlawful under the Fourth Amendment, despite the contention that it had been incidental to a valid arrest. Our reasoning was straightforward:

> The rule allowing contemporaneous searches is justified, for example, by the need to seize weapons and other things which might be used to assault an officer or effect an escape, as well as by the need to prevent the destruction of evidence of the crime—things which might easily happen where the weapon or evidence is on the accused's person or under his immediate control. But these justifications are absent where a search is remote in time or place from the arrest. **Id.**, at 367, 11 L. Ed. 2d at 780.

The same basic principle was reflected in our opinion last Term in *Sibron*. That opinion dealt with *Peters v. New York*, 392 U.S. 40, 20 L. Ed. 2d 917, 88 S. Ct. 1889, as well as with *Sibron's* case, and *Peters* involved a search that we upheld as incident to a proper arrest. We sustained the search, however, only because its scope had been "reasonably limited" by the "need to seize weapons" and "to prevent the destruction of evidence," to which *Preston* had referred. We emphasized that the arresting officer "did not engage in an unrestrained and thoroughgoing examination of *Peters* and his personal effects. He seized him to cut short his flight, and he searched him primarily for weapons." 392 U.S. at 67, 20 L. Ed. 2d at 937.

It is argued in the present case that it is "reasonable" to search a man's house when he is arrested in it. But that argument is founded on little more than a subjective view regarding the acceptability of certain sorts of police conduct, and not on considerations relevant to Fourth Amendment interests. Under such an unconfined analysis, Fourth Amendment protection in this area would approach the evaporation point. It is not easy to explain why, for instance, it is less subjectively "reasonable" to search a man's house when he is arrested on his front lawn—or just down the street—than it is when he happens to be in the house at the time of arrest. As Mr. Justice Frankfurter put it:

Reasonableness of Search

> To say that the search must be reasonable is to require some criterion of reason. It is no guide at all either for a jury or for district judges or the police to say that an "unreasonable search" is forbidden—that the search must be reasonable. What is the test of reason which makes a search reasonable? The test is the reason underlying and expressed by the Fourth Amendment: the history and the experience which it embodies and the safeguards afforded by it against the evils to which it was a response. **United States v. Rabinowitz,** 339 U.S., at 83, 94 L. Ed. at 669 (dissenting opinion).

Thus, although "the recurring questions of the reasonableness of searches" depend upon "the facts and circumstances—the total atmosphere of the case," *id.*, at 63, 66, 94 L. Ed. at 659, 660 (opinion of the Court), those facts and circumstances must be viewed in the light of established Fourth Amendment principles.

It would be possible, of course, to draw a line between *Rabinowitz* and *Harris* on the one hand, and this case on the other. For *Rabinowitz* involved a single room, and *Harris* a four-room apartment, while in the case before us an entire house was searched. But such a distinction would be highly artificial. The rationale that allowed the searches and seizures in *Rabinowitz* and *Harris* would allow the searches and seizures in this case. No consideration relevant to the Fourth Amendment suggests any point of rational limitation, once the search is allowed to go beyond the area from which the person arrested might obtain weapons or evidentiary items. The only reasoned distinction is one between a search of the person arrested and the area within his reach on the one hand, and more extensive searches on the other.

The petitioner correctly points out that one result of decisions such as *Rabinowitz* and *Harris* is to give law enforcement officials the opportunity to engage in searches not justified by probable cause, by the simple expedient of arranging to arrest suspects at home rather than elsewhere. We do not suggest that the petitioner is necessarily correct in his assertion that such a strategy was utilized here, but the fact remains that had he been arrested earlier in the day, at his place of employment rather than at home, no search of his house could have been made without a search warrant. In any event, even apart from the possibility of such police tactics, the general point so forcefully made by Judge Learned Hand in *United States v. Kirschenblatt*, 16 F2d 202, remains:

After arresting a man in his house, to rummage at will among his papers in search of whatever will convict him, appears to us to be indistinguishable from what might be done under a general warrant; indeed, the warrant would give more protection, for presumably it must be issued by a magistrate. True, by hypothesis the power would not exist, if the supposed offender were not found on the premises; but it is small consolation to know that one's papers are safe only so long as one is not at home. **Id.,** at 203.

Rabinowitz and *Harris* have been the subject of critical commentary for many years, and have been relied upon less and less in our own decisions. It is time, for the reasons we have stated, to hold that on their own facts, and insofar as the principles they stand for are inconsistent with those that we have endorsed today, they are no longer to be followed.

Holding. Application of sound Fourth Amendment principles to the facts of this case produces a clear result. The search here went far beyond the petitioner's person and the area from within which he might have obtained either a weapon or something that could have been used as evidence against him. There was no constitutional justification, in the absence of a search warrant, for extending the search beyond that area. The scope of the search was, therefore, "unreasonable" under the Fourth and Fourteenth Amendments, and the petitioner's conviction cannot stand.

Reversed.

CASE STUDY

United States v. Willie Robinson, Jr., 414 U.S. 218 (1973).

Mr. Justice Rehnquist delivered the opinion of the Court.*

Respondent Robinson was convicted in United States District Court for the District of Columbia of the possession and facilitation of concealment of heroin in violation of 26 U.S.C. § 4704(a) (1964 ed.), and 21 U.S.C. § 174 (1964 ed.). He was sentenced to concurrent terms of imprisonment for these offenses. On his appeal to the Court of Appeals for the District of Columbia Circuit, that court first remanded the case to the District Court for evidentiary hearing concerning the scope of the search of respondent's person which had occurred at the time of his arrest. *United States v. Robinson,* 145 U.S.App. D.C. 46, 447 F.2d 1215 (1971). The District Court made findings of fact and conclusions

*Footnotes omitted. Headings added by authors for reader's convenience.

of law adverse to respondent, and he again appealed. This time the Court of Appeals *en banc* reversed the judgment of conviction, holding that the heroin introduced in evidence against respondent had been obtained as a result of a search which violated the Fourth Amendment to the United States Constitution.

Facts of Case. On April 23, 1968, at approximately 11 o'clock P.M., Officer Richard Jenks, a 15-year veteran of the District of Columbia Metropolitan Police Department, observed the respondent driving a 1965 Cadillac near the intersection of 8th and C Streets, Southeast, in the District of Columbia. Jenks, as a result of previous investigation following a check of respondent's operator's permit four days earlier, determined there was reason to believe that respondent was operating a motor vehicle after the revocation of his operator's permit. This is an offense defined by statute in the District of Columbia which carries a mandatory minimum jail term, a mandatory minimum fine, or both. 40 D.C. Code § 302(d).

Jenks signaled respondent to stop the automobile, which respondent did, and all three of the occupants emerged from the car. At that point Jenks informed respondent that he was under arrest for "operating after revocation and obtaining a permit by misrepresentation." It was assumed by the majority of the Court of Appeals, and is conceded by the respondent here, that Jenks had probable cause to arrest respondent, and that he effected a full custody arrest.

In accordance with procedures prescribed in Police Department instructions, Jenks then began to search respondent. He explained at a subsequent hearing that he was "face to face" with the respondent, and "placed [his] hands on [the respondent], my right hand to his left breast like this (demonstrating) and proceeded to pat him down thus (with the right hand)." During this patdown, Jenks felt an object in the left breast pocket of the heavy coat respondent was wearing, but testified that he "couldn't tell what it was" and also that he "couldn't actually tell the size of it." Jenks then reached into the pocket and pulled out the object, which turned out to be a "crumpled up cigarette package." Jenks testified that at this point he still did not know what was in the package:

As I felt the package I could feel objects in the package but I couldn't tell what they were. . . . I knew they weren't cigarettes.

The officer then opened the cigarette pack and found 14 gelatin capsules of white powder which he thought to be, and which later analysis proved to be, heroin. Jenks then continued his search of respondent to completion, feeling around his waist and trouser legs, and examining the remaining pockets. The heroin seized from the respondent was admitted into evidence at the trial which resulted in his conviction in the District Court.

Warrantless Search Incident to Lawful Arrest. The opinion for the plurality judges of the Court of Appeals, written by Judge Wright, the concurring opinion of Judge Bazelon, and the opinion for the dissenting judges, written by Judge Wilkey, gave careful and comprehensive treatment to the authority of a police officer to search the person of one who has been validly arrested and taken into custody. We conclude that the search conducted by Jenks in this case did not offend the limits imposed by the Fourth Amendment, and we therefore reverse the judgment of the Court of Appeals.

I.

It is well settled that a search incident to a lawful arrest is a traditional exception to the warrant requirement of the Fourth Amendment. This general exception has historically been formulated into two distinct propositions. The first is that a search may be made of the *person* of the arrestee by virtue of the lawful arrest. The second is that a search may be made of the area within the control of the arrestee.

Examination of this Court's decisions in the area show that these two propositions have been treated quite differently. The validity of the search of a person incident to a lawful arrest has been regarded as settled from its first enunciation, and has remained virtually unchallenged until the present case. The validity of the second proposition, while likewise conceded in principle, has been subject to differing interpretations as to the extent of the area which may be searched.

Because the rule requiring exclusion of evidence obtained in violation of the Fourth Amendment was first enunciated in *Weeks v. United States*, 232 U.S. 383, 34 S. Ct. 341, 58 L. Ed. 652 (1914), it is understandable that virtually all of this Court's search and seizure law has been developed since that time. In *Weeks*, the Court made clear its recognition of the validity of a search incident to a lawful arrest:

> What then is the present case? Before answering that inquiry specifically, it may be well by a process of exclusion to state what it is not. It is not an assertion of the right on the part of the Government, always recognized under English and American law, to search the person of the accused when legally arrested to discover and seize the fruits or evidences of crime. This right has been uniformly maintained in many cases. 1 Bishop on Criminal Procedure, § 211; Wharton, Criminal Plead. and Practice, 8th ed., § 60; **Dillon v. O'Brien and Davis,** 16 Cox C.C. 245. 232 U.S., at 392, 34 S. Ct. at 344.

Agnello v. United States, 269 U.S. 20, 46 S. Ct. 4, 70 L. Ed. 145 (1925), decided 11 years after *Weeks,* repeats the categorical recognition of the validity of a search incident to lawful arrest:

> The right without a search warrant contemporaneously to search persons lawfully arrested while committing crime and to search the place where the arrest is made in order to find and seize things connected with the crime as well as weapons and other things to effect an escape from custody, is not to be doubted. **Id.,** at 30, 46 S. Ct. at 5.

Throughout the series of cases in which the Court has addressed the second proposition relating to a search incident to a lawful arrest—the permissible area beyond the person of the arrestee which such a search may cover—no doubt has been expressed as to the unqualified authority of the arresting authority to search the person of the arrestee. (Citations.)

In *Chimel,* where the Court overruled *Rabinowitz* and *Harris* as to the area of permissible search incident to a lawful arrest, full recognition was again given to the authority to search the person of the arrestee:

> When an arrest is made, it is reasonable for the arresting officer to search the person arrested in order to remove any weapons that the latter might seek to use in order to resist arrest or effect his escape. Otherwise, the officer's safety might well be endangered, and the arrest itself frustrated. In addition, it is entirely reasonable for the arresting officer to search for and seize any evidence on the arrestee's person in order to prevent its concealment or destruction. 395 U.S., at 762–763, 89 S. Ct. at 2040.

Three years after the decision in *Chimel, supra,* we upheld the validity of a search in which heroin had been taken from the person of the defendant, after his arrest on a weapons charge, in *Adams v. Williams,* 407 U.S. 143, 92 S. Ct. 1921, 32 L. Ed. 2d 612 (1972), saying:

> Under the circumstances surrounding Williams' possession of the gun seized by Sgt. Connolly, the arrest on the weapons charge was supported by probable cause, and the search of his person and of the car incident to that arrest was lawful. **Id.,** at 149, 92 S. Ct. at 1925.

Last Term in *Cupp v. Murphy,* 412 U.S. 291, 295, 93 S. Ct. 2000, 2003, 36 L. Ed. 2d 900 (1973), we again reaffirmed the traditional statement of the authority to search incident to a valid arrest.

Thus the broadly stated rule, and the reasons for it, have been repeatedly affirmed in the decisions of this Court since *Weeks v. United States* nearly 60 years ago. Since the statements in the cases speak not simply in terms of an exception to the warrant requirement, but in terms of an affirmative authority to search, they clearly imply that such searches also meet the Fourth Amendment's requirement of reasonableness.

II.

Limited Protective Search for Weapons vs. Search Incident to Lawful Arrest. In its decision of this case, the majority of the Court of Appeals decided that even after a police officer lawfully places a suspect under arrest for the purpose of taking him into custody, he may not ordinarily proceed to fully search the prisoner. He must instead conduct a limited frisk of the outer clothing and remove such weapons that he may, as a result of that limited frisk, reasonably believe the suspect has in his possession. While recognizing that *Terry v. Ohio*, 392 U.S. 1, 88 S. Ct. 1868, 20 L. Ed. 2d 889 (1968), dealt with a permissible "frisk" incident to an investigative stop based on less than probable cause to arrest, the Court of Appeals felt that the principles of that case should be carried over to this probable cause arrest for driving while one's license is revoked. Since there would be no further evidence of such a crime to be obtained in a search of the arrestee, the Court held that only a search for weapons could be justified.

Terry v. Ohio, supra, did not involve an arrest for probable cause, and it made quite clear that the "protective frisk" for weapons which it approved might be conducted without probable cause. 392 U.S., at 21–22, 24–25, 88 S. Ct. at 1879–1880, 1881–1882. The Court's opinion explicitly recognized that there is a "distinction in purpose, character, and extent between a search incident to an arrest and a limited search for weapons":

> The former, although justified in part by the acknowledged necessity to protect the arresting officer from assault with a concealed weapon, **Preston v. United States,** 376 U.S. 364, 367 [84 S. Ct. 881, 883, 11 L. Ed.2d 777] (1964), is also justified on other grounds, **ibid.**, and can therefore involve a relatively extensive exploration of the person. A search for weapons in the absence of probable cause to arrest, however, must, like any other search, be strictly circumscribed by the exigencies which justify its initiation. **Warden v. Hayden,** 387 U.S. 294, 310 [87 S. Ct. 1642, 1652, 18 L. Ed.2d 782] (1967) (Mr. Justice Fortas, concurring). Thus it must be limited to that which is necessary for the discovery of weapons which might be used to harm the officer or others nearby, and may realistically be characterized as something less than a "full" search even though it remains a serious intrusion. . . .
>
> An arrest is a wholly different type of intrusion upon the individual freedom from a limited search for weapons, and the interests each is designed to serve are likewise quite different. An arrest is the initial stage of a criminal

prosecution. It is intended to vindicate society's interest in having its laws obeyed, and it is inevitably accompanied by future interference with the individual's freedom of movement, whether or not trial or conviction ultimately follows. The protective search for weapons, on the other hand, constitutes a brief, though far from inconsiderable, intrusion upon the sanctity of the person. 392 U.S., at 25–26, 88 S. Ct. at 1882.

Terry, therefore, affords no basis to carry over to a probable cause arrest the limitations this Court placed on a stop-and-frisk search permissible without probable cause.

The Court of Appeals also relied on language in *Peters v. New York,* 392 U.S. 40, at 66, 88 S. Ct. 1889, at 1904, 20 L. Ed. 2d 917, a companion case to *Terry.* There the Court held that the police officer had authority to search Peters because he had probable cause to arrest him, and went on to say:

> . . . the incident search was obviously justified "by the need to seize weapons and other things which might be used to assault an officer or effect an escape, as well as by the need to prevent the destruction of evidence of the crime." **Preston v. United States,** 376 U.S. 364, 367 [84 S. Ct. 881, 11 L. Ed.2d 777] (1964). Moreover, it was reasonably limited in scope by these purposes. Officer Laskey did not engage in an unrestrained and thorough-going examination of Peters and his personal effects, 392 U.S., at 67, 88, S. Ct. at 1905.

It is of course possible to read the second sentence from this quotation as imposing a novel limitation on the established doctrine set forth in the first sentence. It is also possible to read it as did Mr. Justice Harlan in his concurring opinion:

> The second possible source of confusion is the Court's statement that "Officer Laskey did not engage in an unrestrained and thorough-going examination of Peters and his personal effects." Ante, at 1905. Since the Court found probable cause to arrest Peters, and since an officer arresting on probable cause is entitled to make a very full incident search, I assume that this is merely a factual observation. As a factual matter, I agree with it. 392 U.S., at 77, 88 S. Ct. at 1909.

We do not believe that the Court in *Peters* intended in one unexplained and unelaborated sentence to impose a novel and far reaching limitation on the authority to search the person of an arrestee incident to his lawful arrest. While the language from *Peters* was quoted with approval in *Chimel v. California, supra,* 395 U.S., at 764, 89 S. Ct. at 2040, it is preceded by a full exposition of the traditional and unqualified authority of the arresting officer to search the arrestee's person. 395 U.S., at 763, 89 S. Ct. at 2040. We do not believe that either *Terry* or *Peters,* when considered in the light of the previously discussed statements of this Court, justified the sort of limitation upon that authority which the Court of Appeals fashioned in this case.

III.

Virtually all of the statements of this Court affirming the existence of an unqualified authority to search incident to a lawful arrest are dicta. We would not therefore be foreclosed by principles of *stare decisis* from further examination into history and practice in order to see whether the sort of qualifications imposed by the Court of Appeals in this case were in fact intended by the Framers of the Fourth Amendment or recognized in cases decided prior to *Weeks*. Unfortunately such authorities as exist are sparse. Such common-law treatises as Blackstone's Commentaries and Holmes' Common Law are simply silent on the subject. Pollock and Maitland, in their History of English Law, describe the law of arrest as "rough and rude" before the time of Edward the First, but do not address the authority to search incident to arrest. II Pollock and Maitland, at 582.

The issue was apparently litigated in the English courts in *Dillon v. O'Brien*, 16 Cox C.C. 245 (Exch. Ireland, 1887), cited in *Weeks v. United States, supra*. There Baron Palles said:

> But the interest of the state in the person charged being brought to trial in due course necessarily extends, as well to the preservation of material evidence of his guilt or innocence, as to his custody for the purpose of trial. His custody is of no value if the law is powerless to prevent the abstraction or destruction of this evidence, without which a trial would be no more than an empty forum. But if there be a right to production or preservation of this evidence, I cannot see how it can be enforced otherwise than by capture. 16 Cox C.C. 245, 250.

Spalding v. Preston, 21 Vt. 9 (1848), represents an early holding in this country that evidence may be seized from one who is lawfully arrested. In *Closson v. Morrison*, 47 N.H. 482, 484 (1867), the Court made the following statement:

> We think that an officer would also be justified in taking from a person whom he has arrested for crime, any deadly weapon he might find upon him, such as a revolver, a dirk, a knife, a sword cane, a slung shot, or a club, though it had not been used or intended to be used in the commission of the offense for which the prisoner had been arrested, and even though no threats of violence towards the officer had been made. A due regard for his own safety on the part of the officer, and also for the public safety, would justify a sufficient search to ascertain if such weapons were carried on the person of the prisoner, or were in his possession, and if found, to seize and hold them until the

prisoner should be discharged, or until they can otherwise be properly disposed of. **Spalding v. Preston**, 21 Vt. 9, 16.

So we think it might be with money or other articles of value, found upon the prisoner, by means of which, if left in his possession, he might procure his escape, or obtain tools, or implements, or weapons with which to effect his escape. We think the officer arresting a man for crime, not only may, but frequently should, make such searches and seizures; then in many cases they might be reasonable and proper, and courts would hold him harmless for so doing, when he acts in good faith, and from a regard to his own or the public safety, or the security of his prisoner. 47 N.H., at 484–485.

Similarly in *Holker v. Hennessey*, 141 Mo. 527, 42 S.W. 1090 (1897), the Supreme Court of Missouri says:

Generally speaking, in the absence of a statute, an officer has no right to take any property from the person of the prisoner except such as may afford evidence of the crime charged, or means of identifying the criminal, or may be helpful in making an escape. **Id.**, at 539, 42 S.W. at 1093.

Then Chief Judge Cardozo of the New York Court of Appeals summarized his understanding of the historical basis for the authority to search incident to arrest in these words:

The basic principle is this: Search of the person is unlawful when the seizure of the body is a trespass, and the purpose of the search is to discover grounds as yet unknown for arrest or accusation [citation omitted]. Search of the person becomes lawful when grounds for arrest and accusation have been discovered, and the law is in the act of subjecting the body of the accused to its physical dominion.

The distinction may seem subtle, but in truth it is founded in shrewd appreciation of the necessities of government. We are not to strain an immunity to the point at which human nature rebels against honoring it in conduct. The peace officer empowered to arrest must be empowered to disarm. If he may disarm, he may search, lest a weapon be concealed. The search being lawful, he retains what he finds if connected with the crime. **People v. Chiagles**, 237 N.Y. 193, 197, 142 N.E. 583, 584 (1923).

While these earlier authorities are sketchy, they tend to support the broad statement of the authority to search incident to arrest found in the successive decisions of this Court, rather than the restrictive one which was applied by the Court of Appeals in this case. The scarcity of case law before *Weeks* is doubtless due in part to the fact that the exclusionary rule there enunciated had been first adopted only 11 years earlier in Iowa; but it would seem to be also due in part to the fact that the issue was regarded as well-settled.

The Court of Appeals in effect determined that the *only* reason
supporting the authority for a *full* search incident to lawful arrest was
the possibility of discovery of evidence or fruits. Concluding that there
could be no evidence or fruits in the case of an offense such as that with
which respondent was charged, it held that any protective search would
have to be limited by the conditions laid down in *Terry* for a search
upon less than probable cause to arrest. Quite apart from the fact that
Terry clearly recognized the distinction between the two types of
searches, and that a different rule governed one than governed the
other, we find additional reason to disagree with the Court of Appeals.

The justification or reason for the authority to search incident to a
lawful arrest rests quite as much on the need to disarm the suspect in
order to take him into custody as it does on the need to preserve evidence on his person for later use at trial. *Agnello v. United States, supra;
Abel v. United States,* 362 U.S. 217, 80 S. Ct. 683, 4 L. Ed. 2d 668
(1960). The standards traditionally governing a search incident to lawful arrest are not, therefore, commuted to the stricter *Terry* standards
by the absence of probable fruits or further evidence of the particular
crime for which the arrest is made.

*No Exception for Arrests in Traffic Cases; All Custodial Arrests
Alike.*   Nor are we inclined, on the basis of what seems to us to be a
rather speculative judgment, to qualify the breadth of the general authority to search incident to a lawful custodial arrest on an assumption
that persons arrested for the offense of driving while their license has
been revoked are less likely to be possessed of dangerous weapons than
are those arrested for other crimes. It is scarcely open to doubt that the
danger to an officer is far greater in the case of the extended exposure
which follows the taking of a suspect into custody and transporting
him to the police station than in the case of the relatively fleeting contact resulting from the typical *Terry*-type stop. This is an adequate
basis for treating all custodial arrests alike for purposes of search justification.

*Ad hoc Judgment; Reasonableness of Search Incident to Lawful
Arrest.*   But quite apart from these distinctions, our more fundamental
disagreement with the Court of Appeals arises from its suggestion that
there must be litigated in each case the issue of whether or not there
was present one of the reasons supporting the authority for a search of
the person incident to a lawful arrest. We do not think the long line of
authorities of this Court dating back to *Weeks,* nor what we can glean
from the history of practice in this country and in England, requires
such a case by case adjudication. A police officer's determination as to
how and where to search the person of a suspect whom he has arrested
is necessarily a quick *ad hoc* judgment which the Fourth Amendment

does not require to be broken down in each instance into an analysis of each step in the search. The authority to search the person incident to a lawful custodial arrest, while based upon the need to disarm and to discover evidence, does not depend on what a court may later decide was the probability in a particular arrest situation that weapons or evidence would in fact be found upon the person of the suspect. A custodial arrest of a suspect based on probable cause is a reasonable intrusion under the Fourth Amendment; that intrusion being lawful, a search incident to the arrest requires no additional justification. It is the fact of the lawful custodial arrest which establishes the authority to search, and we hold that in the case of a lawful custodial arrest a full search of the person is not only an exception to the warrant requirement of the Fourth Amendment, but is also a "reasonable" search under that Amendment.

IV

Holding. The search of respondent's person conducted by Officer Jenks in this case and the seizure from him of the heroin, were permissible under established Fourth Amendment law. While thorough, the search partook of none of the extreme or patently abusive characteristics which were held to violate the Due Process Clause of the Fourteenth Amendment in *Rochin v. California,* 342 U.S. 165, 72 S. Ct. 205, 96 L. Ed. 183 (1952). Since it is the fact of custodial arrest which gives rise to the authority to search, it is of no moment that Jenks did not indicate any subjective fear of the respondent or that he did not himself suspect that respondent was armed. Having in the course of a lawful search come upon the crumpled package of cigarettes, he was entitled to inspect it; and when his inspection revealed the heroin capsules, he was entitled to seize them as "fruits; instrumentalities, or contraband" probative of criminal conduct. *Harris v. United States, supra,* 331 U.S., at 154–155, 67 S. Ct. at 1103–1104; *Warden v. Hayden,* 387 U.S. 294, 299, 307, 87 S. Ct. 1642, 1646, 1650 (1967); *Adams v. Williams, supra,* 407 U.S., at 149, 92 S. Ct. at 1924. The judgment of the Court of Appeals holding otherwise is reversed.

Reversed.

Syllabus*

Having, as a result of a previous check of respondent's operator's permit, probable cause to arrest respondent for driving while his license was revoked, a police officer made a full-custody arrest of respondent

*The syllabus constitutes no part of the opinion of the Court.

for such offense. In accordance with prescribed procedures, the officer made a search of respondent's person, in the course of which he found in an inside coat pocket a cigarette package containing heroin. The heroin was admitted into evidence at the District Court trial, which resulted in respondent's conviction for a drug offense. The Court of Appeals reversed on the ground that the heroin had been obtained as a result of a search in violation of the Fourth Amendment. *Held*: In the case of a lawful custodial arrest a full search of the person is not only an exception to the warrant requirement of the Fourth Amendment, but is also a "reasonable" search under that Amendment. Pp. 471–477.**

1.   A search incident to a valid arrest is not limited to a frisk of the suspect's outer clothing and removal of such weapons as the arresting officer may, as a result of such frisk, reasonably believe the suspect has in his possession, and the absence of probable fruits or further evidence of the particular crime for which the arrest is made does not narrow the standards applicable to such a search. *Terry v. Ohio*, 392 U.S. 1, 88 S. Ct. 1868, 20 L. Ed. 2d 889 distinguished. Pp. 473–474; 476–477.

2.   A custodial arrest of a suspect based on probable cause is a reasonable intrusion under the Fourth Amendment and requires no additional justification, such as the probability in a particular arrest situation that weapons or evidence would in fact be found upon the suspect's person; and whether or not there was present one of the reasons supporting the authority for a search of the person incident to a lawful arrest need not be litigated in each case. Pp. 476–477.

3.   Since the custodial arrest here gave rise to the authority to search, it is immaterial that the arresting officer did not fear the respondent or suspect that he was armed. P. 477.

CASE STUDY

James E. Gustafson v. Florida, 414 U.S. 260 (1973).

Mr. Justice Rehnquist delivered the opinion of the Court.*

Facts of Case.   Petitioner James Gustafson was convicted in a Florida trial court for unlawful possession of marijuana. At his trial the State introduced into evidence marijuana which had been seized from him during a search incident to his arrest on a charge of driving without an operator's license. The District Court of Appeal of Florida, Fourth Dis-

---

**Page numbers in the opinion.
*Footnotes omitted. Headings added by authors for reader's convenience.

trict, reversed petitioner's conviction, holding that the search which had led to the discovery of the marijuana was unreasonable under the Fourth and Fourteenth Amendments. *Gustafson v. State*, 243 So. 2d 615 (4th D.C.A. Fla. 1971). The Supreme Court of Florida in turn reversed that decision, *State v. Gustafson*, 258 So. 2d 1 (Fla. 1972), and petitioner sought certiorari in this Court. We granted certiorari.

For the reasons set forth below, we affirm the judgment of the Supreme Court of Florida.

At approximately 2 A.M., on January 12, 1969, Lieutenant Paul R. Smith, a uniformed municipal police officer of Eau Gallie, Florida, was on a routine patrol in an unmarked squad car when he observed a 1953 white Cadillac, bearing New York license plates, driving south through the town. Smith observed the automobile weave across the center line and back to the right side of the road "three or four" times. Smith testified that he observed the two occupants of the Cadillac look back; after they apparently saw the squad car, the car drove across the highway and behind a grocery store, and then headed south on another city street.

At that point Smith turned on his flashing light and pulled the Cadillac over to the side of the road. After stopping the vehicle, Smith asked petitioner, the driver, to produce his operator's license. Petitioner informed Smith that he was a student and that he had left his operator's license in his dormitory room in the neighboring city of Melbourne, Florida. Petitioner was then placed under arrest for failure to have his vehicle operator's license in his possession. It was conceded by the parties below and in this Court that the officer had probable cause to arrest upon learning that petitioner did not have his license in his possession, and that he took petitioner into custody in order to transport him to the stationhouse for further inquiry.

Smith then proceeded to search the petitioner's person. Smith testified that he patted down the clothing of the petitioner, "outside and inside, I checked the belt, the shirt pockets and all around the belt, completely around the inside." Upon completing his patdown, he testified, he placed his hand into the left front coat pocket of the coat petitioner was wearing. From that pocket he extracted a "long chain" and a Benson and Hedges cigarette box. Smith testified that he then "opened [the cigarette box] and it appeared there were marijuana cigarettes in the box. I had been shown this in training at the police department and these appeared to be marijuana to me."

I.

Petitioner urges that there could be no evidentiary purpose for the search conducted by Smith, and therefore the authority to search for weapons incident to a lawful arrest is controlled by the standards laid down in *Terry v. Ohio*, 392 U.S. 1 (1968). Petitioner contends that this case is different from *United States v. Robinson, ante,* p. 218, in that petitioner had experienced no previous encounters with the officer in this case, and the offense for which he was arrested was "benign or trivial in nature," carrying with it no mandatory minimum sentence as did the offense for which Robinson was arrested. Petitioner points out that here, unlike *Robinson,* there were no police regulations which required the officer to take petitioner into custody, nor were there police department policies requiring full scale body searches upon arrest in the field. Petitioner also points to the fact that here, as in *Robinson,* the officer expressed no fear for his own well-being or for that of others in dealing with the petitioner.

We have held today in **United States v. Robinson** that "it is the fact of the lawful arrest which establishes the authority to search, and . . . in the case of a lawful custodial arrest a full search of the person is not only an exception to the warrant requirement of the Fourth Amendment, but is also a 'reasonable' search under that Amendment." Our decision in *Robinson* indicates that the limitations placed by *Terry v. Ohio, supra,* on protective searches conducted in an investigatory stop situation based on less than probable cause are not to be carried over to searches made incident to lawful custodial arrests. We stated in *Robinson:*

> The justification or reason for the authority to search incident to a lawful arrest rests quite as much on the need to disarm the suspect in order to take him into custody as it does on the need to preserve evidence on his person for later use at trial. **Agnello v. United States, supra** [269 U.S. 20, 46 S. Ct. 4, 70 L. Ed. 145]; **Abel v. United States,** 362 U.S. 217, [80 S. Ct. 683, 4 L. Ed.2d 668] (1960). The standards traditionally governing the search incident to lawful arrest are not, therefore, commuted to stricter **Terry** standards by the absence of probable fruits or further evidence of the particular crime for which the arrest is made.

Neither *Chimel v. California,* 395 U.S. 752, 89 S. Ct. 2034, 23 L. Ed. 2d 685 (1969), nor *Peters v. New York,* 392 U.S. 40, 88 S. Ct. 1889, 20 L. Ed. 2d 917 (1968), relied upon by petitioner, purported to limit the traditional authority of the arresting officer to conduct a full search of the person of an arrestee incident to a lawful custodial arrest. *United States v. Robinson, ante,* at 225–226, 228–229. Indeed, as our decision in *Robinson* indicates, not only has this been established Fourth Amendment law since the decision in *Weeks v. United States,* 232 U.S. 383, 34 S. Ct. 341, 58 L. Ed. 652 (1914), but it was also the rule both at common law and in the early development of American law. *United States v. Robinson, ante,* at 230–233.

Warrantless Search Incident to Lawful Arrest. Though the officer here was not required to take the petitioner into custody by police regulations as he was in *Robinson,* and there did not exist a departmental policy establishing the conditions under which a full scale body search should be conducted, we do not find these differences determinative of the constitutional issue. *Id.,* at 223 n.2. It is sufficient that the officer had probable cause to arrest the petitioner and that he lawfully actuated the arrest, and placed the petitioner in custody. In addition, as our decision in *Robinson* makes clear, the arguable absence of "evidentiary" purpose for a search incident to a lawful arrest is not controlling. *Id.,* at 233. "The authority to search a person incident to a lawful custodial arrest, while based upon the need to disarm and to discover evidence, does not depend on what a court may later decide was the probability in a particular arrest situation that weapons or evidence would in fact be found upon the person of the suspect." *Id.,* at 235.

II.

Holding. We hold therefore that upon arresting petitioner for the offense of driving his automobile without a valid operator's license, and taking him into custody, Smith was entitled to make a full search of petitioner's person incident to that lawful arrest. Since it is the fact of custodial arrest which gives rise to the authority to search, it is of no moment that Smith did not indicate any subjective fear of the petitioner or that he did not himself suspect that the petitioner was armed. Having in the course of his lawful search come upon the box of cigarettes, Smith was entitled to inspect it; and when his inspection revealed the homemade cigarettes which he believed to contain an unlawful substance, he was entitled to seize them as "fruits, instrumentalities or contraband" probative of criminal conduct. *Harris v. United States,* 331 U.S. 145, 154–155, 67 S. Ct. 1098, 1103–1104, 91 L. Ed. 1399 (1947); *Warden v. Hayden,* 387 U.S. 294, 299, 307, 87 S. Ct. 1642, 1650, 18 L. Ed. 2d 782 (1967); *Adams v. Williams,* 407 U.S. 143, 149, 92 S. Ct. 1921, 1925, 32 L. Ed. 2d 612 (1972); *United States v. Robinson, ante,* at 236. The judgment of the Supreme Court of Florida is therefore affirmed.

Affirmed.

Mr. Justice Stewart, concurring.

It seems to me that a persuasive claim might have been made in this case that the custodial arrest of the petitioner for a minor traffic offense violated his rights under the Fourth and Fourteenth Amendments. But no such claim has been made. Instead, the petitioner has fully conceded the constitutional validity of his custodial arrest. That being so, it follows that the incidental search of his person was also constitutionally valid. To hold otherwise would, as the Court makes clear in this case, and in *United States v. Robinson, ante,* p. 218, mark an abrupt departure from settled constitutional precedent.

Syllabus

During the course of a patdown search of the person of petitioner, who had been arrested for not having his driver's license in his possession, the arresting officer seized marijuana cigarettes, for the unlawful possession of which petitioner was subsequently tried and convicted. The State Supreme Court upheld the conviction, concluding that the search leading to the discovery of the marijuana, which was used as evidence in petitioner's trial, was not unreasonable.

Held: The full search of the person of the suspect made incident to a lawful custodial arrest did not violate the Fourth and Fourteenth Amendments, *United States v. Robinson,* 414 U.S. 260, and it is of no constitutional significance that, contrary to the situation in *Robinson,* police regulations did not require that petitioner be taken into custody or establish the conditions under which a full-scale body search should be conducted, nor, as in *Robinson,* is it relevant that the arresting officer had no subjective fear of petitioner or suspect that he was armed, since it is the fact of custodial arrest which gives rise to the authority to search. Pp. 491–492**

CASE STUDY

Warden v. Hayden, 387 U.S. 294 (1967).

Opinion of the Court, delivered by Mr. Justice Brennan.*

We review in this case the validity of the proposition that there is under the Fourth Amendment a "distinction between merely evidentiary materials, on the one hand, which may not be seized either under the authority of a search warrant or during the course of a search incident to arrest, and on the other hand, those objects which may validly be seized including the instrumentalities and means by which a crime is committed, the fruits of crime such as stolen property, weapons by which escape of the person arrested might be effected, and property the possession of which is a crime."

Facts of Case.   A Maryland court sitting without a jury convicted respondent of armed robbery. Items of his clothing, a cap, jacket, and

*Footnotes omitted. Headings added by authors for reader's convenience.
**Pages in opinion.

trousers, among other things, were seized during a search of his home, and were admitted in evidence without objection. After unsuccessful state court proceedings, he sought and was denied federal habeas corpus relief in the District Court for Maryland. A divided panel of the Court of Appeals for the Fourth Circuit reversed. 363 F. 2d 647. The Court of Appeals believed that *Harris v. United States*, 331 U.S. 145, 154, sustained the validity of the search, but held that respondent was correct in his contention that the clothing seized was improperly admitted in evidence because the items had "evidential value only" and therefore were not lawfully subject to seizure. We granted certiorari. 385 U.S. 926. We reverse.

I.

About 8 A.M. on March 17, 1962, an armed robber entered the business premises of the Diamond Cab Company in Baltimore, Maryland. He took some $363 and ran. Two cab drivers in the vicinity, attracted by shouts of "Holdup," followed the man to 2111 Cocoa Lane. One driver notified the company dispatcher by radio that the man was a Negro about 5'8" tall, wearing a light cap and dark jacket, and that he had entered the house on Cocoa Lane. The dispatcher relayed the information to police who were proceeding to the scene of the robbery. Within minutes, police arrived at the house in a number of patrol cars. An officer knocked and announced their presence. Mrs. Hayden answered, and the officers told her they believed that a robber had entered the house, and asked to search the house. She offered no objection.

The officers spread out through the first and second floors and the cellar in search of the robber. Hayden was found in an upstairs bedroom feigning sleep. He was arrested when the officers on the first floor and in the cellar reported that no other man was in the house. Meanwhile an officer was attracted to an adjoining bathroom by the noise of running water, and discovered a shotgun and a pistol in a flush tank; another officer who, according to the District Court, "was searching the cellar for a man or the money" found in a washing machine a jacket and trousers of the type the fleeing man was said to have worn. A clip of ammunition for the pistol and a cap were found under the mattress of Hayden's bed, and ammunition for the shotgun was found in a bureau drawer in Hayden's room. All these items of evidence were introduced against respondent at his trial.

II.

Reasonableness of Search: "Hot Pursuit." We agree with the Court of Appeals that neither the entry without warrant to search for the robber, nor the search for him without warrant was invalid. Under the circumstances of this case, "the exigencies of the situation made that course imperative." *McDonald v. United States*, 335 U.S. 451, 456. The police were informed that an armed robbery had taken place, and that the suspect had entered 2111 Cocoa Lane less than five minutes before they reached it. They acted reasonably when they entered the house and began to search for a man of the description they had been given and for weapons which he had used in the robbery or might use against them. The Fourth Amendment does not require police officers to delay in the course of an investigation if to do so would gravely endanger their lives or the lives of others. Speed here was essential, and only a thorough search of the house for persons and weapons could have insured that Hayden was the only man present and that the police had control of all weapons which could be used against them or to effect an escape.

We do not rely upon *Harris v. United States, supra*, in sustaining the validity of the search. The principal issue in *Harris* was whether the search there could properly be regarded as incident to the lawful arrest, since Harris was in custody before the search was made and the evidence seized. Here, the seizures occurred prior to or immediately contemporaneous with Hayden's arrest, as part of an effort to find a suspected felon, armed, within the house into which he had run only minutes before the police arrived. The permissible scope of search must, therefore, at the least, be as broad as may reasonably be necessary to prevent the dangers that the suspect at large in the house may resist or escape.

It is argued that, while the weapons, ammunition, and cap may have been seized in the course of a search for weapons, the officer who seized the clothing was searching neither for the suspect nor for weapons when he looked into the washing machine in which he found the clothing. But even if we assume, although we do not decide, that the exigent circumstances in this case made lawful a search without warrant only for the suspect or his weapons, it cannot be said on this record that the officer who found the clothes in the washing machine was not searching for weapons. He testified that he was searching for the man or the money, but his failure to state explicitly that he was searching for weapons, in the absence of a specific question to that effect, can hardly be accorded controlling weight. He knew that the robber was armed and he did not know that some weapons had been found at the time he opened the machine. In these circumstances the inference that he was in fact also looking for weapons is fully justified.

III.

Question: "Mere Evidence." We come, then, to the question whether, even though the search was lawful, the Court of Appeals was correct in holding that the seizure and introduction of the items of clothing violated the Fourth Amendment because they are "mere evidence." The distinction made by some of our cases between seizure of items of evidential value only and seizure of instrumentalities, fruits, or contraband has been criticized by courts and commentators. The Court of Appeals, however, felt "obligated to adhere to it." 363 F. 2d, at 655. We today reject the distinction as based on premises no longer accepted as rules governing the application of the Fourth Amendment.

We have examined on many occasions the history and purposes of the Amendment. It was a reaction to the evils of the use of the general warrant in England and the writs of assistance in the Colonies, and was intended to protect against invasions of "the sanctity of a man's home and the privacies of life," *Boyd v. United States*, 116 U.S. 616, 630, from searches under indiscriminate, general authority. Protection of these interests was assured by prohibiting all "unreasonable" searches and seizures, and by requiring the use of warrants, which particularly describe "the place to be searched, and the persons or things to be seized," thereby interposing "a magistrate between the citizen and the police," *McDonald v. United States, supra*, 335 U.S., at 455.

Nothing in the language of the Fourth Amendment supports the distinction between "mere evidence" and instrumentalities, fruits of crime, or contraband. On its face, the provision assures the "right of the people to be secure in their persons, houses, papers, and effects, . . ." without regard to the use to which any of these things are applied. This "right of the people" is certainly unrelated to the "mere evidence" limitation. Privacy is disturbed no more by a search directed to a purely evidentiary object than it is by a search directed to an instrumentality, fruit, or contraband. A magistrate can intervene in both situations, and the requirements of probable cause and specificity can be preserved intact. Moreover, nothing in the nature of property seized as evidence renders it more private than property seized, for example, as an instrumentality; quite the opposite may be true. Indeed, the distinction is wholly irrational, since, depending on the circumstances, the same "papers and effects" may be "mere evidence" in one case and "instrumentality" in another. See Comment, 20 U. Chi. L. Rev. 319, 320–22 (1953).

Search Warrants. In *Gouled v. United States*, 255 U.S. 298, 309, the Court said that search warrants "may not be used as a means of gaining access to a man's house or office and papers solely for the purpose of making search to secure evidence to be used against him in a criminal or penal proceeding. . . ." The Court derived from *Boyd v. United States, supra*, the proposition that warrants "may be resorted to only when a primary right to such search and seizure may be found in the interest which the public or the complainant may have in the property to be seized, or in the right to the possession of it, or when a valid exercise of the police power renders possession of the property by the accused unlawful and provides that it may be taken," 255 U.S., at 309; that is, when the property is an instrumentality or fruit of crime, or contraband. Since it was "impossible to say, on the record . . . that the Government had any interest" in the papers involved "other than as evidence against the accused, . . ." "to permit them to be used in evidence would be, in effect, as ruled in the *Boyd Case*, to compel the defendant to become a witness against himself." *Id.*, at 311.

Nontestimonial Evidence. The items of clothing involved in this case are not "testimonial" or "communicative" in nature, and their introduction therefore did not compel respondent to become a witness against himself in violation of the Fifth Amendment. *Schmerber v. California*, 384 U.S. 757. This case thus does not require that we consider whether there are items of evidential value whose very nature precludes them from being the object of a reasonable search and seizure.

The Fourth Amendment ruling in *Gouled* was based upon the dual, related premises that historically the right to search for and seize property depended upon the assertion by the Government of a valid claim of superior interest, and that it was not enough that the purpose of the search and seizure was to obtain evidence to use in apprehending and convicting criminals. The common law of search and seizure after *Entick v. Carrington*, 19 How. St. Tr. 1029, reflected Lord Camden's view, derived no doubt from the political thought of his time, that the "great end, for which men entered into society, was to secure their property." *Id.*, at 1066. Warrants were "allowed only where the primary right to such a search and seizure is in the interest which the public or complainant may have in the property seized." Lasson, *The History and Development of the Fourth Amendment to the United States Constitution* 133–34. Thus stolen property—the fruits of crime—was always subject to seizure. And the power to search for stolen property was gradually extended to cover "any property which the private citizen was not permitted to possess," which included instrumentalities of crime (because of the early notion that items used in crime were forfeited to the State) and contraband. Kaplan, "Search and Seizure: A No-Man's Land in the Criminal Law," 49 Calif. L. Rev. 474, 475. No separate governmental interest in seizing evidence to apprehend and convict criminals was recognized, it was required that some property interest be asserted. The remedial structure also reflected these dual premises.Trespass, replevin, and the other means of redress for persons aggrieved by searches and seizures, depended upon proof of a superior property interest. And since a lawful seizure presupposed a superior claim, it was inconceivable that a person could recover property lawfully seized. As Lord Camden pointed out in *Entick v. Carrington, supra*, at 1066, a general warrant enabled "the party's own property [to be] seized before and without conviction, and he has no power to reclaim his goods, even after his innocence is cleared by acquittal."

Fourth Amendment Protection of Privacy, Not Property. The premise that property interests control the right of the Government to search and seize has been discredited. Searches and seizures may be "unreasonable" within the Fourth Amendment even though the Government asserts a superior property interest at common law. We have recognized that the principal object of the Fourth Amendment is the protection of privacy rather than property, and have increasingly discarded fictional and procedural barriers rested on property concepts. See *Jones v. United States,* 362 U.S. 257, 266; *Silverman v. United States,* 365 U.S. 505, 511. This shift in emphasis from property to privacy has come about through a subtle interplay of substantive and procedural reform. The remedial structure at the time even of *Weeks v. United States,* 232 U.S. 383, was arguably explainable in property terms. The Court held in *Weeks* that a defendant could petition *before* trial for the return of his illegally seized property, a proposition not necessarily inconsistent with *Adams v. New York,* 192 U.S. 585, which held in effect that the property issues involved in search and seizure are collateral to a criminal proceeding. The remedial structure finally escaped the bounds of common law property limitations in *Silverthorne Lumber Co. v. United States,* 251 U.S. 385, and *Gouled v. United States, supra,* when it became established that suppression might be sought during a criminal trial, and under circumstances which would not sustain an action in trespass or replevin. Recognition that the role of the Fourth Amendment was to protect against invasions of privacy demanded a remedy to condemn the seizure in *Silverthorne,* although no possible common law claim existed for the return of the copies made by the Government of the papers it had seized. The remedy of suppression, necessarily involving only the limited, functional consequence of excluding the evidence from trial, satisfied that demand.

The development of search and seizure law since *Silverthorne* and *Gouled* is replete with examples of the transformation in substantive law brought about through the interaction of the felt need to protect privacy from unreasonable invasions and the flexibility in rulemaking made possible by the remedy of exclusion. We have held, for example, that intangible as well as tangible evidence may be suppressed, *Wong Sun v. United States,* 371 U.S. 471, 485–86, and that an actual trespass under local property law is unnecessary to support a remedial violation of the Fourth Amendment, *Silverman v. United States, supra.* In determining whether someone is a "person aggrieved by an unlawful search and seizure" we have refused "to import into the law . . . subtle distinctions, developed and refined by the common law in evolving the body of private property law which, more than almost any other branch of law, has been shaped by distinctions whose validity is largely historical." *Jones v. United States, supra*, 362 U.S., at 266. And with particular relevance here, we have given recognition to the interest in privacy despite the complete absence of a property claim by suppressing the very items which at common law could be seized with impunity: stolen goods, *Henry v. United States*, 361 U.S. 98; instrumentalities, *Beck v. Ohio*, 379 U.S. 89; *McDonald v. United States, supra*; and contraband, *Trupiano v. United States*, 334 U.S. 699; *Aguilar v. Texas*, 378 U.S. 108.

Nexus: Seized Evidence and Criminal Conduct. The premise in *Gouled* that government may not seize evidence simply for the purpose of proving crime has likewise been discredited. The requirement that the Government assert in addition some property interest in material it seizes has long been a fiction, obscuring the reality that government has an interest in solving crime. *Schmerber* settled the proposition that it is reasonable, within the terms of the Fourth Amendment, to conduct otherwise permissible searches for the purpose of obtaining evidence which would aid in apprehending and convicting criminals. The requirements of the Fourth Amendment can secure the same protection of privacy whether the search is for "mere evidence" or for fruits, instrumentalities or contraband. There must, of course, be a nexus—automatically provided in the case of fruits, instrumentalities or contraband—between the item to be seized and criminal behavior. Thus in the case of "mere evidence," probable cause must be examined in terms of cause to believe that the evidence sought will aid in a particular apprehension or conviction. In so doing, consideration of police purposes will be required. *Cf. Kremen v. United States*, 353 U.S. 346. But no such problem is presented in this case. The clothes found in the washing machine matched the description of those worn by the robber and the police therefore could reasonably believe that the items would aid in the identification of the culprit.

The remedy of suppression, moreover, which made possible protection of privacy from unreasonable searches without regard to proof of a superior property interest, likewise provides the procedural device necessary for allowing otherwise permissible searches and seizures conducted solely to obtain evidence of crime. For just as the suppression of evidence does not entail a declaration of superior property interest in the person aggrieved, thereby enabling him to suppress evidence unlawfully seized despite his inability to demonstrate such an interest (as with fruits, instrumentalities, contraband), the refusal to suppress evidence carries no declaration of superior property interest in the State, and should thereby enable the State to introduce evidence lawfully seized despite its inability to demonstrate such an interest. And, unlike the situation at common law, the owner of property would not be rendered remediless if "mere evidence" could lawfully be seized to prove crime.

For just as the suppression of evidence does not in itself necessarily entitle the aggrieved person to its return (as, for example, contraband), the introduction of "mere evidence" does not in itself entitle the State to its retention. Where public officials "unlawfully seize *or hold* a citizen's realty or chattels, recoverable by appropriate action at law or in equity, . . ." the true owner may "bring his possessory action to reclaim that which is wrongfully withheld." *Land v. Dollar*, 330 U.S. 731, 738. (Emphasis added.) See *Burdeau v. McDowell*, 256 U.S. 465, 474.

The survival of the *Gouled* distinction is attributable more to chance than considered judgment. Legislation has helped perpetuate it. Thus, Congress has never authorized the issuance of search warrants for the seizure of mere evidence of crime. See *Davis v. United States*, 328 U.S. 582, 606 (dissenting opinion of Mr. Justice Frankfurter). Even in the Espionage Act of 1917, where Congress for the first time granted general authority for the issuance of search warrants, the authority was limited to fruits of crime, instrumentalities, and certain contraband. 40 Stat. 228. *Gouled* concluded, needlessly it appears, that the Constitution virtually limited searches and seizures to these categories. After *Gouled*, pressure to test this conclusion was slow to mount. Rule 41(b) of the Federal Rules of Criminal Procedure incorporated the *Gouled* categories as limitations on federal authorities to issue warrants, and *Mapp v. Ohio*, 367 U.S. 643, only recently made the "mere evidence" rule a problem in the state courts. Pressure against the rule in the federal courts has taken the form rather of broadening the categories of evidence subject to seizure, thereby creating considerable confusion in the law. See, e.g., Note, 54 Geo. L. J. 593, 607–21 (1966).

Holding. The rationale most frequently suggested for the rule preventing the seizure of evidence is that "limitations upon the fruit to be gathered tend to limit the quest itself." *United States v. Poller*, 43 F. 2d 911, 914 (C.A. 2d Cir. 1930). But privacy "would be just as well served by a restriction on search to the even-numbered days of the month. . . . And it would have the extra advantage of avoiding hair-splitting questions. . . ." Kaplan, *op. cit. supra*, at 479. The "mere evidence" limitation has spawned exceptions so numerous and confusion so great, in fact, that it is questionable whether it affords meaningful protection. But if its rejection does enlarge the area of permissible searches, the intrusions are nevertheless made after fulfilling the probable cause and particularity requirements of the Fourth Amendment and after the intervention of "a neutral and detached magistrate. . . ." *Johnson v. United States*, 333 U.S. 10, 14. The Fourth Amendment allows intrusions upon privacy under these circumstances, and there is no viable reason to distinguish intrusions to secure "mere evidence" from intrusions to secure fruits, instrumentalities, or contraband.

The judgment of the Court of Appeals is reversed.

Separate Opinions*

Mr. Justice Black and Mr. Justice Fortas concur in the result. Mr. Justice Fortas preparing a separate opinion. Mr. Justice Douglas dissents.

Opinion of Mr. Justice Fortas, with whom the Chief Justice joins, concurring.

While I agree that the Fourth Amendment should not be held to require exclusion from evidence of the clothing as well as weapons and ammunition found by the officers during the search, I cannot join in the majority's broad—and in my judgment, totally unnecessary—repudiation of the so-called "mere evidence" rule.

Reasonableness of Search: "Hot Pursuit." Our Constitution envisions that searches will ordinarily follow procurement by police of a valid search warrant. Such warrants are to issue only on probable cause, and must describe with particularity the persons or things to be seized. There are exceptions to this rule. Searches may be made incident to a lawful arrest, and—as today's decision indicates—in the course of "hot pursuit." But searches under each of these exceptions have, until today, been confined to those essential to fulfill the purpose of the exception: that is, we have refused to permit use of articles the seizure of which could not be strictly tied to and justified by the exigencies which excused the warrantless search. The use in evidence of weapons seized in a "hot pursuit" search or search incident to arrest satisfies this criterion because of the need to protect the arresting officers from weapons to which the suspect might resort. The search for and seizure of fruits are, of course, justifiable on independent grounds: The fruits are an object of the pursuit or arrest of the suspect, and should be restored to their true owner. The seizure of contraband has been justified on the ground that the suspect has not even a bare possessory right to contraband. See, *e. g.*, *Boyd v. United States*, 116 U.S. 616, 623–24 (1886); *United States v. Kirschenblatt*, 16 F. 2d 202, 203 (C. A. 2d Cir. 1926) (L. Hand, J.).

Similarly, we have forbidden the use of articles seized in such a search unless obtained from the person of the suspect or from the immediate vicinity. Since a warrantless search is justified only as incident to an arrest or "hot pursuit," this Court and others have held that its scope does not include permission to search the entire building in which the arrest occurs, or to rummage through locked drawers and closets, or to search at another time or place. *James v. Louisiana*, 382 U.S. 36 (1965); *Stoner v. California*, 376 U.S. 483, 486–87 (1964); *Preston v. United States*, 376 U.S. 364, 367 (1964); *United States v. Lefkowitz*, 285 U.S. 452 (1932); *Go-Bart Co. v. United States*, 282 U.S. 344, 358

---

*Footnotes omitted. Headings added by authors for reader's convenience.

(1931); *Agnello v. United States,* 269 U.S. 20, 30–31 (1925); *United States v. Kirschenblatt, supra.*

In the present case, the articles of clothing admitted into evidence are not within any of the traditional categories which describe what materials may be seized, either with or without a warrant. The restrictiveness of these categories has been subjected to telling criticism, and although I believe that we should approach expansion of these categories with the diffidence which their imposing provenance commands, I agree that the use of identifying clothing worn in the commission of a crime and seized during "hot pursuit" is within the spirit and intendment of the "hot pursuit" exception to the search-warrant requirement. That is because the clothing is pertinent to identification of the person hotly pursued as being, in fact, the person whose pursuit was justified by connection with the crime. I would frankly place the ruling on that basis. I would not drive an enormous and dangerous hole in the Fourth Amendment to accommodate a specific and, I think, reasonable exception.

As my Brother Douglas notes, *post,* opposition to general searches is a fundamental of our heritage and of the history of the Anglo-Saxon legal principles. Such searches, pursuant to "writs of assistance," were one of the matters over which the American Revolution was fought. The very purpose of the Fourth Amendment was to outlaw such searches, which the Court today sanctions. I fear that in gratuitously striking down the "mere evidence" rule, which distinguished members of this Court have acknowledged as essential to enforce the Fourth Amendment's prohibition against general searches, the Court today needlessly destroys, root and branch, a basic part of liberty's heritage.

Opinion of Mr. Justice Douglas, dissenting.

We start with the Fourth Amendment which provides:

The right of the people to be secure in their persons, houses, papers, and effects, against unreasonable searches and seizures, shall not be violated, and no Warrants shall issue, but upon probable cause, supported by Oath or affirmation, and particularly describing the place to be searched, and the persons or things to be seized.

Fourth Amendment: Zones of Privacy. This constitutional guarantee, now as applicable to the States (*Mapp v. Ohio,* 367 U.S. 643) as to the Federal Government, has been thought, until today, to have two faces of privacy:

1. One creates a zone of privacy that may not be invaded by the police through raids, by the legislators through laws, or by magistrates through the issuance of warrants.

2. A second creates a zone of privacy that may be invaded either by

the police in hot pursuit or by a search incident to arrest or by a warrant issued by a magistrate on a showing of probable cause.

The *first* has been recognized from early days in Anglo-American law. Search warrants, for seizure of stolen property, though having an ancient lineage, were criticized even by Coke. Institutes Bk. 4, pp. 176–77.

As stated by Lord Camden in *Entick v. Carrington*, 19 How. St. Tr. 1029, 1067, even warrants authorizing seizure of stolen goods were looked upon with disfavor but "crept into the law by imperceptible practice." By the time of Charles II they had burst their original bounds and were used by the Star Chamber to find evidence among the files and papers of political suspects. Thus in the trial of Algernon Sidney in 1683 for treason "papers, which were said to be found in my [Sidney's] house, were produced as another witness" (9 How. St. Tr. 818, 901) and the defendant was executed. *Id.*, at 906–907. From this use of papers as evidence there grew up the practice of the Star Chamber empowering a person "to search in all places, where books were printing, in order to see if the printer had a licence; and if upon such search he found any books which he suspected to be libellous against the church or state, he was to seize them, and carry them before the proper magistrate." *Entick v. Carrington, supra*, at 1069. Thus the general warrant became a powerful instrument in proceedings for seditious libel against printers and authors. *Ibid.* John Wilkes led the campaign against the general warrant. *Boyd v. United States*, 116 U.S. 616, 625. Wilkes won (*Entick v. Carrington, supra*, decided in 1765); and Lord Camden's opinion not only outlawed the general warrant (*id.*, at 1072) but went on to condemn searches "for evidence" with or without a general warrant:

> There is no process against papers in civil causes. It has been often tried, but never prevailed. Nay, where the adversary has by force or fraud got possession of your own proper evidence, there is no way to get it back but by action.
>
> In the criminal law such a proceeding was never heard of; and yet there are some crimes, such for instance as murder, rape, robbery, and house-breaking, to say nothing of forgery and perjury, that are more atrocious than libelling. But our law has provided no paper-search in these cases to help forward the conviction.
>
> Whether this procedeth from the gentleness of the law towards criminals, or from a consideration that such a power would be more pernicious to the innocent than useful to the public, I will not say.
>
> It is very certain, that the law obligeth no man to accuse himself; because the necessary means of compelling self-accusation, falling upon the innocent as well as the guilty, would be both cruel and unjust; and it should seem, that search for evidence is disallowed upon the same principle. There too the innocent would be confounded with the guilty. **Id.**, at 1073.

Thus Lord Camden decided two things: (1) that searches for evidence violated the principle against self-incrimination; (2) that general warrants were void.

This decision, in the very forefront when the Fourth Amendment was adopted, underlines the construction that it covers something other than the form of the warrant and creates a zone of privacy which no government official may enter.

The complaint of Bostonians, while including the general warrants, went to the point of police invasions of personal sanctuaries:

"A List of Infringements and Violations of Rights" drawn up by the Boston town meeting late in 1772 alluded to a number of personal rights which had allegedly been violated by agents of the crown. The list included complaints against the writs of assistance which had been employed by royal officers in their searches for contraband. The Bostonians complained that "our houses and even our bed chambers are exposed to be ransacked, our boxes, chests, and trunks broke open, ravaged and plundered by wretches, whom no prudent man would venture to employ even as menial servants." Rutland, The Birth of the Bill of Rights 25 (1955).

The debates concerning the Bill of Rights did not focus on the precise point with which we here deal. There was much talk about the general warrants and the fear of them. But there was also some reference to the sanctity of one's home and his personal belongings, even including the clothes he wore. Thus in Virginia, Patrick Henry said:

The officers of Congress may come upon you now, fortified with all the terrors of paramount federal authority. Excisemen may come in multitudes; for the limitation of their numbers no man knows. They may, unless the general government be restrained by a bill of rights, or some similar restriction, go into your cellars and rooms, and search, ransack, and measure, every thing you eat, drink, and wear. They ought to be restrained within proper bounds. 3 Elliot's Debates 448–49.

This indicates that the Fourth Amendment has the dual aspect that I have mentioned. Certainly the debates nowhere suggest that it was concerned only with regulating the form of warrants.

This is borne out by what happened in the Congress. In the House the original draft read as follows:

The right of the people to be secured in their persons, houses, papers, and effects, shall not be violated by warrants issuing without probable cause, supported by oath or affirmation, and not particularly describing the place to be searched and the persons or things to be seized. 1 Annals of Cong. 754.

That was amended to read "The right of the people to be secure in their persons, houses, papers, and effects, against unreasonable seizures and searches," etc. *Ibid.* Mr. Benson, Chairman of a Committee of Three to arrange the amendments, objected to the words "by warrants issuing" and proposed to alter the amendment so as to read "and no warrant shall issue." *Ibid.* But Benson's amendment was defeated. *Ibid.* And if the story had ended there, it would be clear that the Fourth Amendment touched only the form of the warrants and the manner of their issuance. But when the Benson Committee later reported the Fourth Amendment to the House, it was in the form he had earlier proposed and was then accepted. 1 Annals of Cong. 779. The Senate agreed. Senate Journal August 25, 1789.

Thus it is clear that the Fourth Amendment has two faces of privacy, a conclusion emphasized by Lasson, The History and Development of the Fourth Amendment to the United States Constitution 103 (1937):

> As reported by the Committee of Eleven and corrected by Gerry, the Amendment was a one-barrelled affair, directed apparently only to the essentials of a valid warrant. The general principle of freedom from unreasonable search and seizure seems to have been stated only by way of premise, and the positive inhibition upon action by the Federal Government limited consequently to the issuance of warrants without probable cause, etc. That Benson interpreted it in this light is shown by his argument that although the clause was good as far as it went, **it was not sufficient**, and by the change which he advocated to obviate this objection. The provision as he proposed it contained **two** clauses. The general right of security from unreasonable search and seizure was given a sanction of its own and the amendment thus intentionally given a broader scope. That the prohibition against "unreasonable searches" was intended, accordingly, to cover something other than the form of the warrant is a question no longer left to implication to be derived from the phraseology of the Amendment.

Lord Camden's twofold classification of zones of privacy was said by Cooley to be reflected in the Fourth Amendment:

> The warrant is not allowed for the purpose of obtaining evidence of an intended crime; but only after lawful evidence of an offense actually committed. Nor even then is it allowable to invade one's privacy for the sole purpose of obtaining evidence against him, except in a few special cases where that which is the subject of the crime is supposed to be concealed, and the public or the complainant has an interest in it or in its destruction. Constitutional Limitations 431–32 (7th ed. 1903).

And that was the holding of the Court in *Boyd v. United States,* 116 U.S. 616, decided in 1886. Mr. Justice Bradley reviewed British history, including *Entick v. Carrington, supra,* and American history under the Bill of Rights and said:

> The search for and seizure of stolen or forfeited goods, or goods liable to duties and concealed to avoid the payment thereof, are totally different things from a search for and seizure of a man's private books and papers for the purpose of obtaining information therein contained, or of using them as evidence against him. The two things differ **toto coelo**. In the one case, the government is entitled to the possession of the property: in the other it is not. **Id.**, at 623.

What Mr. Justice Bradley said about stolen or forfeited goods or contraband is, of course, not accurate if read to mean that they may be seized at any time even without a warrant or not incident to an arrest that is lawful. The right to seize contraband is not absolute. If the search leading to discovery of an illicit article is not incidental to a lawful arrest or not authorized by a search warrant, the fact that contraband is discovered does not make the seizure constitutional. *Trupiano v. United States*, 334 U.S. 699, 705; *McDonald v. United States*, 335 U.S. 451, *Henry v. United States*, 361 U.S. 98, 103; *Beck v. Ohio*, 379 U.S. 89; *Aguilar v. Texas*, 378 U.S. 108.

That is not our question. Our question is whether the Government, though armed with a proper search warrant or though making a search incident to an arrest, may seize, and use at the trial, testimonial evidence, whether it would otherwise be barred by the Fifth Amendment or would be free from such strictures. The teaching of *Boyd* is that such evidence, though seized pursuant to a lawful search, is inadmissible.

That doctrine had its full flowering in *Gouled v. United States*, 255 U.S. 298, where an opinion was written by Mr. Justice Clarke for a unanimous Court that included both Mr. Justice Holmes and Mr. Justice Brandeis. The prosecution was for defrauding the Government under procurement contracts. Documents were taken from defendant's business office under a search warrant and used at the trial as evidence against him. Stolen or forged papers could be so seized, the Court said; so could lottery tickets; so could contraband; so could property in which the public had an interest, for reasons tracing back to warrants allowing the seizure of stolen property. But the papers or documents fell in none of those categories and the Court therefore held that even though they had been taken under a warrant, they were inadmissible at the trial as not even a warrant, though otherwise proper and regular, could be used "for the purpose of making search to secure evidence" of a crime. *Id.*, at 309. The use of those documents against the accused might, of course, violate the Fifth Amendment. *Id.*, at 311. But whatever may be the intrinsic nature of the evidence, the owner is then "the unwilling source of the evidence" (*id.*, at 306), there being no difference so far as the Fifth Amendment is concerned "whether he be obliged to supply evidence against himself or whether such evidence be obtained by an illegal search of his premises and seizure of his private papers." *Ibid.*

We have, to be sure, breached that barrier, *Schmerber v. California*, 384 U.S. 757, being a conspicuous example. But I dissented then and renew my opposing view at this time. That which is taken from a person without his consent and used as testimonial evidence violates the Fifth Amendment.

That was the holding in *Gouled*; and that was the line of authority followed by Judge Simon Sobeloff, writing for the Court of Appeals for reversal in this case. 363 F. 2d 647. As he said, even if we assume that the search was lawful, the articles of clothing seized were of evidential value only and under *Gouled* could not be used at the trial against petitioner. As he said, the Fourth Amendment guarantees the right of the people to be secure "in their persons, houses, papers, and effects, against unreasonable searches and seizures." Articles of clothing are covered as well as papers. Articles of clothing may be of evidential value as much as documents or papers.

Fourth Amendment: Right to Privacy.   Judge Learned Hand stated a part of the philosophy of the Fourth Amendment in *United States v. Poller*, 43 F. 2d 911, 914:

> It is only fair to observe that the real evil aimed at by the Fourth Amendment is the search itself, that invasion of a man's privacy which consists in rummaging about among his effects to secure evidence against him. If the search is permitted at all, perhaps it does not make so much difference what is taken away, since the officers will ordinarily not be interested in what does not incriminate, and there can be no sound policy in protecting what does. Nevertheless, limitations upon the fruit to be gathered tend to limit the quest itself. . . .

The right of privacy protected by the Fourth Amendment relates in part of course to the precincts of the home or the office. But it does not make them sanctuaries where the law can never reach. There are such places in the world. A mosque in Fez, Morocco, that I have visited, is by custom a sanctuary where any refugee may hide, safe from police intrusion. We have no such sanctuaries here. A policeman in "hot pursuit" or an officer with a search warrant can enter any house, any room, any building, any office. The privacy of those *places* is of course protected against invasion except in limited situations. The full privacy protected by the Fourth Amendment is, however, reached when we come to books, pamphlets, papers, letters, documents, and other personal effects. Unless they are contraband or instruments of the crime, they may not be reached by any warrant nor may they be lawfully seized by the police who are in "hot pursuit." By reason of the Fourth Amendment the police may not rummage around among these personal effects, no matter how formally perfect their authority may appear to be. They may not seize them. If they do, those articles may not be used in evidence. Any invasion whatsoever of those personal effects is "unreasonable" within the meaning of the Fourth Amendment. That is the teaching of *Entick v. Carrington, Boyd v. United States,* and *Gouled v. United States.*

Some seek to explain *Entick v. Carrington* on the ground that it dealt with seditious libel and that any search for political tracts or letters under our Bill of Rights would be unlawful *per se* because of the First Amendment and therefore "unreasonable" under the Fourth. That argument misses the main point. A prosecution for seditious libel would of course be unconstitutional under the First Amendment because it bars laws "abridging the freedom of speech, or of the press." The First Amendment also has a penumbra, for while it protects only "speech" and "press" it also protects related rights such as the right of association. See *NAACP v. Alabama* 357 U.S. 449, 460, 462; *Bates v. Little Rock,* 361 U.S. 516, 523; *Shelton v. Tucker,* 364 U.S. 479, 486; *Louisiana v. NAACP,* 366 U.S. 293, 296; and *NAACP v. Button,* 371 U.S. 415, 430–31. So it could be held, quite apart from the Fourth Amendment, that any probing into the area of opinions and beliefs would be barred by the First Amendment. That is the essence of what we said in *Watkins v. United States,* 354 U.S. 178, 197:

> Clearly, an investigation is subject to the command that the Congress shall make no law abridging freedom of speech or press or assembly. While it is true that there is no statute to be reviewed, and that an investigation is not a law, nevertheless an investigation is part of lawmaking. It is justified solely as an adjunct to the legislative process. The First Amendment may be invoked against infringement of the protected freedoms by law or by law-making.

But the privacy protected by the Fourth Amendment is much wider than the one protected by the First. *Boyd v. United States* was a forfeiture proceeding under the customs revenue law and the paper held to be beyond the reach of the Fourth Amendment was an invoice covering the imported goods. 116 U.S., at 617–19, 638. And as noted *Gouled v. United States* involved a prosecution for defrauding the Government under procurement contracts and the papers held protected against seizure, even under a technically proper warrant, were (1) an unexecuted form of contract between defendant and another person; (2) a written contract signed by defendant and another person; and (3) a bill for disbursement and professional services rendered by the attorney to the defendant. 255 U.S., at 306–7.

The constitutional philosophy is, I think, clear. The personal effects and possessions of the individual (all contraband and the like excepted) are sacrosanct from prying eyes, from the long arm of the law, from any rummaging by police. Privacy involves the choice of the individual to disclose or to reveal what he believes, what he thinks, what he possesses. The article may be a nondescript work of art, a manuscript of a book, a personal account book, a diary, invoices, personal clothing, jewelry, or whatnot. Those who wrote the Bill of Rights believed that every individual needs both to communicate with others and to keep his affairs to himself. That dual aspect of privacy means that the individual should have the freedom to select for himself the time and circumstances when he will share his secrets with others and decide the extent of that sharing. This is his prerogative not the States'. The Framers, who were as knowledgeable as we, knew what police surveillance meant and how the practice of rummaging through one's personal effects could destroy freedom.

It was in that tradition that we held in *Griswold v. Connecticut*, 381 U.S. 479, that lawmakers could not, as respects husband and wife at least, make the use of contraceptives a crime. We spoke of the pronouncement in *Boyd v. United States* that the Fourth and Fifth Amendments protected the person against all governmental invasions "of the sanctity of a man's home and the privacies of life." 116 U.S., at 630. We spoke of the "right to privacy" of the Fourth Amendment upheld by *Mapp v. Ohio*, 367 U.S. 643, 656, and of the many other controversies "over these penumbral rights of 'privacy and repose.' " 381 U.S., at 485. And we added:

> Would we allow the police to search the sacred precincts of marital bedrooms for telltale signs of the use of contraceptives? The very idea is repulsive to the notions of privacy surrounding the marriage relationship.
>
> We deal with a right of privacy older than the Bill of Rights—older than our political parties, older than our school system. Marriage is a coming together for better or for worse, hopefully enduring, and intimate to the degree of being sacred. It is an association that promotes a way of life, not causes; a harmony in living, not political faiths; a bilateral loyalty, not commercial or social projects. Yet it is an association for as noble a purpose as any involved in our prior decisions. **Id.**, at 485–86.

This right of privacy, sustained in *Griswold*, is kin to the right of privacy created by the Fourth Amendment. That there is a zone that no police can enter—whether in "hot pursuit" or armed with a meticulously proper warrant—has been emphasized by *Boyd* and by *Gouled*. They have been consistently and continuously approved. I would adhere to them and leave with the individual the choice of opening his private effects (apart from contraband and the like) to the police or keeping their contents a secret and their integrity inviolate. The existence of that choice is the very essence of the right of privacy. Without it the Fourth Amendment and the Fifth are ready instruments for the police state that the Framers sought to avoid.

SUMMARY

The cases given in this chapter examine the Fourth Amendment doctrine of reasonableness in stop-and-frisk situations, balancing the investigative stops of suspicious persons by police against the individual's right to privacy; establish the right of police to conduct limited protective searches for weapons; spell out the limited scope of warrantless searches; define the authority of police to make full body searches incident to any lawful custodial arrest, including arrests for traffic offenses; and bring "mere evidence" into the category of nontestimonial evidence subject to search and seizure.

DISCUSSION QUESTIONS

1. How would you define an arrest? A "stop?"
2. What criteria is established in *Terry v. Ohio* for evaluating and justifying a "stop?" In *Adams v. Williams?*
3. Why does the court's opinion in *Terry v. Ohio* approve of a "frisk" under circumstances indicating a "search" would be unreasonable?
4. How does the opinion of Justice Harlan in *Terry v. Ohio* differ from the opinion of the court? The opinion of Justice Douglas?
5. How would you define "hot pursuit?"
6. Why was the search and seizure described in *Warden v. Hayden* termed "reasonable" in the court's opinion?
7. How does the court's opinion in *Warden v. Hayden* distinguish evidence which can be seized under the authority of a search warrant or a search incident to arrest?
8. What is the limitation on warrantless searches incidental to arrest?
9. Is the full body search by an arresting officer restricted when the arrest is for a minor violation such as a traffic offense?
10. Explain the difference between *Terry, Robinson,* and *Gustafson.*

GLOSSARY

AD HOC (JUDGEMENT).   Pertaining to, or for the sake of, this case alone.

DICTA, DICTUM.   Judicial opinion not essential to a court's decision on the question under review.

En Banc.   Together, all the judges of a court "sit" and hear a case.

Field Interrogation.   Questioning of suspicious person stopped by police.

Nexus.   Connection; tie; link.

Protean.   Variable; readily assuming different shapes or forms.

Rubric.   A form or thing established or settled; formally specified; a class or category.

Stare Decisis.   Rule of precedents; principle that once the law of a specific case has been decided it should serve as a definite and known rule for the future (unless decision in error, or mistake).

11

The Exclusionary Rule

CHAPTER OBJECTIVES

1. This chapter uses a chronological arrangement of case law to conceptualize the steady growth of the exclusionary rule as a legal process to control police misbehavior and illegal conduct; describes

2. The use of the Fourteenth Amendment and its due process clause to restrain state agents and align their evidence-gathering methods with standards set for federal agents.

3. Pertinent cases are identified and outlines are given of the decisions related to excluding evidence tainted by illegal or improper searches and seizures, interrogations, and lineups. Also explored are the forbidding of the use of illegally secured evidence;

4. The legal mechanics of suppressing tainted evidence subject to exclusion by judicial ruling, and

5. The potential revisions of the exclusionary rule.

The exclusionary rule is designed to discourage law enforcement agents from violating constitutional guarantees while gathering evidence.

The rule does this by rejecting any illegally obtained evidence. Police have not hesitated to violate procedural rules in gathering evidence for the ultimate purpose of using such evidence in court to prove, with the aid of the prosecutor, the guilt of the accused person. Their work, however, is wasted when the tainted evidence is suppressed before trial or is not admitted into evidence at trial. The exclusionary rule compels respect for constitutional guarantees by removing the incentive for disregarding them.

Before the growth of the exclusionary rule, there was no effective way of **restraining agents of law enforcement** while gathering evidence for use in court. Under the rule of common law, illegally obtained evidence was admissible. If it could be shown that the evidence was pertinent to the issue, the court did not take notice of how it was obtained.

The exclusion of logically relevant evidence in criminal prosecutions is justified by the public policy expressed in the Constitution. The exclusionary rule has been slow in its emergence and application to the states and their courts, and has been under constant attack from police and prosecuting attorneys. The concepts of home rule and state criminal justice, as well as the ageless problem of resolving the conflict between the government power and the protection of citizens from misuse of that power, were heavy handicaps in developing the rules for suppressing illegally obtained evidence.

The exclusionary rule has shaped the conduct of all agents of law enforcement into a new pattern of reasonableness and fundamental fairness in connection with searches and seizures, confessions, and other critical stages of a criminal case, from the focusing of a case through arrest to trial. This rule has also preserved the moral force of law and the integrity of the judiciary. Law enforcement agents are asked to act out the adversary role in a way that will earn the respect of the community. If they fail to do so, the "imperative of **judicial integrity**" demands that their conduct be negated by the courts.

The basic merit of the exclusionary rule is that it affords every person—innocent and possibly guilty—the Constitutional guarantees enacted to protect all citizens of the United States—and it now does so in both federal and state courts.

In developing the exclusionary rule, the United States Supreme Court acted initially under its authority over United States court proceedings and over federal agents who used these courts to prosecute violations of federal law. The Court hesitated to extend federalism into the local criminal justice field by forcing state courts and state officials to abide by the federal rules of procedure. The failure of state authorities to use some other effective methods to compel state agents to comply with the provisions of the Constitution in gathering evidence, and the continual refusal of most state appellate courts to reject illegal evidence, led to the Supreme Court's action in *Weeks, Mapp, Wade,* and *Miranda.* These four cases established procedural safeguards to protect three essential areas of individual liberty: the right to privacy, to an attorney, and to protection against self-incrimination.

FEDERAL AGENTS AND PROCEEDINGS

In 1914, in *Weeks v. United States,*[1] the United States Supreme Court held that the private papers of an accused, which had been seized by federal officers during a warrantless search of his home, were inadmissible as evidence in the federal courts because they had been obtained through an illegal search and seizure in violation of the Fourth Amendment.

This decision established the exclusionary rule as the best means for **discouraging lawless searches** and seizures by federal agents. The majority opinion noted that exclusion is implicit in the right to privacy created by the Fourth Amendment and, that if the constitutional guarantees against unreasonable searches and seizures are to have significance, they must be enforced. If such guarantees had been effectively enforced by means other than excluding evidence before 1914, there would have been little justification for initiating this judicial rule. However, experience had demonstrated that administrative, criminal, and civil remedies were not effective in suppressing lawless searches and seizures by federal agents.

A few of the states became "exclusionary" in conformity with the Week's doctrine. In these exclusionary states, law enforcement agents who had obtained evidence during an unreasonable search could not use it in their state courts, but they could turn it over to federal authorities for prosecution under federal law. This became known as the **"silver platter" doctrine.** The doctrinal justification for this procedure was that the federal courts could admit this evidence because federal agents had had nothing to do with the illegal search and seizure. The rationale was given that the turnover from state to federal agents legitimized the illegal evidence.

In their opinion in *Elkins v. United States,*[2] in 1960, the Court rejected this silver platter doctrine and stopped the traffic in illegal searches aimed at nullifying state and federal laws. The Court's majority opinion in *Elkins* said that the act of a federal court sitting in an exclusionary state and admitting evidence lawlessly seized by state agents not only frustrated state policy but did so in a particularly inappropriate way: "For by admitting the unlawfully seized evidence the federal court

[1]232 U.S. 383 (1914).
[2]364 U.S. 206 (1960).

serves to defeat the state's effort to assure obedience to the Federal Constitution."

In a comment by Mr. Justice Frankfurter in a 1943 case, *McNabb v. United States*,[3] the Court indicated its attitude toward federal criminal justice and of **police interrogations:**

> Judicial supervision of the administration of criminal justice in the federal courts implies the duty of establishing and maintaining civilized standards of procedure and evidence. Such standards are not satisfied merely by observance of those minimal historic safeguards for securing trial by reason which are summarized as "due process" of law and below which we reach what is really trial by force.

In *McNabb*, the arresting officers delayed Benjamin McNabb's arraignment after his arrest and secured a confession from him during this period of detention which violated a federal law requiring prompt arraignment of arrestees. The Court's opinion pointed to legislative recognition that police must act with reasonable promptness to show legal cause for the arrest to safeguard both innocent and guilty arrestees. Its comment about this law was: "It aims to avoid all the implications of secret interrogations of persons accused of crime. It reflects not a sentimental but a sturdy view of law enforcement. It outlaws easy but self-defeating ways in which brutality is substituted for brains as an instrument of crime detection."

In 1957, the court was confronted with a case similar to *McNabb*. In this case, *Mallory v. United States*,[4] a unanimous Court reaffirmed its position in *McNabb*. Andrew R. Mallory was a 19-year-old youth of limited intelligence. He was arrested in the early afternoon hours in Washington, D.C., and accused of forcible rape. He was questioned for about a half hour, and asked to submit to a lie detector test. He was given the test about four hours later, and after slightly less than two hours of testing, Mallory confessed. At about midnight, he finished dictating his confession to a typist. He was not told of his right to counsel and that he might keep silent, nor was he warned that any statement made by him might be used against him. He was arraigned before a U.S. Commissioner the following morning. In a subsequent trial, Mallory was convicted of rape.

In its review, the Court conceded that a brief delay was justified under the federal law specifying arraignment of arrestees "without unnecessary delay,"[5] but concluded that the delay must not be designed to give federal agents an opportunity to extract a confession. The court

---

[3]318 U.S. 322 (1943).
[4]354 U.S. 449 (1957).
[5]**Federal Rules of Criminal Procedure**, Section 5(a).

ruled against the concept of **investigative arrests or detention**: "Whomever the police arrest they must arrest on 'probable cause.' It is not a function of the police to arrest, as it were, at large and to use an interrogating process at police headquarters in order to determine whom they should charge before a committing magistrate on 'probable cause.'"

STATE AGENTS AND PROCEEDINGS

In 1961, the country's highest court gave up its campaign to encourage state authorities to use methods other than exclusion to protect the constitutional right to privacy, justly concluding this right had not been adequately protected from the intrusions of state agents in the "non-exclusion" states. In the landmark decision in *Mapp v. Ohio*,[6] the U.S. Supreme Court held that the constitutional prohibition against unreasonable searches and seizures under the Fourth Amendment was enforceable against the states under the due process clause of the Fourteenth Amendment.

For a long time, the Court believed exclusion vital to this protection in federal proceedings, but was reluctant to extend its supervision to state courts. As early as 1949, in *Wolf v. Colorado*,[7] the justices expressed this reluctance in the following words:

> There are, moreover, reasons for excluding evidence unreasonably obtained by the federal police which are less compelling in the case of police under state or local authority. The public opinion of a community can far more effectively be exerted against oppressive conduct on the part of police directly responsible to the community itself than can local opinion, sporadically aroused, be brought to bear upon remote authority pervasively exerted throughout the country.

Freedom from arbitrary intrusion by state agents, however, was not achieved by the remedies suggested for states by the Wolf doctrine. The legal stumbling block to imposing minimum standards on the states by U.S. Supreme Court action was the doctrine that the first eight amendments to the Constitution were directed only to the federal government and its agents and were not adopted to limit state governments or state agents.

In 1833, Mr. Chief Justice Marshall delivered the opinion of the court in *Barron v. Baltimore*.[8] The following segment of his opinion indicated the court's concept of **federalism** at that time:

---

[6]367 U.S. 643 (1961).
[7]338 U.S. 25 (1949).
[8]Barron v. Baltimore, U.S. Supreme Court Reports 7 Peters 243 (1833).

The Constitution was ordained and established by the people of the United States for themselves, for their own government, and not for the government of the individual states. Each state established a constitution for itself, and in that constitution provided such limitations and restrictions on the powers of its particular government as its judgment dictated. The people of the United States framed such a government for the United States as they supposed best adapted to their situation, and best calculated to promote their interests. The powers they conferred on this government were to be exercised by itself; and the limitations on power, if expressed in general terms, are naturally and, we think, necessarily applicable to the government created by the instrument.

The 1961 Court, in *Mapp*,[9] cleared away this road block by reasoning that the due process clause of the Fourteenth Amendment, adopted after the civil war, was meant to impose the **Bill of Rights limitations on state governments** as well as the federal government.

The **facts in Mapp** were as follows: Three Cleveland police officers came to Mapp's home in that city after receiving information that "a person [was] hiding out in the home, who was wanted for questioning in connection with a recent bombing, and that there was a large amount of policy paraphernalia being hidden in the home." Miss Mapp and her daughter by a former marriage lived on the top floor of the two-family dwelling. When they arrived at the house, the officers knocked on the door and demanded entrance but Miss Mapp, after telephoning her attorney, refused to admit them without a search warrant. They advised headquarters of the situation and began surveillance of the house.

The officers again asked to be admitted about three hours later after four or more additional officers had arrived. When Miss Mapp did not come to the door immediately, at least one of the several doors to the house was forcibly opened and the policemen gained admittance. A police officer testified, "We did pry the screen door to gain entrance." Miss Mapp demanded to see the search warrant. A paper, claimed to be a warrant, was held up by one of the officers. She grabbed the "warrant" and placed it in her bosom. After a struggle in which the officers recovered the piece of paper, they handcuffed Miss Mapp because she had been "belligerent" in resisting their official rescue of the "warrant" from her person. Miss Mapp, in handcuffs, was then forcibly taken upstairs to her bedroom where the officers searched a dresser, a chest of drawers, a closet, and some suitcases. They also looked into a photo album and through some of her personal papers. The search spread to the rest of the second floor including the child's bedroom, the living room, the kitchen, and a dinette. The basement of the building and a trunk found there were also searched. Some obscene materials, for pos-

[9]Mapp v. Ohio, 367 U.S. 643 (1961).

session of which she was ultimately convicted, were discovered in the course of that widespread search.

At the trial, no search warrant was produced by the prosecution, nor was the failure to produce one explained or accounted for. At best, "there is, in the record, considerable doubt as to whether there ever was any warrant for the search of defendant's home." The Ohio Supreme Court affirmed the conviction. The United States Supreme Court noted probable jurisdiction and reviewed the action of the lower courts.

The Court's review of the right to privacy in this case noted that this right was enforceable against the **states** through the due process clause of the Fourteenth Amendment by the same **sanction of exclusion** that was used against the federal agents, saying:

> Moreover, our holding that the exclusionary rule is an essential part of both the Fourth and Fourteenth Amendments is not only the logical dictate of prior cases, but it also makes very good sense. There is no war between the Constitution and common sense. Presently, a federal prosecutor may make no use of evidence illegally seized, but a state's attorney across the street may, although he supposedly is operating under the enforceable prohibitions of the same amendment. Thus the state, by admitting evidence unlawfully seized, serves to encourage disobedience to the Federal Constitution which it is bound to uphold. Moreover, as was said in Elkins "the very essence of a healthy federalism depends upon the avoidance of needless conflict between state and federal courts."

Control of police power, preservation of judicial integrity, and re-iteration of the right to privacy were the objectives of this landmark decision. These goals are apparent in the concluding words of the majority opinion:

> The ignoble shortcut to conviction left open to the state tends to destroy the entire system of constitutional restraints on which the liberties of the people rest. Having once recognized that the right to privacy embodied in the Fourth Amendment is enforceable against the states, and that the right to be secure against rude invasions of privacy by state officers is, therefore, constitutional in origin, we can no longer permit that right to remain an empty promise. Because it is enforceable in the same manner and to like effect as other basic rights secured by the Due Process Clause, we can no longer permit it to be revocable at the whim of any police officer who, in the name of law enforcement itself, chooses to suspend its enjoyment. Our decision, founded on reason and truth, gives to the individual no more than that which the Constitution guarantees him, to the police officer no less than that to which honest law enforcement is entitled, and, to the courts, that judicial integrity so necessary in the true administration of justice.

The judgment of the Supreme Court of Ohio is reversed and the cause remanded for further proceedings not inconsistent with this opinion. Reversed and remanded.

The exact nature of the supervisory power of the United States Supreme Court over the administration of criminal justice in state courts is best illustrated by the Court's standards for protecting constitutional rights. The Court's standards for protecting these rights in federal proceedings are now matched by the standards in state proceedings. The unity of the Court's standards for admitting evidence when there is a dispute as to whether it was secured during an illegal **search and seizure,** is illustrated by the concluding words of the majority opinion in the case of *Ker v. California*:[10]

> We have no occasion here to decide how many of the situations, in which by the exercise of our supervisory power over the conduct of federal officers we would exclude evidence, are also situations which would require the exclusion of evidence from state criminal proceedings under the constitutional principles extended to the states by Mapp. But where the conduct effecting an arrest so clearly trangresses those rights guaranteed by the Fourth Amendment as does the conduct which brought about the arrest of these petitioners, we would surely reverse the judgment if this were a federal prosecution involving federal officers. Since our decisions in Mapp has made the guarantees of the Fourteenth Amendment co-extensive with those of the Fourth Amendment we should pronounce precisely the same judgment upon the conduct of these state officers.

The Court's concern for minimum standards next found the inequality of legal representation offensive and violative of the constitutional admonition that every person accused of crime has the **right to be represented by legal counsel.** The Court recognized the widespread practice that allowed an attorney for those who could afford one, but ignored the constitutional right to legal assistance if the accused was unable to hire an attorney. In *Gideon v. Wainwright,*[11] the Court found the vehicle for extending these minimum standards through the Sixth Amendment, and ruled that every defendant who desires an attorney should have one, even if counsel must be appointed at state expense for indigent defendants.

In 1967, in *Wade v. United States,*[12] the Court again extended its supervision over state agents and proceedings. In *Wade,* the critical stage at which an accused is entitled to legal assistance was moved forward to the time of the **post-indictment lineup.** Again, seeking to deter violations of accused persons' constitutional rights the Court warned police

[10]374 U.S. 23 (1963).
[11]372 U.S. 335 (1963).
[12]388 U.S. 218 (1967).

and prosecutors that courtroom identification of a defendant would be barred unless the defendant's counsel was present at this prior identification. Wade was as much entitled to the aid of legal counsel while being viewed by eyewitnesses as at the trial itself. The danger the Court sought to avoid was and is the possibility of identification by suggestion. The Court recognized that the main source of unjust convictions is mistaken identification, and has sought to standardize the lineup, or other identification procedures, by providing that defense counsel may be present to independently criticize any suggestive procedures.

In 1972 a differently balanced Supreme Court, in *Kirby v. Illinois*,[13] limited any extension of *Wade's* critical stage doctrine at which an accused is entitled to an attorney at post-indictment lineups, ruling that accused persons are not entitled to counsel until prosecution against them has been initiated, and differentiating between post-arrest and post-charge lineups.

The reasoning behind the Supreme Court's determination to outlaw pretrial practices by state agents that violate constitutional privileges and protection, and to exclude any evidence obtained by such actions, may be traced through the court's firm stand in *McNabb* and *Mallory*— cases in which conduct by federal agents was ruled likely to coerce confessions—and an 1896 case—*Brown v. Walker*.[14] This case involved that clause of the Fifth Amendment which declares that no person "shall be compelled in any criminal case to be a witness against himself." The majority opinion contained the following background data on the privilege against self-incrimination:

The maxim, **Nemo tenetur seipsum accusare,** had its origin in a protest against the inquisitorial and manifestly unjust methods of interrogating accused persons, which has long obtained in the continental system, and, until the expulsion of the Stuarts from the British throne in 1688, and the erection of additional barriers for the protection of the people against the exercise of arbitrary power, was not uncommon even in England. While the admissions or confessions of the prisoner, when voluntarily and freely made, have always ranked high in the scale of incriminating evidence, if an accused person be asked to explain his apparent connection with a crime under investigation, the ease with which the questions put to him may assume an inquisitorial character, the temptation to press the witness unduly, to brow-beat him if he be timid or reluctant, to push him into a corner, and to entrap him into fatal contradictions, which is so painfully evident in many of the earlier state trials, notably in those of Sir Nicholas Throckmorton and Udal, the Puritan minister, made the system so odious as to give rise to a demand for its total abolition. The change in the English criminal procedure in that particular seems to be founded upon no statute and no judicial opinion, but upon a general and silent

---

[13]406 U.S. 682 (1972).
[14]161 U.S. 591 (1896).

acquiescence of the courts in a popular demand. But, however adopted, it has become firmly imbedded in English as well as in American jurisprudence. So deeply did the inequities of the ancient system impress themselves upon the minds of the American colonists that the states with one accord, made a denial of the right to question an accused person a part of their fundamental law; so that a maxim, which in England was a mere rule of evidence, became clothed in this country with the impregnability of a constitutional enactment.

In federal prosecutions, the issue of voluntary confessions is controlled by the **Fifth Amendment's privilege against self-incrimination.** This is the basic requirement set forth in *Bram v. United States.*[15]

The high court's ultimate dissatisfaction with constitutional violations of an accused's rights before trial climaxed in *Miranda v. Arizona.*[16] It extended the doctrine of the *Mapp* case to the Fifth Amendment and imposed its standards on state agents and courts through the "due process clause" of the Fourteenth Amendment and implemented the Sixth Amendment's guarantee of legal help.

Miranda's requirements are more than the mere provision that the accused has a procedural right not to have a coerced confession used against him at trial. In many ways, *Miranda* is similar to *Mapp.* The Court, through *Miranda*, seeks to prevent illegally secured confessions by forewarning police against actions which will result in the confession being excluded from evidence. *Miranda's* trio of warnings (notice of the right to silence, of any statement being used against its maker, and of the right to counsel) put the span of time between the focusing of police attention on a suspect to his arraignment in court in the same category as the arrest-to-arraignment period of threat which developed the *Mc-Nabb-Mallory* rule for federal agents and proceedings.

DERIVATIVE USE OF ILLEGAL EVIDENCE

The rule of exclusion for evidence seized during an illegal search was expanded in 1920 in the U.S. Supreme Court's decision in *Silverthorne Lumber Company v. United States.*[17] This decision supported the exclusionary rule by plainly stating that the essence of the provision **forbidding illegal acquisition of evidence** in violation of the Fourth Amendment is that not only shall such evidence be rejected in court, but that it shall not be used at all.

Frederick W. Silverthorne and his father were indicted, arrested, and detained by U.S. agents. During this initial detention period, U.S.

[15]168 U.S. 532 (1897).
[16]384 U.S. 436 (1966).
[17]251 U.S. 385 (1920).

agents went to the office of the Silverthorne Lumber Company, operated by the defendants, and without a shadow of authority, searched the premises and seized all the books and papers they found there. The Silverthornes made a timely application to the U.S. District Court for the return of the unlawfully seized books and papers, and the prosecutor was forced to return the original books and papers. But first the prosecutor made photographs and copies of the seized evidence. Subsequently, the prosecutor served the Silverthorne firm with a subpoena to produce the original books and papers in court. Their refusal resulted in a court order of compliance, and their continued refusal to obey this order led to a judgment of contempt and a fine of $250. In response to a writ of error filed by the Silverthornes, the judgment was reversed, with Mr. Justice Holmes delivering the Court opinion. The proposition involved in this case is summed up in this opinion as follows:

> The government now, while in form repudiating and condemning the illegal seizure, seeks to maintain its right to avail itself of the knowledge obtained by that means which otherwise it would not have. The proposition could not be presented more nakedly. It is that although, of course, its seizure was an outrage which the government now regrets, it may study the papers before it returns them, copy them, and then may use the knowledge that it has gained to call upon the owners in a more regular form to produce them; that the protection of the constitution covers the physical possession but not any advantages the government can gain over the object of its pursuit by doing the forbidden act. Weeks v. United States, 232, U.S. 383 (1914), to be sure, had established that laying the papers directly before a grand jury is unwarranted, but it is taken to mean two steps are required instead of one. In our opinion such is not the law. It reduces the Fourth Amendment to a form of words.

The *Silverthorne* opinion recognized the exigencies of criminal investigation by pointing out that any knowledge of the illegally gathered facts obtained from an "independent source" could be used to prove those facts. There is no doubt the source must have no connection with the warrantless search or its fruits, in this case, the examination of the seized books and papers. The Court warned in *Silverthorne* that: "The knowledge gained by the government's own wrong cannot be used by it in the way proposed."

Further, in a 1925 prosecution for conspiracy to violate a drug possession law, evidence obtained in an illegal search was held not admissible in the prosecution's case in chief nor in rebuttal during cross-examination of the defendant. The facts in this case, *Agnello v. United States*,[18] were as follows: Frank Agnello and others were convicted of conspiracy to sell cocaine in violation of federal law. Among the items

[18]269 U.S. 20 (1925).

of evidence proffered by the government in its case in chief was a can of cocaine that had been seized by U.S. agents in Agnello's bedroom some time after his arrest. At the time of the search Agnello was in custody elsewhere, and the place searched was not the place where Agnello had been arrested. This evidence was excluded on the ground that the search and seizure had been made without a search warrant. On direct examination, Agnello was not asked and did not testify about this can of cocaine. In cross-examination, however, he was asked if he had ever seen this evidence ("Did you ever see narcotics before?"), and he answered no after the trial judge overruled defense counsel's objection.

The court held that this line of questioning, after the prosecutor had failed in his efforts to introduce the unlawfully seized evidence in its case in chief, was nothing more than an attempt to smuggle illegal evidence into the court record. After Agnello's expected denial of the above question, the prosecutor attempted to introduce the can of cocaine illegally seized in Agnello's bedroom. The judgment against Agnello was set aside, and a new trial ordered, on the grounds he had done nothing to waive his constitutional protection or justify cross-examination about the evidence obtained by the unlawful search, and the admission of such testimony was an error that prejudiced Agnello's rights.

The doctrine **barring derivative evidence** tainted by illegal origin from federal courts was further expanded when the U.S. Supreme Court ruled, in *Nardone v. United States*,[19] that once the accused established that any evidence was unlawfully procured, the trial court must give the accused an opportunity to prove that a substantial portion of the case against him was based on such unlawfully procured evidence.

After Nardone's original trial, his conviction was reversed because illegally intercepted telephone messages were a vital part of the prosecution's proof of guilt. Nardone was again convicted in a new trial, and the Court agreed to review his appeal to determine whether the trial judge had improperly refused to allow the accused to ask the prosecution about the uses to which it had put the information contained in the illegal wire-tapping which had caused Nardone's original conviction to be reversed. The court's opinion noted that, as in the *Silverthorne* case, facts improperly obtained do not "become sacred and inaccessible." If knowledge of them is gained from an independent source they may be proved like any others, but the knowledge gained by the Government's own wrong cannot be used by it simply because it is used derivatively.

In reversing Nardone's second conviction, the Court's majority indicated the sensible way of handling this problem: "The burden is, of course, on the accused in the first instance to prove to the trial court's satisfaction that wire-tapping was unlawfully employed. Once that is

---

[19]308 U.S. 338 (1939).

established—as was plainly done here—the presiding judge must give opportunity, however closely confined, to the accused to prove that a substantial portion of the case against him was the fruit of the poisonous tree. This leaves ample opportunity to the Government to convince the trial court that its proof had an independent origin. And if such a claim is made after the trial is under way, the judge must likewise be satisfied that the accused could not at an earlier stage have had adequate knowledge to make his claim."

COLLATERAL USE DOCTRINE

An exception to the exclusionary rule has become known as the collateral use doctrine. This rule allows the introduction of illegally obtained and otherwise inadmissible evidence for the limited purpose of impeaching the credibility of a defendant in a criminal action when he assumes the role of a witness. In a 1954 case, *Walder v. United States*,[20] Walder was indicted in the United States District Court for purchasing heroin. Claiming that the heroin capsule had been obtained through an unlawful search and seizure, Walder moved to suppress it. The motion was granted, and shortly thereafter, on the government's motion, the case against him was dismissed. In January of 1952, Walder was indicted again, this time for four other illicit transactions in narcotics. The government's case consisted principally of testimony by two drug addicts who claimed to have procured the illicit stuff from Walder under the direction of federal agents. The only witness for the defense was the defendant himself. He denied any narcotics dealings with the two government informers and attributed the testimony against him to personal hostility.

During direct examination, Walder was questioned and testified as follows:

Q: Now, first, Mr. Walder, before we go further in your testimony, I want you to tell the Court and jury whether, not referring to these informers in this case, but whether you have ever sold any narcotics to anyone?

A: I have never sold any narcotics to anyone in my life.

Q: Have you ever had any narcotics in your possession, other than what may have been given to you by a physician for an ailment?

A: No.

Q: Now, I will ask you one more thing. Have you ever handled or given any narcotics to anyone as a gift or in any other manner without the receipt of any money or any other compensation?

A: I have not.

[20]347 U.S. 62 (1954).

Q: Have you ever even acted as, say, have you acted as a conduit for the purpose of handling what you knew to be a narcotic from one person to another?

A: No, sir.

On cross-examination, in response to a question by government counsel referring to this direct testimony, Walder again said that he had never purchased, sold, or possessed any narcotics. Over the defendant's objection, the government then questioned him about the heroin capsule unlawfully seized from his home, in his presence, during a prior arrest in February 1950. The defendant stoutly denied that any narcotics had been taken from him at that time. (This denial squarely contradicted an affidavit filed by the defendant in the earlier proceedings in connection with his motion to suppress the evidence unlawfully seized.) The government then put on the stand one of the officers who had participated in the unlawful search and seizure and also the chemist who had analyzed the heroin capsule that had been seized.

The trial judge admitted this evidence, but carefully charged the jury that it was not to be used to determine whether the defendant had committed the crimes charged, but solely for the purpose of **impeaching the defendant's credibility**. The defendant was convicted.

The Court's opinion shows a basic aversion to perjury while upholding the exclusionary rule. The opinion concludes with the following paragraphs:

1. The Government cannot violate the Fourth Amendment—in the only way the government can do anything, namely through its agents—and use the fruits of such unlawful conduct to secure a conviction. (**Weeks v. United States, supra.**) Nor can the Government make indirect use of such evidence for its case (Silverthorne Lumber Company v. United States, 251 U.S. 385), or support a conviction on evidence obtained through leads from the unlawfully obtained evidence (Nardone v. United States, 308 U.S. 388). All these methods are outlawed, and convictions obtained by means of them are invalidated, because they encourage the kind of society that is obnoxious to free men.

2. It is one thing to say that the Government cannot make an affirmative use of evidence unlawfully obtained. It is quite another to say that the defendant can turn the illegal method by which evidence in the Government's possession was obtained to his own advantage, and provide himself with a shield against contradiction of his untruths. Such an extension of the Weeks' doctrine would be a perversion of the Fourth Amendment.

Take the present situation. Of his own accord, the defendant went beyond a mere denial of complicity in the crimes of which he was charged and made the sweeping claim that he had never dealt in or possessed any narcotics. Of course, the Constitution guarantees a defendant the fullest opportunity to meet the accusation against him. He must be free to deny all the elements of the case against him without thereby giving leave to the Government to introduce by way of rebuttal evidence illegally secured by it, and therefore not available for its case in chief. Beyond that, however, there is hardly justification for letting the defendant affirmatively resort to perjurious testimony in reliance on the Government's disability to challenge his credibility.

The situation here involved is to be sharply contrasted with that presented by **Agnello v. United States**, 269 U.S. 20 (1925). There the Government, after having failed in its efforts to introduce the tainted evidence in its case in chief, tried to smuggle it in on cross-examination by asking the accused the broad question, "Did you ever see narcotics before?" After eliciting the expected denial, it sought to introduce evidence of narcotics, located in the defendant's home by means of an unlawful search and seizure in order to discredit the defendant.

In 1971 the United States Supreme Court decided *Harris v. New York*[21] which extended the court's attitude in *Walder* to *Miranda* violation confessions, admissions, or statements. Harris was not properly advised of his rights under *Miranda* and did give incriminating statements as a result of interrogation by police. At his trial the prosecution did not attempt to introduce the statements taken in violation of *Miranda*. During the defense case Harris' testimony was different from the statements he had made to the police. He was cross-examined concerning the statements he had given in violation of *Miranda* and the Court allowed impeachment with the introduction of the relevant extrajudicial statement:

It is one thing to say that the government cannot make an affirmative use of evidence unlawfully obtained. It is quite another to say that the defendant can turn the illegal method by which evidence in the government's possession was obtained to his own advantage, and provide himself with a shield against contradiction of his untruths. Such an extension of the **Weeks** doctrine would be a perversion of the Fourth Amendment.[22]

The Court further stated that the defendant had no right to commit perjury and that it was proper to utilize the traditional truth-testing devices to aid the jury in assessing his credibility.

MOTION TO SUPPRESS

The procedure for **suppressing illegally obtained evidence** is usually controlled by detailed statute. If these procedures are not followed, the illegally obtained evidence may be admitted as evidence against the defendant.

Jurisdictions vary in the details of procedure, but each state pro-

---

[21]401 U.S. 222 (1971).
[22]Harris v. New York, 401 U.S. 222 (1971), p. 224.

vides a procedure for raising and resolving the issue of whether or not the evidence should be excluded. At least twenty states generally follow the federal procedure. Rule 41 of the Federal Rules of Criminal Procedure provides the following exclusive method of suppressing evidence:

> **Motion for Return of Property and to Suppress Evidence.** A person aggrieved by an unlawful search and seizure may move the district court for the district in which the property was seized for the return of the property and to suppress for use as evidence anything so obtained on the ground that: (1) the property was illegally seized without warrant, or (2) the warrant is insufficient on its face, or (3) the property seized is not that described in the warrant, or (4) there was not probable cause for believing the existence of the grounds on which the warrant was issued, or (5) the warrant was illegally executed. The judge shall receive evidence on any issue of fact necessary to the decision of the motion. If the motion is granted the property shall be restored unless otherwise subject to lawful detention and it shall not be admissible in evidence at any hearing or trial. The motion to suppress evidence may also be made in the district where the trial is to be had. The motion shall be made before trial or hearing unless opportunity therefore did not exist or the defendant was not aware of the grounds for the motion, but the court in its discretion may entertain the motion at the trial or hearing.
>
> **Scope and Definition.** This rule does not modify any act, inconsistent with it, regulating search, seizure and the issuance and execution of search warrants in circumstances for which special provision is made. The term 'property' is used in this rule to include documents, books, papers and any other tangible objects.

California's procedure is both exclusive and comprehensive.[23] In a felony case, a motion may be made at the preliminary examination, tested on a motion to set aside the information, and aligned with a petition for a writ of prohibition to the appellate court. It may be repeated with an evidentiary hearing on a written motion made to the trial court prior to trial, and an appeal by either party to the ruling of the court. If the motion is granted in favor of the defendant and the prosecution appeals, the defendant may be released on his own recognizance. The court—if additional evidence is produced—may also allow the question of suppression to be raised again at the trial. However, without good cause the issue is lost unless raised at the pretrial hearing, or, if raised, has been denied at such hearing.

ATTACKING THE EXCLUSIONARY RULE

Whenever evidence gathered by police has been excluded at the subsequent prosecution, there has been the outcry that the court is letting the

23California Penal Code, Sections 995 and 1538.5.

guilty criminal go free. In 1922 when the Chicago police had coerced a confession from a defendant and the court excluded that confession and would not allow it in evidence at the trial of the defendant, a high police official made the following comment to the newspapers: "Ninety-five percent of the work of the department will be nullified if the [court] policy is permitted to prevail. Few, if any, prisoners confess except after lengthy examination. We are permitted to do less every day, pretty soon there won't be a police department."[24]

The official was obviously a bit premature and perhaps over-reacting. There is, however, considerable sentiment and substance to the argument that the criminal should not go free merely because the policeman blunders. Few in or outside of law enforcement advocate that there be no limit to police authority and activity, but most contend there are ways other than exclusion to preserve our individual rights and lawful police activity.

The attack on exclusion was given prestige and direction in 1964 by Warren E. Burger in a law review article:

> I suggest that the notion that suppression of evidence in a given case effectively deters the future action of the particular policeman or of policemen generally was never more than wishful thinking on the part of the Courts.[25]

Justice Burger further commented that the spectacle of freeing the guilty because of the exclusionary rule destroys public respect for the law and the courts.

In 1967 the President's Commission on Law Enforcement and Administration of Justice gave additional substance to the numerous but scattered complaints of the police and prosecution agencies:

> In the Federal system, as well as in many States, the existing rule, now the subject of reconsideration by the Supreme Court, is that search warrants may be used only to seize contraband or the fruits or instrumentalities of crime. If evidence is seized illegally, it cannot be used in court. In the words of a Supreme Court decision: "They may not be used as a means of gaining access to a man's house or office and papers solely for the purpose of making search to secure evidence to be used against him in a criminal or penal proceeding." (**Gouled v. United States,** 255 U.S. 298 (1921), p. 309). If evidence is seized illegally, it cannot be used in court.
>
> These limitations on proof of guilt are not universal; many countries operate effective and humane criminal systems without putting so great a burden on the prosecution. America's adherence to these principles not only demands complex and time-consuming court procedures but also in some cases forecloses the proof of facts altogether. Guilty criminals may be set free because

[24]People v. Rogers, 136 N.E. 470, 474 (1922).
[25]Burger, "Who Will Watch the Watchman?" **14 American University Law Review**, 1, no. 12 (1964).

the court's exclusionary rules prevent the introduction of a confession or of seized evidence. Crimes may never even be detected because restrictions on the methods of investigation insulate criminal conduct from the attention of the police.[26]

Again in 1971, Justice Burger, as the Chief Justice of the United States Supreme Court, stated in an opinion:

> Inadvertent errors of judgment that do not work any grave injustice will inevitably occur under the pressure of police work. These honest mistakes have been treated in the same way as deliberate and flagrant **Irvine**-type violations of the Fourth Amendment. For example, in **Miller v. United States**, 357 U.S. 301, 309–310 (1958), reliable evidence was suppressed because of a police officer's failure to say a "few more words" during the arrest and search of a known narcotics peddler.
>
> Freeing either a tiger or a mouse in a schoolroom is an illegal act, but no rational person would suggest that these two acts should be punished in the same way.
>
> I submit that society has at least as much right to expect rationally graded responses from judges in place of the universal "capital punishment" we inflict on all evidence when police error is shown in its acquisition.[27]

In 1973 a select committee appointed directly by the governor of California drew together the arguments opposing the exclusionary rule and made a recommendation to the governor:

> In line with the recommendations of Chief Justice Burger and several other experts in the field, we recommend enactment of law which abolishes the exclusionary rule and creates a better remedy, permitting the victim of an unlawful search or seizure to collect damages from the agency which employed the offending officer.
>
> This better remedy stops the suppression of reliable evidence and freeing criminals for police mistakes. It makes the public entity liable for damages from an unlawful search or seizure. It provides priority to obtain prompt redress and provides attorney's fee so everyone will be able to afford to pursue a valid claim. It retains punitive damages and criminal prosecution where appropriate against officers guilty of malicious, fraudulent, oppressive, or criminal conduct. It returns the emphasis to the ascertainment of the truth.[28]

The California Governor's Committee summarized the arguments against the exclusionary rule:

26The President's Commission on Law Enforcement and Administration of Justice, **The Challenge of Crime in a Free Society** (Washington, D.C.: U.S. Government Printing Office, 1967), pp. 125–26.
27**Bivins v. Six Unknown Federal Narcotic Agents**, 403 U.S. 388, 418–419 (1971); See also **Irvine v. California**, 347 U.S. 128 (1954).
28**Report of the Governors Select Committee on Law Enforcement Problems: Protecting the Law Abiding, Controlling Crime in California**, (Sacramento, Cal.: State Printing Office, 1973), p. 52.

Obstacles to Effective Deterrence:

1. There is no penalty against the officer or agency
2. Exclusion may be months or years later
3. Law is complex and confused
4. Officer can't understand and comply with rules when even Supreme Court judges can't agree on what the rules are
5. No effect on bulk of police work which is not directed toward prosecution
6. Many decisions are so unreasonable they do not inspire respect and compliance
7. Because most exclusions involve inadvertent violations, officers tend to excuse all violations as trivial and technical

Other Defects of the Exclusionary Rule:

1. Suppresses the truth
2. Frees guilty criminals
3. Destroys respect for law and courts
4. Offends justice by benefiting guilty but not innocent victims
5. Causes great delay in justice
6. Makes capricious distinctions between equally guilty defendants
7. Diverts trial away from the determination of guilt
8. Creates overwhelming trial and appellate workload
9. Motion to suppress may pressure prosecutor into a bad plea bargain
10. Officer may confer immunity for serious crimes
11. Does not differentiate between honest mistakes and flagrant violations
12. Does not differentiate between releasing murderers and releasing drunks
13. Says releasing a murderer is less serious than a police mistake
14. Cure is worse than the ill[29]

The Committee's solution and the claimed advantage of their solution are also summarized:

A Better Solution:

1. Abolish the exclusionary rule
2. Make the public entity liable for ordinary damages for unlawful searches and seizures, plus attorney's fees

[29] Ibid., p. 146.

3.   Provide court trial, to avoid possible jury sympathy for police officers and bias against guilty victims

4.   Encourage use of search warrants by excluding liability for searches pursuant to a warrant

5.   Set a minimum award of $250

6.   Provide priority so victims can obtain prompt redress

7.   Retain punitive damages and criminal prosecution, where applicable, against any officers guilty of malicious, fraudulent, or oppressive conduct

Advantages of the Alternative:

1.   The individual does not bear the burden of actions taken for public benefit

2.   Criminal trials are returned to their proper purpose

3.   Financial responsibility should stimulate police training and supervision to avoid liability

4.   Gives a remedy to innocent victims, and treats guilty victims the same as innocent ones, instead of exalting the guilty

5.   *Stops freeing the guilty*

6.   *Returns emphasis to ascertainment of the truth*[30]

The search for a balance between the power of government and the right of the individual against unlawful intrusion, and the further right of citizens to the protection by government from intrusions of criminals, is continuing and ongoing. The future of our system of justice in America depends upon the preservation of both rights. The exclusionary rule has had its impact but cannot now be judged as a solution to this problem. Perhaps the recommendations of the California Governor's Committee offer new means for resolving this problem; perhaps the solution will be necessarily deferred until more innovative means are suggested.

SUMMARY

The exclusionary rule compels respect for constitutional guarantees against self-incrimination, unreasonable searches and seizures, and improper police lineups by removing the incentive to disregard these safeguards. Illegal evidence gathering by police is wasted effort when the tainted evidence is suppressed before trial or excluded at trial. The exclusionary rule is a judicial technique that gives to the accused his constitutional rights, to the police guidelines for national standards of law-

30Ibid.

ful behavior, and to the courts a reaffirmation of judicial integrity. The trend to restrain police has been a reactive process over many years in response to specific illegal, overt police behavior. The term "handcuffing the police" has been used in criticizing the exclusionary rule, but it has proven itself as an effective means of balancing the power of the government against the rights of the individual.

DISCUSSION QUESTIONS

1. Why was the U.S. Supreme Court reluctant to extend federal rules on invasion of privacy to state courts and proceedings dealing with state agents?

2. Why did the Court outlaw the "silver platter" routine?

3. Explain the "fruit of the poisoned tree" concept of derivative evidence. Why should evidence justly classified solely as fruits of lawless procedures not be used at all?

4. What is meant by the denial of a defendant's "license for perjury" in the collateral use of evidence tainted by illegality?

5. Outline several benefits accruing to the administration of justice as a result of the exclusionary rule and the growing acceptance of pretrial motions to suppress.

6. Outline the arguments against the exclusionary rule.

7. What are the alternatives to the exclusionary rule?

8. What innovative action is likely to achieve the objectives of the exclusionary rule without its many disadvantages?

GLOSSARY

AFFIDAVIT. Sworn written statement.

FRUITS OF THE POISONED TREE DOCTRINE. Doctrine barring the use of derivative evidence tainted by illegal origin (See *Silverthorne v. United States* in Chapter 11.).

IRVINE-TYPE VIOLATIONS. Purposeful violations of the constitution by police officer.

NEMO TENETUR SEIPSUM ACCUSARE. No one is bound to accuse himself.

Evidence: Arrests, Searches and Seizures

12

CHAPTER OBJECTIVES

1. Chapter 11 lists and describes the controls of police behavior in arrest situations and searches and seizures;

2. Details the procedure and requirements for warrants (arrest, search);

3. Emphasizes the role of the issuing magistrate as seeing that summary police action does not interfere with the rights of citizens; and

4. Develops the reliable informant concept as relevant to evidence of probable cause.

Lawful searches are governed by the doctrine of reasonableness and probable cause embodied in the **Fourth Amendment**. Unreasonable intrusions by police are likely to invalidate evidence necessary to prove the guilt of a person responsible for a criminal act. The Fourth Amendment protects people and their property from **unreasonable search and seizure**. In order to make this protection effective, the law presently prohibits the use of evidence seized illegally against the victim of the unreasonable search and seizure.

Under reasonable circumstances a police officer may interfere with a person's freedom of action and detain him for investigation or arrest him as the person responsible for a specific crime. A police officer may justify a reasonable intrusion to conduct a protective search or to search for and seize fruits and instrumentalities of crime or mere evidence connected with a crime or criminal. Evidence, however, may be tainted by illegality if the police unreasonably interfere with the constitutional liberties of the person stopped, arrested, "frisked," or searched when the articles or objects of evidence are seized.

Court decisions no longer permit extensive searches incidental to lawful arrests, searches to justify arrests, or sham or pretext arrests to justify searches.

The critical area is reasonableness. A uniform rule permitting a search in every case of a valid arrest would greatly simplify the work of police investigators and clarify a nebulous area of admissibility of evidence. However, a uniform approach to a complex problem precludes consideration of the reasonableness of any particular search. A single uniform standard for searches and seizures accompanying arrests would jeopardize the protection the Fourth Amendment was designed to provide each of us. Whenever it happens, a search is a once-only happening to be reviewed not on any broad rule of uniformity but rather on its merits as a particular event brought about by police action which the police involved must justify.

If there is any movement toward uniformity, it is in the concept that the officer must obtain a search warrant. A police officer who searches for and seizes evidence without a search warrant must show exceptionally compelling reasons for his actions. With each decision, the Supreme Court shows more clearly its desire to place an impartial judge between the police officer and the privacy of the individual.[1]

The Fourth Amendment[2] has two major clauses. One concerns reasonableness and the other probable cause. The first clause of the Fourth Amendment establishes a standard of reasonableness applicable to all searches and seizures, and arrests. The second clause establishes the level of reasonableness in situations best termed "warrant areas"— where the intrusion is made not for the protection of the officer, but for the purpose of collecting evidence for use at the trial of the arrestee.

---

[1]Chimel v. United States, 395 U.S. 752 (1969). Katz v. United States 389 U.S. 347 (1967). United States v. U.S. District Court, 407 U.S. 297 (1973).

[2]"The right of the people to be secure in their persons, houses, papers, and effects, against unreasonable searches and seizures, shall not be violated, and no warrants shall issue, but upon probable cause, supported by oath or affirmation, and particularly describing the place to be searched, and the persons or things to be seized."

In 1967, the United States Supreme Court held that it was reasonable, within the terms of the Fourth Amendment's protection against unreasonable searches and seizures, to conduct otherwise prohibited searches for the purpose of obtaining evidence which would aid in apprehending and convicting criminals so long as there was a link—always present in the case of fruits or instrumentalities of crime or contraband —between the article of evidence and the criminal.[3]

PROBABLE CAUSE

A simple assertion of police suspicion is not in itself a sufficient basis for a magistrate's finding of probable cause.[4]

All the definitions of probable cause require, in substance, that there be reasonable grounds for belief of guilt—a belief that is supported by evidence and inclines the mind to assume guilt, but which may leave some room for doubt. Probable cause exists when the person taking or planning action knows of fact or circumstances sufficient to justify a man of reasonable caution in believing that an offense has been or is being committed. Quite often, it is difficult to distinguish between mere suspicion and probable cause. Many situations confronting police investigators are ambiguous. Some errors in judgment are not unexpected. These mistakes, however, must be the errors of reasonable men, acting on facts to arrive at their conclusions of probability.[5]

Belief in the existence of probable cause is best based on the direct observations and knowledge of the police officer involved, but hearsay evidence may be the basis for believing probable cause exists. A police officer may rely on information received through an informant if the informant's statement is corroborated by other matters the officer knows about.[6]

Probable cause is the standard against which a particular decision to search for, and possibly seize evidence, is measured to see if it meets the constitutional requirement of reasonableness.

REASONABLENESS

Reasonableness is determined by balancing the need to search against the invasion of privacy the search entails. Wherever a man may be, he is entitled to know that he will remain free from unreasonable searches

---

[3]Warden v. Hayden, 387 U.S. 294 (1967).
[4]Apinelli v. United States, 393 U.S. 410 (1969).
[5]Brinegar v. United States, 338 U.S. 160 (1949).
[6]Jones v. United States, 362 U.S. 257 (1960).

and seizures. The Fourth Amendment was aimed at the abhorred practice of breaking in and searching homes and other buildings and seizing people's personal belongings without warrants issued by magistrates. The issue of reasonableness is determined by asking whether the invasion is justified by the evidence of criminality. The facts available to the police officer at the time of the search and seizure must be sufficient to warrant the action taken and its urgency.[7]

Today's judiciary requires a greater showing of reasonableness than was necessary in a 1949 case of bootlegging from a "wet" to a "dry" state. The dialogue accepted was:

Q: How much liquor have you got in the car this time?
A: Not too much.[8]

The right, without a search warrant, to search with appropriately given consent, to contemporaneously search persons lawfully arrested, or to search premises entered in "hot pursuit" of a suspect, are exceptions to the rule that the Fourth Amendment requires adherence to judicial processes, and that searches without judicial process are in themselves unreasonable under the Fourth Amendment.[9] Vehicles usually have a special status in relation to search warrants because of their mobility, but only when they are suspected of transporting contraband.[10]

Courts scrutinize the claims of police about consent. Consent to enter and search premises must be affirmatively shown to have been secured freely and voluntarily. Any trace of coercion ruins reliance on consent as authority for a search and seizure.[11] Quite often, consent may be secured from a person not in control of the premises or not authorized by the resident involved to grant consent to a search.[12] When any doubt exists, application for a search warrant is more than justified in order to avoid tainting the evidence likely to be seized. Courts do not approve of unrealistic claims that the person who consented to the search had "apparent authority."

The factual situations spelling out the degree of reasonableness required in making arrests and conducting hot-pursuit and arrest-based searches have remarkable variety. Each case must be judged on its individual circumstances. Factors found important in court decisions should serve as guidelines to police in learning to recognize what is reasonable in any particular situation.

[7]Chimel v. California, 395 U.S. 752 (1970).
[8]Brinegar v. United States, 338 U.S. 160 (1949).
[9]Katz v. United States, 389 U.S. 347 (1967). Warden v. Hayden, 387 U.S. 294 (1967).
[10]Carroll v. United States, 267 U.S. 132 (1925).
[11]Bumper v. North Carolina, 391 U.S. 543 (1968).
[12]Stoner v. California, 376 U.S. 483 (1964).

A search which is reasonable when it begins may violate the Fourth Amendment by virtue of its intolerable intensity or **scope.**

Two cases illustrate police searches that were so intense that the courts considered them unreasonable: (1) The contents of an entire cabin were seized after a search incidental to the arrest.[13] (2) The stomach of the arrestee was pumped out to recover two capsules of illegal drugs.[14]

The seizure of the entire contents of a small house by FBI agents, in *Kremen v. California,* may have been warranted by the remote rural area in which the house was located and the investigative necessity of processing a great deal of the collected evidence in a scientific crime laboratory. On its merits, however, it was ruled that this search was unreasonable.

The scope of the search must be strictly tied to, and justified by, the circumstances that rendered it permissible when the search began. It cannot be founded on subjective viewpoints sensitive to the evidentiary needs of investigators. It must be founded on a constitutional frame of reference—the reasonableness clause of the Fourth Amendment. For this reason, there is little or no justification for searching an arrestee's home or office, if either is the place of arrest. In the ordinary arrest it should be sufficient to search the arrestee and the area immediately within his control to provide physical protection to police from an accessible weapon or to prevent destruction of evidence within the reasonable reach of the arrestee.[15] If there is reason to believe there is other evidence in the general area, police should secure the area, obtain a search warrant, and then a search of the area may be conducted.

In *Rochin v. California,* however, there is little disagreement that the stomach-pumping was unreasonable. The facts in Rochin were as follows: Police officers investigating the illegal sale of habit-forming drugs were alerted to the activities of Rochin by information from underworld sources. Two officers forced the door of Rochin's room. Rochin was found there, sitting on the bed. The officers then asked Rochin about two capsules of suspect drugs visible on a nightstand alongside Rochin's bed. ("Whose stuff is this?") Rochin seized the capsules and put them in his mouth. The officers attempted to extract the capsules, but Rochin had apparently swallowed them. The officers then handcuffed Rochin and took him to a nearby hospital where a doctor, at the request of the two police officers, forced an emetic solution through a tube into Rochin's stomach, against his will. Two capsules of an illegal drug, morphine, were recovered when the emetic solution caused Rochin

[13]Kremen v. United States, 353 U.S. 346 (1957).
[14]Rochin v. California, 342 U.S. 165 (1952).
[15]Chimel v. California, 395 U.S. 752 (1970).

to vomit. Rochin was charged with illegal possession of morphine. He was convicted, and appealed his conviction.

The ground for his appeal was that an unreasonable search had invalidated the evidence on which his conviction was based. The opinion of the court labeled stomach-pumping a major and unreasonable intrusion. "The proceedings by which this conviction was obtained," the opinion states, "do more than offend some fastidious squeamishness or private sentimentalism about combatting crime too energetically. This is a conduct that shocks the conscience."

LAWFUL ARRESTS

Arrest is defined as the taking of a person into custody for the purpose of bringing him before a court in a criminal action (infrequently, in a civil action) in the manner authorized and specified by law. An arrest is made by an actual restraint or by submission.

The law of arrest, which is important to searches and seizures, developed from common-law doctrines. In the United States, it is mainly authorized by statute. Either a peace officer or a private person may arrest. However, a duty to arrest in appropriate circumstances is imposed on peace officers—the "sworn" employees of criminal justice agencies.

Peace officers are usually defined by local law as persons employed by law enforcement or other criminal justice agencies with a sworn duty to enforce statutes enacted to control crime and to provide for the apprehension and punishment of criminally liable persons. A peace officer may arrest with or without a warrant for felonies or misdemeanors (or traffic violations and other acts termed minor offenses and below the grade of misdemeanor) committed in his presence; or for a felony (but not a misdemeanor) committed out of his presence when he has reasonable grounds for believing the arrestee is the wanted felon. An arresting officer with reasonable grounds for his belief that the person he arrests has committed a felony is protected even if it later appears that no felony was, in fact, committed.

A peace officer may legally make an arrest with a warrant as long as he acts without malice, reasonably believes that the person arrested is the subject of the warrant, and makes the arrest at the time of day or night permitted by federal or local law or authorized in the warrant by endorsement of the issuing magistrate. Generally, felony arrest warrants can be served without any restrictions as to time of day, or day of the week. Misdemeanor warrants are normally restricted to daytime service, and Sundays service may be prohibited.

The legality of an arrest without a warrant depends upon its reasonableness. An arrest without a warrant lacks the safeguards provided by an objective predetermination that probable cause exists. Instead, the far less reliable procedure of an after-the-event justification is substituted. This procedure is likely to be subtly influenced by the familiar shortcomings of hindsight judgment. An officer who arrests without a warrant should act only on the basis of information as reliable and detailed as he would need if he *were* seeking a warrant.[16]

A misdemeanor arrest without a warrant lacks reasonable cause unless something happens in the arresting officer's presence to justify his belief that a crime has been or is being committed by the arrestee. Arresting officers in misdemeanor cases, therefore, must react to personal observation and knowledge. No amount of second-person information or report is allowed—no matter how credible the information or reliable the informant. In this connection, an offense is committed within the presence of an officer if he perceives the activity of the arrestee with his own eyes or with any of his five senses.

Felony arrests may be legal even without activity in the arresting officer's presence, but the officer must have reasonable cause to believe the suspect has committed a felony. Reasonable belief need not be based on the officer's personal knowledge. It may be based on second-hand sources of known trustworthiness and reliability supported by the officer's expertise.

Federal agents act under the authority of Title 18, *United States Code*, the "Crimes and Criminal Procedure" section of federal law. The arrest powers granted to FBI agents are typical of the authority granted to federal agents. These agents may serve warrants and make arrests without warrant for any offense against the United States committed in their presence, or for any felony that may be prosecuted under the laws of the United States if they have reasonable grounds to believe that the person to be arrested has committed or is committing such a felony.[17]

In a trade-off from common-law doctrine, **private persons** may arrest for acts committed in their presence that are misdemeanors or felonies under local law. Some states allow private persons to make arrests for felonies not committed in their presence if a felony has, in fact, been committed, and the person making the arrest knows or reasonably believes, the person arrested committed it.[18]

Some people are immune to arrest. For instance, out-of-state witnesses are immune from criminal arrests for crimes committed prior to their return to the state as a testifying witness. Legislators and militiamen are immune from civil arrest within the narrow limits associated with their work.

[16]Beck v. Ohio, 379 U.S. 89 (1964).
[17]Title 18, **United States Code**, Section 3052.
[18]California Penal Code, Section 837.

THE ARREST WARRANT

A **warrant of arrest** is simply a court order commanding that the individual named therein be taken into custody and brought before the court. The warrant usually contains:

1. *Officers Designated to Execute the Warrant:* Federal arrest warrants are usually directed to federal agents. Local warrants are generally directed to state peace officers.

2. *Name of Person to be Arrested:* The name of the person to be arrested, if known, is specified in the warrant. If the real name of the person is unknown, an alias, nickame or a fictitious name is allowed. "John Doe" and "Jane Doe" warrants are not allowed in some jurisdictions, but when they are accompanied by some descriptive words which describe the specific individual sought, they are generally issued. This is normally required when any fictitious name is used.

3. *Designation of Crime:* The warrant describes the accusation of crime. It is sufficient to designate it in general terms as robbery, arson, or grand theft.

4. *Signature of Magistrate:* To be valid, a warrant of arrest must be personally signed by the magistrate. It usually bears the impress of the court seal as well.

5. *Return:* Space for the return is provided on the warrant. This is the report to the issuing judge of action taken. The arresting officer must enter the time, date, and place he received the warrant and made arrest (if any) and sign his name and title. He is responsible for delivering the completed warrant to the issuing judge at the time he delivers the arrestee, if an arrest has been made.

An **arrest warrant** is sought by application to an appropriate judicial officer. The person seeking the warrant must appear before the judicial officer and justify his application under oath. An **affidavit** to secure a criminal arrest warrant must contain: (1) Information which, if true, directly indicates the commission of the crime charged, and the person committing it, and (2) reliable data about the source of this information.[19] The application is usually made in the form of a complaint and, like an indictment or information, it is an accusatory pleading. If the application (complaint) satisfies the presiding judge at the hearing that the offense complained of has been committed, and if there are reasonable grounds for believing the defendant committed it, the judge must issue a warrant to arrest the defendant.

An application for an arrest warrant can be made on the basis of information and belief, as well as personal knowledge. The complainant

[19]Jaben v. United States, 381 U.S. 214 (1965).

must believe the facts stated in his application and given under oath, and indicate that the information has been actually received from a trustworthy and reliable source.

BENCH WARRANTS

A **bench warrant** is slightly different from a warrant of arrest. It can be issued to compel the appearance of a witness or the presence of the defendant. It is used, after indictments or the filing of informations, to apprehend an accused who is not in custody. It is also issued, on the application of the prosecuting attorney, for the arrest of a defendant who has been released on bail, but who has failed to appear for judgment.

THE SEARCH WARRANT

A **search warrant** is an order in writing, in the name of the people, signed by a magistrate, and directed to a peace officer, commanding him to search for specified personal property in a particular place and to bring it before the magistrate. If the warrant is void, searches and seizures pursuant to it are illegal, and articles of evidence obtained as a result are not admissible against the person involved.

A search warrant may be issued when:

1. The property was stolen or embezzled
2. The property or things were used in committing a felony
3. The property or things are possessed by someone who intends to use them in committing a public offense, or have been delivered to someone for concealment
4. The property or things to be seized consists of items or evidence that tend to show a felony has been committed or tend to show that a particular person has committed a felony.

A search warrant is also obtained by application to an appropriate judicial officer. The application for a search warrant requires a deposition or **affidavit** showing probable cause for believing that something falling within one of the categories mentioned above is in a certain place. This application must provide the magistrate with sufficient facts to show that reliance on such information is reasonable. The facts may be known by the police officer seeking the warrant, or based on knowledge he received from others. When the information comes from an informant, there must be some evidence of the informant's personal knowledge and reliability. The magistrate must be satisfied that the facts alleged in the application support the conclusion that one of the grounds for issuing a search warrant exists and that there is **probable cause** for believing it exists. The magistrate can, if he wishes, examine the applicant and any witnesses produced under oath. Probable cause is determined on the basis of whether or not the applicant has reasonable cause for believing the truth of the alleged facts.

The search warrant must meet the following criteria:

1. *Particularity:* The warrant must contain a description of the place or person to be searched and property sought with some particularity. The words "or other evidence" cannot be used to justify seizure of evidence not specifically described.

2. *Procedure of Service:* The search warrant must be directed to a peace officer (others may assist him). Conditions of forcible entry may be specified. Service at night may be approved when the magistrate, upon a showing of good cause, believes such service is justified. A time limit is usually set within which the warrant must be executed. The seizure of property under authority of a search warrant requires that an officer taking the property give a detailed receipt to the person found in possession. If no person is found in possession, he should leave a receipt where the property was found.

3. *Return:* The peace officer executing the search warrant must make a return (report) under oath and deliver to the magistrate an inventory of all property seized. This must be done publicly or in the presence of the person from whom the property was taken. The inventory usually is a duplicate copy of the required receipt, and the return is frequently the police arrest or offense report. The use of such reports does not taint this procedure, but rather enhances it because they contain the stories of the incidents written in the course of official business.[20]

THE RELIABLE INFORMER CONCEPT

The reliable informer concept justifies police action when police may lack personal knowledge.

In 1806 the Supreme Court expressed the view that oaths and affirmations to secure warrants either for arrest or for search and seizure must state facts with a sufficient definiteness that civil damages could be assessed against the person swearing or a criminal penalty imposed upon one falsely signing such statements.[21] Chief Justice Marshall noted

[20]Paul B. Weston and Kenneth M. Wells, **Criminal Investigation: Basic Perspectives**, 2nd ed. (Englewood Cliffs, N.J.: Prentice-Hall, Inc., 1974), Chapter 25, pp. 427–47.
[21]**Ex parte Burford**, 3 Cranch 448.

this point by writing: "If the charge against him (Burford) was malicious, or grounded on perjury, whom could he sue for the malicious prosecution? Or whom could he indict for perjury?"

In 1959, in *Draper v. United States*,[22] the Supreme Court held that there was probable cause for arresting Draper without a warrant, and for making a search incidental to the arrest, on the basis of information the arresting officers had received by telephone from a reliable informant. The only personal knowledge the arresting officer had at the time of the arrest was that the suspect met the description given by the informant and was alighting from a train as the informant said he would be, and was within the time span mentioned by the informant. When stopped, arrested, and searched he was found to be in possession of illegal narcotics as stated by the informant.

In 1960, in the case of *Jones v. United States*[23] the U.S. Supreme Court ruled that an affidavit is not to be deemed insufficient by virtue of the fact that it sets out, not the affiant's observations, but those of another, as long as a substantial basis for believing the hearsay is presented. In his affidavit in this case, the police investigator, Detective Didone of the Metropolitan (Washington, D.C.) Police Department swore there was a basis for accepting the informant's story: The informant had previously given accurate information; his story was corroborated by other sources of information; and the suspect Jones was known by police to be a narcotics user.

In 1967, in *McCray v. Illinois*, McCray was arrested, searched, and convicted for the illegal possession of heroin found in the course of a search. The arresting officers justified the search on the basis of information from an informant whose reliability had been established. In sustaining the informer privilege in this case the Court commented that the arresting officers acted "in good faith upon credible information supplied by a reliable informant."[24]

Although a great deal has been written about the doubtful character of the so-called reliable informant and his dubious motives for informing, it is the informer's record for reliable performance on which he is evaluated. A reliable informant who gives the police information on which to base probable cause for summary action, or for an affidavit for a warrant to arrest or search, is necessarily a steady source of information. The informant's reliability is personally known to the police officer, and the officer is prepared to state that the informant in question has given similar information on past occasions, and that this information has proven to be accurate.

---

[22]358 U.S. 307 (1959).
[23]362 U.S. 257 (1960).
[24]386 U.S. 300 (1967).

ARREST-BASED SEARCHES

Traditionally, officers and agents of law enforcement agencies have believed that **searches and seizures incidental to or accompanying a lawful arrest** are reasonable. Probable cause and reasonableness of this type of intrusion was believed to flow from the circumstances which led to and justified arrest. This belief has generally been in harmony with prevailing rules of decisional law. Majority opinions in cases recently reviewed by the United States Supreme Court have both supported and limited this right to search and seize. The basic conflict is between searches and an accused's constitutional rights (primarily his right to be let alone).

In each case in which there is a search for evidence at the time of arrest, the circumstances must indicate both a bona fide arrest and a search merely incidental to the apprehension.

When a valid arrest is made the **scope of the search** is now limited to the person of the arrestee and the area within the immediate control of the prisoner at the time of arrest, from which he might gain possession of a weapon, or of destructible evidence. A weapon, if discovered, can be seized because the prisoner might use it to assault the officer or to escape. Articles of evidence are seized to prevent their concealment or destruction. This is the doctrine of *Chimel v. California.*[25]

All too often, limitations such as those imposed on police officers by *Chimel* are misunderstood by investigators. As a result, legally significant evidence is tainted beyond hope by procedures which the court has said are forbidden by the Fourth Amendment.

In this decision, the Court noted that the doctrine that a warrantless search "incidental to a lawful arrest" may generally extend to the entire area considered to be in the "possession" or "control" of the person arrested developed from the case of *United States v. Rabinowitz,*[26] but the Court said that this doctrine was wrong. "That doctrine," the majority opinion states, "at least in the broad sense in which it was applied by the California courts in this case, can withstand neither historical nor rational analysis." Further, quoting its decision in *Terry v. Ohio,* the Court outlined its position on these searches:

> 1. We emphasized that the police must, whenever practicable, obtain advance judicial approval of searches and seizures through the warrant process.
> 2. The scope of a search must be strictly tied to and justified by the circumstances which rendered its initiation permissible.

[25]395 U.S. 752 (1970). See case study in Chapter 10.
[26]339 U.S. 56 (1950).

3.   The practice of searching a man's house when he is arrested in it is founded on little more than a subjective view regarding the acceptability of certain sorts of police conduct and not on the considerations of the Fourth Amendment.

4.   There is ample justification, however, for a search of the arrestee's person and the area within his immediate control. This is the area from within which he might gain possession of a weapon or destructible evidence.

5.   There is no comparable justification, however, for routinely searching rooms other than that in which an arrest occurs, or—for that matter —for searching through all the desk drawers or other concealed areas in that room itself.[27]

In 1973 the United States Supreme Court, in two cases decided on the same day, set guidelines for arrest-based search.[28] Arrests in both cases were based upon traffic-offense stops[29] which the Court defined as custodial arrests (full-custody arrests). Both arresting officers conducted a full search of the prisoners. The search in each case resulted in the discovery of contraband, which in turn led to a felony possession conviction. The Court commented that the effect of these decisions is to authorize police to fully search the person of an arrestee if the arrest has been valid and the arrestee has been placed in custody, despite the fact the arrest may be for a minor offense. The Court held all arrests to be alike. The Court described this as a custodial arrest, distinguishable from an investigative stop as in *Terry v. Ohio*,[30] and the search is not confined to the frisk necessary for the self-protection of the officer.

A custodial arrest of a suspect based upon probable cause is a reasonable intrusion under the Fourth Amendment; that intrusion being lawful, a search incident to the arrest requires no additional justification. It is the fact of the lawful arrest which establishes the authority to search, and we hold that in the case of a lawful custodial arrest a full search of the person is not only an exception to the warrant requirement of the Fourth Amendment but also a "reasonable" search under that Amendment.[31]

English and American law has always recognized the right, on the part of arresting officers, to search the person of an accused who has been legally arrested to discover and seize fruits or evidence of crime.[32] When a man is legally arrested for an offense, whatever is found

[27]395 U.S. 752 (1970), p. 762.
[28]United States v. Robinson, 414 U.S. 218 (1973); Gustafson v. Florida, 414 U.S. 260 (1973).
[29]Operating a vehicle after revocation of license (**Robinson**); no license in possession of operator (**Gustafson**).
[30]392 U.S. 1 (1968).
[31]United States v. Robinson, 414 U.S. 218 (1973).
[32]Weeks v. United States, 232 U.S. 383 (1914).

on his person, or in his control, which may be used to prove the offense may be seized and held as evidence in the prosecution.[33]

ENTRY

The laws of many states differ on the exact circumstances under which a police officer may break and enter a dwelling, but there is some uniformity when the purpose of the entry is (1) to arrest for a felony; (2) to prevent the flight of the person to be arrested, (3) to prevent such a person from destroying evidence, or (4) considered necessary by the police officer because his life or the life of someone inside is endangered. Entry, however, requires **notice**. Such action by federal agents to execute a search warrant must follow the provisions of Title 18, *United States Code*, which allows an agent to break and enter forcibly "if, after notice of his authority and purpose, he is refused admittance or when necessary to liberate himself or a person aiding him in the execution of the warrant." State agents are more likely to obtain court approval of their entry when they can testify that they expressly announced their purpose in demanding admission or can cite facts indicating their certainty that the person involved already knew their purpose.[34]

Sometimes, the method of entry may suggest that notice or demand is unnecessary, as when officers enter through an unlocked door. However, the opening of an unlocked door is a breaking and notice and demand is required. In one case, *Sabbath v. United States*,[35] United States Customs agents knocked on the door of an apartment, waited a few moments, and then entered the apartment. The case was reversed because of the agents' failure to announce their authority and purpose. Failure to give notice by raiding police to occupants of a residence has resulted in raids being carried out in the wrong premises. In addition, the entry of armed unidentified persons into a home might be resisted forcibly by some householders, with unlimited possibilities for tragedy.

STOP AND FRISK

The stop-and-frisk routine is less than an arrest. It is a "stop" only, and the search is a **superficial patdown for weapons**. A police officer is alerted to suspicious conduct and stops the suspect, "frisking" him because it is usually reasonable, under the circumstances, to fear the suspect is armed and may attack his questioner. To justify this type of

---

[33]Carroll v. United States, 267 U.S. 132 (1925); United States v. Robinson, 414 U.S. 218 (1973).
[34]Miller v. United States, 357 U.S. 301 (1958).
[35]391 U.S. 585 (1968). See also People v. Rosalas, 68 Cal. 2d 299 (1968).

intrusion, the police officer must be able to point to specific and definite facts which, together with rational inferences from those facts, reasonably warrant the intrusion. The Court, in *Terry v. Ohio*,[36] established the objective **standard** to be followed in these cases: "Would the facts warrant a man of reasonable caution in the belief the action taken was appropriate?"

When a police officer observes unusual conduct which leads him reasonably to conclude, in the light of his experience, that criminal activity may be afoot and that the person he is dealing with may be armed and presently dangerous; when, in the course of investigating this behavior, he identifies himself as a policeman and makes reasonable inquiries; and when nothing in the initial stages of the encounter serves to dispel his reasonable fear for his own or other's safety, he is entitled, for the protection of himself and others in the area, to conduct a carefully limited search of the outer clothing of such a person in an attempt to discover weapons that might be used to assault him. Such a search is reasonable under the Fourth Amendment, and any weapons seized may properly be introduced in evidence against the person from whom they were taken.[37]

SUMMARY

Probable cause and reasonableness balance the conflict between police intrusions and an individual's privacy: Is the intrusion justified by the evidence of criminality? Warrants position a magistrate between the police and the citizen; this judicial officer must be satisfied that police applicants have justified their requests for prior judicial approval of contemplated police action. The reliable informant concept is developed as relevant to evidence of probable cause. Peace officers are given more authority in arrest situations than are private persons; this authority is based on objective reasoning and officer safety in stop-and-frisk cases. In detailing the scope of warrantless searches incident to a lawful arrest, the lawfulness of the arrest is cited as justification for a full body search, despite the less serious nature of some offenses for which arrests are made by police.

DISCUSSION QUESTIONS

1. Why is it important for a policeman to have up to date knowledge of arrest and search-and-seizure laws?

[36]392 U.S. 1 (1968). See case study in Chapter 10.
[37]Terry v. Ohio, 392 U.S. 1 (1968); People v. Waters, 30 Cal. App. 3rd 354 (1973).

2.   What may an officer do to investigate a suspicious individual short of arrest?
3.   How extensively may an officer search while making a lawful arrest? When making a limited protective search for weapons?
4.   What is probable cause?
5.   What are the laws pertaining to a citizen's arrest?
6.   What is a search warrant? How is it obtained? What is its importance?
7.   What role should informants play in arrest and search?

GLOSSARY

Ex Parte.   On one side only; no adverse party in proceedings.

Peace Officer.   A "sworn" police officer, sheriff's deputy, or state investigator; usually named by job title in state statutes giving peace officers power to carry out their sworn duty.

Return (Search Warrant).   A report of police action when executing a search warrant, including an inventory of property seized and a description of the place found.

13 Confessions and Admissions

CHAPTER OBJECTIVES

1. Confessions and admissions are defined in this chapter;
2. The controls on police behavior during police interrogations are listed and described; and
3. The circumstances indicating whether a confession or admission is voluntary or involuntary are detailed, with the exclusion of involuntary statements. The thesis that
4. Involuntary confessions are basically untrustworthy is expressed, and
5. The involuntary-confession aspect of plea negotiations and the acceptance of guilty pleas described; procedural safeguards against judicial compulsion are also cited. Finally,
6. The contribution of *Miranda v. Arizona* toward upgrading police interrogation standards is pointed out.

A **confession** is a statement—verbal, written, or both—by a person accused of crime saying that he is guilty of the specific crime with which he is charged. An extrajudicial confession is a statement made out of court to any person. A judicial confession is usually a plea of guilty made in court or at a coroner's inquest. A plea of guilty accepted at a prior arraignment, hearing or trial is considered an extrajudicial confession at a subsequent trial.

A reading of appellate opinions in the **"confession cases"** can lead to a broad knowledge of interrogation techniques that may violate an accused's rights. Many of these cases, reversing previous lower court decisions, set forth the doctrine that involuntary confessions should not be admitted into evidence against the person making them, not only because no one should be compelled to incriminate himself,[1] but also because of the unreliability of any coerced confession.

An **admission** is less than a confession. The facts admitted as true only raise the inference of guilt when viewed in connection with other evidence or circumstances. The term "damaging" is used frequently to modify the word "admission." This illustrates how these statements do little more than connect some aspect of the crime with the person making the admission.

THE JACKSON-DENNO HEARING

It is up to the trial judge to determine **whether a confession is voluntary**. The standard of proof for admitting confessions places a heavy burden on the prosecution. On the issue of voluntariness, the role of the trial judge has been outlined by the U.S. Supreme Court in *Jackson v. Denno*.[2] In this landmark case the court ruled: It is both practical and desirable that, in cases to be tried thereafter, a proper determination of voluntariness be made before allowing the confession to be presented as evidence to the jury which is adjudicating guilt or innocence.

Jackson shot and killed a police officer following a robbery in a New York hotel. He was badly wounded in the robbery. His confession was made to police and to an assistant prosecutor shortly after he was admitted to the hospital for treatment, but before surgery. He was convicted of first-degree murder on a web of evidence based in part on his confession. His petition for relief was reviewed by the United States Supreme Court. Jackson contended that he was in pain during the police

---

[1]No person shall be held to answer for a capital, or otherwise infamous crime, unless on a presentment or indictment of a Grand jury, except in cases arising in the land or naval forces, or in the Militia, when in actual service in time of War or public danger; nor shall any person be subject for the same offence to be twice put in jeopardy of life or limb; **nor shall be compelled in any criminal case to be a witness against himself**, nor be deprived of life, liberty, or property, without due process of law; nor shall private property be taken for public use, without just compensation.—Amendment V, U.S. Constitution (emphasis added).
[2]378 U.S. 368 (1964).

interrogation, was refused water, and was told he would not be let alone until he had answered all the questions of the police. The evidence showed that the hospital staff had administered demerol and scopolamine and that Jackson had lost a great deal of blood. The state denied that the drugs had had any effect on his statements and presented evidence to indicate the prisoner was denied water because of his impending operation. Under the New York rules, a confession could be submitted to the jury with instructions to disregard it if they found the confession to be involuntary, or to determine its reliability and weigh it accordingly if they found the confession voluntary. The jury in Jackson's case returned a verdict of guilty. The U.S. Supreme Court reversed this conviction, saying that New York's procedure did not afford a reliable determination of the voluntariness of the confession, and that it was not clear whether the jury had found the confession to be voluntary or involuntary. The danger, the Court pointed out, was that the jury might believe the confession and find it difficult to understand the policy forbidding reliance on a coerced-but-true confession.

THE ISSUE OF VOLUNTARINESS

A confession is judged to be **involuntary** when it is induced by: (1) promise and hope of reward or benefit, (2) coercion (violence, threats or fear), (3) judicial compulsion.

Promise and Hope of Reward; Coercion

In attempting to lay the foundation before introducing a confession as evidence, the questioner conducting the direct examination will usually probe this area of promises and hope of reward, and coercion, with three or four simple questions:

Q: Either before or during the questioning of the defendant were any promises of reward or benefit made to persuade him to confess?
A: No.
Q: Was there any force or threats of force made against him or his family if he failed to answer your questions?
A: No.
Q: Were his answers freely and voluntarily made?
A: Yes.

Promises on which the accused person can depend must be made by a person in authority, and almost any employee of a criminal justice agency has been defined as a person in authority. An accused individual's belief or hope that confessing will gain some advantage is often one of the factors that lead him to admit guilt even though his hope is not induced by the promise of a public official. Such belief or hope does not make a confession involuntary when it originates in the mind of the accused, or is suggested by a friend, relative, or legal counsel. It is not uncommon for a guilty individual to react this way to the threat inherent when police investigation focuses on his criminal activities.

In one case, statements made by a convicted defendant to a probation officer during a pre-sentence interview were held to be involuntary when proffered as evidence. The convicted defendant in the case[3] had pled guilty to a single charge of robbery, after being indicted on several felony charges. He made damaging admissions to a probation officer during a pre-sentence interview, but he then withdrew his guilty plea and pled not guilty to all three felony charges in the indictment. The probation officer testified at the subsequent trial about the content of the admissions, and said that all convicted persons interviewed by him were informed that they would not be recommended for release on probation if they did not tell the truth. The defendant was convicted on all three charges. However, the California Supreme Court reversed the action of the trial court, saying the defendant's admissions were involuntary and, therefore, inadmissible as evidence against him.

On the issue of coercion, the question in each case is whether the defendant's will was overborne at the time he confessed.[4] Inquiry into the voluntariness of a confession involves finding out (1) the crude historical facts—the occurrences and events surrounding the confession; and (2) the internal, "psychological" facts (through reconstructing what the accused's state of mind must have been—this often requires imagination and a great deal of inference).[5]

The probability of truth or falsity of the confession is not in issue during this dual inquiry. The attention of the judge conducting the inquiry should be focused, for the purposes of the Constitution, on the question of whether the questioners behaved in such a way as to overbear the accused's will to resist and bring about a confession that was not freely self-determined.[6]

Judicial Compulsion—Guilty Pleas

Judicial compulsion is inherent in the sentencing function of the judiciary. It is not any express pressure upon any one accused person. It is the result of the judicial role. For this reason, it must be shown that

[3]People v. Quinn, 61 Cal. 551 (1964). See also People v. Siemsen, 153 Cal. 387 (1908).
[4]Lynumn v. Illinois, 372 U.S. 528 (1963).
[5]Culombe v. Connecticut, 367 U.S. 568 (1961).
[6]Rogers v. Richmond, 365 U.S. 534 (1961).

judicial confessions (pleas of guilty) are not influenced by fear or hope of leniency, or lack of knowledge of all the implications of such action. Because this inherent judicial compulsion is a thing of value in plea negotiation, it must be shown that the plea did not result from misrepresentation or over-persuasion during plea negotiations. Finally, there must be some evidence that the accused understood the crime charged and the possible sentence, and that the plea was not the result of ignorance or misunderstanding.

The **plea negotiation** has finally become a respectable method of disposition of criminal cases. It has always been a fact in the practical administration of justice and obtained its questionable reputation because it was carried on without express judicial sanction and secretly. This very secrecy caused defendant complaints of judicial compulsion to plead guilty owing to alleged promises made by prosecutors or judges, transmitted to them by their own attorneys; the complaint being expressed when the defendant claimed the promise was not kept.

Beginning in the late 1960s and culminating in the early 1970s, cases throughout the country brought plea negotiation out into open court where the promises made became part of the court record. Illustrative of these cases was *People v. West.*[7] Dale West entered a *nolo contendre* as the result of a plea bargain, and subsequently appealed on the basis that his plea had been coerced and not "voluntary" because of the promises involved in the bargain. The California Supreme Court took the opportunity to fully discuss the propriety (and necessity) of plea bargaining:

> We undertake here to confirm the legality of the plea bargain and set up procedures for its acceptance or rejection in the strong light of full disclosure. In a day when courts strive to simplify trial procedures and to achieve speedier dispatch of litigation, we believe that the recognition of the legal status of the plea bargain will serve as a salutary time saver as well as a means to dispel the procedural obscurantism that now enshrouds it. The grant of legal status to the plea bargain should enable the court in each case to reach a frank, open and realistic appraisal of its propriety.

The Effect and Procedures:

1. A plea of guilty or *nolo contendre* is not rendered "involuntary" merely because it is the product of plea bargaining between defendant and the state.

2. Counsel should disclose any plea bargain to the court, and the terms of that agreement should become part of the record of the case.

3. The court may accept a bargained plea of guilty, or *nolo contendre*

[7]3 Cal. 3d 595 (1970).

to any lesser offense reasonably related to the offense charged in the accusatory pleading.[8]

The questions trial judges often ask at hearings about the accuracy of a guilty plea illustrate the requirement being enforced in many courts: voluntariness and accuracy.[9]

Before an accused person enters a plea of guilty, the sentencing judge asks the defendant about the **voluntariness** of his plea and his **understanding of its nature** and consequences. The following line of questioning explores this area in a murder-robbery case:

COURT: (Addressing the defendant.) You come up here with your attorney. Your attorney has indicated you want to withdraw your plea of not guilty as to the charges, and we'll take them one at a time. Do you want to withdraw your plea of not guilty as to the first count?

DEFENDANT: Yes, sir.

COURT: That's the count charging you with the murder of Vernice Bowen. You do withdraw your plea of not guilty?

DEFENDANT: Yes, I do.

COURT: Counsel, do you concur in the withdrawal of the plea of not guilty as indicated?

MR. SMITH (defense attorney):   Yes, your Honor.

COURT: All right, I'll grant you permission to withdraw your plea of not guilty. You understand the nature of the charges against you in this court?

DEFENDANT: Yes, sir, I do.

COURT: You've discussed this all with Mr. Smith, have you?

DEFENDANT: Yes, I have.

COURT: Your attorney has explained your constitutional rights to you, has he?

DEFENDANT: Yes, sir.

COURT: Are you changing your plea freely and voluntarily, without threat or fear to yourself or to anyone closely related to or associated with you?

DEFENDANT: Yes, your Honor.

COURT: Has anyone made you any promise of a lesser sentence, or probation, reward or immunity, or anything else, in order to induce you to change your plea?

It is at this point in the court's questioning of the defendant that any promises made pursuant to a plea bargain are explained to the defendant there in open court and on the record. The defendant is asked if he is under the impression that there have been any other or different

---

[8]People v. West, 3 Cal. 3d 595 (1970), p. 611.
[9]Donald J. Newman, **Conviction: The Determination of Guilt or Innocence Without Trial** (Boston, Mass.: Little Brown & Co., 1966), p. 27.

promises made in connection with his plea or change of plea. If the defendant believes there were other commitments he has the opportunity then to express that belief. If such commitments were made they are confirmed then on the record; if the defendant's understanding of the commitments made is mistaken, the court will not accept his plea, or a change of plea, until he has had an opportunity to fully confer with his attorney and decide whether he wishes to accept the commitments offered in exchange for his plea or change of plea. If the defendant does enter his plea of guilty based upon commitments which the court later determines cannot be kept, he is allowed by the court to withdraw the plea of guilty and enter a not guilty plea without prejudice attaching from his prior guilty plea.[10]

COURT: You understand that the matter of sentence is to be determined by the jury or by the court in this case?

DEFENDANT: Yes, I do.

COURT: You are charged with murder. Are you changing your plea to guilty? Is that going to be—

MR. SMITH: Yes, your Honor.

COURT: Are you changing your plea to guilty because in truth and in fact you are guilty, and for no other reason, Mr. T——?

DEFENDANT: Yes, sir.

COURT: Do you waive a further reading of the indictment as to count one?

MR. SMITH: Yes, your Honor.

COURT: What is your plea, Mr. T ——?

DEFENDANT: Guilty.

(The court repeated this process for the other counts in this indictment, and then took up the question of the degree of guilt.)

COURT: All right. The court will find that the degree of murder as to count one is first degree.

DISTRICT ATTORNEY: Your Honor, I think on that matter, if the defense is willing, we'd be willing to stipulate to that.

COURT: I think so. I understood there would be a stipulation that it was first degree, is that right?

MR. SMITH: So stipulated.

DEPUTY DISTRICT ATTORNEY: The People so stipulate; does the defendant?

COURT: Mr. T——, I think since you've entered your plea, you've got to concur also that this is murder in the first degree.

DEFENDANT: Yes.

MR. SMITH: Your Honor, it is my understanding that murder in the first degree is stipulated to, since the robbery count would be first-

[10]People v. West, 3 Cal 3d 595 (1970), and citations to other jurisdictions extensively set forth in that decision.

degree robbery, and this is a murder committed in the course of a robbery or attempted robbery.

COURT: Well, I don't know if the district attorney wants to be limited to that or not.

DEPUTY DISTRICT ATTORNEY: My feeling is that I would assume that the defense attorney has explained to his client, and I would appreciate it if the court would inquire of the defendant whether he fully understands what we are now talking about, and it has been explained to him, so that he would stipulate.

COURT: I think so. This has been explained to you, about murder in the first degree if it's committed while committing a robbery? You understand that, is that right, Mr. T——?

DEFENDANT: Yes.

COURT: With that in mind, do you agree that this is murder in the first degree?

DEFENDANT: Yes, I do.

DEPUTY DISTRICT ATTORNEY: Your Honor, may we go back to count number three? There's a further matter charged there, and I think that should be established as to degree.

COURT: Yes, (addressing the defendant). I think in the third count I neglected to ask you if at the time of the commission of the offense— it says: "said defendant was armed with a deadly weapon, to wit, a .410 gauge shotgun." Do you admit that you were so armed?

DEFENDANT: Yes, I do.

STANDARDS FOR POLICE INTERROGATION

The case of *Miranda v. Arizona*[11] is the controlling case on the **standards of police interrogation**. In dealing with statements obtained through interrogation, the court did not purport to find all such confessions inadmissible. The majority opinion of the court in this case points out that any statement given freely and voluntarily without any compelling influences is, of course, admissible in evidence. "Volunteered statements of any kind are not barred by the Fifth Amendment and their admissibility is not affected by our holding today." Police are not required to stop a person who enters a police station and states that he wishes to confess to a crime, or to silence a person who calls the police to offer a confession or any other statement he desires to make.

The majority opinion also spells out circumstances which will safeguard the integrity of the confessions secured by interrogation. This segment of the opinion states that unless other fully effective means are devised to inform accused persons of their **right of silence** and to assure

[11]384 U.S. 436 (1966).

a continuous opportunity to exercise this right, the following measures are required: Before questioning, the person must be told that (1) he has a right to remain silent, that any statement he does make may be used as evidence against him, and (2) he has a right to the presence of an attorney, either retained or appointed.

The defendant may waive these rights, provided the **waiver** is made voluntarily, knowingly, and intelligently. If, however, he indicates in any manner and at any stage of the process that he wishes to consult with an attorney before speaking, there can be no questioning. Also, if the individual indicates in any manner that he does not wish to be interrogated, the police may not question him. The mere fact that he may have answered some questions or volunteered some statements on his own does not deprive him of the right to refrain from answering any further inquiries until he has consulted with an attorney and thereafter consents to be questioned.

The United States Supreme Court in 1974 with a newly balanced court reexamined the *Miranda* decision in the case of *Michigan v. Tucker,* __U.S.__; 41 L. Ed. 2d 182 (1974). The case itself was not a direct assault on Miranda because it involved an interrogation which was held after *Escobedo v. Illinois* had required advice and before *Miranda v. Arizona*[12] had set down rules for such advice, which included informing the suspect he could have an attorney appointed for him if he couldn't afford to hire one. There was also a question of the fruits of such interrogation being admitted at the trial of Thomas Tucker.

Neither the arguments of counsel nor the decision of the court in *Michigan v. Tucker* reflected a concern under the Sixth Amendment's right to counsel, but instead concentrated upon the Fifth Amendment's right against compulsory self-incrimination. The emphasis of the court was the evil which preceded the Miranda decision: "Not whether a defendant had waived his privilege against compulsory self-incrimination but seemingly whether his statement was voluntary . . . examining the circumstances of interrogation to determine whether the processes were so unfair or unreasonable as to render a subsequent confession involuntary."[13]

A coalition of justices appointed to the Supreme Court after the *Miranda* decision (Chief Justice Burger, Justices Rehnquist, Powell, and Blackman), and Justices Stewart and White, who dissented to the *Miranda* opinion, here placed a limiting interpretation on the philosophy of and the rules set out in the *Miranda* case.

The major thrust of *Michigan v. Tucker* and the rationale for its decision are shown by the following extracts from the majority opinion:

---

[12]378 U.S. 478 (1964); 384 U.S. 436 (1966).
[13]__U.S.__; 41 L. Ed. 2d 182 at 191.

It was not until this Court's decision in Miranda that the privilege against compulsory self-incrimination, was seen as the principal protection for a person facing police interrogation. This privilege was thought to offer a more comprehensive and less subjective protection than the doctrine of previous cases. . . .

Thus the Court in Miranda, for the first time, expressly declared that the Self-Incrimination Clause was applicable to state interrogations at a police station, and that a defendant's statements might be excluded at trial despite their voluntary character under traditional principles.

To supplement this new doctrine, and to help police officers conduct interrogations without facing a continued risk that valuable evidence would be lost, the Court in Miranda established a set of specific protective guidelines, now commonly known as the Miranda rules. The Court declared that "the prosecution may not use statements, whether exculpatory or inculpatory, stemming from custodial interrogation of the defendant unless it demonstrates the use of procedural safeguards effective to secure the privilege against self-incrimination."

The Court recognized that these procedural safeguards were not themselves rights protected by the Constitution but were instead measures to insure that the right against compulsory self-incrimination was protected. . . .

The suggested safeguards were not intended to "create a constitutional straightjacket," but rather to provide practical reinforcement for the right against compulsory self-incrimination.

A comparison of the facts in this case with the historical circumstances underlying the privilege against compulsory self-incrimination strongly indicates that the police conduct here did not deprive respondent of his privilege against compulsory self-incrimination as such, but rather failed to make available to him the full measure of procedural safeguards associated with that right since Miranda. Certainly no one could contend that the interrogation faced by respondent bore any resemblance to the historical practices at which the right against compulsory self-incrimination was aimed.

The police had "warned [respondent] that he had the right to remain silent," and the record in this case clearly shows that respondent was informed that any evidence taken could be used against him." The record is also clear that respondent was asked whether he wanted an attorney and that he replied that he did not. Thus, his statements could hardly be termed involuntary as that term has been defined in the decisions of this Court. Additionally, there were no legal sanctions, such as the threat of contempt, which could have been applied to respondent had he chosen to remain silent. He was simply not exposed to "the cruel trilemma of self-accusation, perjury, or contempt." Murphy v Waterfront Commission, 378 U.S. 52, 55, 12 L. Ed. 2d 678, 84 S. Ct. 1594 (1964).

Our determination that the interrogation in this case involved no compulsion sufficient to breach the right against compulsory self-incrimination does not mean there was not a disregard, albeit an inadvertent disregard, of the procedural rules later established in Miranda. The question for decision is how sweeping the judicially imposed consequences of this disregard shall be. . . .

But we have already concluded that the police conduct at issue here did not abridge respondent's constitutional privilege against compulsory self-incrimination, but departed only from the prophylactic standards later laid down by this Court in Miranda to safeguard that privilege.

Just as the law does not require that a defendant receive a perfect trial, only a fair one, it cannot realistically require that policemen investigating serious crimes make no errors whatsoever. The pressures of law enforcement and the vagaries of human nature would make such an expectation unrealistic. Before we penalize police error, therefore, we must consider whether the sanction serves a valid and useful purpose.[14]

The court implies, but does not decide, that the "valid and useful purpose" may be to deter future police behavior which would deny the guarantee of the 5th Amendment's right against compulsory self-incrimination. This implication may well lead to a "totality of the circumstances" test leaning heavily upon whether the failure to advise tends to promote compulsory self-incrimination and is wilfull conduct by the police. A future decision could decide that exclusion is not necessary for a *Miranda* violation unless the above additional test is also violated.

LEGISLATIVE GUIDELINES—CONFESSIONS AND ADMISSIONS

Title III of the Omnibus Crime Control and Safe Streets Act of 1968[15] provides for the projected admissibility of confessions and statements on the preliminary fact issues of voluntariness.

This law reads as follows:

(a) In any criminal prosecution brought by the United States or by the District of Columbia, a confession, as defined in subsection (e) hereof, shall be admissible in evidence if it is voluntarily given. Before such confession is received in evidence, the trial judge shall, out of the presence of the jury, determine any issue as to voluntariness. If the trial judge determines that the confession was voluntarily made it shall permit the jury to hear relevant evidence on the issue of voluntariness and shall instruct the jury to give such weight to the confession as the jury feels it deserves under all the circumstances.

(b) *Voluntariness of Confession**. The trial judge in determining the issue of voluntariness shall take into consideration all the circumstances surrounding the giving of the confession, including (1) the time elapsing between arrest and arraignment of the defendant making the confession, if it was made after arrest and before arraignment, (2) whether such defendant knew the nature of the offense with which he was charged or of which he was suspected

---

[14]**Michigan v. Tucker**, 41 L. Ed. 2d 182 at 192–94 (1974).
[15]Public Law 90–351 (1968).
*Heads added by authors.

at the time of making the confession, (3) whether or not such defendant was advised or knew that he was not required to make any statement and that any such statement could be used against him, (4) whether or not such defendant had been advised prior to questioning of his right to the assistance of counsel; and (5) whether or not such defendant was without the assistance of counsel when questioned and when giving such confession. The presence or absence of any of the above-mentioned factors to be taken into consideration by the judge need not be conclusive on the issue of voluntariness of the confession.

(c) *Delay in Arraignment of Arrestee.* In any criminal prosecution by the District of Columbia, a confession made or given by a person who is a defendant therein, while such person was under arrest or other detention in the custody of any law-enforcement officer or law-enforcement agency, shall not be inadmissible solely because of delay in bringing such person before a commissioner or other officer empowered to commit persons charged with offenses against the laws of the United States or of the District of Columbia if such confession is found by the trial judge to have been made voluntarily and if the weight to be given the confession is left to the jury and if such confession was made or given by such person within six hours immediately following his arrest or other detention: **Provided**, that the time limitation contained in this subsection shall not apply in any case in which the delay in bringing such person before such commission or other officer beyond such six-hour period is found by the trial judge to be reasonable considering the means of transportation and distance to be traveled to the nearest available such commissioner or other officer.

(d) *Confession Without Interrogation; Non-Custodial Confession.* Nothing contained in this section shall bar the admission in evidence of any confession made or given voluntarily by any person to any other person without interrogation by anyone, or at any time at which the person who made or gave such confession was not under arrest or other detention.

(e) *Confession Defined.* As used in this section, the term "confession" means any confession of guilt of any criminal offense or any self-incriminating statement made or given orally or in writing.

This legislation was enacted by Congress as a reaction to, and a legislative attempt to overrule, the decisions of *Escobedo v. Illinois*[16] and *Miranda v. Arizona*.[17] It is of doubtful constitutionality in the areas which conflict with and purport to change the impact of those cases, because the holdings in both cases were constitutionally based. In its concluding segments, this section of the law seeks to restore the doctrine of **"totality of circumstances"** in reviewing confessions secured during police interrogation. The totality of circumstances doctrine was blamed,

[16]378 U.S. 478 (1964).
[17]384 U.S. 436 (1966).

in part, for the many confession cases presented to the U.S. Supreme Court which resulted in the series of court decisions restricting some former practices of police interrogators. Police may not deliberately refuse to warn accused persons of ·their constitutional rights or prevent them from having the assistance of legal counsel; just as they are not free to use physical or psychological coercion in any form.

SUMMARY

Statements given voluntarily without any compelling influences such as promises or hope of reward, coercion, or judicial compulsion are admissible in evidence. The basic issue is voluntariness; involuntary confessions are basically untrustworthy and violative of the Fifth Amendment's privilege against self-incrimination. The United States Supreme Court's decision in *Miranda v. Arizona* established standards for police interrogators requiring the accused to be warned of his constitutional right to silence (Fifth Amendment) and right to legal counsel (Sixth Amendment). One major court decision, *Michigan v. Tucker*, limits the *Miranda* doctrine, but legislation designed to limit the impact of *Miranda* upon police interrogation practices are likely to be modified by future case law. *Miranda* established standards, no more than procedural safeguards, aligned with the constitutional rights of persons accused of crime.

DISCUSSION QUESTIONS

1. What is the difference between a confession and an admission? Is the difference important for admissibility rules?
2. Who initially passes on the admissibility of a defendant's confession or admission?
3. What must the court determine before accepting a guilty plea?
4. What is coercion?
5. What are the present standards for police interrogation?
6. What was the legislative intent in enacting legislation establishing guidelines for judicial review of police interrogation?
7. What is the extent of the U.S. Supreme Court decision in 1974 that limited the doctrine of *Miranda*?

GLOSSARY

APPOINTED ATTORNEY. Legal counsel provided by a court for defendants without funds to hire private counsel.

CONFESSION CASES. A series of United States Supreme Court decisions concerned with illegal or improper police interrogations.

14 Discovery and Disclosure

CHAPTER OBJECTIVES

1. Chapter 14 will define pretrial discovery and establish the rationale for disclosure of evidence gathered by police to defense counsel as within the concept of a fair trial.

2. The kind of evidence within the scope of discovery will be described, and

3. Counterdiscovery (defense to prosecutor) will be revealed as a threat to defendant's privilege against self-incrimination; a case study is presented to probe whether or not a notice-of-alibi law is violative of this privilege. Also discussed will be

4. The conflict that exists between the police policies of keeping the identity of informants confidential and the rights of a defendant when disclosure of an informant's identity is necessary for a fair trial.

The procedure for making available to participants in a criminal action the data underlying the in-court testimony of witnesses or exhibits of evidence is known as criminal discovery and disclosure. **Discovery is a pretrial procedure** by which one party requests the production of evidence possessed by the opposition. One of the inequities of common-law procedure was that it afforded no adequate machinery for one party to obtain from his adversary any disclosure of facts material to the issue—either by compelling him to make admissions in his pleading, or to testify at or before the trial, or to furnish documents material to the issue for inspection. To remedy these defects, the courts of chancery entertained the bill of discovery, that is, a bill which sought no relief other than the discovery of facts known by the defendant or the discovery of deeds, writings or other things in the defendant's possession or power.

The **concept of a fair trial** is inherent in the constitutional provisions which provide procedural safeguards for a person accused of crime. Allowing the accused and his attorney, at their leisure, to look over the evidence against the accused and allowing them to learn the identity of the police informer and to peruse the records of intercepted communications are among the means by which American courts make certain an investigation and an accusation of criminal behavior will end in a fair trial for the accused.

The need for a truthful verdict in a criminal trial outweighs the community's need for evidence with any surprise value at trial. Because the prosecutor, as representative of the government, also has a duty to the accused to see that justice is done, it is unconscionable to allow him to undertake prosecution and then invoke the government's privileges to deprive the accused of anything that might be material to his defense.[1] This is the rationale for discovery and disclosure in criminal cases. It is a balancing between the rights of accused persons and the interests of the community.

The American Bar Association's *Code of Professional Responsibility* states the prosecutor's responsibility as follows: "A public prosecutor or other governmental lawyer in criminal litigation shall make timely disclosure to counsel for the defendant, or to the defendant if he has no counsel, of the existence of evidence known to the prosecutor or other government lawyer, that tends to negate the guilt of the accused, mitigate the degree of his offense, or reduce the punishment."

PRETRIAL DISCOVERY

Pretrial discovery offers an opportunity to inspect an opponent's evidence. Not all jurisdictions have established extensive areas of **discovery,**

[1]United States v. Reynolds, 345 U.S. 1 (1953).

but in most jurisdictions the defendant can request production of one or more items of evidence in the hands of the prosecutor or police by making an appropriate request in the court that has jurisdiction to try the case. If the motion is granted, the court will order the prosecutor to produce specific evidence for inspection by the defense. If discovery is denied, the justification is usually avoidance of some particular evil. Some states favor granting discovery, only withholding it for cause. Federal courts allow extensive discovery to defendants in accordance with the Federal Rules of Criminal Procedure (Rule 16). There is little doubt that the rules of pretrial discovery are being liberalized in all jurisdictions.

Extensive discovery rights have originated slowly but have gained impetus from judicial beliefs that the objective of a criminal action is the ascertainment of the truth and that a major role to this goal is a well-informed defense counsel. Legislators have adopted this judicial premise and enacted laws regarding pretrial discovery in many states and at the federal level. Although the rationale for discovery by the defense is the belief that the exchange of information enhances the possibility of a fair trial, its growth may be credited to recognition of a need for balancing the meager capacity of the defense for investigation with the massive investigatory apparatus of police and prosecutor, and **rejection of the "sporting theory" of justice** in which surprise was part of the game.

From time to time, the prosecutor has sought to extend *his* rights to discovery. In some areas, this thrust has met with success, particularly when the defense has indicated in some fashion that it intends to use an affirmative defense such as an alibi. In *Williams v. Florida*,[2] the U.S. Supreme Court reviewed a Florida alibi disclosure statute and found such statute and concept constitutional.

However, the attempt to convert pretrial discovery into a real two-way process has foundered on the defendant's right to remain silent and his privilege against self-incrimination. The **prosecution's rights to counterdiscovery** can hardly be expanded to overcome the absolute right of an accused person not to bring forth evidence that will incriminate him.

In 1885, the U.S. Supreme Court nullified legislation requiring that a citizen produce certain evidence or forfeit certain goods, saying the law was a compulsion in violation of the Fifth and Fourteenth Amendments.[3] More recently, a case involving policemen convicted of a conspiracy to obstruct justice in relation to corrupt practices in traffic law enforcement in New Jersey was reversed by the U.S. Supreme Court. During the investigation, the accused officers were informed of a New

---

[2]399 U.S. 78 (1970). See case study at end of this chapter.
[3]Boyd v. United States, 116 U.S. 616 (1885).

Jersey statute providing for forfeiture of their jobs by public employees who invoked the privilege against self-incrimination on an official matter. They were told that if they refused to talk they would lose their jobs. They talked. Their statements were then used against them at their trial. The court's opinion suggested the choice was nothing more than forfeiture of job and livelihood or self-incrimination, saying that this option was the antithesis of free choice to speak or be silent and "was likely to exert such pressure upon the individual as to disable him from making a free and rational choice."[4]

Discovery is available to the defense despite its potential for perjury and the intimidation or elimination of witnesses. These **hazards** can be neutralized by cross-examination and prompt judicial action. Minimizing the harmful aspects of discovery allows achievement of its main goal—an adequately informed defense counsel.

Police **investigators must expect discovery** and learn to cope with its problems. It should be expected that the defendant's statements and any police reports, photographs, or sketches that record the criminal act the defendant is charged with will be subject to discovery. This is also true of physical evidence, reports of identification and laboratory technicians, lists of witnesses, and witness' statements.

Illustrative of the **scope of discovery** in various states are the items now subject to production and inspection in California:

1. Written, typed, or signed statements of the accused
2. Transcripts of recorded statements of the accused
3. The right to hear recordings of electronic devices (such as tape recordings) of the accused
4. Written statements of prosecution witnesses
5. Transcripts of statements of prosecution witnesses
6. Written statements or transcripts thereof used by the prosecution to impeach an accused's witness
7. The right to hear recordings of statements of prosecution witnesses
8. The right to interview witnesses without interference from the prosecution
9. The names and addresses of eyewitnesses to a crime in the hands of the prosecution
10. Coroner's and pathologist's reports
11. Scientific reports, specimens, and samples in the hands of the prosecution
12. Blood tests
13. Police reports
14. Police notes of conversations with prosecution witnesses
15. Photographs used in identifying an accused

4Garrity v. New Jersey, 385 U.S. 493 (1967).

16. Documents in the hands of the prosecution such as receipts that are material to the crime charged

DISCLOSURES—INFORMANTS

Police investigators depend on a great variety of people for information about crime and criminals. So-called amateur informants supply information about one crime, one criminal or one criminal group. Citizenship and revenge are the two terminals along the continuum of amateur motivation. On the other hand, the professional informant is a wholesaler of data about the commission of crimes. He is knowledgeable about underworld or subversive activities, and his motivation is plain profit in most cases—except for cases involving national security and there is little doubt of basic patriotism in these instances because the total monies paid out have never been really sufficient to justify the hazards inherent in the role of informer. Although some amateur informants may fear adverse social reactions or civil actions for defamation of character, most informants worry about death or injury—to themselves or to their families.

Disclosing the identity of informants raises many problems similar to pretrial discovery. It also requires a balancing between the rights of the accused and the interests of the community. The accused certainly has a right to prepare and present his defense against the accusation. In a system of criminal justice committed to the resolution of doubt by adversary proceedings, the right to confront witnesses must be guaranteed. There is also a bona fide public interest in protecting the flow of information about crime and criminals to police. Wholesale disclosure will certainly curtail soures of information.

This has led to the **"informer's privilege,"** a privilege which does not extend to the informant who is a participant in the criminal transaction. The accused cannot be made helpless at trial, unable to subject any witness to effective examination. To deny the accused the identity of an informant-participant deprives him of the right of effective cross-examination which is an essential safeguard accompanying the defendant's right to confront the witnesses against him or to produce witnesses in his own behalf.[5]

The **role of the informant-participant** is not that of a mere informant, but rather that of a material witness to the transaction or criminal act. Refusal to identify such an informant would deprive the defendant of a fair trial because the informant-participant is likely to be a material witness on the ultimate issue of guilt or innocence. The prosecutor must,

[5]Pointer v. Texas, 380 U.S. 400 (1965).

therefore, disclose the informant's identity or face dismissal of the case by the trial judge.[6]

Roviero v. United States[7] is a case in which the rights of the individual prevailed and the informer's privilege was rejected. In this case the informant in a drug possession-and-sale case was actually involved in the criminal transaction despite the fact that he did not purchase the drugs. He was a material witness on the issue of guilt or innocence. The issue in *Roviero* was whether the informant's name should be disclosed. Roviero picked up "John Doe," the informant, in his automobile. Roviero was seated in Doe's automobile. As the auto was driven around nearby streets, his conversation with Doe was overheard by police officer Bryson, who had previously concealed himself in the trunk of Doe's car. Doe stopped his car after this talk and Roviero alighted, walked to a nearby tree, picked up a package and returned to the car, and spoke to Doe. At this point in the transaction, Federal Narcotics Agent Durham, who had been keeping Doe's car under visual surveillance, alighted from his own vehicle and seized Roviero and the suspect package, and signaled to his associate, Bryson, in the trunk of Doe's car. Bryson stepped out and saw the agent with the package alongside of Roviero. The testimony of Bryson as to the conversation between Doe and Roviero was admitted into evidence, as was the testimony of Agent Durham about what he had observed. This evidence was supported by expert testimony that the suspect package contained illegal opium. The identity of John Doe was not revealed nor was he produced in court. Roviero was convicted.

In reviewing and reversing Roviero's conviction, the Court's opinion stated:

> John Doe had cooperated with law enforcement personnel in establishing the criminal transaction and took a prominent part in it. Petitioner Roviero's opportunity at trial to cross-examine Police Officer Bryson and Narcotics Agent Durham was not a substitute to examining the man who had been with him and took part in the transaction. The desirability of Doe's testimony was that it might have disclosed entrapment. He might have cast doubt upon Roviero's identity as well as the identity of the package. Only Roviero and Doe could explain, amplify or contradict Bryson's report of their talk. The use of the substance of this talk as overheard by Officer Bryson emphasizes the unfairness of nondisclosure in this case.

The identity of an informant need not be disclosed when the question is whether there was **probable cause** for an arrest or a search, rather than the fundamental issue of guilt or innocence. When it appears that law enforcement officers making the search or arrest relied on facts

---

[6]People v. Lawrence, 149 Cal. App. 2d 435 (1957).
[7]353 U.S. 53 (1957).

supplied by an informant they had reason to trust, there is no constitutional requirement that the informant's identity be disclosed at any preliminary hearing.

This is the doctrine of *McCray v. Illinois.*[8] In this case, the two officers making a warrantless arrest on information supplied by an informant testified, in open court, fully and in detail as to what the informant had told them about the defendant and as to why they had reason to believe the informant was reliable and his information was trustworthy. Both officers were under oath, each withstood a searching cross-examination, and the presiding judge was obviously satisfied that truthful statements were made by each officer.

California has in its Evidence Code a section that is an excellent example of the basic concepts of **official information and its confidentiality and protection from disclosure** in the interests of justice. This section reads as follows:

Identity of Informant—A public entity has a privilege to refuse to disclose official information and to prevent another from disclosing such information if the privilege is claimed by a person authorized by the public entity to do so and:

1. Disclosure is forbidden by an act of the Congress of the United States or a statute of this state; or

2. Disclosure of the information is against the public interest, because there is a necessity for preserving the confidentiality of the information that outweighs the necessity for disclosure in the interest of justice; but no privilege may be claimed under this paragraph if any person authorized to do so has consented that the information be disclosed in the proceeding. In determining whether disclosure of the information is against the public interest, the interest of the public entity as a party in the outcome of the proceeding may not be considered.

Except as provided in this section, a public entity has a privilege to refuse to disclose the identity of a person who has furnished information in confidence to an agent of law enforcement purporting to disclose a violation of a law of the United States or of this state or of a public entity in this state, and to prevent another from disclosing such identity, if the privilege is claimed by a person authorized by the public entity to do so and:

1. Disclosure is forbidden by an act of the Congress of the United States or a statute of this state; or

2. Disclosure of the identity of the informer is against the public interest because there is a necessity for preserving the confidentiality of his identity that outweighs the necessity for disclosure in the interest of justice; but no privilege may be claimed under this paragraph if any person authorized to do so has consented that the information be disclosed in

[8]386 U.S. 300 (1967).

the proceeding. In determining whether disclosure of the information of the informer is against the public interest, the interest of the public entity as a party in the outcome of the proceeding may not be considered.

This section applies only if the information is furnished in confidence by the informer to:

1.   A law enforcement officer;
2.   A representative of an administrative agency charged with the administration of enforcement of the law alleged to be violated; or
3.   Any person for the purpose of transmittal to a person listed in paragraph (1) or (2).

There is no privilege under this section to prevent the informer from disclosing his identity.[9]

DISCLOSURE—REPORTS AND RECORDS

In 1957, the landmark case of *Jencks v. United States*[10] established the right of a defendant to inspect reports shown to relate to the testimony of witnesses.

Jencks, a labor union official, was convicted, in federal court, of falsely swearing to a National Labor Relations Act affidavit about being a non-Communist. The basis of Jencks' appeal involved the government's two principal witnesses, both members of the Communist Party and informants who were paid by a federal investigative agency (FBI) to make oral or written reports while engaged in Communist Party activities. They made such reports to the FBI which contained information about Jencks participating in Communist Party activities with the two informants. At trial, both witnesses testified to such activities by Jencks. Counsel for Jencks made timely and appropriate motions that the government be required to produce these reports for defense inspection and use in cross-examination of both informant-witnesses. These motions were denied by the trial judge. Jencks was convicted.

In this case the Supreme Court said: "We hold that the criminal action must be dismissed when the government, on the grounds of privilege, elects not to comply with an order to produce, for the accused's inspection and for admission in evidence, relevant statements or reports in its possession of government witnesses touching the subject matter of their testimony at trial." In concluding its opinion, the Court noted that the government must decide whether the consequences of allowing the crime to go unpunished are greater than the dangers of possible disclosure of state secrets and other confidential information.

---

[9]California Evidence Code, Sec. 1040; Rule 510; Federal Rules of Evidence.
[10]353 U.S. 657 (1957).

The Jencks doctrine permits the defense to inspect reports related to testimony without first showing that the reports and testimony conflict, and allows the defense to inspect the documents in order to decide whether to use them in the defense case. Only the defense can make a judgment about the value of using such reports to discredit the government witnesses—and thus further the accused's defense—and to make this decision defense counsel must see the reports. "Justice," the court noted, "requires no less."

In 1969, the United States Supreme Court reviewed three cases involving disclosure of electronic surveillance records.[11] The petitioners in one of these cases, *Alderman v. United States*, were convicted of conspiring to transmit murderous threats in interstate commerce, while petitioners Ivanov and Butenko were convicted of conspiring to transmit information relating to the national defense of the United States to the Soviet Union. The court review joined all three cases because the questions in each were nearly identical. The court held that a defendant had "standing" to object to evidence obtained by unlawful electronic surveillance only if he was a party to the overheard conversation or if, whether or not he was present, the conversations occurred on his premises. On the question of whether the evidence against any of the petitioners grew out of illegally overheard conversations or conversations occurring on his premises, the court found and ordered that:

1. Surveillance records as to which any petitioner had standing to object should be turned over to him without being screened privately by the trial judge,

2. The trial judges, through lack of time or unfamiliarity, were unable to provide the scrutiny which the Fourth Amendment exclusionary rule requires,

3. Petitioners were entitled to a hearing, findings and conclusions: (a) on the question of whether the electronic surveillance violated their Fourth Amendment rights, and (b) whether the nature and relevance of any conversations overheard and recorded during such surveillance related to the convictions in these cases.

CASE STUDY

Johnny Williams v. State of Florida, 399 U.S. 78 (1970).

Mr. Justice White delivered the opinion of the Court.*

Facts of Case. Prior to his trial for robbery in the State of Florida, petitioner filed a "Motion for a Protective Order," seeking to be excused

---

[11]Alderman v. United States, Ivanov v. United States, Butenko v. United States, 394 U.S. 165 (1969).

*Extract only (segment of opinion relating to six-man jury omitted), footnotes omitted. Headings added by authors for reader's convenience.

from the requirements of Rule 1.200 of the Florida Rules of Criminal Procedure. That rule requires a defendant, on written demand of the prosecuting attorney, to give notice in advance of trial if the defendant intends to claim an alibi, and to furnish the prosecuting attorney with information as to the place where he claims to have been and with the names and addresses of the alibi witnesses he intends to use. In his motion petitioner openly declared his intent to claim an alibi, but objected to the further disclosure requirements on the ground that the rule "compels the Defendant in a criminal case to be a witness against himself" in violation of his Fifth and Fourteenth Amendment rights. The motion was denied.

Florida's notice-of-alibi rule** is in essence a requirement that a defendant submit to a limited form of pretrial discovery by the State whenever he intends to rely at trial on the defense of alibi. In exchange for the defendant's disclosure of the witnesses he proposes to use to establish that defense, the State in turn is required to notify the defendant of any witnesses it proposes to offer in rebuttal to that defense. Both sides are under a continuing duty promptly to disclose the names and addresses of additional witnesses bearing on the alibi as they become available. The threatened sanction for failure to comply is the exclusion at trial of the defendant's alibi evidence—except for his own testimony —or, in the case of the State, the exclusion of the State's evidence offered in rebuttal of the alibi.

In this case, following the denial of his Motion for a Protective Order, petitioner complied with the alibi rule and gave the State the name and address of one Mary Scotty. Mrs. Scotty was summoned to the office of the State Attorney on the morning of the trial, where she gave pretrial testimony. At the trial itself, Mrs. Scotty, petitioner, and petitioner's wife all testified that the three of them had been in Mrs. Scotty's apartment during the time of the robbery. On two occasions during cross-examination of Mrs. Scotty, the prosecuting attorney confronted her with her earlier deposition in which she had given dates and times that in some respects did not correspond with the dates and times given at trial. Mrs. Scotty adhered to her trial story, insisting that she had been mistaken in her earlier testimony. The State also offered in rebuttal the testimony of one of the officers investigating the robbery who claimed that Mrs. Scotty had asked him for directions on the afternoon in question during the time when she claimed to have been in her apartment with petitioner and his wife.

We need not linger over the suggestion that the discovery permitted the State against petitioner in this case deprived him of "due process" or a "fair trial." Florida law provides for liberal discovery by

---

**Florida statute set out as an appendix to this opinion.

the defendant against the State, and the notice-of-alibi rule is itself carefully hedged with reciprocal duties requiring state disclosures to the defendant. Given the ease with which an alibi can be fabricated, the State's interest in protecting itself against an eleventh-hour defense is both obvious and legitimate. Reflecting this interest, notice-of-alibi provisions, dating at least from 1927, are now in existence in a substantial number of States.

Rejection of Sporting Theory. In addition to Florida, at least 15 States appear to have alibi-notice requirements of one sort or another. See Arizona Rule Crim. Proc. 192 B (1965); Ind. Ann. Stat. §§ 9–1631 to 9–1633 (1956); Iowa Code § 777.18 (1966); Kan. Stat. Ann. § 62–1341 (1964); Mich. Comp. Laws §§ 768.20, 768.21 (1948); Minn. Stat. § 630.14 (1967); N.J. Rule 3.5–9 (1958); N.Y. Code Crim. Proc. § 295–l (1958); Ohio Rev. Code Ann. § 2945.58 (1954); Okla. Stat., Tit. 22, § 585 (1969); Pa. Rule Crim. Proc. 312 (1970); S.D. Comp. Laws §§ 23–37–5, 23–37–6 (1967); Utah Code Ann. § 77–22–17 (1953); Vt. Stat. Ann., Tit. 13, §§ 6561, 6562 (1959); Wis. Stat. § 955.07 (1961). The adversary system of trial is hardly an end in itself; it is not yet a poker game in which players enjoy an absolute right always to conceal their cards until played. We find ample room in that system, at least as far as "due process" is concerned, for the instant Florida rule, which is designed to enhance the search for truth in the criminal trial by insuring both the defendant and the State ample opportunity to investigate certain facts crucial to the determination of guilt or innocence.

Fifth Amendment Privilege Against Self-Incrimination. Petitioner's major contention is that he was "compelled . . . to be a witness against himself" contrary to the commands of the Fifth and Fourteenth Amendments because the notice-of-alibi rule required him to give the State the name and address of Mrs. Scotty in advance of trial and thus to furnish the State with information useful in convicting him. No pretrial statement of petitioner was introduced at trial; but armed with Mrs. Scotty's name and address and the knowledge that she was to be petitioner's alibi witness, the State was able to take her deposition in advance of trial and to find rebuttal testimony. Also, requiring him to reveal the elements of his defense is claimed to have interfered with his right to wait until after the State had presented its case to decide how to defend against it. We conclude, however, as has apparently every other court that has considered the issue, that the privilege against self-incrimination is not violated by a requirement that the defendant give notice of an alibi defense and disclose his alibi witnesses.

Alibi Defense. The defendant in a criminal trial is frequently forced to testify himself and to call other witnesses in an effort to re-duce the risk of conviction. When he presents his witnesses, he must reveal their identity and submit them to cross-examination which in itself may prove incriminating or which may furnish the State with leads to incriminating rebuttal evidence. That the defendant faces such a dilemma demanding a choice between complete silence and presenting a defense has never been thought an invasion of the privilege against compelled self-incrimination. The pressures generated by the State's evi-dence may be severe but they do not vitiate the defendant's choice to present an alibi defense and witnesses to prove it, even though the at-tempted defense ends in catastrophe for the defendant. However "testi-monial" or "incriminating" the alibi defense proves to be, it cannot be considered "compelled" within the meaning of the Fifth and Fourteenth Amendments.

Very similar constraints operate on the defendant when the State requires pretrial notice of alibi and the naming of alibi witnesses. Nothing in such a rule requires the defendant to rely on an alibi or pre-vents him from abandoning the defense; these matters are left to his unfettered choice. That choice must be made, but the pressures that bear on his pretrial decision are of the same nature as those that would induce him to call alibi witnesses at the trial: the force of historical fact beyond both his and the State's control and the strength of the State's case built on these facts. Response to that kind of pressure by offering evidence or testimony is not compelled self-incrimination transgressing the Fifth and Fourteenth Amendments.

Notice-of-Alibi Rule. In the case before us, the notice-of-alibi rule by itself in no way affected petitioner's crucial decision to call alibi witnesses or added to the legitimate pressures leading to that course of action. At most, the rule only compelled petitioner to accelerate the timing of his disclosure, forcing him to divulge at an earlier date infor-mation that the petitioner from the beginning planned to divulge at trial. Nothing in the Fifth Amendment privilege entitles a defendant as a matter of constitutional right to await the end of the State's case before announcing the nature of his defense, any more than it entitles him to await the jury's verdict on the State's case-in-chief before decid-ing whether or not to take the stand himself.

Holding. Petitioner concedes that absent the notice-of-alibi rule the Constitution would raise no bar to the court's granting the State a continuance at trial on the ground of surprise as soon as the alibi wit-ness is called. Nor would there be self-incrimination problems if, during that continuance, the State was permitted to do precisely what it did here prior to trial: take the deposition of the witness and find rebuttal evidence. But if so utilizing a continuance is permissible under the Fifth and Fourteenth Amendments, then surely the same result may be accomplished through pretrial discovery, as it was here, avoiding the necessity of a disrupted trial. We decline to hold that the privilege against compulsory self-incrimination guarantees the defendant the right to surprise the State with an alibi defense.

Appendix to Opinion of the Court

Florida Rule Crim. Proc. 1.200:

Notice-of-alibi Law: Florida.   Upon the written demand of the prosecuting attorney, specifying as particularly as is known to such prosecuting attorney, the place, date and time of the commission of the crime charged, a defendant in a criminal case who intends to offer evidence of an alibi in his defense shall, not less than ten days before trial or such other time as the court may direct, file and serve upon such prosecuting attorney a notice in writing of his intention to claim such alibi, which notice shall contain specific information as to the place at which the defendant claims to have been at the time of the alleged offense and, as particularly as is known to defendant or his attorney, the names and addresses of the witnesses by whom he proposes to establish such alibi. Not less than five days after receipt of defendant's witness list, or such other times as the court may direct, the prosecuting attorney shall file and serve upon the defendant the names and addresses (as particularly as are known to the prosecuting attorney) of the witnesses the State proposes to offer in rebuttal to discredit the defendant's alibi at the trial of the cause. Both the defendant and the prosecuting attorney shall be under a continuing duty to promptly disclose the names and addresses of additional witnesses which come to the attention of either party subsequent to filing their respective witness lists as provided in this rule. If a defendant fails to file and serve a copy of such notice as herein required, the court may exclude evidence offered by such defendant for the purpose of proving an alibi, except the testimony of the defendant himself. If such notice is given by a defendant, the court may exclude the testimony of any witness offered by the defendant for the purpose of proving an alibi if the name and address of such witness as particularly as is known to defendant or his attorney is not stated in such notice. If the prosecuting attorney fails to file and serve a copy on the defendant of a list of witnesses as herein provided, the court may exclude evidence offered by the state in rebuttal to the defendant's alibi evidence. If such notice is given by the prosecuting attorney, the court may exclude the testimony of any witness offered by the prosecuting attorney for the purpose of rebutting the defense of alibi if the name and address of such witness as particularly as is known to the prosecuting attorney is not stated in such notice. For good cause shown the court may waive the requirements of this rule.

Mr. Justice Black, dissenting.*

The core of the majority's decision is an assumption that compelling a defendant to give notice of an alibi defense before a trial is no different from requiring a defendant, after the State has produced the evidence against him at trial, to plead alibi before the jury retires to consider the case. This assumption is clearly revealed by the statement that "the pressures that bear on [a defendant's] pretrial decision are of the same nature as those that would induce him to call alibi witnesses at the trial: the force of historical fact beyond both his and the State's control and the strength of the State's case built on these facts." *Ante*, at 85, 26 L. Ed. 2d at 452. That statement is plainly and simply wrong as a matter of fact and law, and the Court's holding based on that statement is a complete misunderstanding of the protections provided for criminal defendants by the Fifth Amendment and other provisions of the Bill of Rights.

Hazards to Defense in Notice-of-Alibi Rule. When a defendant is required to indicate whether he might plead alibi in advance of trial, he faces a vastly different decision from that faced by one who can wait until the State has presented the case against him before making up his mind. Before trial the defendant knows only what the State's case *might* be. Before trial there is no such thing as the "strength of the State's case"; there is only a range of possible cases. At that time there is no certainty as to what kind of case the State will ultimately be able to prove at trial. Therefore any appraisal of the desirability of pleading alibi will be beset with guesswork and gambling far greater than that accompanying the decision at the trial itself. Any lawyer who has actually tried a case knows that, regardless of the amount of pretrial preparation, a case looks far different when it is actually being tried than when it is only being thought about.

The Florida system, as interpreted by the majority, plays upon this inherent uncertainty in predicting the possible strength of the State's case in order effectively to coerce defendants into disclosing an alibi defense that may never be actually used. Under the Florida rule, a defendant who might plead alibi must, at least 10 days before the date of trial, tell the prosecuting attorney that he might claim an alibi or else the defendant faces the real threat that he may be completely barred from presenting witnesses in support of his alibi. According to the Court, however, if he gives the required notice and later changes his

*Extracts only; footnotes omitted. Headings added by authors for reader's convenience.

mind "[n]othing in such a rule requires [him] to rely on an alibi or prevents him from abandoning the defense; these matters are left to his unfettered choice." *Ante*, at 84, 26 L. Ed. 2d 451. Thus in most situations defendants with any possible thought of pleading alibi are in effect compelled to disclose their intentions in order to preserve the possibility of later raising the defense at trial. Necessarily few defendants and their lawyers will be willing to risk the loss of that possibility by not disclosing the alibi. Clearly the pressures on defendants to plead an alibi created by this procedure are not only quite different from the pressures operating at the trial itself, but are in fact significantly greater. Contrary to the majority's assertion, the pretrial decision cannot be analyzed as simply a matter of "timing," influenced by the same factors operating at the trial itself.

The Court apparently also assumes that a defendant who has given the required notice can abandon his alibi without hurting himself. Such an assumption is implicit in and necessary for the majority's argument that the pretrial decision is no different from that at the trial itself. I, however, cannot so lightly assume that pretrial notice will have no adverse effects on a defendant who later decides to forego such a defense. Necessarily the defendant will have given the prosecutor the names of persons who may have some knowledge about the defendant himself or his activities. Necessarily the prosecutor will have every incentive to question these persons fully, and in doing so he may discover new leads or evidence. Undoubtedly there will be situations in which the State will seek to use such information—information it would probably never have obtained but for the defendant's coerced cooperation.

Notice-of-Alibi Rule Violates Fifth Amendment. It is unnecessary for me, however, to engage in any such intellectual gymnastics concerning the practical effects of the notice-of-alibi procedure, because the Fifth Amendment itself clearly provides that "no person . . . shall be compelled in any criminal case to be a witness against himself." If words are to be given their plain and obvious meaning, that provision, in my opinion, states that a criminal defendant cannot be required to give evidence, testimony, or any other assistance to the State to aid it in convicting him of crime. *Cf. Schmerber v. California*, 384 U.S. 757, 773, 16 L. Ed. 2d 908, 921, 86 S. Ct. 1826 (1966) (Black, J., dissenting). The Florida notice-of-alibi rule in my opinion is a patent violation of that constitutional provision because it requires a defendant to disclose information to the State so that the State can use that information to destroy him. It seems to me at least slightly incredible to suggest that this procedure may have some beneficial effects for defendants. There is no need to encourage defendants to take actions they think will help them. The fear of conviction and the substantial cost or inconvenience resulting from criminal prosecutions are more than sufficient incentives to make defendants want to help themselves. If a defendant thinks that making disclosure of an alibi before trial is in his best interests, he will obviously do so. And the only time the State needs the compulsion provided by this procedure is when the defendant has decided that such disclosure is likely to hurt his case.

Power of Government vs. Individual. It is no answer to this argument to suggest that the Fifth Amendment as so interpreted would give the defendant an unfair element of surprise, turning a trial into a "poker game" or "sporting contest," for that tactical advantage to the defendant is inherent in the type of trial required by our Bill of Rights. The Framers were well aware of the awesome investigative and prosecutorial powers of government and it was in order to limit those powers that they spelled out in detail in the Constitution the procedure to be followed in criminal trials. A defendant, they said, is entitled to notice of the charges against him, trial by jury, the right to counsel for his defense, the right to confront and cross-examine witnesses, the right to call witnesses in his own behalf, and the right not to be a witness against himself. All of these rights are designed to shield the defendant against state power. None are designed to make convictions easier and taken together they clearly indicate that in our system the entire burden of proving criminal activity rests on the State. The defendant, under our Constitution, need not do anything at all to defend himself, and certainly he cannot be required to help convict himself. Rather he has an absolute, unqualified right to compel the State to investigate its own case, find its own witnesses, prove its own facts, and convince the jury through its own resources. Throughout the process the defendant has a fundamental right to remain silent, in effect challenging the State at every point to: "Prove it!"

The Bill of Rights thus sets out the type of constitutionally required system that the State must follow in order to convict individuals of crime. That system requires that the State itself must bear the entire burden without any assistance from the defendant. This requirement is clearly indicated in the Fifth Amendment itself, but it is equally apparent when all the specific provisions of the Bill of Rights relating to criminal prosecutions are considered together. And when a question concerning the constitutionality of some aspect of criminal procedure arises, this Court must consider all those provisions and interpret them together. The Fifth Amendment prohibition against compelling a defendant to be a witness against himself is not an isolated, distinct provision. It is part of a system of constitutionally required procedures, and its true meaning can be seen only in light of all those provisions. "Strict construction" of the words of the Constitution does not mean that the Court can look only to one phrase, clause, or sentence in the Constitution and expect to find the right answer. Each provision has clear and definite meaning, and various provisions considered together may have an equally clear and definite meaning. It is only through sensitive attention to the specific words, the context in which they are used, and the history surrounding the adoption of those provisions that the true meaning of the Constitution can be discerned.

This constitutional right to remain absolutely silent cannot be avoided by superficially attractive analogies to any so-called "compulsion" inherent in the trial itself that may lead a defendant to put on evidence in his own defense. Obviously the Constitution contemplates that a defendant can be "compelled" to stand trial, and obviously there will be times when the trial process itself will require the defendant to do something in order to try to avoid a conviction. But nothing in the Constitution permits the State to add to the natural consequences of a trial and compel the defendant in advance of trial to participate in any way in the State's attempt to condemn him.

Concept of Fair Trial. A criminal trial is in part a search for truth. But it is also a system designed to protect "freedom" by insuring that no one is criminally punished unless the State has first succeeded in the admittedly difficult task of convincing a jury that the defendant is guilty. That task is made more difficult by the Bill of Rights, and the Fifth Amendment may be one of the most difficult of the barriers to surmount. The Framers decided that the benefits to be derived from the kind of trial required by the Bill of Rights were well worth any loss in "efficiency" that resulted. Their decision constitutes the final word on the subject, absent some constitutional amendment. That decision should not be set aside as the Court does today.

II.

On the surface this case involves only a notice-of-alibi provision, but in effect the decision opens the way for a profound change in one of the most important traditional safeguards of a criminal defendant. The rationale of today's decision is in no way limited to alibi defenses, or any other type or classification of evidence. The theory advanced goes at least so far as to permit the State to obtain under threat of sanction complete disclosure by the defendant in advance of trial of all evidence, testimony, and tactics he plans to use at that trial. In each case the justification will be that the rule affects only the "timing" of the disclosure, and not the substantive decision itself. This inevitability is clearly revealed by the citation to *Jones v. Superior Court*, 58 Cal, 2d 56, 372 P2d 919 (1962), *ante*, at 83, n 13, 26 L. Ed. 2d 451. In that case, the theory of which the Court today adopts in its entirety, a defendant in a rape case disclosed that he would rely in part on a defense of impotency. The prosecutor successfully obtained an order compelling the defendant to reveal the names and addresses of any doctors he consulted and the medical reports of any examinations relating to the claimed incapacity. That order was upheld by the highest court in California. There was no "rule" or statute to support such a decision, only the California Supreme Court's sense of fairness, justice, and judicial efficiency. The majority there found no barrier to the judicial creation of pretrial discovery by the State against the defendant, least of all a barrier raised by any constitutional prohibition on compelling the defendant to be a witness against himself.

The dangerous implications of the Jones rationale adopted today are not, however, limited to the disclosure of evidence that the defendant has already decided he will use at trial. In *State v. Grove*, 65 Wash. 2d 525, 398 P2d 170 (1965), the Washington Supreme Court, relying on Jones, held that a defendant in a murder trial could be compelled to produce a letter he had written his wife about the alleged crime, even though he had no thought at all of using that evidence in his own behalf. These cases are sufficient evidence of the inch-by-inch, case-by-case process by which the rationale of today's decision can be used to transform radically our system of criminal justice into a process requiring the defendant to assist the State in convicting him, or be punished for failing to do so.

There is a hint in the State's brief in this case—as well as, I fear, in the Court's opinion—of the ever-recurring suggestion that the test of constitutionality is the test of "fairness," "decency," or in short the Court's own views of what is "best." Occasionally this test emerges in disguise as an intellectually satisfying "distinction" or "analogy" designed to cover up a decision based on the wisdom of a proposed procedure rather than its conformity with the commands of the Constitution. Such a course, in my view, is involved in this case. This decision is one more step away from the written Constitution and a radical departure from the system of criminal justice that has prevailed in this country. Compelling a defendant in a criminal case to be a witness against himself in any way, including the use of the system of pretrial discovery approved today, was unknown in English law, except for the unlamented proceedings in the Star Chamber courts—the type of proceedings the Fifth Amendment was designed to prevent. For practically the first 150 years of this Nation's history no State considered adopting such procedures compelling a criminal defendant to help convict himself, although history does not indicate that our ancestors were any less intelligent or solicitous of having a fair and efficient system of criminal justice than we are. History does indicate that persons well familiar with the dangers of arbitrary and oppressive use of the criminal process were determined to limit such dangers for the protection of each and every inhabitant of this country. They were well aware that any individual might some day be subjected to criminal prosecution, and it was in order to protect the freedom of *each* of us that they restricted the Government's ability to punish or imprison *any* of us. Yet in spite of the history of oppression that produced the Bill of Rights and the strong reluctance of our governments to compel a criminal defendant to assist in his own conviction, the Court today reaches out to embrace and sanctify at the first opportunity a most dangerous departure from the Constitution and the traditional safeguards afforded persons accused of crime. I cannot accept such a result and must express my most emphatic disagreement and dissent.

SUMMARY

Discovery is a pretrial procedure primarily for the defense. It requires the prosecution to produce evidence developed by police generally. Its rationale is that the lack of surprise at trial promotes the chance of a fair trial for the accused. The hazards of discovery are the potential for perjury or harassment of witnesses, but these hazards can be reduced or eliminated by cross-examination and judicial action. The Fifth Amendment privilege against self-incrimination precludes any extensive two-way discovery, with even notice-of-alibi laws being suspect. Disclosure of the identity of informants is required in some cases to insure a fair trial, despite police reluctance to reveal the names of people providing information. There is a differentiation between the informants who supplies data for probable cause and what is described as the informant-participant who is involved in the issue of guilt or innocence. The court's majority opinion in the case study supports the use of notice-of-alibi laws; the dissenting opinion opposes such legislation as violative of First and Fourteenth Amendment rights of the accused.

DISCUSSION QUESTIONS

1. What is discovery?
2. What is the extent of discovery in your jurisdiction?
3. Should there be discovery? Why?
4. What are the arguments for and against making discovery a "two-way street?"
5. What are the rules concerning the disclosure of an informant's identity?
6. What reasons are given for disclosure of the identity of informants?
7. Prepare a syllabus of *Williams v. Florida*.

GLOSSARY

INFORMER'S PRIVILEGE.   Right of police to avoid disclosure of identity of informants to protect them from retaliation and to enhance continuance of the flow of information about crime and criminals from informants to police.

SPORTING THEORY.   A spinoff from the American legal system's trial-by-adversary concept (fight theory), with surprise being part of the strategy of the prosecution.

Evidence
of
15 Electronic
Surveillances

CHAPTER OBJECTIVES

1. In Chapter 15, the judicial review of electronic surveillances and the methods used for such surveillances are described.
2. Criteria are developed that are useful in evaluating the admissibility of evidence secured as the result of wiretapping or electronic eavesdropping; and
3. A case study is presented to emphasize the emerging trend in electronic surveillance case law: the requirement for prior judicial approval (antecedent justification).

Evidence gathered through electronic surveillances must be viewed as the fruit of wiretapping and eavesdropping. Both the content of the overheard wire and oral communications and the identity of the participants fall into this category. The use of this type of evidence against accused persons in criminal proceedings has led to a long series of legislative and judicial attempts to resolve the conflict between the constitutional privacy of individuals and the public goal of protecting all citizens against criminal behavior. Federal and state laws of varying-but-similar content are a morass of restrictions ,and permissiveness. Generally, wiretapping is banned and eavesdropping is suspect, with various levels of privilege accorded agents of law enforcement.

Eavesdropping is an area of conflict. Legislators made wiretapping a crime, but still, judges often held the fruit of such surveillance to be lawful evidence. More recently, courts have held electronic surveillances to be unlawful and have refused to allow the evidence of intercepted communications to be used against the aggrieved person. Legislators, meanwhile, have enacted an extensive law allowing electronic surveillance. The United States Congress, in Title III, *Omnibus Crime Control and Safe Streets Act of 1968*, established procedural guidelines for law enforcement agents conducting such surveillances. This is the area of future conflict.

Constitutional protection against evidence secured by electronic surveillances seems to be based on the right to be let alone. Mr. Justice Brandeis, in a dissenting opinion in an early wiretapping case,[1] noted that the makers of our Constitution undertook to secure conditions favorable to the pursuit of happiness, saying:

> They conferred, as against the government, the right to be let alone—the most comprehensive of rights and the right most valued by civilized man. To protect that right, every unjustifiable intrusion by the government upon the privacy of the individual, whatever the means employed, must be deemed a violation of the Fourth Amendment. And the use, as evidence in a criminal proceeding, of facts ascertained by such intrusion must be deemed a violation of the Fifth Amendment.

Mr. Justice Holmes, dissenting in the same case, joined with Brandeis in applying the maxim of "unclean hands" to wiretapping. This maxim which comes from the courts of equity is usually applied in civil litigation between private parties. Here, the principle prevails in criminal proceedings. The rule is not one of action, but of inaction: The court will not come to the aid of, or grant judgment for, the party who proffers evidence when he has violated the law in collecting the evidence. This maxim may be thought of as abstract thinking about ethical conduct in legal process and law enforcement, but when Justice Brandeis associated it with his comment that wiretapping was a "dirty business," he pinpointed a community attitude toward wiretapping that exists today and militates against the use in court of any evidence based on electronic surveillance.

The aggrieved person is entitled to suppression of evidence origi-

[1] Olmstead v. United States, 277 U.S. 438 (1928).

nating in electronic surveillance that violates the Fourth Amendment's protection against unreasonable searches.[2]

ADMISSIBILITY—TOTALITY OF CIRCUMSTANCES

The legal significance of any evidence obtained through an electronic surveillance depends on the total circumstances of the surveillance. The totality of circumstances to be considered in a case involving electronic surveillance are:

1. The need for using this type of investigative technique.
2. The probable cause for "search and seizure"
3. The point in time during the criminal proceeding that the interception occurred—whether it happened while the case was "focusing," during the lineup, or after indictment and information

To establish the need for electronic surveillance, the situation should indicate that normal investigative methods are inadequate. The continued operations of organized crime have been cited as justification for the use of electronic surveillance by law enforcement agencies.[3] The urgency of the situation outweighs dangers that may result from the lack of notice inherent in these interceptions. Such a showing of urgent need to avoid notice—and the law enforcement objectives of electronic surveillances depend on secrecy—is quite important because of the inherent dangers in eavesdropping.[4]

The existence and establishment of **probable cause** are vital to preserving the legal significance of *any* evidence gathered in the course of search and seizure. Electronic surveillances are searches and seizures within the meaning of the Fourth Amendment and therefore probable cause and a return or inventory of some kind must be affirmatively shown. This requires specific identification of the parties involved; their connection with a specific crime; the specific facility (wire or oral communication) to be monitored and its designation by location or other means; a description of the communications the surveillance is aimed at; and a termination clause indicating whether the "search" is prosecutorial (terminating when its evidence objective is first obtained), or investigative and not to be terminated until the objective of identifying accomplices and co-conspirators has been achieved.

The point in time during the investigation that interception takes

[2]Alderman v. United States, 394 U.S. 165 (1969).
[3]**Omnibus Crime Control and Safe Streets Act of 1968** (Public Law 90–351), Title III, Section 801 (c).
[4]Berger v. New York, 388 U.S. 41 (1967).

place is critical to the legal significance of lawfully intercepted wire and oral communications. The time of arraignment, following indictment and arrest may be used as a base point for viewing the span of time prior to a criminal trial. In the *Massiah* case,[5] the time in which an oral communication was electronically intercepted was a deciding issue. In the original indictment, it was alleged that Massiah and a co-defendant named Colson had acted in concert to violate a federal law forbidding the possession of illegal drugs. Massiah retained legal counsel, pleaded not guilty, and was released on bail. Colson, also released on bail, decided to cooperate with the prosecution. His automobile was wired for sound, utilizing a microphone and short-distance radio transmitter. Colson and Massiah, without any notice to Massiah of Colson's new role as government informer, had a conversation in Colson's wired automobile while it was parked on a New York City street. By prearrangement with Colson, a government agent, who was equipped with an appropriate radio receiver and stationed a short distance from the parked car, overheard the lengthy conversation between the two co-defendants. The agent subsequently testified, at trial, to several incriminating portions of this interception, despite defense objection. Massiah was convicted. His case was reversed on review by the United States Supreme Court, with the opinion stating that this action only reflected a constitutional principle established as long ago as *Powell v. Alabama*[6]—the principle that the period between arraignment and the beginning of a trial is perhaps the most critical period of the proceedings, and that during this time the accused is as much entitled to counsel as he is at the trial itself.

The *Massiah* case was decided in the same year as the *Escobedo* case,[7] 1964, and is really based on policy underlying the *Escobedo* decision and reinforced in 1966 by the Court's ruling in *Miranda v. Arizona*[8]—namely, that a suspect may not be questioned without "informed consent." In the *Massiah* case, the police tried to get around this restriction by, in effect, conducting the interrogation through a third party, but the Court balked at the subterfuge.

The totality of circumstances to be considered in electronic surveillance cases spans possible violations of the rights of an accused person against unreasonable search or seizure, self-incrimination, or denial of legal counsel. The way Fourth, Fifth, and Sixth Amendment rights are affected by the total circumstances of any one case is splendidly illustrated by the final paragraph of the majority opinion in the *Massiah* case. This concluding fragment reads:

[5]Massiah v. United States, 377 U.S. 210 (1964).
[6]287 U.S. 45 (1932).
[7]Escobedo v. Illinois, 378 U.S. 478 (1964).
[8]384 U.S. 436 (1966).

We do not question that in this case, as in many cases, it was entirely proper to continue an investigation of the suspected criminal activities of the defendant and his alleged confederates, even though the defendant had already been indicted. All that we hold is that the defendant's own incriminating statements, obtained by federal agents under the circumstances here disclosed, could not constitutionally be used by the prosecution as evidence against **him** at his trial.[9]

The total circumstances of an interception also encompass the possibility that the communication may be privileged. Conversations about social, business, and personal affairs are often private and privileged—such as communications between physician and patient, lawyer and client, husband and wife, or others in a confidential relationship. Evidence proffered in these areas must withstand preliminary examination as to the existence of a privilege which would bar admission of the contents of the conversation.

PARTICIPANT MONITORING TO BOLSTER CREDIBILITY

When the issue in dispute hinges on the substance of a conversation, the triers of fact are often faced with the classic courtroom dilemma: Who is telling the truth about a conversation between two persons? When the versions given by the participants conflict, the triers of fact are faced with a credibility problem. If one of the participants is an informant or some other witness whose credibility is doubtful, a recording device appears to be an ideal instrument to bolster the credibility of the witness.

The case of *Osborn v. United States*[10] shows the rationale followed by the United States Supreme Court in approving this type of electronic surveillance. The use of a recording device in this case had two justifications: (1) the prosecution had made a serious charge against a defense attorney, and (2) a testimonial contest between the only two people who knew the truth was highly undesirable because one was a government informer, the other an attorney of previous good repute.

Z. T. Osborn, Jr., a Nashville (Tennessee) lawyer, was convicted in a United States District Court of trying to bribe a member of a jury panel in a prospective criminal trial. Osborn was one of the defense attorneys for James R. Hoffa, a labor leader, against whom a federal criminal prosecution was pending in Nashville. In preparing to defend Hoffa, Osborn needed an investigator and hired a Nashville police officer named

[9]Massiah v. United States, 377 U.S. 210 (1964).
[10]385 U.S. 323 (1966).

Robert Vick. Osborn had hired Vick for similar work during his off-duty time about a year earlier in another case involving the same defendant (Hoffa). The accusation against Osborn charged that between November 6th and 15th, 1963, he "did unlawfully, knowingly, wilfully and corruptly endeavor to influence, obstruct and impede the due administration of justice," and that he "did request, counsel and direct Robert D. Vick to contact Ralph A. Elliot, who was, and was known by the said Osborn to be, a member of the petit jury panel scheduled to be drawn to hear the trial (of Hoffa), and to offer and promise to pay the said Ralph A. Elliot $10,000 to induce the said Elliot to vote for an acquittal, if the said Elliot should be selected to sit on the petit jury in the said trial." The compelling evidence against Osborn was Vick's testimony and a tape recording of a conversation between Vick and Osborn. Osborn's conviction was confirmed by the Court of Appeals. The United States Supreme Court granted his request for review primarily to consider whether his conviction rested on unconstitutionally acquired evidence.

The prosecution in this case resulted from the use of Vick as a federal informant. Vick claimed he had met with federal agents (FBI) several times and had agreed to report any illegal activities he might encounter, and that he was not "doubled"—an employed agent who is turned into a double agent by another employer seeking information about his first employer. On November 7th, he met with Osborn and mentioned that he knew several of the prospective jurors, and, during the conversation that followed, the possibility of "approaching" a juror was discussed.

Vick reported this conversation to federal agents and submitted an affidavit of his report. The relevant portion of Vick's affidavit read as follows:

> On November 7, 1963, I was in Mr. Osborn's office going over the results of my investigation. I was aware that the jury panel which I had been investigating was the panel assigned to Judge William E. Miller. Mr. Osborn and I got into a discussion of the jury panel assigned to Judge Frank Gray. This jury panel list had previously been shown to me by John Polk, an investigator for Mr. Osborn. Polk told me at this time that he was investigating the jury panel assigned to Judge Gray. At that time, I mentioned to Polk that I knew three of the people on the jury panel. In discussing the panel with Mr. Osborn, I again mentioned that I knew three of the people on the jury panel. Mr. Osborn said, "You do?" Why didn't you tell me?" I told Mr. Osborn I had told John Polk and assumed that John Polk had told him. Mr. Osborn said that Polk had not told him and suggested that we discuss the matter further. Mr. Osborn asked me how well I knew the three prospective jurors. I told him that I knew Mr. Ralph A. Elliot, Springfield, Tennessee, the best since he was my first cousin. Mr. Osborn asked me whether I knew him well enough to talk to him

about anything. I said I thought I did. Mr. Osborn then said, "Go contact him right away. Sit down and talk to him and get him on our side. We want him on the jury." I told Mr. Osborn that I thought Mr. Elliot was not in very good financial position and Mr. Osborn said, "Good, go see him right away."

On November 8th, two judges (Miller and Gray) of the Federal District Court reviewing Vick's affidavit, delivered to them by the prosecution, authorized the FBI agents to conceal a recorder on Vick in order to determine from recordings of further conversations between Vick and Osborn whether Vick's affidavit was truthful.

Subsequently, Vick visited Osborn and talked to him, but the recorder was not functioning. However, on November 11, the prosecution presented a written statement by Vick about this conversation and the recorder's malfunctioning, and Judge Miller authorized continued use of the recorder under the original conditions, proper surveillance and supervision to see that the recording was not faked in any way, with every precaution taken to make sure that the recorder was used in a fair manner.

This time the recorder worked and the government produced the tape as a return on the court's order. It was later used at trial. An extract of the final portion of the taped conversation between Osborn and Vick indicates the compelling nature of this type of evidence:

OSBORN: Then it's a deal. What we'll have to do—When it gets down to the trial date, when we know the date—tomorrow, for example, if the Supreme Court rules against us—and well, within a week, we'll know when the trial comes. Then, he has to be certain that when he gets on he's got to know that he'll just be talking to you and nobody else.

VICK: Social strictly.

OSBORN: Oh yeah.

VICK: I've got my story all fixed on that.

OSBORN: Then he will have to know where to—He will have to know where to come.

VICK: Well, er—

OSBORN: And, he'll have to know when.

VICK: Do you want to see him yourself? You want me to handle it or what?

OSBORN: You're gonna handle it yourself.

VICK: All right. You want to know it when he's ready, when I think he's ready for the five thousand? Is that right?

OSBORN: Well, no, when he gets on the panel, once he gets on the jury. Provided he gets on the panel.

VICK: Yeah. Oh, yeah. That's right. That's right. Well now, he's on the number one group.

OSBORN: I know, but now—

VICK: But you don't know whether that would be the one.

OSBORN: Well, I know this, that if we go to trial before that jury he'll be on it, but suppose the government challenges him over being on another hung jury.

VICK: Oh, I see.

OSBORN: So we have to be certain that he makes it on the jury.

VICK: I think it's in our favor, see. I think that'll work to our favor.

OSBORN: That's why I'm so anxious that they accept him.

VICK: I think they would, too. I don't think they would have a reason in the world to challenge him. I don't think that I'm under any surveillance or suspicion or anything like that.

OSBORN: I don't think so.

VICK: That's right.

OSBORN: All right, so we'll leave it to you. The only thing to do would be to tell him. In other words, your next contact with him would be to tell him if he wants that deal, he's got it.

VICK: O.K.

OSBORN: The only thing it depends upon is his being accepted on the jury. If the government challenges him, there will be no deal.

VICK: All right. If he is seated.

OSBORN: If he's seated.

VICK: He can expect five thousand and—

OSBORN: Immediately.

The court's opinion noted that this case did not involve third-party eavesdropping, the surreptitious surveillance of a private conversation by an outsider, rather, it involved one party to a conversation making a record of what was said. The majority opinion (7–1) held that the use of a recording device was permissible and consequently the recording itself was properly admitted as evidence at trial. The concluding segment of this opinion sums up the court's rationale for this decision:

The situation which faced the two judges of the District Court when they were presented with Vick's affidavit on November 8, and the motivations which prompted their authorization of the recorder, are reflected in the words of Chief Judge Miller. As he put it, "The affidavit contained information which reflected seriously upon a member of the bar of this court, who had practiced in my court ever since I have been on the bench. I decided that some action had to be taken to determine whether this information was correct or whether it was false. It was the most serious problem that I have had to deal with since I have been on the bench. I could not sweep it under the rug." So it was that, in response to a detailed factual affidavit alleging the commission of a specific criminal offense directly and immediately affecting the administration of justice in the federal court, the judges of that court jointly authorized the use of a recording device for the narrow and particularized purpose of ascertaining the truth of the affidavit's allegations. As the district judges recognized, it was imperative to determine whether the integrity of their court was being undermined, and highly undesirable that this determination should hinge on the inconclusive outcome of a testimonial contest between the only two people in the world who knew the truth—one an informer, the other a lawyer of previous good repute. There could hardly be a clearer example of "the procedure of antecedent justification before a magistrate that is central to the Fourth Amendment as a precondition of lawful electronic surveillance."

A requirement for warrants in participant monitoring is likely to be the rule rather than the exception. However, participant monitoring to bolster credibility without a warrant has not been ruled out. This type of recording is not eavesdropping in any proper sense of the word. It is best described as the use of an electronic device to obtain reliable evidence of a conversation by one of the participants. It is the recorded memory of a witness who participated in the conversation.

CONSENSUAL THIRD-PARTY EAVESDROPPING

Each party to a telephone conversation takes the risk that the other party may have an extension telephone and may allow another to overhear the conversation. The communication itself is not privileged and one party may not force the other to secrecy merely by using the telephone. Either party may record the conversation and publish it. In *Rathbun v. United States*,[11] the Court upheld the admission in evidence of a policeman's testimony about a conversation he had overheard on an extension telephone with the consent of a party to the conversation, who was also the subscriber to the telephone service and the extension user.

Listening on an extension telephone doesn't seem to be a great deal different from using a "party line" to overhear a conversation. However, the party line telephone hookup is quite different from a single telephone with an extension paid for by a single subscriber. Listening in on a party line involves more than the possibility of one subscriber taking part in a telephone conversation and allowing someone else to listen in over an authorized extension that the subscriber-participant has paid for.

Although it is true that the telephone party-line service offers an opportunity to overhear conversations between others, misuse of this opportunity has been classed as a forbidden interception within the meaning of Section 605 of the Federal Communications Act. A case illustrating this rule is *Lee v. Florida*.[12] Lee sought telephone service for his residence in Orlando, Florida, and the local telephone company ad-

[11] 355 U.S. 107 (1957).
[12] 392 U.S. 378 (1968).

vised him that only party-line service was available. Lee had no option. He accepted and was given a telephone on a four-party line. A week later the Orlando police had the telephone company install a telephone in a nearby house and hook it up to Lee's party line. The police hookup was installed for the purpose of overhearing and recording Lee's incoming and outgoing calls. The police eavesdropped for more than a week. Neither Lee nor any other participant consented to having the conversations overheard. Several of the recordings were admitted into evidence at Lee's trial for violating Florida's antigambling (lottery) law. The Court ruled that the evidence gained by this interception should be excluded because the federal statute proscribing the divulging of an intercepted communication applies to the states, just as the rule excluding the fruits of illegal searches and seizures was applied to the states in *Mapp v. Ohio*.[13]

Lack of physical penetration of the premises is no longer an important factor in electronic surveillances. At one time, "spike" microphones and induction devices were relevant when eavesdropping cases were decided on the basis of trespass. Electronic surveillances that did not involve trespass under local property laws were believed to be outside the protection of the Fourth Amendment,[14] but in *Katz v. United States*,[15] the United States Supreme Court ruled that the Fourth Amendment protects people and not simply areas. In reviewing the interception of Katz's conversations in a public telephone booth by federal agents, the court concluded the "trespass" doctrine was no longer controlling. Once this concept of privacy is recognized, the court commented, "it will become clear that the protection afforded by the Fourth Amendment cannot turn upon the presence or absence of a physical intrusion into any given enclosure."

ANTECEDENT JUSTIFICATION

Electronic Surveillance as Search and Seizure

The majority opinion of the United States Supreme Court in *Katz v. United States*,[16] concedes that the law enforcement agents had developed a strong **probable cause** for their third-party eavesdropping, but the court reversed Katz's conviction in the trial court because of the agents' failure to secure prior court approval of their electronic surveillance. In pointing out the need for a warrant to authorize such an in-

[13]367 U.S. 643 (1961).
[14]Silverman v. United States, 365 U.S. 505 (1961).
[15]389 U.S. 347 (1967).
[16]389 U.S. 347 (1967).

vasion of privacy, the court noted: "Wherever a man may be, he is entitled to know that he will remain free from unreasonable searches and seizures. The government agents here ignored the procedure of antecedent justification that is central to the Fourth Amendment, procedure that we hold to be a constitutional precondition of the kind of electronic surveillance involved in this case."

The court's action in the *Katz* case was foreshadowed when it nullified a New York State law which allowed nonconsensual third-party eavesdropping in accordance with a court order. In *Berger v. New York*,[17] the Court's opinion highlighted the necessity of a warrant being issued on a showing of probable cause in the following words:

> The Fourth Amendment commands that a warrant issue not only upon probable cause supported by oath or affirmation, but also "particularly describing the place to be searched, and persons or things to be seized." New York's statute lacks this particularization. It merely says that a warrant may issue on reasonable grounds to believe that evidence of crime may be obtained by the eavesdropping. It lays down no requirement for particularity in the warrant as to what specific crime has been or is being committed, nor the "place to be searched," or "the persons or things to be seized" as specifically required by the Fourth Amendment. The need for particularity and evidence of reliability in the showing required when judicial authorization of a search is sought is especially great in the case of eavesdropping. By its very nature, eavesdropping involves an intrusion on privacy that is broad in scope. In **Osborn [Osborn v. United States**, 385 U.S. 323 (1966)] the recording device was, as the Court said, authorized under the most precise and discriminate circumstances, circumstances which fully met the requirement of particularity of the Fourth Amendment. The invasion was lawful because there was sufficient proof to obtain a search warrant to make the search for the limited purpose outlined in the order of the judges. Through these "precise and discriminate" procedures the order authorizing the use of the electronic device afforded similar protections to those which are present in the use of conventional warrants authorizing the seizure of tangible evidence. Among other safeguards, the order described the type of conversation sought with particularity, thus indicating the specific objective of the government in entering the constitutionally protected area and the limitations placed upon the officer executing the warrant. Under it the officer could not search unauthorized areas; likewise, once the property sought, and for which the order was issued, was found the officer could not use the order as a passkey to further search. In addition, the order authorized one limited intrusion rather than a series or a continuous surveillance. And, we note that a new order was issued when the officer sought to resume the search and probable cause was shown for the succeeding one. Moreover, the order was executed by the officer with dispatch, not over a prolonged and extended period. In this manner no greater invasion of privacy was permitted than was necessary under the circumstances. Finally the officer

---

[17]388 U.S. 41 (1967).

was required to and did make a return on the order showing how it was executed and what was seized. Through these strict precautions the danger of an unlawful search and seizure was minimized.

INTERCEPTION OF WIRE AND ORAL COMMUNICATIONS

In 1968, Congress found it necessary to define the circumstances and conditions under which the interception of wire and oral communications may be authorized and the contents of intercepted communications may be used as evidence, and to prohibit unauthorized interception of such communications. The stated purpose of Title III, *Omnibus Crime Control and Safe Streets Act of 1968*, is to safeguard the **privacy of wire and oral communications.** Potential evidence is the basis for authorizing interception of wire or oral communications under this law, and the federal or local prosecutor is named as the public official who may apply to federal or state courts respectively, for appropriate court orders when such interception may provide evidence of specified crimes justifying the use of this investigative technique. The use of intercepted wire and oral communications is tied to the public duties of law enforcement officials and the in-court use of collected information.

Under this act, the procedures to be followed in obtaining a court order authorizing the interception of wire or oral communications provides for the judicial antecedent justification called for in *Osborn* and *Katz*, the particularity and overall reasonableness required in the *Berger* opinion, and the general rules suggested to justify an invasion of privacy in these three controlling decisions. However, the law also recognizes an "emergency situation" involving conspiracies threatening the national security or characteristic of organized crime, and rules are established for after-the-fact judicial review of such emergency interceptions.

Case Law. In the 1972 case of *United States v. United States District Court*[18] the U.S. Supreme Court dealt specifically with the domestic aspects of the national security portion of the Omnibus Crime Control and Safe Streets Act.[19] The Court did not accept the theory that the act defined the president's power in the area of national security. The case is an excellent discourse on the separation of powers problems involved in the sensitive area of the government's power in national security investigations and intrusions into the privacy of the individual citizen. The Court rejected the attorney general's claim that government had the right to make this surveillance without judicial approval because of the president's inherent power.

[18] 407 U.S. 297 (1972). See case study at end of chapter.
[19] 18 U.S.C., Section 2510–2520.

The public concern over the challenges and issues involved in the electronic surveillances of today and the future is expressed in the **declared legislative policy** of California:

> The Legislature hereby declares that advances in science and technology have led to the development of new devices and techniques for the purpose of eavesdropping upon private communications and that the invasion of privacy resulting from the continual and increasing use of such devices and techniques has created a serious threat to the free exercise of personal liberties and cannot be tolerated in a free and civilized society.
>
> The Legislature by this chapter intends to protect the right of privacy of the people of this state.
>
> The Legislature recognizes that law enforcement agencies have a legitimate need to employ modern listening devices and techniques in the investigation of criminal conduct and the apprehension of lawbreakers. Therefore, it is not the intent of the Legislature to place greater restraints on the use of listening devices and techniques by law enforcement agencies than existed prior to the effective date of this chapter.[20]

CASE STUDY

United States v. United States District Court, 407 U.S. 297 (1972).

Mr. Justice Powell delivered the opinion of the Court.*

The issue before us is an important one for the people of our country and their Government. It involves the delicate question of the President's power, acting through the Attorney General, to authorize electronic surveillance in internal security matters without prior judicial approval. Successive Presidents for more than one-quarter of a century have authorized such surveillance in varying degrees, without guidance from the Congress or a definitive decision of this Court. This case brings the issue here for the first time. Its resolution is a matter of national concern, requiring sensitivity both to the Government's right to protect itself from unlawful subversion and attack and to the citizen's right to be secure in his privacy against unreasonable Government intrusion.

Facts of Case. This case arises from a criminal proceeding in the United States District Court for the Eastern District of Michigan, in which the United States charged three defendants with conspiracy to destroy Government property in violation of 18 U.S.C. § 371. One of the defendants, Plamondon, was charged with the dynamite bombing of an office of the Central Intelligence Agency in Ann Arbor, Michigan.

[20]California Penal Code, Section 630.
*Footnotes and lengthy citations omitted. Headings added by authors for reader's convenience.

During pretrial proceedings, the defendants moved to compel the United States to disclose certain electronic surveillance information and to conduct a hearing to determine whether this information "tainted" the evidence on which the indictment was based or which the Government intended to offer at trial. In response, the Government filed an affidavit of the Attorney General, acknowledging that its agents had overheard conversations in which Plamondon had participated. The affidavit also stated that the Attorney General approved the wiretaps "to gather intelligence information deemed necessary to protect the nation from attempts of domestic organizations to attack and subvert the existing structure of the Government." The logs of the surveillance were filed in a sealed exhibit for in camera inspection by the District Court.

On the basis of the Attorney General's affidavit and the sealed exhibit, the Government asserted that the surveillance was lawful, though conducted without prior judicial approval, as a reasonable exercise of the President's power (exercised through the Attorney General) to protect the national security. The District Court held that the surveillance violated the Fourth Amendment, and ordered the Government to make full disclosure to Plamondon of his overheard conversations. 321 F. Supp. 1074 (ED Mich. 1971).

The Government then filed in the Court of Appeals for the Sixth Circuit a petition for a writ of mandamus to set aside the District Court order, which was stayed pending final disposition of the case. After concluding that it had jurisdiction, that court held that the surveillance was unlawful and that the District Court had properly required disclosure of the overheard conversations, 444 F2d 651 (CA6 1971).

I.

Legislation. Title III. of the Omnibus Crime Control and Safe Streets Act, 18 U.S.C. §§ 2510–2520, authorizes the use of electronic surveillance for classes of crimes carefully specified in 18 U.S.C. § 2516. Such surveillance is subject to prior court order. Section 2518 sets forth the detailed and particularized application necessary to obtain such an order as well as carefully circumscribed conditions for its use. The Act represents a comprehensive attempt by Congress to promote more effective control of crime while protecting the privacy of individual thought and expression. Much of Title III was drawn to meet the constitutional requirements of electronic surveillance enunciated by this Court in *Berger v. New York*, 388 U.S. 41, 18 L. Ed. 2d 1040, 87 S. Ct. 1873 (1967), and *Katz v. United States*, 389 U.S. 347, 19 L. Ed. 2d 576, 88 S. Ct. 507 (1967).

Together with the elaborate surveillance requirements in Title III, there is the following proviso, 18 U.S.C. § 2511(3):

Nothing contained in this chapter or in section 605 of the Communications Act of 1934 (48 Stat. 1143; 47 U.S.C. 605) shall limit the constitutional power of the President to take such measures as he deems necessary to protect the Nation against actual or potential attack or other hostile acts of a foreign power, to obtain foreign intelligence information deemed essential to the security of the United States, or to protect national security information against foreign intelligence activities. **Nor shall anything contained in this chapter be deemed to limit the constitutional power of the President to take such measures as he deems necessary to protect the United States against the overthrow of the Government by force or other unlawful means, or against any other clear and present danger to the structure or existence of the Government.** The contents of any wire or oral communication intercepted by authority of the President in the exercise of the foregoing powers may be received in evidence in any trial hearing or other proceeding only where such interception was reasonable, and shall not be otherwise used or disclosed except as is necessary to implement that power. (Emphasis supplied.)

The Government relies on § 2511(3). It argues that "in excepting national security surveillances from the Act's warrant requirement Congress recognized the President's authority to conduct such surveillances without prior judicial approval." Brief for U.S. 7, 28. The section thus is viewed as a recognition or affirmance of a constitutional authority in the President to conduct warrantless domestic security surveillance such as that involved in this case.

We think the language of § 2511(3), as well as the legislative history of the statute, refutes this interpretation. The relevant language is that:

Nothing contained in this chapter . . . shall limit the constitutional power of the President to take such measures as he deems necessary to protect . . .

against the dangers specified. At most, this is an implicit recognition that the President does have certain powers in the specified areas. Few would doubt this, as the section refers—among other things—to protection "against actual or potential attack or other hostile acts of a foreign power." But so far as the use of the President's electronic surveillance power is concerned, the language is essentially neutral.

Section 2511(3) certainly confers no power, as the language is wholly inappropriate for such a purpose. It merely provides that the Act shall not be interpreted to limit or disturb such power as the President may have under the Constitution. In short, Congress simply left presidential powers where it found them. This view is reinforced by the general context of Title III. Section 2511(1) broadly prohibits the use of electronic surveillance "except as otherwise specifically provided in this chapter." Subsection (2) thereof contains four specific exceptions. In each of the specified exceptions, the statutory language is as follows: "It shall not be unlawful . . . to intercept" the particular type of communication described.

The language of subsection (3), here involved, is to be contrasted with the language of the exceptions set forth in the preceding subsection. Rather than stating that warrantless presidential uses of electronic surveillance "shall not be unlawful" and thus employing the standard language of exception, subsection (3) merely disclaims any intention to limit the constitutional power of the President.

The express grant of authority to conduct surveillances is found in § 2516, which authorizes the Attorney General to make application to a federal judge when surveillance may provide evidence of certain offenses. These offenses are described with meticulous care and specificity.

Where the Act authorizes surveillance, the procedure to be followed is specified in § 2518. Subsection (1) thereof requires application to a judge of competent jurisdiction for a prior order of approval, and states in detail the information required in such application. Subsection (3) prescribes the necessary elements of probable cause which the judge must find before issuing an order authorizing an interception. Subsection (4) sets forth the required contents of such an order. Subsection (5) sets strict time limits on an order. Provision is made in subsection (7) for "an emergency situation" found to exist by the Attorney General (or by the principal prosecuting attorney of a State) "with respect to conspiratorial activities threatening the national security interest." In such a situation, emergency surveillance may be conducted "if an application for an order approving the interception is made . . . within forty-eight hours." If such an order is not obtained, or the application therefor is denied, the interception is deemed to be a violation of the Act.

Interpretation.   In view of these and other interrelated provisions delineating permissible interceptions of particular criminal activity upon carefully specified conditions, it would have been incongruous for Congress to have legislated with respect to the important and complex area of national security in a single brief and nebulous paragraph. This would not comport with the sensitivity of the problem involved or with the extraordinary care Congress exercised in drafting other sections of the Act. We therefore think the conclusion inescapable that Congress only intended to make clear that the Act simply did not legislate with respect to national security surveillances.

One could hardly expect a clearer expression of congressional neutrality. The debate above explicitly indicates that nothing in § 2511(3) was intended to *expand* or to *contract* or to *define* whatever presidential surveillance powers existed in matters affecting the national security. If we could accept the Government's characterization of § 2511(3) as a congressionally prescribed exception to the general requirement of a warrant, it would be necessary to consider the question of whether the surveillance in this case came within the exception and, if so, whether the statutory exception was itself constitutionally valid. But viewing § 2511(3) as a congressional disclaimer and expression of neutrality, we hold that the statute is not the measure of the executive authority asserted in this case. Rather, we must look to the constitutional powers of the President.

II.

It is important at the outset to emphasize the limited nature of the question before the Court. This case raises no constitutional challenge to electronic surveillance as specifically authorized by Title III of the Omnibus Crime Control and Safe Streets Act of 1968. Nor is there any question or doubts as to the necessity of obtaining a warrant in the surveillance of crimes unrelated to the national security interest. *Katz v. United States*, 389 U.S. 347, 19 L. Ed. 2d 576, 88 S. Ct. 507 (1967); *Berger v. New York*, 388 U.S. 41, 18 L. Ed. 2d 1040, 87 S. Ct. 1873 (1967). Further, the instant case requires no judgment on the scope of the President's surveillance power with respect to the activities of foreign powers, within or without his country. The Attorney General's affidavit in this case states that the surveillances were "deemed necessary to protect the nation from attempts of *domestic organizations* to attack and subvert the existing structure of Government" (emphasis supplied).

There is no evidence of any involvement, directly or indirectly, of a foreign power.

Fourth Amendment Requirement of Reasonableness in Search and Seizure.

Our present inquiry, though important, is therefore a narrow one. It addresses a question left open by *Katz, supra*, at 358 n 23, 19 L. Ed. 2d at 586.

Whether safeguards other than prior authorization by a magistrate would satisfy the Fourth Amendment in a situation involving the national security. . . .

The determination of this question requires the essential Fourth Amendment inquiry into the "reasonableness" of the search and seizure in question, and the way in which that "reasonableness" derives content and meaning through reference to the warrant clause.

We begin the inquiry by noting that the President of the United States has the fundamental duty, under Art II, § 1, of the Constitution, to "preserve, protect, and defend the Constitution of the United States." Implicit in that duty is the power to protect our Government against those who would subvert or overthrow it by unlawful means. In the discharge of this duty, the President—through the Attorney General— may find it necessary to employ electronic surveillance to obtain intelligence information on the plans of those who plot unlawful acts against the Government. The use of such surveillance in internal security cases has been sanctioned more or less continuously by various Presidents and Attorneys General since July 1946.

Herbert Brownell, Attorney General under President Eisenhower, urged the use of electronic surveillance both in internal and international security matters on the grounds that those acting against the Government "turn to the telephone to carry on their intrigue. The success of their plans frequently rests upon piecing together shreds of information received from many sources and many nests. The participants in the conspiracy are often dispersed and stationed in various strategic positions in government and industry throughout the country."

Though the Government and respondents debate their seriousness and magnitude, threats and acts of sabotage against the Government exist in sufficient number to justify investigative powers with respect to them. The covertness and complexity of potential unlawful conduct against the Government and the necessary dependency of many conspirators upon the telephone make electronic surveillance an effective investigatory instrument in certain circumstances. The marked acceleration in technological developments and sophistication in their use have resulted in new techniques for the planning, commission, and concealment of criminal activities. It would be contrary to the public interest for Government to deny to itself the prudent and lawful employment of those very techniques which are employed against the Government and its law-abiding citizens.

Civil Liberties and Government Power. It has been said that "the most basic function of any government is to provide for the security of the individual and of his property." *Miranda v. Arizona,* 384 U.S. 436, 539, 16 L. Ed. 2d 694, 761, 86 S. Ct. 1602, 10 A.L.R. 3d 974 (1966) (White, J., dissenting). And unless Government safeguards its own capacity to function and to preserve the security of its people, society itself could become so disordered that all rights and liberties would be endangered. As Chief Justice Hughes reminded us in *Cox v. New Hampshire,* 312 U.S. 569, 574, 85 L. Ed. 1049, 1052, 61 S. Ct. 762, 133 A.L.R. 1396 (1941):

> Civil liberties, as guaranteed by the Constitution, imply the existence of an organized society maintaining public order without which liberty itself would be lost in the excesses of unrestrained abuses.

But a recognition of these elementary truths does not make the employment by Government of electronic surveillance a welcome development—even when employed with restraint and under judicial supervision. There is, understandably, a deep-seated uneasiness and apprehension that this capability will be used to intrude upon cherished privacy of law-abiding citizens.

We look to the Bill of Rights to safeguard this privacy. Though physical entry of the home is the chief evil against which the wording of the Fourth Amendment is directed, its broader spirit now shields private speech from unreasonable surveillance. *Katz v. United States, supra; Berger v. New York, supra; Silverman v. United States,* 365 U.S. 505, 5 L. Ed. 2d 734, 81 S. Ct. 679, 97 A.L.R. 2d 1277 (1961). Our decision in Katz refused to lock the Fourth Amendment into instances of actual physical trespass. Rather, the Amendment governs "not only the seizure of tangible items, but extends as well to the recording of oral statements . . . without any 'technical trespass under . . . local property law.'" *Katz, supra,* at 353, 19 L. Ed. 2d at 583. That decision implicitly recognized that the broad and unsuspected governmental incursions into conversational privacy which electronic surveillance entails necessitate the application of Fourth Amendment safeguards.

National security cases, moreover, often reflect a convergence of First and Fourth Amendment values not present in cases of "ordinary" crime. Though the investigative duty of the executive may be stronger in such cases, so also is there greater jeopardy to constitutionally protected speech. "Historically the struggle for freedom of speech and press in England was bound up with the issue of the scope of the search and seizure power."

History abundantly documents the tendency of Government—however benevolent and benign its motives—to view with suspicion those who most fervently dispute its policies. Fourth Amendment protections become the more necessary when the targets of official surveillance may be those suspected of unorthodoxy in their political beliefs. The danger to political dissent is acute where the Government attempts to act under so vague a concept as the power to protect "domestic security." Given the difficulty of defining the domestic security interest, the danger of abuse in acting to protect that interest becomes apparent. Senator Hart addressed this dilemma in the floor debate on § 2511(3):

> As I read it—and this is my fear—we are saying that the President, on his motion, could declare—name your favorite poison—draft dodgers, Black Muslims, the Ku Klux Klan, or civil rights activists to be a clear and present danger to the structure or existence of the Government.

The price of lawful public dissent must not be a dread of subjection to an unchecked surveillance power. Nor must the fear of unauthorized official eavesdropping deter vigorous citizen dissent and discussion of Government action in private conversation. For private dissent, no less than open public discourse, is essential to our free society.

III.

As the Fourth Amendment is not absolute in its terms, our task is to examine and balance the basic values at stake in this case: the duty of Government to protect the domestic security, and the potential danger posed by unreasonable surveillance to individual privacy and free expression. If the legitimate need of Government to safeguard domestic security requires the use of electronic surveillance, the question is whether the needs of citizens for privacy and free expression may not be better protected by requiring a warrant before such surveillance is undertaken. We must also ask whether a warrant requirement would unduly frustrate the efforts of Government to protect itself from acts of subversion and overthrow directed against it.

Search Warrants. Though the Fourth Amendment speaks broadly of "unreasonable searches and seizures," the definition of "reasonableness" turns, at least in part, on the more specific commands of the warrant clause. Some have argued that "the relevant test is not whether it is reasonable to procure a search warrant, but whether the search was reasonable," *United States v. Rabinowitz,* 339 U.S. 56, 66, 94 L. Ed. 653, 660, 70 S. Ct. 430 (1950). This view, however, overlooks the second clause of the Amendment. The warrant clause of the Fourth Amendment is not dead language. Rather, it has been "a valued part of our constitutional law for decades, and it has determined the result in scores and scores of cases in courts all over this country. It is not an inconvenience to be somehow 'weighed' against the claims of police efficiency. It is, or should be, an important working part of our machinery of government, operating as a matter of course to check the 'well-intentioned but mistakenly overzealous executive officers' who are a part of any system of law enforcement."

Over two centuries ago, Lord Mansfield held that common-law principles prohibited warrants that ordered the arrest of unnamed individuals whom the *officer* might conclude were guilty of seditious libel. "It is not fit," said Mansfield, "that the receiving or judging of the information should be left to the discretion of the officer. The magistrate ought to judge; and should give certain directions to the officer."

The Concept of a Neutral and Detached Magistrate. Lord Mansfield's formulation touches the very heart of the Fourth Amendment directive: that, where practical, a governmental search and seizure should represent both the efforts of the officer to gather evidence of wrongful acts and the judgment of the magistrate that the collected evidence is sufficient to justify invasion of a citizen's private premises or conversation. Inherent in the concept of a warrant is its issuance by a "neutral and detached magistrate." *Coolidge v. New Hampshire, supra,* at 453, 29 L. Ed. 2d at 575; *Katz v. United States, supra,* at 356, 19 L. Ed. 2d at 585. The further requirement of "probable cause" instructs the magistrate that baseless searches shall not proceed.

These Fourth Amendment freedoms cannot properly be guaranteed if domestic security surveillances may be conducted solely within the discretion of the executive branch. The Fourth Amendment does not contemplate the executive officers of Government as neutral and disinterested magistrates. Their duty and responsibility is to enforce the laws, to investigate, and to prosecute. *Katz v. United States, supra,* at 359–360, 19 L. Ed. 2d at 586, 587 (Douglas, J., concurring). But those charged with this investigative and prosecutorial duty should not be the sole judges of when to utilize constitutionally sensitive means in pursuing their tasks. The historical judgment, which the Fourth Amendment accepts, is that unreviewed executive discretion may yield too readily to pressures to obtain incriminating evidence and overlook potential invasions of privacy and protected speech.

It may well be that, in the instant case, the Government's surveillance of Plamondon's conversations was a reasonable one which readily would have gained prior judicial approval. But this Court "has never sustained a search upon the sole ground that officers reasonably expected to find evidence of a particular crime and voluntarily confined their activities to the least intrusive means consistent with that end." *Katz, supra,* at 356–357, 19 L. Ed. 2d at 585. The Fourth Amendment contemplates a prior judicial judgment, not the risk that executive discretion may be reasonably exercised. This judicial role accords with our basic constitutional doctrine that individual freedoms will best be preserved through a separation of powers and division of functions among the different branches and levels of Government. The independent check upon executive discretion is not satisfied, as the Government argues, by "extremely limited" post-surveillance judicial review. Indeed, post-surveillance review would never reach the surveillances which failed to result in prosecutions. Prior review by a neutral and detached magistrate is the time-tested means of effectuating Fourth Amendment rights.

It is true that there have been some exceptions to the warrant requirement. But those exceptions are few in number and carefully delineated; in general, they serve the legitimate needs of law enforcement officers to protect their own well-being and preserve evidence from destruction. Even while carving out those exceptions, the Court has reaffirmed the principle that the "police must, whenever practicable, obtain advance judicial approval of searches and seizures through the warrant procedure."

Government Argument. The Government argues that the special circumstances applicable to domestic security surveillances necessitate a further exception to the warrant requirement. It is urged that the requirement of prior judicial review would obstruct the President in the discharge of his constitutional duty to protect domestic security. We are told further that these surveillances are directed primarily to the collecting and maintaining of intelligence with respect to subversive forces, and are not an attempt to gather evidence for specific criminal prosecutions. It is said that this type of surveillance should not be subject to traditional warrant requirements which were established to govern investigation of criminal activity, not ongoing intelligence gathering.

The Government further insists that courts "as a practical matter would have neither the knowledge nor the techniques necessary to determine whether there was probable cause to believe that surveillance was necessary to protect national security." These security problems, the Government contends, involve "a large number of complex and subtle factors" beyond the competence of courts to evaluate.

As a final reason for exemption from a warrant requirement, the Government believes that disclosure to a magistrate of all or even a significant portion of the information involved in domestic security surveillances "would create serious potential dangers to the national security and to the lives of informants and agents. . . . Secrecy is the essential ingredient in intelligence gathering; requiring prior judicial authorization would create a greater 'danger of leaks, . . . because in addition to the judge, you have the clerk, the stenographer and some other officer like a law assistant or bailiff who may be apprised of the nature' of the surveillance."

These contentions in behalf of a complete exemption from the warrant requirement, when urged on behalf of the President and the national security in its domestic implications, merit the most careful consideration. We certainly do not reject them lightly, especially at a time of worldwide ferment and when civil disorders in this country are more prevalent than in the less turbulent periods of our history. There is, no doubt, pragmatic force to the Government's position.

Holding. But we do not think a case has been made for the requested departure from the Fourth Amendment standards. The circumstances described do not justify complete exemption of domestic security surveillance from prior judicial scrutiny. Official surveillance, whether its purpose be criminal investigation or ongoing intelligence gathering, risks infringement of constitutionally protected privacy of speech. Security surveillances are especially sensitive because of the inherent vagueness of the domestic security concept, the necessarily broad and continuing nature of intelligence gathering, and the temptation to utilize such surveillances to oversee political dissent. We recognize, as we have before, the constitutional basis of the President's domestic security role, but we think it must be exercised in a manner compatible with the Fourth Amendment. In this case we hold that this requires an appropriate prior warrant procedure.

We cannot accept the Government's argument that internal security matters are too subtle and complex for judicial evaluation. Courts regularly deal with the most difficult issues of our society. There is no reason to believe that federal judges will be insensitive to or uncomprehending of the issues involved in domestic security cases. Certainly courts can recognize that domestic security surveillance involves different considerations from the surveillance of "ordinary crime." If the threat is too subtle or complex for our senior law enforcement officers to convey its significance to a court, one may question whether there is probable cause for surveillance.

Nor do we believe prior judicial approval will fracture the secrecy essential to official intelligence gathering. The investigation of criminal activity has long involved imparting sensitive information to judicial officers who have respected the confidentialities involved. Judges may be counted upon to be especially conscious of security requirements in national security cases. Title III of the Omnibus Crime Control and Safe Streets Act already has imposed this responsibility on the judiciary in connection with such crimes as espionage, sabotage, and treason, § 2516(1) (a) and (c), each of which may involve domestic as well as foreign security threats. Moreover, a warrant application involves no public or adversary proceedings: it is an ex parte request before a magistrate or judge. Whatever security dangers clerical and secretarial personnel may pose can be minimized by proper administrative measures, possibly to the point of allowing the Government itself to provide the necessary clerical assistance.

Thus, we conclude that the Government's concerns do not justify departure in this case from the customary Fourth Amendment requirement of judicial approval prior to initiation of a search or surveillance. Although some added burden will be imposed upon the Attorney General, this inconvenience is justified in a free society to protect constitutional values. Nor do we think the Government's domestic surveillance powers will be impaired to any significant degree. A prior warrant establishes presumptive validity of the surveillance and will minimize the burden of justification in post-surveillance judicial review. By no means of least importance will be the reassurance of the public generally that indiscriminate wiretapping and bugging of law-abiding citizens cannot occur.

Scope of Decision. We emphasize, before concluding this opinion, the scope of our decision. As stated at the outset, this case involves only the domestic aspects of national security. We have not addressed, and express no opinion as to, the issues which may be involved with respect to activities of foreign powers or their agents. Nor does our decision rest on the language of § 2511(3) or any other section of Title III of the Omnibus Crime Control and Safe Streets Act of 1968. That Act does not attempt to define or delineate the powers of the President to meet domestic threats to the national security.

Moreover, we do not hold that the same type of standards and procedures prescribed by Title III are necessarily applicable to this case. We recognize that domestic security surveillance may involve different policy and practical considerations from the surveillance of "ordinary crime." The gathering of security intelligence is often long range and involves the interrelation of various sources and types of information. The exact targets of such surveillance may be more difficult to identify than in surveillance operations against many types of crime specified in Title III. Often, too, the emphasis of domestic intelligence gathering is on the prevention of unlawful activity or the enhancement of the Government's preparedness for some possible future crisis or emergency. Thus, the focus of domestic surveillance may be less precise than that directed against more conventional types of crime.

Given these potential distinctions between Title III criminal surveillances and those involving the domestic security. Congress may wish to consider protective standards for the latter which differ from those already prescribed for specified crimes in Title III. Different standards may be compatible with the Fourth Amendment if they are reasonable both in relation to the legitimate need of Government for intelligence information and the protected rights of our citizens. For the warrant application may vary according to the governmental interest to be enforced and the nature of citizen rights deserving protection. As the Court said in *Camara v. Municipal Court,* 387 U.S. 523, 534–535, 18 L. Ed. 2d 930, 939, 87 S. Ct. 1727 (1967):

> In cases in which the Fourth Amendment requires that a warrant to search be obtained, "probable cause" is the standard by which a particular decision to search is tested against the constitutional mandate of reasonableness. . . . In determining whether a particular inspection is reasonable—and thus in determining whether there is probable cause to issue a warrant for that inspection—the need for the inspection must be weighed in terms of these reasonable goals of code enforcement.

It may be that Congress, for example, would judge that the application and affidavit showing probable cause need not follow the exact requirements of § 2518 but should allege other circumstances more appropriate to domestic security cases; that the request for prior court authorization could, in sensitive cases, be made to any member of a specially designated court (e.g., the District Court or Court of Appeals for the District of Columbia); and that the time-and-reporting requirements need not be so strict as those in § 2518.

The above paragraph does not, of course, attempt to guide the congressional judgment but rather to delineate the present scope of our own opinion. We do not attempt to detail the precise standards for domestic security warrants any more than our decision in Katz sought to set the refined requirements for the specified criminal surveillances which now constitute Title III. We do hold, however, that prior judicial approval is required for the type of domestic security surveillance involved in this case and that such approval may be made in accordance with such reasonable standards as the Congress may prescribe.

As the surveillance of Plamondon's conversations was unlawful, because conducted without prior judicial approval, the courts below correctly held that *Alderman v. United States*, 394 U.S. 165, 22 L. Ed. 2d 176, 89 S. Ct. 961 (1969), is controlling and that it requires disclosure to the accused of his own impermissibly intercepted conversations. As stated in *Alderman*, "the trial court can and should, where appropriate, place a defendant and his counsel under enforceable orders against unwarranted disclosure of the materials which they may be entitled to inspect." 394 U.S. at 185, 22 L. Ed. 2d, at 193.

The judgment of the Court of Appeals is hereby
Affirmed.

SUMMARY

Evidence from electronic surveillance is the overheard content of oral communications and the identity of participants in the conversations. The circumstances of the interception, including methodology, determines whether or not such evidence will be admissible. A recording device is now an acceptable instrument to bolster the credibility of a witness. Each party to a telephone conversation risks divulgement by another participant. An electronic surveillance is a search and seizure within the scope of the Fourth Amendment. Fourth Amendment protection no longer depends upon whether there was a physical intrusion into any enclosure, but instead depends upon an intrusion into the privacy of an individual. Failure to secure prior court approval of an electronic surveillance is likely to ruin any further admissibility of conversations overheard by electronic interception. Police must apply in court, using the same application-affidavit process common to requests for arrest or search warrants, for prior judicial approval. When the police procedures used violate the protection of the Fourth Amendment against unreasonable searches, the aggrieved person is entitled to the suppression of the evidence illegally obtained.

DISCUSSION QUESTIONS

1. What danger to privacy is inherent in the uncontested entry of electronic surveillances?
2. Explain the danger to fair trials and due process inherent in the use of "seized" conversations.
3. Describe the "aggrieved person" who can seek to suppress electronic surveillances alleged to violate constitutional safeguards.
4. Is prior judicial approval necessary in participant monitoring of informer-suspect conversations? In consensual third-party eavesdropping? What differences do you see between the two?
5. Trace the history of legislative-judicial conflict over wiretapping.
6. What are the similarities or differences between the use of paid informants and electronic surveillances?
7. What are the three major aspects of the totality of circumstances doctrine for evaluating the likely legal significance of overheard wire and oral communications?
8. Why do the rules of evidence regarding the confidentiality of privileged communications apply to overheard conversations?
9. Are the objectives of participant monitoring different from those of consensual third-party eavesdropping? From nonconsensual third-party eavesdropping?
10. Discuss the statement: Fourth Amendment freedoms cannot properly be guaranteed if domestic security surveillances may be conducted solely within the discretion of the executive branch of government.

GLOSSARY

ANTECEDENT JUSTIFICATION (POLICE ACTION). Prior court approval.

DIRTY BUSINESS. Term used to describe wiretapping in *Olmstead v. United States.*

DOUBLED (AGENT). Action of "turning" an agent employed by an adverse party into an associate who will provide information about his first employer (adverse party).

IN CAMERA. Not in open court; private; judicial chambers.

SPIKE MICROPHONE. When driven into the wall of a premises, a spike microphone has the capability of picking up sounds on the other side of the wall; similar to induction microphones (which pick up conversations without direct wiring in telephonic interceptions), and "shotgun" or "tubular" microphones, which have a long-range directional pickup capability. No physical intrusion into the premises involved is necessary when these eavesdropping devices are used.

16

The Defense Case

CHAPTER OBJECTIVES

1. This final chapter will focus attention on the defense case. It will also

2. Describe common defenses, with a discussion of

3. The *total evidence* concept of evidence of guilt and the evidence necessary to disprove common defenses. In addition,

4. The theme that only the total amount of evidence has real legal significance will be emphasized.

It is wise for a person working within one area of the administration of justice to learn and know about areas other than his own particular specialty. It is particularly valuable for an investigator to know and understand the various affirmative defenses available to a person accused of crime and the evidence that may be admitted at his trial to create in the minds of the jurors a "reasonable doubt" of his guilt.

It should be repeated here regarding the **burden of proof** that the quantity and quality of evidence produced by the defendant need only be strong enough to create a reasonable doubt, while the quantity and quality of the prosecutors' evidence must have the compelling strength to convince the jurors of guilt beyond a reasonable doubt.

The circumstances under which people are accused of crime differ. Sometimes it is difficult for a defendant and his attorney to develop an adequate response to the criminal charge. More often, the nature of the case and the circumstances surrounding it structure the defense case. In any event, the basic affirmative defenses to an accusation of crime include an attack on identification evidence, through claims of alibi, lack of intent or motive, or entrapment; and defenses based on consent of the victim or insanity.

IDENTITY

Evidence produced on this basic defense may consist of alibi; lack of motive; inability of witnesses to see or to accurately identify on the basis of their perceptions; suggestions by others which influence the identification; weakness, or absence, of a connecting link in the chain of circumstances supposedly connecting the accused to the event.

The vagaries of identifying witnesses and the inherent suggestibility of lineups have been treated elsewhere in this volume. This is a vast area in which the defense may attack the credibility of the witness, his identification, and police procedures.

ALIBI

An alibi is a claim that the defendant was elsewhere at the time of the crime. It is a possibility in every case in which the defendant is not caught in the very act of crime charged. Witnesses testifying to an alibi may include a mother, a wife, a friendly bartender, or an individual unknown to the defendant previously, but now willing to corroborate his story because of some chance encounter at the time of the crime. Besides people who may testify to seeing the accused, there may be such things as receipts, tickets, or other time-placing items of evidence possessed by the accused which will be admitted to help the jury determine whether he was at the scene of the crime when it happened or whether he was elsewhere. One item of alibi evidence that is seemingly credible and unimpeachable may be, and many times is, sufficient to cast **reasonable doubt** on the accusing identification.

LACK OF MOTIVE

Lack of motive may be a circumstance in conflict with **identification evidence.** Evidence of motives, such as greed, revenge, jealousy, family dispute, and sex, may be admissible against an accused as circumstantial evidence of guilt. The reverse is also true—a person without a motive may be inferred to be innocent of the crime.

Lack of motive is often important in cases in which direct evidence is weak, and a chain of **circumstantial evidence** connects the defendant with the crime. To convict on circumstantial evidence alone, the evidence presented should, to a moral certainty, exclude every theory except that of guilt.[1] Thus, if the defendant can propound a reasonable theory of innocence from the prosecution evidence alone or combined with other circumstances impeaching various of the prosecution circumstances, he should prevail. In jury trials, the triers of fact will be instructed, in these circumstances, to follow the law by the trial judge. He will remind them that the defendant is entitled to an acquittal if the people fail to establish guilt beyond a reasonable doubt.

CRIMINAL INTENT (MENS REA)

Where an affirmative defense is based on the absence of necessary intent, the accused will generally admit the physical act of the crime while denying a criminal state of mind.

As a general proposition, there must be a union (or uniting) of the physical act and criminal intent (or gross negligence) in order for a crime to be committed. An act without intent or an intent without an act are generally not crimes. Therefore, evidence which will tend to infer intent or lack of it is admissible and most important.

For instance, in a burglary prosecution in California, the elements which must be proven are: (1) the identity of the culprit; (2) the fact that a building was broken into; (3) and an intention to steal or commit another felony—assault, rape, or the like. (In other states, the element of "entering" a building is also essential.) Thus, evidence that the accused took, or started to take, property from the building; or that he assaulted or had the means to assault; or that he raped or attempted to rape will be admissible evidence that, at the time he broke in, he intended to commit the particular crime. On the other hand, if evidence is produced that the defendant was intoxicated at the time he broke in and that he promptly went to sleep inside the premises without taking or moving any of the property within the building, this would be evidence that he had no intent to steal. If, after gaining entry, he discovered someone there, and immediately fled, this would be admissible evidence from which the jury could infer he had no intent to assault or rape.

Intoxication alone (if to a sufficient degree) will be evidence that the accused could not and did not form a criminal intent. However, if

[1]State v. Maley (W. Va.) 153 SE 2d 827.

intoxication is offered as a defense, evidence may be admitted, if available, to show that the defendant intended and planned the crime before he became intoxicated.

Intent may also be a vital factor in determining the degree of a crime. Evidence which leads to the inference that a particular state of mind was lacking may reduce the seriousness of a murder charge to second-degree murder or manslaughter.

A particular accused may try to show that he was so ignorant of the law, or of some crucial fact, that there is good reason to doubt he acted with criminal intent. Generally, a mistake of law, even though based on advice of counsel, will not be a defense, nor will evidence of such a mistake be admissible. However, various states have different rules in this field and there is strong reason to allow evidence of *good faith* reliance on the advice of persons who should reasonably know the law in order to show lack of intent.[2]

Where specific intent is a necessary element, the general rule seems to be that good-faith ignorance of the law will negate the existence of that intent. For instance, an honest claim of title and belief in ownership may be a defense to a theft charge (lack of felonious intent) even though the claim is based on a misconception of the law or the defendant's right under the law.[3]

Evidence of an honest mistake or ignorance of fact, based on reasonable grounds, and of such a nature that the conduct would have been lawful had the facts been as they were reasonably supposed to be, will generally be admissible as bearing on the issue of criminal intent. An erroneous belief in the type of crime being committed or the identity of the victim, even though reasonable, will not be a defense.[4]

If the only intent necessary for the commission of a crime is intent to do the act, mistake may not be a defense. However, when the intent necessary is an intention to do wrong, the courts will allow evidence of mistake as an affirmative defense.[5]

ENTRAPMENT

The name of this defense is misleading. It probably should be named "seduction." There is nothing in the law which indicates the policeman may not "trap" the criminal. The basis for this defense is evidence that shows the crime or plan originated in the mind of a policeman. Thus, if

[2]Long v. State (Del. 1949) 65 A 2d 489. People v. Ferguson (Cal. 1933) 134 Cal. App 41, 24P.2d 965.
[3]Baugh v. State (Ind. 1929) 165 NE. 434.
[4]McGehee v. State (Miss. 1885) 62 Miss. 772. People v. Weaver (Cal. 1945) 163 P. 2d 456.
[5]VonBrown v. State (Tex. 1959) 322 SW 2d 626.

the plan to break into a building originated in the mind of the burglar, and the policeman went along with it in order to gain evidence of the crime, there would be no entrapment.[6] On the other hand, if the offense were planned by a police officer who procured its commission by the defendant, and if the defendant would not otherwise have committed the crime except for trickery, persuasion or fraud by the officer, this will constitute entrapment.[7]

In cases where an undercover agent solicits the act (for example, sale of narcotics), the issue or question of entrapment will have to be decided by the triers of fact.[8] The mere fact that the officer gives the defendant an opportunity to commit the crime is not an entrapment. Thus, if the officer gives a seller of narcotics an opportunity to ply his trade, there is no entrapment. Such circumstances are similar to the cases in which the officer plays the role of an unconscious drunk in order to catch "drunk rollers" at their business. There is no entrapment when the police agents play such passive roles.

Entrapment is an affirmative defense. Thus, the defendant has the burden of coming forward with the evidence.[9] The arresting officer's testimony by itself may be sufficient to convict without corroboration because the officer is not a true accomplice.[10]

CONSENT

Consent may or may not be a defense to an accusation of crime. This depends on the nature of the crime charged.

Consent is a defense when the crime itself requires that it be against the will of the victim. When rape is charged, the evidence must show that intercourse was against the will of the victim. Lack of consent is an **essential element** of the crime. In the crime of robbery, if the essential elements include "against the will" of the victim, any proof of consent would require a not guilty verdict as to the crime of robbery.[11]

Other crimes are committed whether or not consent is given. Therefore, in sex crimes against children, evidence of consent would not be allowed because consent has no bearing on this crime. Murder may not be consented to, and evidence that the victim asked to be killed will not be admitted because this is not relevant or material to the charge.

A third category of crimes is more complicated and varying cir-

[6]State v. Currie (N.D. 1905) 102 NW 875.
[7]People v. Lindsey (Cal. 1949) 205 P. 2d 1114.
[8]U.S. v. Moses (1955) 220 F. 2d 166.
[9]People v. Terry (Cal. 1955) 282 P. 2d 19.
[10]State v. Neely (Mont. 1931) 300 P. 561. People v. Collins (Cal. 1878) 53 Cal. 185.
[11]People v. Gibsen (N.Y. 1922) 134 NE 531.

cumstances will determine whether consent is or is not a defense. Participants in a boxing match or a football game may not be the victims of an assault or battery. But prosecution for a fight on the public streets, whether mutually agreed to or not, may not be avoided by evidence of consent because the fight was also a breach of peace or had a tendency to create such a breach. Neither participant can consent to the breach of peace in order to thwart a criminal prosecution.

MENTAL DISORDER

There are two defenses which may be urged on the basis of a mental disorder at the time of the crime.

Legal insanity will relieve the defendant from legal responsibility for the crime. The term **legal insanity** may be defined in any of three ways depending on where the criminal action took place.

The test for legal insanity most common in the United States is generally this: "At the time of the committing of the act, the party accused was laboring under such a defect of reason, from disease of the mind, as not to know the nature and quality of the act he was doing; or, if he did know it, that he did not know he was doing what was wrong."[12] Many states, while still using this basic test, have modified it in light of modern developments. One such modification is this: "First, did the defendant have sufficient mental capacity to know and understand what he was doing, and second, did he know and understand that it was wrong and a violation of the rights of others. To be sane and thus responsible to the law for the act committed, the defendant must be able to know and understand the nature and quality of his act and to distinguish between right and wrong at the time of the commission of the offense."[13]

A few states have rejected the M'Naughten rule stated above, and have fashioned new definitions and tests. The American Law Institute's model Penal Code proposed the following: "A person is not responsible for criminal conduct if at the time of such conduct as a result of mental disease or defect he lacks substantial capacity either to appreciate the criminality (wrongfulness) of his conduct or to conform his conduct to the requirements of law."[14]

An additional test formulated in an 1870 New Hampshire case, *State v. Pike*[15] has been adopted in the District of Columbia circuit of

---

[12]Daniel M'Naughten's case, House of Lords 1843, 8 Eng. Rep. 718.
[13]People v. Wolff 61 Cal. 2d 795 (1964).
[14]Section 4.01 adopted in substance in Vermont, Illinois, Missouri, and generally known as the Currens Rule, United States v. Currens (1961) 290 F. 2 751.
[15]49 N. H. 399.

the Federal Court. Under this test: "An accused is not criminally responsible if his unlawful act was the product of mental disease or mental defect."[16]

Evidence showing either legal sanity or insanity may arise from the particular facts and circumstances of the crime (evidence showing knowledge of wrongfulness, such as hiding or fleeing), testimony of persons who had an opportunity to observe the defendant's behavior, and from persons qualified to testify to mental diseases, disorders and defects.

A second defense, available when the mental disorder is not severe enough to be considered legal insanity, is the capacity of the defendant to hold certain necessary states of mind due to his mental disorder. In *People v. Conley*[17] the rule, as it applied to homicide, was stated this way: (1) "If because of mental defect, disease, or intoxication, the defendant is unable to comprehend his duty to govern his actions in accord with the duty imposed by law, he does not act with malice aforethought and cannot be guilty of murder. (2) It has long been settled that evidence of diminished mental capacity whether caused by intoxication, trauma, or disease can be used to show that a defendant did not have a specific mental state essential to an offense."

The **doctrine of diminished capacity** recognizes that there is a mental disorder, short of legal insanity, which is disabling and should reduce the responsibility even though it does not eliminate it entirely. The facts and circumstances of the offense, the defendant's actions, and the testimony of qualified experts in the field of psychology and psychiatry may be proffered as evidence of such reduced capacity.

THE TOTAL EVIDENCE CONCEPT

The affirmative defenses briefly discussed should give the investigator an idea of an area he must consider before he labels a case completely prepared. Investigators gather and communicate to the prosecuting attorney the bits and pieces of evidence (both testimony and articles or objects of evidence) which point to the defendant as having committed a particular crime. Yet, investigators must also gather and report admissible evidence which will prevent the defendant from successfully asserting any of the affirmative defenses available to him.

Under this "total evidence" concept, a case is ready when there is sufficient legally admissible, available, and credible evidence to prove the offense charged beyond a reasonable doubt, and there is available

---

[16]Durham v. United States (1954) 214 F2 862.
[17](Cal. 1966) 411 P. 2d 911.

sufficient legally admissible and credible evidence to overcome the common defenses to crime, from mistaken identification to insanity.

To some extent the total evidence concept rests on the duty and obligation of police investigators. It is the duty of a police investigator to present to the prosecutor and to the court, and to the jury in jury trials, all of the evidence in his possession bearing on the guilt or innocence of the defendant. A police investigator's primary responsibility is to collect all of the evidence he can uncover about the true facts of a criminal event and the guilt or innocence of the person or persons involved.

When an accused person is criminally responsible for the crime charged, this diligence in collecting evidence, and in fulfilling the responsibility of police investigators allows an investigation to be closed with results. When an investigator knows about police procedures that can ruin carefully collected evidence, and knows about evidence that cannot be admissible when proffered, then all the evidence he collects will have legal significance and will be usable in court to prove the guilt of the person accused of crime.

The burden of proof is not placed on the defendant in criminal cases. The "people" have this burden and must prove guilt beyond a reasonable doubt. **Proof is the outcome or effect of evidence**. Guilt beyond a reasonable doubt is the result of convincing and compelling evidence—evidence presented in court by the police and prosecutor who represent the "people."

SUMMARY

A police officer's primary responsibility is to collect all the evidence he can uncover about the true facts of a criminal event. Prior to prosecution, police must be certain there is sufficient legally admissible, available, and credible evidence to overcome the common defenses to crime and to prove the offense(s) charged beyond a reasonable doubt. The burden of proof on the issue of guilt or innocence is upon the prosecution; only convincing and compelling evidence can become the proof necessary to satisfy this burden and overcome the basic presumption that a person accused of crime is innocent until proven guilty beyond a reasonable doubt.

DISCUSSION QUESTIONS

1. How are defenses based on alibi and on lack of intent similar? How do they differ?

2.   Explain good-faith ignorance of the law as a potential defense.

3.   What are the legal limits of entrapment? When does this situation become a defense to crime?

4.   Cite one or more crimes in which evidence that the victim did not give consent would be required. Cite one in which consent or lack of consent would have no bearing. Try to explain the underlying differences that account for this distinction.

5.   Explain the "Currens Rule" and the standard it imposes for excusing responsibility for a crime because of mental disease or defect.

6.   Define the total evidence concept.

GLOSSARY

MENS REA.   Criminal intent.

Selected Bibliography

Books

Cahn, William, *Mock Trial.* Chicago, Ill.: National District Attorneys Association, 1974.

California Evidence Code Manual, Sacramento, Cal.: California Continuing Education of the Bar, 1966.

Drinker, Henry S., *Legal Ethics.* New York: Columbia University Press, 1953.

Ehrlich, J. W., *The Lost Art of Cross-Examination.* New York: G. P. Putnam's Sons, 1970.

Fricke, Charles W., and Arthur L. Alarcon, *California Criminal Evidence,* 8th ed., Los Angeles: Legal Book Corp., 1971.

Fryer, William T., ed., *Selected Writings on the Law of Evidence and Trial.* St. Paul, Minn.: West Publishing Co., 1957.

George, James, Jr., *Constitutional Limitations on Evidence in Criminal Cases.* Ann Arbor, Mich.: Institute of Continuing Legal Education, The University of Michigan Law School, 1966.

Heafey, Edwin A., Jr., *California Trial Objections.* Sacramento, Cal.: California Continuing Education of the Bar, 1967.

Heffron, Floyd N., *Evidence for the Patrolman.* Springfield, Ill.: Charles C. Thomas, 1958.

Inbau, Fred E., Marvin E. Aspen, and Frank Carrington, *Evidence Law for the Police*. Philadelphia: Chilton Book Co., 1972.

Kerr, Harry P., *Opinion and Evidence: Cases for Argument and Discussion*. New York: Harcourt Brace Jovanovich, 1962.

Klein, Irving J., *Law of Evidence for Police*. St. Paul, Minn.: West Publishing Co., 1973.

Klotter, John C., and Carl L. Meier, *Criminal Evidence for Police*. Cincinnati: The W. H. Anderson Co., 1971.

Louisell, David W., John Kaplan, and Jon R. Waltz, *Principles of Evidence and Proof*. Mineola, N.Y.: The Foundation Press, Inc., 1968.

Maguire, John M., Jack B. Weinstein, James H. Chadbourn, and John H. Mansfield, *Cases and Materials on Evidence*, with 1967 Supplement. Brooklyn, N.Y.: The Foundation Press, Inc., 1965.

McBain, James P., *California Evidence Manual*, 2nd ed., St. Paul, Minn.: West Publishing Co., 1960.

McCormack, Charles T., *Handbook of the Law of Evidence*. St. Paul, Minn.: West Publishing Co., 1954.

Mendelson, Irving, *Defending Criminal Cases*. New York: Practicing Law Institute, 1967.

Moenssens, Andre A., Edward Moses, Fred E. Inbau, *Scientific Evidence in Criminal Cases*. Mineola, N.Y.: The Foundation Press, Inc., 1973.

Morgan, Edmund M., *Basic Problems of Evidence*, vols. I and II. Philadelphia: American Law Institute, 1957.

Newman, Donald J., *Conviction: The Determination of Guilt or Innocence Without Trial*. Boston: Little, Brown, 1966.

Richardson, James R., *Scientific Evidence for Police Officers: Scientific Tests and Experiments; Specific Methods of Proof*. Cincinnati: The W. H. Anderson Co., 1963.

Rothblatt, Henry B., *Successful Techniques in the Trial of Criminal Cases*. Englewood Cliffs, N.J.: Prentice-Hall, Inc., 1961.

Rothstein, Paul F., *Evidence in a Nutshell*. St. Paul, Minn.: West Publishing Co., 1970.

Scott, Charles C., *Photographic Evidence: Preparation and Presentation*. Kansas City, Mo.: Vernon Law Book Co., 1942.

Solottolo, A. Lawrence, *Modern Police Service Encyclopedia*. New York: Arco Publishing Co., 1962.

Spellman, Howard Hilton, *Direct Examination of Witnesses*. Englewood Cliffs, N.J.: Prentice-Hall, Inc., 1968.

Sobel, Nathan R., *Eyewitness Identification: Legal and Practical Problems*. New York: Clark Boardman Co., Ltd., 1972.

Stephens, Otis H., *The Supreme Court and Confessions of Guilt*. Knoxville, Tenn.: The University of Tennessee Press, 1973.

Stryker, Lloyd Paul, *The Art of Advocacy: A Plea for the Renaissance of the Trial Lawyer*. New York: Simon and Schuster, 1954.

Tierney, Kevin, *Courtroom Testimony: A Policeman's Guide*. New York: Funk and Wagnalls, 1970.

Tobias, Marc Weber, and David R. Petersen, *Pretrial Criminal Procedure: A Survey of Constitutional Rights*. Springfield, Ill.: Charles C. Thomas, 1972.

Tompkins, Dorothy C., *The Confession Issue—From McNabb to Miranda: A Bibliography*. Berkeley, Cal.: Institute of Governmental Studies, University of California, Berkeley, 1968.

Tracy, John Evarts, *Handbook of the Law of Evidence*. Englewood Cliffs, N.J.: Prentice-Hall, Inc., 1952.

Underhill, H. C., *Criminal Evidence*, 4th ed., rev. and ed. by John Lewis Niblack. Indianapolis: The Bobbs-Merrill Co., 1935.

United States Supreme Court, *Proposed Rules of Evidence for United States Courts and Magistrates*, 1973.

Walls, H. J., *Forensic Science*. New York: Praeger, 1968.

Wellman, Francis L., *The Art of Cross-Examination*, 4th ed. New York: Macmillan, 1936.

Weston, Paul B., and Kenneth M. Wells, *Criminal Investigation: Basic Perspectives*, 2nd ed. Englewood Cliffs, N.J.: Prentice-Hall, Inc., 1974.

———, *Fundamentals of Evidence*. Englewood Cliffs, N.J.: Prentice-Hall, Inc., 1972.

Williams, John B., *California Criminal Evidence*. Beverly Hills, Cal.: Glencoe Press, 1969.

Witkin, B. E., *California Evidence*, 2nd ed., with 1972 Supplement, San Francisco: Bancroft-Whitney, 1966 and 1972.

Zagel, James, *Confessions and Interrogations After Miranda*. Chicago: National District Attorneys Association, 1972.

Articles

Delgado, Richard, "Underprivileged Communications: Extension of the Psychotherapist-Patient Privilege to Patients of Psychiatric Social Workers," *California Law Review*, 61, no. 4 (June 1973), 1050–71.

Dershowitz, Alan M., and John Hart Ely, "Harris v. New York: Some Anxious Observations on the Candor and Logic of the Emerging Nixon Majority," *The Yale Law Journal*, 80, no. 6 (May 1971), 1198–1227.

Greenberg, Peter S., "The Balance of Interests Theory: A Selective Analysis of Supreme Court Action Since *Camara* and *See*," *California Law Review*, 61, no. 4 (June 1973), 1011–47.

Kaus, Otto M., and Ronald E. Mallen, "The Misguiding Hand of Counsel—Reflections on Criminal Malpractice," *UCLA Law Review*, 21, no. 4 (June 1974), 1191–1232.

Oaks, Dallin H., "Studying the Exclusionary Rule in Search and Seizure," *The University of Chicago Law Review*, 37, no. 4 (Summer 1970), 665–757.

Rosett, Arthur, "The Negotiated Guilty Plea," *The Annals*, 374 (November 1967), 70–81.

Tribe, Lawrence H., "Triangulating Hearsay," *Harvard Law Review*, 87, no. 5 (March 1974), 957–74.

———, "Effect of *Mapp v. Ohio* on Police Search-and-Seizure Practices in Narcotics Cases," *Columbia Journal of Law and Social Problems*, 4, no. 1 (March 1968), 87–104.

Citation of Cases—Guide

Cases decided by the United States Supreme Court are cited by reference to the official reports: for example, *Jackson v. Denno* is cited as 378 U.S. 368 (1964), indicating that the case is reported in volume 378 of *U.S. Reports* at page 368 and that the decision was made in 1964. Within the cases reported, however, additional citations are given. These are usually to the *United States Supreme Court Reports* of the Lawyers Cooperative Publishing Co., cited as "L. Ed." or "L. Ed. 2nd," and the *Supreme Court Reporter* of West Publishing Co., cited as "Sup. Ct." or "S. Ct." The numerals contained in these references also refer to the volume and page numbers.

Cases in which decisions were made in other federal courts, or appellate and district courts, are similarly cited: for example, *Johns v. Smyth*, 176 F. Supp. 949 (1959), indicating that the case is reported in volume 176 of the *Federal Supplement* of West Publishing Co., at page 949, and that the decision is dated in 1959. Within the cases reported, however, additional data are given in such citations to indicate the court involved. For instances, *Johns v. Smyth* would be identified as a case from the United States District Court of the Eastern District of Virginia by the additional notation: (E.D.Va.).

Cases in which the decisions were made in state courts are identified in similar fashion, with the name of the state included in abbreviated form, and with volume and page numbers of both the state reports and the regional reports: for example, *People v. Bob*, 29 Cal. 2nd 321, 175 P. 2nd 12 (1946), indicates that the case will be found in both *California Reports, 2nd Series* and in the *Pacific Reporter, 2nd Series*. California cases may also be cited to the *California Reporter* ("Cal. Rptr."), the complete reporter for all California cases.

Glossary

Acquittal. Court or jury certification of the innocence of a defendant during or after trial.

Ad Hoc (Judgment). Pertaining to, or for the sake of, this case alone.

Admissibility. Determination of whether evidence, exhibits, or testimony will be allowed in trial; inadmissible evidence cannot be allowed and is therefore not presented in court and is not heard or examined by the triers of fact.

Admission. A statement inconsistent with innocence of a crime; defendant admits a damaging fact.

Advocacy. Defending, assisting, or pleading for another; to defend by argument.

Advocate. One who renders legal advice and pleads the cause of another before a court or tribunal; one who speaks in favor of another.

Affidavit. Sworn written statement.

Antecedent Justification (Police Action). Prior court approval.

Appeal. Judicial review; a post-conviction step in judicial proceedings. After the decision of a trial court, the removal of the case (cause) to a higher court with authority to review the decision of the lower court for the purpose of obtaining a retrial.

APPOINTED ATTORNEY. Legal counsel provided by a court for defendants without funds to hire private counsel.

AUTOPSIC (EVIDENCE). Evidence as a result of viewing an object or thing.

BAIL. Release of a defendant upon his written agreement to appear in court as required. Cash or other security may be required.

BALLISTICS. Science of the motion of projectiles; firearms identification; the scientific examination of evidence found at crime scenes and connected with firearms; firearms, spent bullets, empty cartridge or shell cases, and cartridges and shells.

BENCH. The presiding judge (and his position at the front of the courtroom).

BEST EVIDENCE RULE. The best evidence of the content of writing is the writing itself.

CASE IN CHIEF. The main case of the prosecution or defense; their original array of evidence.

CITATION. Reference to an authority; U.S. Supreme Court decisions give the case name, the volume and page numbers (*U.S. Reports*), and the year in which the case was decided.

CONFESSION. A statement acknowledging guilt; defendant's statement that he committed the crime charged.

CONFESSION CASES. A series of United States Supreme Court decisions concerned with illegal or improper police interrogations.

CONSPIRACY (CRIMINAL). A combination of two or more persons for the purpose of committing, by joint effort, an unlawful act or using unlawful means for the commission of a lawful act.

CORPOREAL. Of or pertaining to the human body.

CRIMINAL ACT. Act or omission prohibited by law.

CRIMINAL INTENT. A determination of the mind; an intelligent purpose to do an act prohibited as criminal by law; *mens rea*.

CRIMINALISTICS. Scientific discipline directed to the recognition, identification, individualization, and evaluation of physical evidence by the application of the natural sciences in matters of law and science. The application of science to the examination of physical evidence; linked to forensic science, the general application of science to the solution of crimes. Evidence technicians represent a sub-classification of this field.

CROSS-EXAMINATION. Questioning of witness by counsel for opposing party; follows the *direct examination* of a witness by the party calling the witness to court.

DECLARANT. A person who makes a declaration (statement).

DICTA, DICTUM. Judicial opinion not essential to a court's decision on the question under review.

DIRTY BUSINESS. Term used to describe wiretapping in *Olmstead v. United States.*

DISCOVERY. Disclosure by the prosecution of certain evidence regarding a defendant in a pending trial. There is limited disclosure by the defense. Term is generally identified with defense pretrial request to prosecutor to disclose facts of the police case against defendant.

DIVERSION. Finding alternatives to formal action within the criminal justice system.

DOUBLED (AGENT). Action of "turning" an agent employed by an adverse party into an associate who will provide information about his first employer (adverse party).

EN BANC. Together, all the judges of a court "sit" and hear a case.

EXEMPLAR (HANDWRITING). A specimen (of handwriting); an example; a model.

EX PARTE. On one side only; no adverse party in proceedings.

EXPERTS. Capable of being qualified in court as expert witnesses; men and women of science educated in art or science, or persons possessing special or unusual knowledge acquired from practical experience.

EXPERT WITNESS. An individual, with reference to a particular subject, who possesses knowledge not acquired by ordinary persons; a man of science or a person possessing special or peculiar knowledge acquired from practice and experience.

FIELD INTERROGATION. Questioning of suspicious person stopped by police.

FORENSIC. Related to courts of justice.

FORENSIC SCIENCE. Application of scientific knowledge to the solution of crimes and in support of the investigation of crime. (See Criminalistics)

FOUNDATION (OF TESTIMONY). Establishing the fact that the opportunity of a witness to observe was sufficient to afford a reasonable basis for the proposed testimony.

FRUITS OF THE POISONED TREE DOCTRINE. Doctrine barring the use of derivative evidence tainted by illegal origin (See *Silverthorne v. United States* in Chapter 11).

GRAND JURY. A certain number of persons selected according to law and sworn to the duty of receiving complaints and accusations of crime in criminal cases, to hear evidence presented by the "state," and to return indictments when they are satisfied a trial is warranted. The term "grand" developed because, at common law, the number of persons on this jury was set at not less than twelve nor more than twenty-three, while the ordinary *trial jury* (petit jury, as distinguished from grand jury) was a body of twelve persons.

GUILTY. The result of a guilty verdict in a criminal prosecution (jury or judge); the result of judicial acceptance of a guilty plea; the opposite of innocence.

HABEAS CORPUS. A name for writs seeking to bring a party in custody before a court or judge to examine into the lawfulness of imprisonment. Its sole function is to release from unlawful imprisonment. Technically habeas corpus *ad subjiendum*.

HABEAS CORPUS *ad testificandum*. Directed to a person having legal custody of a prisoner in a jail or prison and ordering him to bring a prisoner to court to testify. ("You have the body to testify.")

HEARSAY. Second-hand evidence; testimony of evidence not based on the personal knowledge of a witness, but information someone else has seen or heard and related to a testifying witness.

IDENTITY. Proof of a person's identity as being the individual alleged in the accusatory pleading.

IMPEACHMENT (OF WITNESS). Attacking the credibility of a witness.

IN CAMERA. Not in open court; private; judicial chambers.

INFAMY. Status of person convicted of crime such as treason and other major felonies. Infamous crimes are those that are scandalous or heinous; usually linked with severe punishment upon conviction.

INFORMER'S PRIVILEGE. Right of police to avoid disclosure of identity of informants to protect them from retaliation and to enhance continuance of the flow of information about crime and criminals from informants to police.

INTELLIGENCE (POLICE). Clandestine or secret collecting and evaluating of information about crime and criminals not normally available through overt investigative techniques.

INTER ALIA. Among other items or things; used when the complete wording of a law is not given.

IRVINE-TYPE VIOLATIONS. Purposeful violations of the constitution by police officer.

JUDICIAL INSTRUCTIONS. A charge to the jury by trial judge; instructions as to the principles of law in a case and their application to the circumstances of the case being tried.

JUVENILES. Persons under a specified age (usually eighteen) who may be processed in a special juvenile court on the issues of neglect and delinquency.

LATENT (FINGERPRINT). Not visible to ordinary visual examination; must be searched for with special skill and equipment. A latent fingerprint can be developed by evidence technicians and preserved as evidence.

MENS REA. Criminal intent.

MODUS OPERANDI (M.O.). Method of operation; used in the identification of criminals by their crime techniques or habitual criminal conduct.

MOTION. Application to court for a legal remedy.

NEMO TENETUR SEIPSUM ACCUSARE. No one is bound to accuse himself.

NEXUS. Connection; tie; link.

NOLO CONTENDERE. No contest; designation of a plea in a criminal action having the legal effect of a guilty plea but which cannot be used elsewhere as an admission.

OBJECTION. Opposition to the introduction of certain evidence or questions during a criminal proceeding, or to judicial rulings. Linked with a "request to strike," to remove from record any portion of the opposed evidence or question already before the triers of fact. The objection is granted when the presiding judge *sustains* it; it is *overruled* when denied.

PEACE OFFICER. A 'sworn" officer, sheriff's deputy, or state investigator; usually named by job title in state statutes giving peace officers power to carry out their sworn duty.

PER SE. By itself.

PHYSICAL EVIDENCE. Things and traces (clue materials) found at crime scenes, upon suspects, or at places or upon persons otherwise related to a criminal investigation.

PLASTIC (FINGERPRINT). A finger impression made in a pliable (plastic) substance.

PRELIMINARY HEARING. A judicial hearing or examination of witnesses to determine whether or not a crime has been committed, and if the evidence presented by the prosecutor is sufficient to warrant the commitment, or bailing, of the accused pending trial.

PRESENTENCE REPORT.   A report by a probation officer of an investigation conducted at court direction into the social and criminal history and resources of a convicted defendant, and containing a recommendation to the sentencing judge concerning the best program of corrections for the offender.

PRESUMPTION.   The inference of one fact from the existence of a related fact.

PRIMA FACIE.   On the face of; at first view; uncontradicted.

PRIVILEGED COMMUNICATION.   A communication between persons in a confidential relationship who are under a special obligation of fidelity and secrecy, and which the law will not allow to be divulged (or inquired into) for the sake of public policy; husband and wife, attorney and client, etc.

PROTEAN.   Variable; readily assuming different shapes or forms.

REBUTTAL.   The answer of the prosecutor to the defense case in chief; an opportunity for the prosecution to repair portion of the prosecution's case damaged by defense evidence.

REJOINDER (SURREBUTTAL).   The answer of the defense to the prosecutor's rebuttal; opportunity for the defense to repair portions of the defense case damaged by prosecution evidence during the rebuttal stage of a trial.

RETURN (SEARCH WARRANT).   A report of police action when executing a search warrant, including an inventory of property seized and a description of the place found.

RUBRIC.   A form or thing established or settled; formally specified; a class or category.

SPIKE MICROPHONE.   When driven into the wall of a premises, a spike microphone has the capability of picking up sounds on the other side of the wall; similar to induction microphones (which pick up conversations without direct wiring in telephonic interceptions), and "shotgun" or tubular microphones, which have a long-range directional pickup capability. No physical intrusion into the premises involved is necessary when these eavesdropping devices are used.

SPORTING THEORY.   A spinoff from the American legal system's trial-by-adversary concept (right theory), with surprise being part of the strategy of the prosecution.

STANDARD.   Desirable or ideal work performance level; work as expected by supervisors and associates; prevailing practices or authoritative recommendations to upgrade prevailing practices.

STARE DECISIS.   Rule of precedents; principle that once the law of a specific case has been decided it should serve as a definite and known rule for the future (unless decision in error, or mistake).

SUBPOENA.   A process commanding the person named therein to appear before a court to testify as a witness.

SUBPOENA *duces tecum*.   A process commanding a witness to bring to court a document or other record in his posession or control which is pertinent to trial issues.

VENUE.   Place or area in which a crime was committed; *situs delicti*. Change of venue is to transfer a pending trial to another county or district.

VOIR DIRE.   In-court preliminary examination of juror or witness when competency, interest, etc., is in dispute.

Case Index

General Index